BANCROFT LIBRARY PUBLICATIONS
BIBLIOGRAPHICAL SERIES

VOLUME II
*Manuscripts Relating Chiefly to
Mexico and Central America*

A Guide to the Manuscript Collections of the Bancroft Library

VOLUME II

EDITED BY GEORGE P. HAMMOND

Published for the Bancroft Library by the
UNIVERSITY OF CALIFORNIA PRESS
BERKELEY AND LOS ANGELES, 1972

UNIVERSITY OF CALIFORNIA PRESS
BERKELEY AND LOS ANGELES, CALIFORNIA

UNIVERSITY OF CALIFORNIA PRESS, LTD.
LONDON, ENGLAND

© 1972 BY THE REGENTS OF THE UNIVERSITY OF CALIFORNIA

ISBN 0–520–01991–1

LIBRARY OF CONGRESS CATALOG CARD NUMBER 63–16986

PRINTED IN THE UNITED STATES OF AMERICA

Foreword

The story of Hubert Howe Bancroft—who opened a San Francisco bookstore in 1856 with little knowledge of the business and very small capital, and became one of the greatest collectors of Western Americana of all time—is a California legend. He had come to California in 1852 as a youth of twenty, his immediate mission to arrange the sale of a shipment of books for his brother-in-law, George H. Derby, of Buffalo, New York. Finding San Francisco greatly overcrowded, he selected the firm of Barton, Reed, and Grimm, commission merchants in Sacramento, for this purpose, then joined his father and brother at Long Bar in the gold-mining region for some months. The extraordinary labors and discomforts of the miner's life, coupled with the disappointing returns, led Bancroft to give up the pursuit of riches in virgin gold and to find a different "mine" more to his liking. His decision was a natural outgrowth of his experience in the book business, slight though it was. So, when an opportunity presented itself in Crescent City, near the Oregon border, then expected to become a new gold-mining center, he became bookkeeper in a general store, at good salary, with the privilege of selling books there on his own account.

Several years later, and after a nostalgic visit to his old home in Ohio, Bancroft opened his own business in San Francisco in December, 1856, at first in association with George L. Kenny, a boyhood friend, but soon as an independent entrepreneur. His remarkable success, now well known, enabled him to pursue with avidity a new avocation—collecting contemporary historical materials relating at first to San Francisco, and then, as his vision grew, to all of California, and finally to the entire North American West, including Mexico and Central America. This enabled him to embrace the old Spanish and Mexican civilization in which California had its origin.

Once having recognized the opportunity for the study of California and its heritage, and having sensed its importance, almost completely ignored until then, Bancroft pursued the collecting of historical sources with great zeal, not only locally in and around San Francisco, the center of population in California, but in frequent visits to the book marts of England and the continent. There he found, to his great surprise, an amazing quantity of the sources he required, sources that seemed to have gathered the dust of the ages in their undisturbed state. No one had any idea of the historical importance of his subject, or of the abundance of materials for the study of its history.

About 1868, after a decade of collecting and when, in a spirit of satisfaction, Bancroft relaxed to estimate his success, he wrote in his Autobiography, *Literary Industries*: "I have ten thousand volumes and over, fifty times more than ever I dreamed were in existence when the collecting began. My library is a *fait accompli. Finis coronat opus.* Here will I rest." But then there came to his desk an inch-thick bookseller's catalogue which raised his blood pressure. It was the *Catalogue de la Riche Bibliothèque de D. José María Andrade. Livres manuscrits et imprimés. . . . 7000 pièces et volumes ayant rapport aux Mexique ou imprimés dans ce pays. . . .*

Bancroft was excited, overwhelmed. "Seven thousand books direct from Mexico, and probably half of them works which should be added to my collection." As he reflected on this surprising development, "A new light broke in upon me. I had never considered that Mexico had been printing books for three and a quarter centuries—one hundred years longer than Massachusetts—and that the earlier works were seldom seen floating about book-stalls and auction-rooms. . . ." It was a unique opportunity. The man of letters who had amassed this collection, Señor Andrade, writer, publisher, and bibliophile, had spent forty years accumulating it, with every facility at his command, and a thorough knowledge of the literature as well as of the places where the sources were most likely to be found. When Maximilian became Emperor of Mexico, he formulated plans for an Imperial Library, to enrich the glory of the country and of his own regime, and he astutely enlisted the services of Andrade and arranged the purchase of the latter's collection as a nucleus for the new venture. Before the transaction could be completed, Maximilian's brief career in Mexico came to an end. In the ensuing confusion, and in a desperate effort to recoup his losses, Andrade managed to bundle his library off to Europe, where it was placed at auction.

Bancroft's excitement knew no bounds. He realized that such an opportunity might never recur. There was not even time to check the catalogue for duplicates in his own library. Since the date of the auction would not permit him to attend in person, he telegraphed his agent in London "to attend the sale and purchase at his discretion." Wise purchasing filled many gaps in Bancroft's library, and in spite of the cost he was delighted with the results, especially later, when he began writing the history of Mexico and Central America. "A sum five times larger than the cost of the books would not have taken them from me after they were in my possession, from the simple fact that though I should live a hundred years I would not see the time when I could buy any considerable part of them at any price." Other European auctions of Mexican materials, similar if not so rich or extensive, followed, and Bancroft bought avidly. He was now deeply committed to enriching his library with the resources for the history of Mexico and Central America, from the very beginnings of knowledge of these areas, and his purchases made at that time still form the nucleus of one of the world's great regional collections.

Once begun, there was no ceasing. Bancroft's great six-volume *History of Mexico* (1883-1888) reflects his achievement in gathering the essential records that made the research and writing possible. But even before that he had greatly expanded his outlook on the development of the New World. In particular, he had become deeply conscious of the history of Central America and the native races, the establishment of European civilization on American shores, the progress and effect of these new influences on the original inhabitants, and the resulting mixture of races and cultures in the succeeding centuries. Bancroft made this theme a major feature of his histories. In 1874-1875, he had published five volumes on *The Native Races*, so that those who read his histories would know something about the people he was dealing with, their origin, background, and subsequent development. The science of anthropology, with which he dealt at some length, had hardly been born in his day; yet his studies of the native races blazed a pioneer path which scholars have followed ever since. These volumes were succeeded by three on *The History of Central America* (1882-1887), and later by two on *The North Mexican States and Texas* (1883-1889). Such massive works required an abundance of source materials, few of which were available until Bancroft undertook to collect them.

Though these studies were made in Bancroft's library in San Francisco, he did a remarkable amount of field work. In 1883, for example, he went to Mexico, not only to become better acquainted with the land, but to meet its leaders, particularly ex-president Porfirio Díaz, who had finished one term in office, and his successor, President Manuel González. Bancroft interviewed Díaz in depth and later published a full-length biography of him (1885). Such visits gave Bancroft an opportunity to establish friendly relations with book-dealers, politicians, and learned men, and enabled him to augment his library greatly. In addition, he sent to Mexico and other countries agents like the gifted Alphonse Pinart, to represent him and make purchases for his collection. Bancroft also employed local agents in these countries to help him acquire the materials indispensable for the writing of his ambitious works.

It should be stressed that Bancroft's collecting zeal embraced manuscript and printed sources, and both were of extreme importance, the one supplementing the other. Upon Bancroft's broad and priceless foundation, The Bancroft Library has continued to build through the years—assiduously gathering a wealth of both printed and manuscript materials. Of the two, manuscripts are infinitely more difficult to describe, catalogue, or locate in library use. Thus it is the aim of this Bibliographical Series on the manuscript sources of The Bancroft Library to provide the scholar with handy reference volumes which will indicate to him whether there is material in the Library pertinent to his particular field of research.

We would rather not dwell on the magnitude of the task we faced in preparing the present volume. At times it seemed insurmountable. There are collections of manuscripts of every conceivable type, in many different languages, ranging in size from one piece to hundreds or even thousands of items. As the work progressed, we came to realize that we must limit our descriptions to the theme and scope of the subjects, rather than analyzing the manuscripts in detail. Under the circumstances, there is bound to be great disparity in the amount of space devoted to each. Sometimes a large group receives only a paragraph of description, while in other cases items are perforce given individual mention. For many of the larger collections, however, the Library has very useful calendars, or "keys," prepared by the Manuscript Division and available to investigators. We have tried to give as much detail as practicable, but in the interest of size and cost of The Guide, we have not attempted to ascertain which of the manuscripts have been printed, in whole or in part, since the research required was simply beyond our means. For the same reason, we have not pursued the provenance of documents, fascinating as such a study would have been.

Contrary to the procedure used in Volume I of this series, we have not divided the material by areas or states; rather, we have placed the entire contents in alphabetical order, normally by author, but in case of doubt of authorship, by subject or title. The investigator will, therefore, find the index of more than usual utility, for in it we have sought to bring out the topics, names of chief persons, subjects, or areas that we considered significant.

In this volume, as in the preceding one, there is a "gray" area of miscellaneous character. While some items may not relate specifically to Mexico and Central America, it has seemed appropriate to include them for the sake of completeness in this survey of the Library's resources. There are documents that concern such topics as French and Spanish Louisiana, the Philippines, various parts of South America, and manuscripts gathered by scholars with special interest in diverse areas. To omit them might have seemed logical, but as they relate in general to the subject of this study, our decision was to include them in order to make it as complete as possible.

It is with much pleasure that I give credit to those who have assisted in this project, which I undertook in 1967. The first was Gwladys Williams, who did a prodigious amount of research in the "Old Bancroft" sources, the materials gathered by Bancroft before his library was purchased by the University of California in 1905, the year before the earthquake and fire in San Francisco.

Miss Williams' successor was Donna Briney, and I profited from her keen and perceptive assistance as we prepared entries for portions of these manuscripts. When family and community responsibilities made too great demands on her time, she was succeeded by Mary Ann Fisher, a former member of the Bancroft staff. To many students and visitors, she will be remembered affectionately as "Quack," from her maiden name, Quackenbush. With her help, the volume went to the printer in the summer of 1971; and she has had major responsibility for preparation of the voluminous index.

Other pursuits kept my collaborator in this series, the late Dale L. Morgan, colleague and long-time member of the Bancroft staff, from participating in preparation of this volume. His contribution to Volume I, however, provided precedents to which we have often turned with gratitude.

Among members of the Bancroft staff whose helpfulness I wish especially to acknowledge are its Director, Dr. James D. Hart; Associate Director Robert H. Becker; Estelle Rebec, head of the Manuscript Division, and her co-workers, Marie Byrne and Ellen Jones. I cannot fail to mention Julia Macleod, former head of that department, on whose knowledge and judgment I was always able to depend. Lorraine P. Mills joined in the chore of proofreading; and the entire Reference Staff, under its head, Dr. John Barr Tompkins, has been most patient throughout as the bundles and cartons of manuscripts were brought to my desk for examination. Nor can I overlook the credit due our typist, Teddi Herron, whose professional skill produced clean copy from the crude drafts as the manuscript took final shape.

It is my pleasure also to acknowledge the support granted by the Committee on Research of the University of California's Academic Senate, Berkeley Campus, on the recommendation of the History Department, for funds to employ a research assistant to help in the preparation of this volume. Without such valuable aid, completion of the study would have been greatly delayed.

GEORGE P. HAMMOND
DIRECTOR EMERITUS

SPECIAL ABBREVIATIONS

A.D.	Autograph Document
A.D.S.	Autograph Document Signed
A.L.	Autograph Letter
A.L.S.	Autograph Letter Signed
A.Ms.	Autograph Manuscript
A.Ms.S.	Autograph Manuscript Signed
ca.	circa
cm.	centimeters
d.	died
D.	Document
D.S.	Document Signed
exp.	exposures
f.	folio
HHB	Symbol for the original H. H. Bancroft collection
L.	Letter
L.S.	Letter Signed
Ms. (or Mss.)	Manuscript (or Manuscripts)
n.d.	no date
n.p.	no place
p.	page or pages
v.	volume or volumes

Mexican and Central American Manuscripts

ABAD, DIEGO JOSÉ, 1727-1779
   Tractatus vnicus de logicis institutionibus, vulgo summulis.
   [Mexico City] 1754.
   84 p. 22 cm.   HHB [M-M 130]
   A summary treatise in Latin on the principles of logic, prepared by the Jesuit, Abad, for his students at the College of San Pedro y San Pablo; composed of a preface and three disputations, with preliminary page explaining the composition of the treatise.

ABBOTT, EMMA, 1850-1891
   Letter of Recommendation. Kansas City. December 13, 1885.
   1 p. L.S. 20 cm.   [Z-Z 100:29]
   Recommending Tillie Ogran, the bearer, as seamstress.

ABERDEEN, GEORGE HAMILTON GORDON, 4TH EARL OF, 1784-1860
   Letter to Charles Bankhead. London. December 31, 1845 [i.e., 1844]
   18 p. (Photocopy) 28 cm.   HHB [M-M 1700:5]
   Letter from the Foreign Secretary to the British minister in Mexico in regard to relations with Mexico and the United States, with special reference to Texas.

ACATLÁN, MEXICO
   Register of Burials. 1632-1734.
   122 p. 21 cm.   HHB [M-M 430]
   Burial register for the parish of Acatlán, in present-day Hidalgo, written in Náhuatl and Spanish. Includes a note on the inspection by Archbishop Francisco Manso y Zúñiga in 1633.

ACATLÁN, MEXICO
   Registers of Marriages and Baptisms. 1567-1621.
   192 p. 30-31 cm.   HHB [M-M 429]
   Baptismal and marriage records kept in Acatlán and vicinity. Includes an introductory statement for the first marriage register, 1529, signed by Fray Tomás de Santa Caterina, and a 1588 count of marriages signed by Ignacio de Barrientos. Entries prior to 1595 are written primarily in Náhuatl, with later entries in Spanish.

ACCOUNT OF TENTHS RECEIVED BY THE LORD ADMIRAL, 1587-1598
   122 exp. (On film)   [Z-G 19]
   Microfilm of Harleian Manuscript 598 in the British Museum.

ACIOPARI, JOSÉ QUERIÉN
   Ratos desgraciados y conversación confidencial de un licenciado Europeo con un oficinista Americano. . . . Memorias de la Real Sociedad Económica de la Habana. Num. 16. Distribuido en 31 de abril de 1818. 1818-1819.
   146 p. Ms. and printed. 19 cm.   HHB [M-M 257]
   The manuscript portion of this volume is a fictitious dialogue, Mexico City, 1819, between a European lawyer and an American clerical employee, criticizing the eulogy of José Pablo Valiente, deceased Minister of the Council of the

Indies, which had been read by Claudio Martínez de Pinillos before the Real Sociedad Económica de la Habana, and subsequently published in the "Memorias" of that society. Outlines unfavorably the career of Valiente, with stress upon his persecution of the Cuban official, José Enrique Aparicio, and upon the latter's claim to damages.

Appended is a printed copy of the "Memorias," Havana, April 31 [*sic*], 1818, which contains, in addition to the eulogy of Valiente, the texts of royal decrees and related documents concerning racial and other problems in Cuba and Florida.

ADAMS, CHARLES FRANCIS, 1835-1915
Letter to C. W. Woolley. Quincy, Massachusetts. May 12, 1891.
2 p. A.L.S. 20 cm. [z-z 100:44]
Describing his caution about political aspirations.

ADAMS, HENRY CARTER, 1851-1921
Letters to Richmond Mayo-Smith. Ann Arbor, Michigan and Washington, D.C. 1887-1890.
10 p. A.L.S. 20 cm. [z-z 153]
Concerning publications and teaching activities.

[ADAMS, WILLIAM]
Notes on a Sojourn in the River Plate region, South America. ca. 1888?
59 p. A.D. 34 cm. [z-d 131]
Description of life and customs in Uruguay and Argentina in the 1860's. With partial draft of lecture on tour of France and Switzerland.

AFECTOS DE UN MORIBUNDO ARREPENTIDO. [N. p., n. d. 18th cent.?]
38 p. 16 cm. HHB [M-M 5]
Religious verses, in the form of *quintillas*, purportedly written by a repentant sinner on the verge of death.

ÁGREDA, DIEGO DE
Representación al Rey en defensa de Miguel José de Azanza. Mexico City. May 20, 1801.
69 p. 30 cm. Contemporary copy. HHB [M-M 6]
Statement in defense of Azanza's record as viceroy of New Spain, submitted by his representative, Ágreda, to King Charles IV. Praises Azanza's administration and appeals from the formal investigation by his successor, Félix Berenguer de Marquina.

AGUADO, PEDRO DE
Recopilación historial resolutoria de Sancta Marta y nuevo Reyno de Granada en las Yndias... Primera Parte. [Nueva Granada, ca. 1568?]
978 p. 32 cm. HHB [M-M 450]
A copy of the opening portion of the history written by Aguado, first Franciscan Provincial of Santa Fé de Bogotá and a participant in Jiménez de Quesada's entry into Nueva Granada. It covers Spanish exploration, conquest, and colonization of that region from the establishment of Santa Marta at the

beginning of the 16th century to 1568, including descriptions of local geography, native life, flora, fauna, and other features.

Part I of Aguado's history was first printed in Bogotá in 1906, as Vol. 5 of the "Biblioteca de Historia Nacional;" Part II was published in Caracas, 1913-1915, by the Venezuelan Academia Nacional de la Historia.

AGUILETA LADRÓN DE GUEVARA, JUAN DE

Residencia of Jerónimo de Vega y Salazar and his Assistants. San José del Parral, Nueva Vizcaya. May 5–June 6, 1654.

51 p. D.S. 32 cm. [M-M 1773]

File on the *residencia* carried out by Aguileta as alcalde mayor and judicial official of San José del Parral, in regard to the services of Vega, former justicia mayor and captain of that mining settlement, and of Vega's assistants. Initiated by order of Enrique Dávila y Pacheco, Governor of Nueva Vizcaya. Contains orders, notifications, a questionnaire for witnesses, testimony, specific charges against Antonio de Alvarado y Salcedo as chief constable and jail warden, Alvarado's refutation thereof, decisions exonerating Vega, Alvarado, and their colleagues from all charges, and related documents.

AHUMADA, JUAN ANTONIO DE

Representación politico legal que hase à N.^{ro} Sor Soberano Dn Phelipe Quinto . . . para que se sirva declarar, no tienen los Españoles Indianos obice para obtener los empleos, politicos, y militares de la America. . . . [Mexico City. ca. 1725]

158 p. D.S. 21 cm. HHB [M-M 155]

Petition addressed to Philip V by Ahumada, attorney of the Real Audiencia in Mexico City, concerning a report that American-born Spaniards are to be barred from public office in the Indies. Sets forth legal and other arguments to show that, on the contrary, political and ecclesiastical posts in the Indies should be reserved exclusively for American Spaniards.

This petition was first printed in Madrid in 1725; reprinted in Mexico City in 1820.

ALATORRE, FRANCISCO

Letters. 1855-1869.

70 folders. L.S., and A.L.S. 21-31 cm. [70/16M]

Letters received by Alatorre, one of Juárez's generals, from Miguel Auza, Santos Degollado, Manuel Doblado, Mariano Escobedo, Gabriel García, Luis García, Jesús González Ortega, Benito Juárez, and Ignacio Zaragoza, relating to Mexican internal struggles and resistance against the French.

ALBIÇURI (ALBIEURI), JUAN DE

Historia de las Missiones Apostolicas, q. los clerigos regulares de la Comp.^{a} de Jesus an echo en las Indias Occidentales del Reyno de la Nueva Vizcaya. Vamupa, Mexico. 1633.

369 p. D.S. 22 cm. HHB [M-M 7]

Review of Sinaloan history, followed by an account of the Jesuit missions in that province and in Michoacán; life and martyrdom of Gonzalo de Tapia.

ALBIZ, JUAN MANUEL COMYN, CONDE DE
> Memorandum de mi excursion a Macharaviaya (Málaga). April 21, 1926.
> 9 p. Typescript and L.S. 27-32 cm. [z-z 102]
> Account of a visit to the birthplace of José de Gálvez, with an excerpt from Pascual Madoz's *Diccionario . . . de España . . .* (Madrid, 1847) and a covering letter to H. I. Priestley, September 5, 1927.

ALCALÁ, FRANCISCO XAVIER DE
> Descripción en bosquexo de . . . la Pvebla de Los Angeles; [y] . . . el Obispado de. . . . [Puebla, Mexico. 1715 or 1716]
> 465 p. 21 cm. HHB [M-M 8]
> In two parts: 1) review, prose interspersed with verse, of the town of Puebla, its history, inhabitants, and natural features, with other information; 2) description of the diocese of Puebla, some events as late as 1765. Two watercolor pictorial maps of the town and diocese of Puebla.

ALCÁNTARA PÉREZ, PEDRO
> Silabario del idioma otomí. . . . [Mexico. 19th century]
> 18 p. Ms. and printed. 23 cm. HHB [M-M 472]
> A guide to pronunciation and spelling of the Otomí language by syllables, prepared by a former professor of the National University of Mexico.

ALCEDO Y BEXARANO, ANTONIO DE, 1736-1812, comp.
> Biblioteca americana; catálogo de los autores que han escrito de la América en diferentes idiomas y noticias de su vida y patria, años en que vivieron y obras que escribieron. . . . Manuscrito inédito. Mexico. 1807.
> 2 vols. 1403 p. Ms. with printed title page. 35 cm. HHB [M-M 509]

ALDRICH, T[HOMAS] B[AILEY], 1836-1907
> Letter to Mr. Osgood. Ponkapog, Massachusetts. May 25, 1880.
> 2 p. A.L.S. 21 cm. [z-z 100:64]
> Declining invitation.

ALESSANDRI RODRÍGUEZ, ARTURO, 1895-
> Letter to Monroe E. Deutsch. Santiago, Chile. March 24, 1941.
> 2 p. L.S. 27 cm. [z-z 100:1]
> Concerning visit of Professor Herbert M. Evans to Chile.

ALVARADO, PEDRO DE, 1485-1541
> Cartas Varias. January 18, 1534–April 29, 1541.
> 42 p. (copies) 33 cm. HHB [M-M 317]
> Six letters of Alvarado: two to the King of Spain, Puerto de la Posesión, Nicaragua, January 18, 1534, and Guatemala City, May 12, 1535; one to Governor Barrionuevo of Tierra Firme, Puerto Viejo, Peru, March 10, 1534; one to the Council of the Indies, Guatemala City, November 20, 1535, on his Pacific exploratory activities, the sale of a portion of his fleet to Diego de

Almagro, etc.; a record, Santiago de Quito, Ecuador, August 26, 1534, of the above-mentioned sale to Almagro; and the instructions, Mexico City, April 29, 1541, issued by Alvarado, jointly with Viceroy Mendoza of New Spain, to guide Gonzalo Dovalle in a voyage of exploration.

ALZATE Y RAMÍREZ, JOSÉ ANTONIO
Memoria sobre la Naturaleza, Cultivo, y Beneficio de la Grana. Mexico. 1771.
284 p. D.S. 31 cm. HHB [M-M 9]
Prepared by order of Viceroy Bucareli. Describes the appearance, life cycle, food habits, varieties, and uses of the cochineal; also production problems, methods of extracting the dye, and its regulation in commerce. Two appendices. Ten colored drawings of the cochineal insect.

AMADEUS, BEATUS, 1420-1482 [?]
Beati Amadei Ordinis Fratrum Minorum Apocalypsis Nova Sensum Habens Apertum et Reseratum per Archangelum Gabrielem. [N. p., n. d.]
270 p. 30 cm. HHB [M-M 10]
Account of the revelations allegedly made by the Archangel Gabriel to Amadeo of Portugal, João da Silva e Menezes; eight "Ecstasies" and fifteen "Sermons," with some appended material. Includes a "Revelation to Saint Bridget," a biographical note on the supposed author, certifications of examination and approval by the Inquisition in Spain and Portugal, and statements of a copyist, Fray Miguel de los Sanctos.

ANDAGOYA, PASCUAL DE, 1495-1548
Carta que escrivió . . . al Rey . . . en contestacion de las 2 Cedulas R.ˢ expedidas en Toledo con fecha de 20 de febrero del mismo año al Governador de Tierra firme. . . . February 20–October 22, 1534.
3 items. 33 cm. HHB [M-M 309]
Andagoya's letter dealt with the administration of Tierra Firme, notably a proposal for changing the site of Panama City. The two cedulas, dated February 20, 1534, commanded that steps be taken to make the Chagres River navigable, to erect structures necessary for a commercial port in Panama City, and that investigations be made concerning the feasibility of connecting the Atlantic and Pacific Oceans.

ANDERSON, ALBIN I
Account of Lingayen Gulf Operations. January, 1945.
5 p. (Typescript) 28 cm. [Z-P 121]

ANDERSON, ROBERT MARSHALL, 1862-1939
Letter to Charles A. Gauld. Circleville, Ohio. December 29, 1936.
6 p. L.S. 22 cm. HHB [M-M 1700:6]
Tells of conditions in northern Mexico during the writer's stay there, 1906-1907, and quotes from Gauld's grandfather's notes on Mexico in 1865-1866. Letterhead of the Rio Grande, Sierra Madre and Pacific Railway.

ANDERSON, THOMAS McARTHUR, 1836-1917
　　Correspondence and Papers. 1864-1900.
　　43 folders. L.S. and D.S. 17-33 cm. [z-p 109]
　　The collection includes records of Anderson's military service during the Civil War but primarily concerns his activities during the Spanish-American War in the Philippines where, as Brigadier and Major General, he commanded the U.S. Volunteers.

ANDONAEGUI, FRANK, 1850-
　　Dictation. [Ensenada, Mexico? N.d.]
　　2 p. 28 cm. HHB [m-m 368]
　　Statement dictated by Andonaegui, first United States consul at Ensenada. Contains data concerning his career, the development of Ensenada, and the operations of the International Company of Mexico.

ANIÑÓN, FELIPE, DE
　　Discurso de Felipe de Aniñón, sobre las utilidades y ventajas que resultarian de mudarse la Navegacion de Nombre de Dios y Panamá al Puerto de Cavallos y Fonseca. [Honduras? 1565?]
　　6 p. 33 cm. HHB [m-m 303]
　　Sets forth the advantages to be derived from substituting the ports of Caballos in Honduras and Fonseca in Guatemala as ports of entry in place of Nombre de Dios and Panama City.

ANTIGUA MADERERÍA DEL CABALLITO, S.A.
　　Accounts of. 1913-1914.
　　See Fernández del Castillo y de Mier, Manuel. [m-b 4]

ANTONIO DE LA ASCENSIÓN, FRAY, fl. 1600
　　Relacion de la jornada que hizo el general Sevastian Vizcayno al descubrimiento de las Californias el año de 1602.
　　127 exp. (On film) [m-m 1833]
　　Original manuscript in the Ayer Collection of the Newberry Library, Chicago.

APRESSA Y GANDRA, DOMINGO DE
　　Domingo de Apressa y Gandra contra Phelipe Pelaez por cantidad de dos mill y seiscientos y noventa y dos p.^{s} de oro comun. . . . San José del Parral, Nueva Vizcaya. January 8, 1675–May 4, 1677.
　　60 p. D.S. 31-32 cm. [m-m 1775]
　　File on collection of debt by the merchant, Apressa, from Felipe Peláez and his wife, María Francisca, coheiress of Francisco de la Parada. Contains certified copies and originals of commitments signed by Peláez, court orders, petitions, and related documents.

ARANA, ANASTASIA DE VERGARA
　　Petition. Mexico City. September, 1794.
　　2 p. D.S. 31 cm. [m-m 1700:83]

Request for payment due her deceased husband. With annotations by Viceroy Miguel Branciforte and the treasurer, Paliza.

ARAUZ, CLEMENTE DE
Informe del Alcalde Mayor de Tegucigalpa . . . sobre el estado de los Sambos-mosquitos y medio de esterminarlos. Guatemala City. October 31, 1735.
18 p. 28 cm. HHB [M-M 441]
Copy of a report from the former Alcalde Mayor of Tegucigalpa, probably addressed to Pedro Ribera y Villalón, Captain General of Guatemala, regarding the resources and depredations of the Sambos-Mosquitos, a mixed Indian-Negro tribe of Honduras and Nicaragua, and their allies. Includes a detailed plan for their extermination.

ARCE Y ECHEAGARAY, JOSÉ MARIANO DE
Instruccion sobre alcavalas. [Mexico City. 1794-1851]
185 p. 31 cm. HHB [M-M 12]
Collection of documents (copies) relating to excise and pulque taxes in New Spain; consists of correspondence of the tax official, Arce, with Viceroy Revilla Gigedo and Customs Director Juan Navarra, April 4-5, 1794; text of instructions for assessing and collecting these taxes, in 154 articles, with index; and various pertinent laws and orders.

ARÉVALO, ANTONIO DE
Descripción del Golfo e Istmo del Darién, con otras noticias interesantes. . . . Cartagena. March 31, 1761.
121 p. 31 cm. HHB [M-M 355]
Descriptive report on the Gulf and Isthmus of Darien, then a part of the Viceroyalty of Nueva Granada, the natives of the region, its history, and plans for constructing a fort on the East coast near the mouth of the Caimán River. Includes estimate of construction costs, and other papers on the proposed fort.

ARIAS, CONDE DE
Note. [N.p., n.d.]
1 p. 15 cm. HHB [M-M 1700:50]
Concerns a *relación* received by the Count.

ARIZA, ANDRÉS DE
Comentos de la Rica y Fertilissima Provincia de el Darién. Santa María la Antigua, Darién, Panama. 1774.
43 p. 32 cm. HHB [M-M 258A]
A report and covering letter of April 5, 1774, with related documents, addressed by the Governor of Darien to Viceroy Manuel Guirior of Nueva Granada and dealing with current conditions in the Province of Darien, the causes of its decline, and possible remedies.
With another copy (M-M 258B) in the handwriting of Alphonse Louis Pinart.

ARNOLD, BENEDICT, 1741-1801
    Order to the Inhabitants of Point Levi[s]. Point aux Trembles. November 28, 1775.
    1 p. A.L.S. (Photocopy) 25 cm. [z-z 100:105]
    Requesting that they prevent any provisions or fuel going to Quebec. From the Archives Provinciales, Musée de Quebec, Canada.

ARÓSTEGUI, NICANOR
    Letter to Manuel Miranda. Zacatecas. October 24, 1839.
    4 p. L.S. 31 cm. [m-m 1700:89]
    Transmitting an official government communication to the administrator of the powder factory in Zacatecas concerning operations of the factory.

ARRIAGA, JULIÁN DE, d. 1776
    Correspondence. Manila, Ferrol (Coruña, Spain), and Cádiz. 1758-1770.
    21 p. L.S. and A.L.S. 21-31 cm. hhb [z-p 3]
    Letters and enclosures addressed to Arriaga, Spanish Minister of Marine Affairs and the Indies, concerning the repair of Philippine fortifications and munitions for various parts of the empire.

ARRILLAGA, JOSÉ JOAQUÍN DE, 1750-1814
    Diario que manifiesta los Reconocimientos q.° á verificado . . . en las Fronteras á la Gentilidad de la Antigua California y margenes del Colorado. Año de 1796.
    3 portfolios, 62, 61, 61 p. D.S. and typescript. 28-31 cm. [m-m 1831]
    Diary of a reconnoitering expedition through the frontier region of Baja California, northward as far as San Diego, and along the Lower Colorado River area. Deals with condition of the Indians, inspection of missions and settlements, and general features of the region. Written at least partly at the mission of San Vicente. June 14–December 9, 1796.
    Accompanied by typescript, and translation by Nellie Van de Grift Sánchez.

ARRILLAGA Y BARCÁRCEL, BASILIO MANUEL, 1791-1867
    Defensa de la Mystica Ciudad de Dios, de la Venerable Madre Sor M.ª de Jesus Agreda. . . . [Mexico] 1844.
    178 p. Ms. and printed. 34 cm. hhb [m-m 13]
    A treatise by the Jesuit, Arrillaga, in defense of the *Mística Ciudad de Dios,* a life of the Virgin written by the Spanish nun, María de Ágreda. Consists of 1) a general history of the work and a review of the arguments on its merits; 2) a specific refutation of criticisms ascribed to Bishop Jacobo Benigno Bossuet, and of articles in the Mexican press based on these criticisms and published in response to a prospectus, advertising serial publication of the *Mística Ciudad* in Mexico. Inscription by the editor, stating that this is the original manuscript, corrected by the author.

ARRIOLA, JUAN JOSÉ DE, 1698-
Vida y Virtudes de la esclarecida Virgen Santa Rosalia de Palermo—Poema Lirico. [Mexico] 1768.
282 p. 22 cm.   HHB [M-M 14]
A biography, in verse, substantially identical in content with M-M 15, but lacking some of the preliminary pages; has watercolor decorations, and engraving of Santa Rosalía pasted in.

ARRIOLA, JUAN JOSÉ DE, 1698-
Vida y virtudes de la esclarecida Virgen y Anacoreta S.ᵗᵃ Rosalía. [Mexico] 1768.
642 p. 22 cm.   HHB [M-M 15]
A biography, in verse, of Santa Rosalía, patron saint of Palermo, composed by the Mexican Jesuit, Arriola. The work, divided into three books, deals with the life of the saint, first in early youth, then in the cave of Quisquina, and finally in Palermo; preceded by a collection of verses, dedication to the Virgin of Guadalupe, and an apologia.

ARTE DE LA LENGUA CHIQUITA. [PUEBLO DE SAN XAVIER DE CHIQUITOS, BOLIVIA. 1718.]
434 p. 25 cm.   HHB [Z-D 4]
Grammar of language of the Chiquita Indians of Bolivia. Transcript, partially in the handwriting of Alphonse L. Pinart, of original manuscript in the Bibliothèque Nationale, Paris.

ARZATE, JOSÉ ANTONIO
Letter to Dr. Antonio López Portillo; with Reply. Mexico City. November 19, 1765.
4 p. A.L.S. 21 cm.   HHB [M-M 403]
A letter from the printing-press official, Arzate, to the ecclesiastic, López Portillo, requesting sanction to print *Fragmentos de la vida y virtudes del Yl.ᵐᵒ y R.ᵐᵒ Sr. . . . Basco de Quiroga*, Bishop of Michoacán. With López Portillo's favorable reply (A.L.S., Mexico City, May 7, 1766) written on the margin, the imprimatur given in Mexico City on June 9, 1766, and an order for registration of the work (Mexico City, December 19, 1766).

ATKINSON, IDA I
Notes on Juan Napoleon Zerman.
1 carton.   [M-R 1]
Notes concerning Juan Napoleon Zerman and his filibustering activities in Mexico, ca. 1850-1900, such as his expedition in support of the Plan de Ayutla of 1854. Together with miscellaneous notes on Mexican history.

AUTOGRAPHS
15 pieces. 4-25 cm.   [Z-R 13]
Autographs of Lawrence Barrett, Struthers Burt, Fitz-Greene Halleck, Samuel Hull, William Hull, Thomas Jefferson (facsimile), Louis Kossuth,

Alexander H. Stephens, John Quincy Adams, James K. Polk, Ulysses S. Grant, Benjamin Harrison, and William H. Taft.

AVENDAÑO SUÁREZ DE SOUSA, PEDRO DE, b. ca. 1654
Fee de Erratas, Respuesta Apologetica à la Dedicatoria Aprovaciones, y Sermòn de la Purificacion, que imprimiô . . . El Doctor Don Diego Suaso, y Coscojales. . . . [Mexico. 1703]
98 p. 21 cm.   HHB [M-M 259]
An attack, in prose and verse, upon the model sermon preached by Suaso, Archdeacon of the Mexico City Cathedral, on February 2, 1703; ascribed on t.p. to "Santiago de Henares," but containing a statement near the end which names as authors Avendaño and one or more collaborators; attributed by Beristáin to Avendaño only.

Except for the transposition of certain opening and closing verses and the addition of the authorship statement, this Ms. is substantially identical with item 2 of "Varios papeles . . ." (M-M 255); for Suaso's sermon, see item 1 of "Varios papeles. . . ."

ÁVILA, JOSÉ MIGUEL DE
Accounts of the Haciendas of Bocas and Illescas. Mexico. 1765-1767.
94 p. 29 cm.   HHB [M-M 215]
Portions of account books for the estates of Bocas and Illescas. Contains 1) José Miguel de Ávila's "Libro Vorador de esta Hazienda de Bocas, perteneciente al Sr Dr Dn Fra.^{co} Espinosa, y Navarixo. . . . October 1, 1765-." These are accounts kept by the steward Ávila for the Hacienda de Bocas, primarily a sheep ranch, originally the property of Francisco Espinosa, one of Ávila's employers. And 2) two statements of accounts for the estate and farm of Illescas, drawn up by José Miguel de Ávila and Antonio Marín de Santa Cruz, stewards, respectively, from September 23, 1766, to October 15, 1767, and from September 14, 1766, to an unspecified date in 1767.

[ÁVILA, JUAN DE DIOS?] [N.p., n.p.]
18 p. 31 cm.   [M-M 1804]
Outline of arithmetical principles and procedure, incomplete, and text of a prayer. Cover sheets contain printed text of a bull of the Santa Cruzada, dated 1799.

ÁVILA Y URIBE, MARIANO GONZÁLEZ DE
Poema Comico Historial—El Indio Mas Venturoso, y Milagro de Milagros. La Aparicion de Nuestra Señora de Guadalupe. [Mexico. N. d.]
118 p. 21 cm.   HHB [M-M 16]
Copy of verse drama, in three acts, depicting the appearance of the Virgin of Guadalupe to the Indian neophyte, Juan Diego, and the subsequent miracles attending the construction of the Church of Guadalupe Hidalgo, under the auspices of Bishop Juan de Zumárraga.

AZANZA, MIGUEL JOSÉ DE, 1746-1826
 Ynstruccion sobre las Provincias de la Nueva España; dada por el Exmo Sr. D. José de Azanza á su sucesor. . . . San Cristóbal, Mexico. April 29, 1800.
 215 p. 31 cm. HHB [M-M 17]
 Report of Viceroy Azanza for his successor, Félix Berenguer de Marquina, divided into two parts: 1) Political, explaining administrative, judicial and commercial problems and plans of the viceroyalty; and 2) Military, especially with reference to Vera Cruz and San Juan de Ulúa. Two maps, one a road map, Puebla, 1798; and one of August, 1779, of the Gulf of N.^{ra} S.^{ra} de Regla on the North Pacific coast.

B   , G   A
 El Espíritu de la Democracia. [Mexico. ca. 1861]
 27 p. 22 cm. HHB [M-M 18-19]
 Monograph in defense of Catholicism, written in connection with deportation of Archbishop Lázaro de la Garza and other prelates from Mexico; points out the spiritual and material contributions of the Church to democratic welfare.

BAJA CALIFORNIA
 Documentos relativos á la administracion de Don Pedro M. Navarrete, Gefe Político y Comandante Militar del Territorio de la Baja California. . . . July 31, 1861–April 13, 1867.
 226 p. 32 cm. HHB [M-M 261]
 Contains a decree of President Juárez, Mexico City, July 31, 1861, relating to elections in Baja California; decrees, petitions, official correspondence, election records, and proclamations, Baja California and San Francisco, 1866, concerned with military and political developments in Baja California under the administration of Pedro M. Navarrete; and two letters, Mazatlán, 1867, from Navarrete to federal authorities regarding the method and consequences of his replacement by Antonio Pedrín.

BAJA CALIFORNIA
 Letters, Documents, and Notes. September 27–December 4, 1847.
 13 folders. 22-55 cm. [M-M 1765]
 Signed originals, copies, and drafts relating to Baja California in 1847 and primarily to the war between Mexico and the United States. Deal with military needs and maneuvers, war-time legislation, the meritorious conduct of various officers, the treachery of Francisco Palacios Miranda, former political head of Baja California, and similar matters. Consist primarily of correspondence and proclamations from Manuel Pineda of the Comandancia General de la Baja California, from Antonio Campuzano of the Comandancia General de Sonora, and from José Matías Moreno and Mauricio Castro, officials in the territorial government of Baja California.
 Written in Baja California and Sonora, with pencilled annotations ascribed to General Henry Wager Halleck. One folder contains brief notes by Halleck on the economics and geography of Baja California.

BAJA CALIFORNIA
  Selected Documents. 1770-1854.
  202 exp. (On film) [M-A 20]
  Threat of piracy in Baja California, 1853-1874; establishment of military posts, 1795-1820, with letters from Diego de Borica and Fernando de Rivera y Moncada; and Indian problems at Mission Santa Gertrudis, 1798.

BALTHROPE, JAMES M
  Letter to a Friend. Paris, Missouri. June 2, 1838.
  4 p. A.L.S. 21 cm. [Z-Z 100:94]
  Concerning conditions in Missouri and Kansas, and describing the raids of Jim Lane Montgomery and his band.

BANCROFT, GEORGE, 1800-1891
  Letters. 1845-1886.
  16 p. A.L.S. 14-23 cm. [Z-Z 120]
  Primarily social correspondence. Accompanied by several pictures of Bancroft.

BANCROFT, HUBERT HOWE, 1832-1918
  Correspondence.
  2 folders in portfolio. HHB [M-M 384]
  Two-page signed letter from General Ramón Corona (1837-1889) dated Mexico City, June 30, 1886, to Bancroft, expressing regret at the destruction of the latter's store by fire.
  Invitation to Bancroft to a Thanksgiving Charity Ball, November 26, 1891, in Mexico City; with two dance programs.

BANCROFT, HUBERT HOWE, 1832-1918
  Mexican Laws. [N.p., n.d.]
  17 p. A.D. 32 cm. HHB [M-M 349]
  Notes on Mexican laws, their origin in Spanish codes, and a review of Mexican compilations, to 1856, with a brief discussion of Mexican courts and legal procedure under the Republic.

BANCROFT, HUBERT HOWE, 1832-1918
  Notes on Mexico in 1883.
  209 p. A.D.S. 25 cm. HHB [M-M 341]
  Journal recording Bancroft's visit to Mexico and return trip to San Francisco, September 1, 1883–March 17, 1884, in company with his daughter Kate and his assistant, A. C. Cabezut. Made in response to a life-long desire to observe Mexico and its people, about which he had been writing for several years. Gives his impressions of the leading figures in the country, and the development and content of Mexican libraries and archives, particularly the Archivo General de la Nación. Contains a copy of a detailed report on the latter institution prepared by Justino Rubio of Mexico City, November 3, 1883.

BANCROFT, HUBERT HOWE, 1832-1918
United States Army in Mexico, 1847-1848. [N.p., n.d.]
5 p. A.D. 32 cm. HHB [M-M 346]
Notes commenting adversely on the conduct of the United States Army, and North Americans generally, in Mexico during the period indicated. Particular attention is given to newspapers published under the auspices of the United States Army at that time.

BANCROFT, MINNIE L (SMITH)
Diary of Mrs. Edward Bancroft. Holly, Michigan. 1884.
141 p. A.D. 10x7 cm. [Z-Z 106]
Entries concerning daily life and experiences as a schoolteacher. Photocopy available.

BANGS, SAMUEL, 1794-ca. 1853
Correspondence of. Monterrey, Saltillo, and Victoria. 1821-1835.
25 letters, 10 imprints, 1 clipping. A.L.S. and D.S. [M-B 14]
Correspondence between Samuel Bangs, first printer of the provinces of Nuevo León and Tamaulipas, with José Alejandro Uro y Lozano, another printer, relating mainly to the sale of printing presses and type to the latter. The imprints include an advertisement of a Ramage press; and manifestos and decrees, the first printed at Saltillo, May 27, 1822, and the last at Monclova, May 13, 1835.

BANNARD, WILLIAM
Letter to E. B. Walsworth. London. June 27, 1843.
4 p. A.L.S. 25 cm. [Z-Z 100:48]
Describing his voyage across the Atlantic.

BAPTISTA, HIERÓNIMO, fl. 1562
De Matrimonio Tractatus. [Mexico. N. d.]
115 p. D.S. 16 cm. HHB [M-M 22]
Treatise on canon law respecting marriage; deals with premarital inquiries, impediments to matrimony, separation of married persons, and related matters. The author, a Franciscan friar, was at one time a resident of the Colegio de Tlatelulco in the Provincia del Santo Evangelio. He is known primarily for his book of sermons in the Matlatzinca language.

BÁRCENA, GALAZO, NÚÑEZ ARICA, AND UROZA FAMILIES
Genealogical Documents, 1591-1714.
514 p. 31 cm. [M-M 1702]
Collection of documents, including petitions, testimony, royal orders and certifications, concerning the above interrelated families of Andalusia, namely, Pedro de Bárcena Jáurigui, Agustina Galazo de Bárcena, Alonzo Núñez Arica, and José de Uroza y Bárcena. Several members of these families settled in Puebla, Mexico, and the bulk of the material emanates from individual peti-

tioners in Puebla and from civil authorities in Spain or Mexico. Primarily contemporary certified copies.

BARING BROTHERS & CO. (LONDON)
The Baring Papers for 1846 to 1850, Relating to the War between the United States and Mexico.
3 folders and 1 vol. (Typescripts and Photocopies) 19-55 cm. [M-M 1727]
Excerpts from the collection for the period 1845-1850, copied or reproduced in 1936 from manuscripts in the Public Archives of Canada, Ottawa.

Folder 1. Typescripts of correspondence and miscellaneous papers, 1846-1850. 210 p. 26 cm.

Folder 2. Photocopies of two originals, letters of Thomas W. Ward and John H. B. Latrobe. Reproduced for the Bancroft Library as samples of the collection. 9 p. 26 cm.

Folder 3. Photocopies of English and French newspaper clippings relating to Mexican affairs, 1845-1849. 27 items. 19-55 cm.

The bound volume consists of carbon copies of the material in Folder 1. 206 p. 26 cm.

BARLOW, SAMUEL LATHAM MITCHILL, 1826-1889
Legal Agreement. St. Louis, Missouri. March 13, 1868.
7 p. D.S. 32 cm. [z-z 144]
Articles of agreement with the heirs of Eliza Clemens for division of property.

BARRUTIA, IGNACIO FRANCISCO
Correspondence. Mexico. April 22-October 10, 1729.
86 p. 30 cm. [M-M 1778]
Copies of official letters and documents received or dispatched by Barrutia, Governor of Nueva Vizcaya, concerning protection against the Tarahumares and other Indians, defense of missions, and Pedro de Rivera's 1724-1728 inspection of frontier presidios.

BATANGAS, PHILIPPINE ISLANDS
Marriage Records. 1738-1777.
2 vols. D.S. 30 cm. [z-p 101]
Records of marriages celebrated in Batangas by priests of the Augustinian Order.

BAUTISTA, JUAN [?], 1555-ca. 1613
Discursos Mexicanos. Mexico. 17th century.
26 p. 23 cm. HHB [M-M 458]
A collection of speeches and conversations in Náhuatl, with headings in Spanish, presenting social formulas and moral precepts. The speakers include a woman on her way to market, a bridal party, various officials, two young nobles, and others of their household. Described in the Ramírez catalogue as

probably fragments from the *Huehuetla(h)tolli* published in 1600, and now largely lost, by the Franciscan, Juan Bautista. Also known as "Huehuetlatolli, Documento A."

BAYARD, THOMAS FRANCIS, 1828-1898
Note to George Hannah. Wilmington, Delaware. November 16, 1883.
1 p. A.L.S. 9 cm. [z-z 100:17]
Card thanking Hannah for lecture ticket.

BEALER, LEWIS WINKLER, 1901-, *comp.*
Materials relating to South America and the West Indies. 1901-1939.
312 p. 20-46 cm. [z-r 9]
Letters and reports, largely statistical, concerning population, trade and commerce, banking, education, transportation and communications, in Bolivia, Peru, Surinam, Guiana, and the islands of Cuba, Puerto Rico, Guadeloupe, Martinique, and St. Pierre et Miquelon. Also a biographical sketch of Paraguayan president, General José Félix Estigarribia.

BEARD, SAMUEL PORTER, 1843-1863
Civil War Diary and Letter. 1862-1863.
107 p. A.D. and A.L.S. 12 and 27 cm. [z-z 117]
Diary, 1862-1863, and letter dated December 12, 1862. With transcripts and notes.

BEAUMONT, PABLO DE LA PURÍSIMA CONCEPCIÓN, fl. 1775
Crónica de la Provincia de S. Pedro y S. Pablo de Mechoacan. Mexico. 1849.
1,183 p. 33 cm. HHB [M-M 23]
Excerpts from Vols. IX, X, and XI of the Mexican National Archives, section on History, outlining the history, religious development, and natural resources of New Spain, with emphasis on the province of Michoacán and the work of the Franciscans. Printed in Mexico in 1873-1874 and again in 1932.

BEDFORD, ED.
Letter to Clarence F. Leighton. Belvedere, Kent, [England]. October 30, 1902.
2 p. A.L.S. 18 cm. [z-z 100:102]
Enclosing check and expressing appreciation of Leighton's help in connection with "Siam affairs."

BEJARANO, FÉLIX FRANCISCO
Informe hecho por el Gobernador [Comandante General] de Veragua . . . sobre las misiones de la Talamanca. Santiago de Veragua[s], Panama. September 15, 1775.
11 p. 28 cm. HHB [M-M 441]
Copy of a report addressed by the Commandant General of Veragua Province to the municipal authorities of Guatemala City, regarding a proposed Franciscan expedition into the territory of the Talamanca Indians. It

discusses the advisability of military assistance for the expedition, describes the territory and its inhabitants, and stresses their enmity with the Mosquito Indians. The document is preceded by copies of the Guatemalan request of March 11, 1775, for the report, and of Bejarano's order, August 6, 1775, for compliance with the request.

Entered by Bancroft under "Costa Rica—Copia del informe. . . ."

BEJARANO, MANUEL G., AND HERNÁNDEZ CHÁZARO, FRANCISCO
Certificate. Naranjal, Veracruz. October 31, 1920.
1 p. D.S. 35 cm.   HHB [M-M 1700:17]
Certificate issued by Judge Bejarano and Court Secretary Hernández of Naranjal, stating that the clay and stone articles in the collection of Custodian Llanos were excavated from a site in that municipality.

BÉLIARDI, AUGUSTIN, ABBÉ
Correspondence and Papers concerning Spanish Finance and Commerce. 1735-1767.
1 box. (Transcripts)   [Z-F 1]
Transcripts of papers of the Abbé Béliardi, "agent du commerce et de le marine a l'espagne, 1757-1771." They relate to the Family Compact; trade with Mexico, Louisiana, the West Indies, and the Philippines; and to war with Great Britain. Originals in the Bibliothèque Nationale, Paris.

BELLUGA Y MONCADA, LUIS ANTONIO DE, CARDINAL, 1662-1743
Memorial que da á su Mag.^{d} el Obispo de Cartagena . . . sobre los Acrecimientos, è impuestos de la Sal. . . . Murcia, Spain. November 29, 1713.
78 p. 31 cm.   HHB [Z-Z 20:2]
Pleas addressed to the King, requesting royal intervention in regard to a decree fixing the minimum price on salt for the clergy and for laymen.

[BENZ, ANTONIO MARÍA, b. 1716?]
Vocabulary of the Pima Language, with Grammatical Notes. Atti (?). [ca. 1796]
74 p. 21 cm.   HHB [M-M 475]
Pima vocabulary and grammatical notes; with criticism of vocabulary in a different handwriting. Incomplete.

BERGOSA Y JORDÁN, ANTONIO, bp.
Letter. Oaxaca, Mexico. June 18, 1802.
2 p. A.L.S. 30 cm.   HHB [M-M 504]
Letter from the Bishop of Antequera (Oaxaca), subsequently Archbishop-elect of Mexico, to the King's Minister, José Antonio de Caballero, enclosing copies of a pastoral epistle for royal approval. (Enclosures not present.)

BERNSTEIN, MAX, 1854-
Dictation. May 16, 1887.
4 p. 29 cm.   HHB [M-M 527]
Copper mining in Baja California, 1879-1885; land claims adjuster for

International Company of Mexico at Ensenada from 1885. Recorded for H. H. Bancroft.

BERRIOZÁBAL, GENERAL FELIPE B, 1827-1900
Papers relating to the Career of. Mexico. 1881.
4 folders in portfolio. 32-34 cm.   HHB [M-M 388]
Four items relating to the career of the Mexican general and statesman, Berriozábal, which contain biographical data and incidental information on military and political events.

1. Anonymous biographical sketch summarizing his military, political, and scientific achievements; Mexico (?), 1881. 10 p. 32 cm.

2. Certification of services rendered by General Berriozábal between February, 1862, and June 23, 1881, with a supplementary statement by General Ignacio Mejía; 10 p.

3. Copies of extracts from Berriozábal's military service record, for the period from July 2, 1847, to September 24, 1881; 10 p.

4. Explanatory list of decorations received and portrait of the general. Mexico, 1881 (?). 3 p.

BERROTARÁN, JOSEPH DE
Expediente on the Campaign of. Nueva Vizcaya. 1749-1750.
184 p. D.S. 31 cm.   [M-M 1784]
Campaign of Joseph de Berrotarán, commander of the presidio of San Francisco de Conchos, Valle de San Bartolomé, for the pacification of Suma, Apache, and other Indians, made by order of the governor of Nueva Vizcaya, Juan Francisco de la Puerta y Barrera, and charges resulting from Berrotarán's alleged failure to obey instructions.

BERTIN, L
Bill from "Bertin, Confiseur" for Various Items. Bolbec, France. March 7, 1850.
1 p. D.S. 13 cm.   [Z-Z 100:42]

BETHLEHEMITES, ORDER OF
Documents relating to. 1788-1816.
5 p. D.S. and printed. 21-31 cm.   [M-M 1865]
Concern the birth of the Infante, Carlos María Isidro (1788), a viceregal order about demonstrations on the return to the throne of Ferdinand VII, and appointment of Juan Ruiz de Apodaca as viceroy of New Spain, 1816.

BIBLE. SELECTIONS
Sacras Lectiones. [Mexico]. February 21, 1596.
318 p. 20 cm.   HHB [M-M 457]
Scriptural passages selected for reading on weekdays, Sundays, and feast days; translated into Náhuatl, with Latin headings and citations. It is preceded by a Church calendar and related material in Náhuatl and Latin.

BIERSTADT, ALBERT, 1830-1902
   Letter to Mr. Moran. December 26, 1867.
   2 p. A.L.S. 20 cm.   [z-z 100:75]
   Thanking him for arranging interview with the Queen and Sir John Cowell.

BLACK, JEREMIAH SULLIVAN, 1810-1883
   Letter to his Son, Chauncey Forward Black. York, Pennsylvania. April 28, [1868?]
   1 p. A.L., initialed. 25 cm.   [z-z 100:32]
   Concerning the printing of a paper he has written. Accompanied by related materials, including a biographical sketch.

BLACK, JOHN
   Certificate. Mexico City. March 4, 1850.
   2 p. D.S. and Printed. 32 cm.   HHB   [M-M 1700:34]
   Document issued by the U.S. Consul in Mexico City, certifying that James R. Norris is a citizen of the United States and requesting permission for him to travel freely in the country.

BLANCO JONS (?), JACINTO
   Orders of the Day. Jalisco. March 6-9, 1849.
   2 p. D.S. 31 cm.   HHB   [M-M 1700:47]
   Assignments to military duty in Zapopan and other places in the state of Jalisco. In the hand of "Bernal."

BLASCO Y GARCÍA, VICENTE, 1735-1813
   Speech before the Catedráticos of the University of Valencia [?]. 18th century.
   3 p. 30 cm.   HHB   [z-z 20:4]
   Upholding the right of the Library's benefactor, Francisco Pérez Bayer, to appoint the University's Chief Librarian.

BLOM, FRANS FERDINAND, 1893-1963
   Notes and Papers concerning Archaeological Research in Middle America.
   12 cartons and 1 package   [z-R 8]
   Diaries, field notes, manuscripts of articles, transcripts and photocopies of documents, periodicals, newspaper clippings, and reports on expeditions and exploration in Palenque, Uxmal, Honduras, Tabasco, and Chiapas.

BLOODGOOD, JOHN
   Draft of Deed to Abram Ackerman for Property in New York City. New York, N.Y. May 9, 1848.
   2 p. 40 cm.   [z-z 100:9]

BOLAÑOS MINING COMPANY
Proceedings at the Annual General Court of Proprietors of. [London] 1827-1845.
2 vols. (On film) [M-B 5]
Reports of the directors on the business operations of the company in the Bolaños mining district, situated between Guadalajara and Zacatecas.

BOLÍVAR, SIMÓN, 1783-1830
Documents. 1822-1828.
3 items. D.S. and Photocopy. 25-33 cm. [Z-D 132]
Photocopy of letter to José Antonio Páez, September 26, 1822, asking for information and hoping for peace; and two signed appointments to office, July 18, 1825, and July 24, 1828.

BOLTON, JUAN
Memoria del Padre Juan Bolton. San Ignacio. April 25, 1710.
2 p. A.L.S. 31 cm. HHB [M-M 1700:67]
Letter of thanks to Padre Juan de Iturderoaga, with list of charitable gifts received.

BONAVÍA Y ZAPATA, BERNARDO
Letters and Documents. Provincias Internas. 1797-1816.
7 folders. 15 p. D.S. 21-30 cm. [M-M 1792]
Seven communications, relating mostly to local affairs, received by Bonavía in his capacity as Governor-Intendant of Durango or as Commandant General of the Provincias Internas. They concern a smallpox epidemic in Papigochi, the absence of guilds and confraternities in Chiripas, development and financing of the new town of Santa Rosalía, questioning of captives taken in the Real de Santa Bárbara, lack of mining in the Basuchil area of Chihuahua, receipt of royal orders abrogating the Spanish constitution, and a disputed land claim in the new settlement of La Cruz.

BONILLA, ANTONIO
Apuntes sobre el Nuevo Mexico. Santa Rosa, New Mexico. September 3, 1776.
24 p. 31 cm. HHB [M-M 167]
Summary account of the conquest, colonization, and conversion of the province of New Mexico, 1600-1776, with suggestions for strengthening the Spanish position there. Appended is a census for the missions of the province, apparently taken from a report by Viceroy Palafox, 1642.
Entered by Bancroft under "New Mexico. Cédulas," and "Nuevo México. Cédulas."

BORAH, WOODROW WILSON, 1912-
Inventories of Parish Archives in the Mixteca Alta, 1682-1954. 1956.
26 p. (Typescript) 28 cm. [70/54m]
Includes the following parishes: Jaltepec, Nochixtlán, Teozacoalco, Teposcolula, Tilantongo, Tlasiaco, and Yanhuitlán.

BÖSE, EMIL, 1868-1927
> Excursions in Mexico. 1906.
> *131 p. and chart. 28 and 18x56 cm.* [M-M 1894]
> Translations of articles describing excursions to Tehuantepec, Tampico, Chavarillo, Santa María Tatetla, Veracruz, and Orizaba, taken during the Tenth International Geological Congress in Mexico in 1906.

BOSTON REGISTER OF SHIPS. 1785-ca. 1880.
> *664 p. (Typescript, carbon) 28 cm.* [Z-R 6]
> A compilation from Boston newspapers of changes of ownership of vessels, etc. Copy made for the Peabody Museum from a card file belonging to the Bostonian Society.

BOURS, TOMÁS ROBINSON & CO.
> Business Papers. Alamos, Mexico. 1863-1919.
> *4 boxes* [M-B 2]
> Correspondence, accounts, bills of lading, freight receipts, checks, promissory notes, customs clearances, and tax records of Bours' mining enterprises in the Sonora district of Mexico.

BOYD, HENRY
> Family Papers. 1850-1915.
> *5 folders. 20 p. L.S. 18-28 cm.* [M-M 1807]
> Four letters from Antonio López de Santa Anna to Henry Boyd, an early advocate of the Panama Canal, about plans for the canal, relations with the British, a California project, and other matters. Also six letters to the University of California from Boyd's son, concerning the sale of his father's maps and letters, 1912-1915.

BOYD FAMILY PAPERS. ca. 1780-1930.
> *1 carton* [Z-Z 115]
> Accounts, land and legal papers, and genealogical notes of the Boyd family of Indiana. Includes miscellaneous correspondence and papers of Dr. Samuel S. Boyd and Civil War diary of William A. Boyd, both officers in the 84th Indiana Volunteers.

BRACKETT, JAMES L
> Deed to Pierre Drouin for Land in Madison County, Illinois. Belleville, Illinois. January 30, 1837.
> *3 p. D.S. 33 cm.* [Z-Z 100:84]

[BRADFORD,   ]
> Sermon. Sheffield, Massachusetts. 1846.
> *28 p. 21 cm.* [Z-Z 100:4]

BRADLEY, ABRAHAM
   Miscellaneous Family Papers. 1766-1851.
   60 p. D.S. 32-42 cm.   [z-z 103]
   Mainly concerning the Bradley family, and land in Fayette County, Ohio, and elsewhere.

BRAMBILA Y ARRIAGA, ANTONIO
   Defensa mui Iusta que hase el maestre de scuela de la S.ta Yglecia de Oaxaca, por el . . . marques de Gelves . . . [Mexico. 1624]
   38 p. 31 cm.   HHB   [M-M 275]
   A defense of the Marqués de Gelves, Viceroy of New Spain, written by an ecclesiastic of the Oaxaca church, evidently shortly after the uprising of January, 1624, which had grown out of the conflict between the Viceroy and Archbishop Serna. Stresses Gelves' beneficence and contrasts it favorably with the provisional régime of the Real Audiencia.
   Entered by Bancroft and Ramírez under "Tumultos de México . . . ."

BRAMER, ELECTA (SNOW), 1796-
   Family Letters. 1818-1838.
   105 p. A.L.S. 19-34 cm.   [z-z 118]
   Mainly describing her experiences teaching in Massachusetts and New York. Included are a few letters from relatives and a biographical sketch of Mrs. Bramer by Achsa Snow Parker.

BREVE EXPLICACION DE LOS MISTERIOS DE N.ª S.ta FE CATHOLICA. [N.p., 18th century?]
   126 p. 23 cm.   HHB   [M-M 264]
   A catechism expounding the mysteries of the Catholic faith. Laid in envelope and portfolio; all margins clipped; ascribed in the Ramírez catalogue to the 18th century.

BREVE NOTICIA DEL ORDEN QUE SE DEVE GUARDAR Y OBSERVAR EN LAS SIEMBRAS DE MAGUEYES, SU ESCARDA, CASTRARLAS Y RASPARLAS, Y LABRAR LOS PULQUES QUE ELLOS PRODUCEN. [N.p., n. d.]
   16 p. 23 cm.   HHB   [M-M 27]
   Anonymous instructions for the cultivation of the maguey plant and the preparation of the fermented juice, pulque.

BREVE RESUMEN DEL DESCUBRIMIENTO DE LA NUEVA-ESPAÑA: DEMARCACION Y DESCRIPCION DE AQUELLAS PROVINCIAS . . . ; ESTADO DE SUS IGLESIAS . . . CON OTRAS NOTICIAS MUY IMPORTANTES DE AQUELLOS DOMINIOS. [Madrid. 1767]
   2 vols. (498, 456 p.) 43 cm.   HHB   [M-M 164-165]
   Anonymous account of the discovery of America, with descriptions of the various provinces of New Spain, the West Indies, the Philippines, the Ladrones, and the Pelew Islands. Covers the period 1492-1767, with special

attention to the history of cathedrals and principal churches, the administration of archdioceses and dioceses, and other ecclesiastical matters. Consists largely of reproductions of the pertinent instruments such as papal bulls and briefs, episcopal proclamations, and lists of bishops, archbishops, and viceroys.

Entered by Bancroft under "Nueva España, Breve Resúmen del Descubrimiento de la."

BRIGGS, LAWRENCE PALMER, 1880-
Papers. 1911-1912.
1 box [z-e 5]

Reports written by Briggs as the first Native Sons of the Golden West Travelling Fellow; material concerning José de Gálvez; notes and transcripts from various archives, chiefly the Archivo General de Indias and the Archivo de Simancas, pertaining to the Falkland Islands and British-Spanish relations; and a plan and manuscript of portions of a projected work on the Falkland Islands.

BRINGAS DE MANZANEDA Y ENCINAS, DIEGO MIGUEL
Papers and Maps. Mexico. 1773-1795.
18 p. (Photocopy and typescript) 28-45 cm. [m-m 1711]

Maps and documents relating to missionary activity in the Provincias Internas, especially Sonora. With typed transcripts of the documents. Originals in private possession.

BRIÓN, LUIS, 1782-1821
Letters relating to the Venezuelan Struggle for Independence. Angostura, etc. 1817-1820.
8 p. L.S., D.S. 25-33 cm. hhb [z-d 2]

BRITISH GUIANA
Documents relating to Land Grants. 1609-1663.
5 items (25 p.) (Photocopy) 31-47 cm. [z-d 136]

Grants and commissions from James I and Charles I and II to Robert Harcourt, Roger North, and Francis Willoughby, Baron Willoughby of Parham. Originals in the Public Record Office, London.

BRITISH WEST INDIES
Documents relating to. 1643-1882.
2 boxes (96 folders) hhb [z-a 3]

Originals, transcripts, and contemporary copies of documents relating to the government of various islands of the British West Indies: Barbados, St. Lucia, St. Christopher, Nevis, Jamaica, Trinidad, Grenada, and others. Included are proclamations, many pertaining to slaves and free Negroes.

The documents have been grouped according to islands, and chronologically within each group. A partial "key" to the collection is available in the Library.

BRODIE, JOHN PRINGLE, 1807-1869
 Journals and Related Material. 1824-1919.
 5 folders in portfolio. (Typescripts) 28 cm. [M-M 1707:1-5]
  Brodie's journals and notes, with relevant letters, grouped as follows:
  Folder 1: J. A. Waldteufel to Herbert E. Bolton. Ukiah, California, October 20-29, 1917; March 11, 1919. 3 p. L.S. Concerns use of the Brodie Mss. and scrapbook by the California Historical Survey Commission.
  Folder 2: John Pringle Brodie. February 27, 1824-May 12(?), 1832. 25 p. Journal of Brodie's 1824 voyage from Scotland to Mexico via the West Indies, aboard the brig *Jane*; fragmentary note on an 1828 trip from Guadalajara to Colima, Mexico; and opening portion of his account concerning a trip from Guadalajara to San Blas and beyond, covering departure from Guadalajara on May 10, 1832, and arrival in Tepic on May 12.
  Folder 3: Brodie's Journal, Mexico, May 10-12(?), 1832. An account of the Guadalajara-San Blas-Tepic trip, describing the countryside, various towns, and the people en route. 8 p. and a carbon copy.
  Folder 4: Brodie's Journal, Mexico, May 13-August 7(?), 1832. Continuation of the account concerning the 1832 trip from Guadalajara, which was extended to Guaymas and Chinapa; describes the Indians of the region, notably the Yaquis and Opatas, and mentions fellow travelers. 51 p. and a carbon copy.
  Folder 5: Brodie's Description of Guadalajara. Guanajuato, Mexico, June 23-July 20, 1831. Notes made during a business trip to Guanajuato. Consists principally of a description of the buildings, customs, and other features of Guadalajara, notably the Lancastrian school directed by Richard Jones, son-in-law of Joseph Lancaster. 15 p. and a carbon copy.
  Folders 2-5 were transcribed from the original Mss., now in the Edward E. Ayer Collection of the Newberry Library, Chicago, for the California Historical Survey Commission, 1917-1919.

BRONIMANN, EMIL
 Papers. ca. 1910-1949
 16 cartons [M-B 19]
  Papers relating to Bronimann's career as an engineer, consisting primarily of maps, plans, diagrams, tracings, sketches, blueprints, etc., of mines, mining camps, roads and railway routes in Chihuahua and other northwestern Mexican states. Included also are reports with related correspondence and plans for some of the engineering projects on which he was engaged; and maps of various towns, cities, and states in Mexico.

BROWN, DAVID
 Letter of Recommendation for. Hampshire County, Virginia. October 27, 1834.
 2 p. D.S. 34 cm. [Z-Z 100:78]
  Recommendation for Brown, "a free man of colour," about to migrate to Ohio. Signed by residents of the county.

BROWN, JAMES
 Pass for Corporal Chase, Company C, 1st Artillery Regiment. Camp Allen. October 11, 1863.
 1 p. D.S. 13 cm. [z-z 100:54]

BUCARELI Y URSÚA, ANTONIO MARÍA, 1717-1779
 Correspondence. 1772-1777.
 1 volume. (Transcripts) 28 cm [z-e 9]
 Typescripts of letters selected by Alfred B. Thomas from the Archivo General de Indias, Seville. A "key" to the collection is available in the Library.

BUCARELI Y URSÚA, ANTONIO MARÍA, 1717-1779
 Document. Mexico City. December 16, 1772
 38 p. D.S. 30 cm. [m-m 1700:78]
 Transmitting report on flood in San Juan del Río, Querétaro, and ordering repairs. Includes statements of town officials.

BUCARELI Y URSÚA, ANTONIO MARÍA, 1717-1779
 Reglamento Provisional para el prest, vestuario, gratificaciones, hospitalidad, recluta, disciplina y total govierno de la tropa que debe guarnecer el Presidio de Nuestra Señora del Carmen de la Isla de Tris . . . [and other documents pertaining to the same presidio]. Mexico City. October 22, 1774-August 2, 1775.
 81 p. Ms. and printed. 31 cm. HHB [m-m 409]
 Printed regulations and instructions for maintenance of the Presidio of Nuestra Señora del Carmen on the island of Tris, discipline of the troops, and establishment and operation of a hospital there. Includes manuscript copies of relevant communications from Viceroy Bucareli to Pedro de Dufau Maldonado, Governor of the Presidio.

BUENOS AIRES (PROV.)
 Proyecto de un puerto en la Bahía de Samborombón, Buenos Aires. ca. 1900-1910.
 20 items. 26-32 cm. [z-d 110]
 Copies of correspondence, reports, drawings, and printed pamphlets concerning a proposed deep-water port on Samborombón Bay. Presumably from the files of Arturo Castaño, engineer and representative of the Port Argentine Great Central Railways Company, Ltd.

BULL, JAMES HUNTER, fl. 1843-1845
 Papers. 1843-1845.
 2 folders (Typescript) 28 cm. [m-m 1754]
 Folder 1. Copies of items ascribed to or concerning Bull, as follows: a letter, Hermosillo, Mexico, September 3, 1843, from William Keith to Abel Stearns, introducing Bull as a visitor to Los Angeles en route to Oregon Territory; a letter, Mexico City, October 9, 1845, from John Black of the U.S. Consular Service to José Antonio Navarro, introducing Bull and requesting assistance for him during a visit to Texas; a report dated November, 1844,

ascribed to Bull, telling of a recent journey through Baja California and describing the countryside, the people, and the missions. 30 p.

Folder 2. Miscellaneous material relating to the contents of Folder 1, as follows: copy of a letter [San Francisco], October 16, 1927, from Frances H. Bull, daughter of James Hunter Bull, to Major Leon French, Secretary-Registrar of the California Society of the Sons of the American Revolution, concerning disposition of her father's papers; a signed letter [San Francisco], December 16, 1927, from French to Professor Fletcher Harper Swift of the University of California at Berkeley, requesting transmittal to Professor Herbert E. Bolton of a copy of a letter from Commodore Bull; an undated memorandum from F. B. (Frances Bull?), explaining why the report on the Baja California material should be ascribed to Bull rather than to Stearns; and a signed letter of transmittal, Berkeley, October 10, 1929, from Swift to Bolton. 4 p.

BURGOA, FRANCISCO DE, 1605-1681

Geográfica descripcion de la Parte Septentrional, del Polo Artico de la America, ... Extractos. Mexico City. 1674.

82 p. 31 cm. HHB [M-M 263]

An English outline, by chapters, of the *Geográfica Descripción*, whose two volumes form a sequel to Burgoa's *Palestra Historial*, the whole work constituting a history of the Dominican Province of Oaxaca during the sixteenth and seventeenth centuries, with some descriptive material on the aborigines. The document has an English translation of the opening portion of Burgoa's preface.

BURKE, EDWARD AUSTIN, d. 193-(?)

Papers. Tegucigalpa, New Orleans, etc. 1883-1936.

332 p. 4½-36 cm. [Z-C 200]

Relate to personal, public, and business affairs in Honduras; letters, contracts, reports, etc. Included are personal letters from various presidents of Honduras, and from Porfirio Díaz of Mexico.

BURT, THOMAS

Sea time & Distance of H.M.S. "Caesar." June 14, 1858-January 27, 1862.

1 p. A.D.S. 29 cm. [Z-Z 100:57]

Record of the *Caesar's* cruises, chiefly in the Mediterranean, with a voyage to the West Indies and Mexico in 1859.

BUSTAMANTE, CARLOS MARIA DE, 1774-1848

Apuntes para la Historia del Gobierno del G.¹ Guadalupe Victoria, primer Presidente de los Estados Unidos Mexicanos. Mexico City. 1830.

870 p. Ms. and printed. 23 cm. HHB [M-M 28]

Adverse account of the administration of Guadalupe Victoria, first president of Mexico, consisting of notes arranged chronologically, 1826-1829, and presented as a warning to his successors. Includes 40 pp. reprinted from *Voz de la Patria*.

BUSTAMANTE, CARLOS MARÍA DE, 1774-1848
 Continuación de la Voz de la Patria. . . . Mexico. 1837-1839.
10 vols. in 5. A.D.S. and printed. 23 cm.   HHB [M-M 49-53]
 Continuation of the 5 volumes of *Voz de la Patria;* contains a record of the principal events in Mexico during the period from October, 1831, to March, 1839, with special attention to the defeat and death of Vicente de Guerrero, the activities of Santa Anna and Valentín Gómez Farías, cholera epidemic of 1833, campaign of General Valentín Canalizo (quoted partly from his own narrative), persecution of the clergy, revolt of Texas and other Mexican possessions, the "Pastry War" with France, 1838-1839; based partly on contemporary journals and partly on personal notes whose importance was enhanced after 1835 by the author's position as deputy from Oaxaca to the National Congress. A substantial portion of the material in Vols. XIII-XIV appears also in Bustamante's *Gabinete Mexicano.*

BUSTAMANTE, CARLOS MARÍA DE, 1774-1848
 Diario de lo especialmente ocurrido en México. August, 1823-August, 1841.
16 reels (13,282 exp., on film).   [M-M 1880]
 Forty volumes of miscellaneous diary entries, printed news sheets, broadsides, government publications, pamphlets, etc. Microfilm of originals in the Biblioteca Pública del Estado, Elías Amador, Zacatecas.
 Manuscripts M-M 29-32 constitute a continuation of this series.

BUSTAMANTE, CARLOS MARÍA DE, 1774-1848
 Diario de lo especialmente ocurrido en Mexico, septiembre de 1841 . . . [a junio de 1843]. Mexico. 1841-1843.
4 vols. A.D.S. and printed. 23-24 cm.   HHB [M-M 29-32]
 Intermittent diary entries, printed news sheets, official and private, and pamphlets covering developments in Mexico from Bustamante's resignation through the adoption of the 1843 Constitutional Bases; stresses Santa Anna, Texas, Central America, and the Constituent Congress of 1842. Printed items include L. Abadiano's verses, "Visita de un Camposanto," a first supplement to Alegre's *Historia de la Compañía de Jesús en Nueva España,* Navarro's catalog of curacies and missions in New Spain, and various broadsides and pamphlets.

[BUSTAMANTE, CARLOS MARÍA DE], 1774-1848 [*comp.?*]
 Diario Esactisimo de lo ocurrido en Mexico en los dias de su invacion por el G.^{ral} Scot, . . . 1676-1849.
10 items. 232 p. Ms. and printed. 32 cm.   HHB [M-M 77-83]
 Compilation of materials relating to Bustamante's work and possibly prepared under his direction, as follows: anonymous diary, Mexico, 1847, on events in Mexico, including the activities of García Torres, owner of the *Monitor Republicano,* during the invasion under General Winfield Scott; entries for May 10-September 21, 1847, and background data extending from December, 1844. Excerpts from the diary of Juan Antonio Rivera, chaplain of the Hospital de Jesús Nazareno in Mexico City; pleas for governmental sup-

port of the Jesuits, with printed copy of a presidential decree to this effect, June 22, 1843; draft of an article on the death of General Morelos; necrology of Dr. Santiago, Mexico City, 1845; official communication on agricultural-export policy, November, 1844; draft of an article on freedom of the press, n. d.; articles by Bustamante on the Count of Aranda's proposal for establishment of a monarchy in Mexico, 1833; reprint of an article by Father Servando Mier on Mexican federation, December 13, 1823; and a printed leaflet, prepared by Bustamante, reviewing the lives of certain emperors of Mexico, 1361-1502, based on old manuscripts used by Lorenzo Boturini.

BUSTAMANTE, CARLOS MARÍA DE, 1774-1848
Gabinete Mexicano: Continuación del Cuadro Histórico de la Revolución Mexicana. . . . Mexico. [1839-1843]
4 vols. A.D.S. and printed. 20-23 cm.   HHB   [M-M 33-36]
Collection of data on events in Mexico from April, 1837, to December, 1844, covering Anastasio Bustamante's second term and Santa Anna's return to power. Based on official and other publications and on the author's personal observations; presented in the form of letters, notes, and journalistic items.

BUSTAMANTE, CARLOS MARÍA DE, 1774-1848
Materiales para la continuación del cuadro histórico de la revolución mexicana. Mexico. 1833-1839.
542 p. A.D.S. 23 cm.   HHB   [M-M 38]
Collection of material for Vols. VII and VIII of his history of the Mexican revolution, August, 1822, to October, 1824, including the period of Agustín de Iturbide and the inauguration of Guadalupe Victoria.

BUSTAMANTE, CARLOS MARÍA DE, 1774-1848
Medidas para la Pacificacion de la America Mexicana. Mexico. 1820-[1839]
374 p. A.D.S. 31 cm.   HHB   [M-M 39]
A treatise on measures for the pacification and development of Mexico; concerns administrative, economic, and social reforms; reformation of the old laws for the Indies; and miscellaneous material on the tobacco trade, schools for Indians, restoration of the Society of Jesus, bankruptcy laws, and other matters.

BUSTAMANTE, CARLOS MARÍA DE, 1774-1848
Memorándum, o sea apuntes p.ª escribir la historia de lo especialmente ocurrido en México. . . . Mexico. 1844-1848.
8 vols. 21-22 cm.   HHB   [M-M 40-47]
A record, in diary form, of the outstanding events affecting the history of Mexico, April, 1844, to September, 1847. Stresses the conflict between Mexico and the United States, treachery of Santa Anna, and the disturbances in Yucatan. Three maps of the battles of Matamoros and Palo Alto.

BUSTAMANTE, CARLOS MARÍA DE, 1774-1848
 Mexico en 1848. Principales sucesos politicos y militares. Mexico. [1847-1848]
 103 p. 22 cm. HHB [M-M 48]
 Collection of notes, chiefly in diary form, on outstanding events in Mexico and Europe, 1847-1848, with particular attention to the occupancy of Mexico by forces of the United States and to their withdrawal. Includes some documents sent to Bustamante by General Pedro de Ampudia, regarding the conduct of General Mariano Arista, and excerpts from current periodicals.

BUSTAMANTE, CARLOS MARÍA DE, 1774-1848
 Ynvasion de Mexico p.r los Anglo-Americanos. [Mexico. ca. 1847]
 345 p. D.S. 22 cm. HHB [M-M 37]
 Incomplete draft, apparently Vol. IV and a portion of Vol. III, of his history of the invasion of Mexico in 1846-1847.

C., M. A. d. l.
 Pastorela en dos Actos. 1828.
 82 p. 21 cm. HHB [M-M 196]
 A semi-allegorical, two-act play in verse, dealing with the announcement of the birth of Christ to a group of shepherds and their homage to him.

CABALLERO, JOSÉ DE
 Estadística del Estado Libre de Sonora y Sinaloa. . . . Mazatlán (Mexico). 1825.
 39 p. D.S. 21-22 cm. HHB [M-M 501]
 Statistical report on the Free State of Sonora and Sinaloa, covering boundaries, topography, civil and religious institutions, ports, products, roads, population, etc. Prepared by a member of the Mexican General Staff in compliance with the Provisional Regulations thereof, and contains a signed introduction dated July 25, and a signed note dated July 27 on a proposed second report. Includes four maps showing respectively the Free State, the port of Guaymas, the port of San Feliz de Mazatlán, and a principal road from the Free State to Mexico City.

CABREDO, RODRIGO DE, d. 1617
 Annual Reports of the Society of Jesus for the Years 1614 and 1615. Mexico. May 1, 1615, and May 1, 1616.
 2 vols. (99, 63 p.). D.S. 30 cm. [M-M 1717]
 Prepared by the Jesuit Provincial of Mexico and Visiting Inspector for Peru, these describe conditions, events, and personnel in the various Jesuit divisions of New Spain. Signature of Cabredo at end of volume I only. Portions of the two volumes are reproduced in "Memorias para la Historia de la Provincia de Sinaloa" (M-M 227).

CALDERÓN DE LA BARCA, PEDRO, AND OTHERS
 Three Comedies. Spain. 17th century.
 142 p. 23 cm. HHB [M-M 462]
 Náhuatl translations or adaptations of three Spanish plays:

1. Pedro Calderón de la Barca (1600-1681), Comedia del gran teatro del mundo . . . , 30 p., n.p., n.d. Translated by Bartolomé de Alba and dedicated to Father Jácome Basilio (mistakenly ascribed to Lope de Vega in the Ramírez catalogue).

2. Antonio Mira de Amescua (fl. 1600), Comedia famosa . . . del animal propheta y dichoso patricida . . . , 78 p., n.p. Translated by Bartolomé de Alba in 1640 (mistakenly ascribed in the heading and in the Ramírez catalogue to Lope de Vega).

3. Lope Félix de Vega Carpio (1562-1635), Comedia . . . intitulada la madre de la mejor . . . , 30 p., n.p., n.d. Anonymous translation, dedicated to the Jesuit, Horacio Carochi.

CALIFORNIA AND THE PROVINCIAS INTERNAS. 1654-1773.
103 exp. (On film) [Z-G 13]
Copies of an account of the provinces of New Spain, written by a Spanish cosmographer, 1654, and descriptions of California by Father Fernando Consag, 1746, and Juan Bautista de Anza, 1773-1774.
Microfilm of documents in the British Museum.

CALIFORNIA DISCOVERIES. MEXICO. 1573-1636.
58 p. 31 cm. HHB [M-M 54]
Portion of a file compiled for the Council of the Indies by order of Viceroy Lope Díaz de Armendáriz relating to exploration rights in Lower California. Contains copy dated November 24, 1635, of Philip II's decree of July 13, 1573, for the regulation of exploration and colonization in the New World, together with related documents of the year 1636.

CALIFORNIA SETTLERS
Warning to the Audiencia of Guadalajara. Mexico City. June 12, 1802.
2 p. 31 cm. HHB [M-M 1700:27]
Call for greater care in the selection of settlers destined for the Californias, in place of the criminals hitherto sent. Preceded by a document, Mexico City, August 17, 1801, in which Borbón, an official of the Treasury, expressed an opinion of the same matter.

CALIFORNIAS
Primer Escuadrón de . . . Primera Compañía. [N.p., ca. 1840]
6 p. 17 cm. HHB [M-M 1700:3]
List of members of the First Company of the California First Squadron. Presumably written in California.

CAMPBELL, W M
Letter to Cyrus [Campbell?], his Brother. "Hd. Quarters 2 Iowa Inft." La Grange, Tennessee. October 5, 1863.
4 p. A.L.S. 21 cm. [Z-Z 100:76]
Concerning the Civil War.

CAMPOS, JUAN
>Appointment. Madrid. January 8, 1802.
>*1 p. D.S. 31 cm.* HHB [M-M 1700:24]
>Royal appointment of Lieutenant Campos to replace the late José Magdonel as Captain of the Tabasco Infantry Militia.

CANARY ISLANDS. GOBIERNO
>Emigration to Cuba. Santa Cruz de Tenerife and Laguna. April 27-May 1, 1853.
>*12 p. Ms. and printed. 31-41 cm.* [Z-A 200:2]
>Permits for emigration of José Suárez, José García, Mateo Gonzales, and Salvador Ángel de la Rosa.

CARLI, GIOVANNI RINALDO, CONTE, 1720-1795
>Cartas Americanas. Nueva edición corregida y aumentada. . . . Traducidas del italiano al castellano. . . . Capo d'Istria. May 9, 1777-December 5, 1779.
>*2 vols. 22 cm.* HHB [M-M 55-56]
>A treatise on the geography, history, and civilizations of the New World, stressing the relationship of its peoples with those of the Old, and tracing a connection through the lost continent of Atlantis. Consists of 25 letters, 24 addressed to Carli's relative, Gerónimo Gravisi, Marchés di Pietra-Pelosa, and one to Father Gregorio de la Fuente of the University of Fabia. Translated by José María Fernández de Herrera y Gómez from the Cremona edition of 1781-1782. See also Fernández de Herrera y Gómez, "Critica. . . ." (M-M 112).

CARLSON, RUTH ELIZABETH (KEARNEY)
>Notes on Baja California. 1944.
>*16 p. (Typescript) 28 cm.* [M-R 4]
>Notes on proposed military colony at Santo Tomás, 1849-1850; on Ensenada filibustering scheme, 1889-1890; biographies of people associated with Lower California colonization ventures; notes on recent economic history.

CAROTHERS, A G
>Sermon. Washington, D.C. January 16, 1853.
>*53 p. A.D.S. 18 cm.* [Z-Z 100:47]
>Dedication sermon for the Fifth Presbyterian Church.

CARRANZA, VENUSTIANO, 1859-1920
>Letters. Veracruz. April 20, 22, 1915.
>*2 p. L.S. 28 cm.* HHB [M-M 1700:15]
>Letter of April 20 to Miguel E. Muñoz in Nogales, Arizona, thanking him for a letter of condolence on the death of the President's brother, General Jesús Carranza; another, dated April 22, addressed to Sra. Dolores Montaño in Veracruz, acknowledging her felicitations on the success of the Constitutionalist Army in Celaya and suggesting an interview on the subject of her son Luis.

CARRERA, FERNANDO DE LA
Arte de la lengua Yunga de los valles del obispado de Truxillo, con un confessionario, y todas las oraciones Christianas, y otras cosas. . . . [Lima, Peru. 1644]
2 vols. 19 cm.   HHB   [Z-D 3]
Copy made by Alphonse Pinart in the library of Joaquín García Icazbalceta. [Cf. Altieri, Radames A. *La Gramática Yunga de F. de la Carrera.* Tucumán, 1939.]

CARRERA, RAFAEL, 1814-1865
Calendar of Selected Documents for Career of. 1838-1865.
1 vol. 25 cm.   [68/89z]
Military rule of Carrera in Guatemala, which he dominated as chief executive for a quarter century. Copied from the Public Record Office, London.

CARRINGTON, J W
Remarks. Mexico. [N.p., n.d.]
11 p. 32 cm.   HHB   [M-M 347]
Remarks of Carrington, at one time translator for the British Legation in Mexico, regarding events leading up to British participation in the invasion of Mexico in 1861, the resulting break in relations with Great Britain, and public affairs during the terms of several Mexican presidents and the reign of Maximilian.

CARVAJAL, RAPHAEL
Letter to Doctor Miller. Brown's Hotel. December 30, 1847.
1 p. A.L.S. 27 cm.   [Z-Z 18]
Requesting that the doctor call to treat his cold.

CASA DE CONTRATACIÓN DE INDIAS, SEVILLE, SPAIN
Documents relating to Personnel Administration. 1779.
9 p. D. and D.S. 21-30 cm.   HHB   [Z-Z 20:3]
A report on individual employees of certain offices, addressed to José de Gálvez, Minister of the Indies, and related correspondence.

CASA FUERTE, JUAN DE ACUÑA Y BEJARANO, MARQUÉS DE, 1658-1734
Document concerning Settlement of Estate of Domingo Ruanco in Santiago de Querétaro. Mexico City. November 5, 1728.
7 p. D.S. 31 cm.   [M-M 1700:76]
With related papers.

CASAS, BARTOLOMÉ DE LAS, bp., 1474-1566
Documents relating to.
9 reels (1,356 exp. On film)   [M-M 1834]
Materials from various sources, chiefly the New York Public Library and the Library of Congress.

CASAS, BARTOLOMÉ DE LAS, bp., 1474-1566
   Extractos de *Historia de las Indias.* Madrid. 1561.
   101 p. 31 cm. HHB [M-M 278]
   Excerpts from Las Casas' *History of the Indies,* dealing principally with the voyages of Columbus. Incomplete.
   The history has been printed several times, with varying volume divisions and under different titles, e.g., *Historia de Yndias, Historia General de las Indias.*

CASAS, BARTOLOMÉ DE LAS, bp., 1474-1566
   Historia Apologetica de las Yndias Occidentales. Extracts. Valladolid, Spain. ca. 1527-ca. 1560.
   247 p. 33 cm. HHB [M-M 122]
   Also known as "Apologética historia sumaria cuanto a las cualidades, disposición, descripción, cielo y suelo de estas tierras, y condiciones naturales, policías, repúblicas, maneras de vivir e costumbres de las gentes de estas Indias occidentales y meridionales, cuyo imperio soberano pertenece á los Reyes de Castilla," and by variants of this longer title. First published in full in Madrid in 1909.
   These excerpts, made for Bancroft from a Ms. in the Library of Congress, deal with the lands, customs, and attributes of the American Indians. The work was originally intended for inclusion in the author's general history of the Indies and was designed to demonstrate the Indians' inherent capacity for assimilating Christian culture as free men.

CASAS, BARTOLOMÉ DE LAS, bp., 1474-1566
   Historia de las Indias. . . . [ca. 1527-1561]
   393 p. 33 cm. HHB [M-M 123]
   Contains excerpts from various parts of the above *Historia;* an outline by chapters of the author's *Historia Apologética;* and an outline by chapters of the *Historia de las Indias.* See also Bartolomé de las Casas, "Extractos de Historia de las Indias" (M-M 278).

CASS, LEWIS, 1782-1866
   Letter to [John Young] Mason. Paris. August 6, 1839.
   1 p. A.L.S. 21 cm. [Z-Z 100:61]
   Inviting him to dine. With autograph of Mason pasted at bottom.

CASTERA, IGNACIO
   Plano de la ciudad de México. . . . [Mexico City]. June 24, 1794.
   1 p. Map. 47x69 cm. [M-M 1879]
   Colored plan of Mexico City, drawn to show the paving assessments that would result from a ruling of Viceroy Revilla Gigedo the Younger, with explanations for use of the plan.

CASTILLO, ANTONIO DEL, fl. 1611
   La Vida del Benerable y muy Religioso P. Fr. Ivan de Castro. . . . [Mexico. N. d.]
   90 p. A.D.S. 15 cm. HHB [M-M 58]

Contains a signed dedication to King Philip III of Spain, prologue, and 13 chapters recording the saintly life of the Augustinian, Juan de Castro, Archbishop of Santa Fé in the kingdom of New Granada and former colleague of the author; with an epitaph in Latin and Spanish composed by Fray Basilio Ponce de León, Knight Commander of Malta. Written between 1611 and 1621.

CASTILLO GADEA, FRAY JUAN DE
Castillo Family Genealogical Documents. 1667-1668.
160 p. D.S. 32 cm. [z-z 138]
Certified copies of records of the Castillo family in Granada, Málaga, Baeza, and other cities of Andalusia, Spain.

CASTRO, MANUEL [DE JESÚS), 1810-
Libro de tomas de razon de los titulos de las tierras de labranza concedidas en la Colonia Militar de Santo Tomas en el año de 1850 y 1851. Baja California. July 5, 1850-September 5, 1851.
2 vols. 7, 44 p. 32 cm. HHB [M-M 262]
An uncompleted record containing copies of land grants issued in 1850-1851 by Castro, Commandant of the Military Colony at Santo Tomás, Baja California, in compliance with a decree of July 20, 1848, and an order of May 3, 1850. Includes grants to José Antonio Chaves, Manuel Díaz, Anastasio Ramírez, and many others, and some miscellaneous documents.

CATLIN, GEORGE, 1796-1872
Correspondence and Papers. 1798-1874.
187 items, and 210 exp. on film. [z-z 114]
Letters, diary, and family papers relating chiefly to Catlin's travels and the execution and exhibition of his Indian portraits. Gift of Mrs. H. G. Roehm.

CAVITE, LUZON, PHILIPPINE ISLANDS
Account of Disciplinary Action against Two Soldiers of the Sixth Infantry Regiment in Cavite. September 10-12, 1852.
10 p. (incomplete). D.S. 15 32 cm. [z-p 116]

CAVITE, LUZON, PHILIPPINE ISLANDS
Estado del Presupuesto de las obras del año prosimo venidero de 1811. . . . Cavite. December 31, 1810.
1 p. D.S. 53x73 cm. [z-p 112]
Budget for the arsenal estimating personnel and wages for the year 1811.

CAVITE, LUZON, PHILIPPINE ISLANDS
Letters to the Jefe de Estado Mayor Apostadero. Cavite. 1895-1896.
5 p. L.S. 23 cm. [z-p 118]
Correspondence concerning the murder of a sailor from the cruiser *Castilla*.

CAVITE, LUZON, PHILIPPINE ISLANDS
Maestranza Eventual Cañonero N.° 17. Mes de Dic.ᵉ de 1861.
4 p. D.S. 30 cm. [z-p 117]
Account of shipyard expenditures.

CAVITE ARSENAL, LUZON, PHILIPPINE ISLANDS
Records. 1815-1839.
22 p. D. and D.S. 20-29 cm. [z-p 113]
Miscellaneous papers relating to the budget and pay record of the arsenal, and to various naval service records.

CEDULARIO Y PAPELES VARIOS. [N. p.] 1675-1819.
3 vols. Ms. and printed. 32-34 cm. HHB [M-M 60-62]
Copies of Spanish royal decrees, Mexican viceregal orders, papal briefs, reports, official correspondence, et cetera, with one original letter (Viceroy Iturrigaray to the Intendant of Guadalajara, Mexico City, June 30, 1803). Concern regulations on various matters in the Indies, such as marriages, property transactions, state and ecclesiastical finances, administrative organization, the University of Guadalajara, judicial procedure, treatment of Indians, public order, and the mining, rum, and tobacco industries; apparently compiled for the Audiencia of Guadalajara. Subject index. Various original signatures. Many items on stamped paper.

CENSUS REPORTS. NUEVA VIZCAYA. 1786-1821.
5 folders. 5 p. D.S. 30-31, 31x42 cm. [M-M 1793]
Census tables and reports for Valle de la Ciénaga de los Olivos, 1786; for the Corps of Dragoons in the jurisdiction of Chihuahua, 1787; for the parish of San Francisco Javier de Satebó and the mission of Santiago de Bobonoyaba, 1799; for the presidio of San Carlos and the Hacienda de Dolores, 1817; and for the Valle de Santa Rosalía, 1821. Included are population figures grouped by race, sex, age, and civil status.

CENTRAL AMERICA
Documents relating to the History of. ca. 1536-1717.
2 reels (On film) [z-c 217]
Documents from various Central American archives, filmed by Philip W. Powell.

CENTRAL AMERICA
Documents relating to the History of. ca. 1678-1822.
6 reels (On film) [z-c 215]
Original documents in various Central American archives, selected for filming by Thomas E. Downey.

CERECEDA, ANDRÉS DE
Letter to the King of Spain. León, Nicaragua. July 20, 1529.
17 p. 33 cm. HHB [M-M 302]
Summary report from the treasurer of the González Dávila-Niño expedition regarding events in Nicaragua and Honduras during the period 1527-1529.

CERECEDA, ANDRÉS DE
   To the King. Trujillo del Pinar, Honduras. June 14, 1533.
   62 p. 33 cm.   HHB   [M-M 318]
   Letter addressed to the King of Spain by the Governor of Honduras, Cerezeda, reporting on events during the period 1530-1533. Gives special attention to the struggle for power of Cerezeda against two rivals, Vasco de Herrera and Diego Méndez, but covers also the arrival and death of Governor Alvítez, local revolts, plans for new settlements in the Naco Valley and elsewhere, the treatment of Indians, and other matters.

CHACÓN [DE LA MOTA], TERESA
   Obra Pia del glorioso Martir Señor San Phelipe de Jesus. Segunda ultima Quenta del Cargo. . . . [Mexico City] 1747.
   19 p. 31 cm.   [M-M 1705]
   Second and final report on the charge entrusted to Andrés de la Mota, deceased presbyter and chaplain of the Mexico City Cathedral, as administrator of the pious foundation in honor of St. Philip the Martyr. It covers the period from November 17, 1733, to August 23, 1747, and was drawn up by Mota's mother, Teresa Chacón de la Mota, on the basis of his records, and submitted by her to Francisco Rodríguez Navarro, cathedral dignitary. Apparently a contemporary copy.

CHAPPE d'AUTEROCHE, JEAN, 1728-1769
   History of the Voyage of Monsieur L'Abbe Chappe to Baja California to Observe the Transit of Venus across the Disk of the Sun, in 1769.
   19 p. 20-24 cm.   [M-M 1713]
   English translation of a summary account of this expedition, by Mr. Pauly, the King's Engineer and Geographer, and one of Chappe d'Auteroche's chief assistants. Describes the epidemic in which Chappe d'Auteroche and others died, and refers also to the kindness of Viceroy Croix. Written by Pauly, apparently in connection with a petition to the King for an increased pension.

CHASE, E   B
   Wagers on the Election of Martin Van Buren. Boston, Massachusetts. April 3, 1840.
   2 p. D S. 10 cm.   [Z-Z 100:37]
   Signed by James T. Fisher, witness.

CHAVERO, ALFREDO, 1841-1906, *comp.*
   Maltratamiento de Indios. Mexico. 1609-1773.
   522 p. Ms. and printed. 32 cm.   HHB   [M-M 135]
   Collection of reports, decrees, correspondence, and related material bearing primarily upon the treatment of Indians in New Spain and the difficulties encountered there by Franciscans and Jesuits. The volume contains 28 separate items, as follows:
   1) A statement, ca. 1724, by Cristóbal Domínguez, guardian of the convent of San Francisco de México, protesting the collection of certain tribute by

the secular clergy; 2) instructions of Joseph de la Vallina, Franciscan provincial, November 11, 1752, on investigation of complaints regarding obsequies; 3) draft of a proposal by a Mexican Jesuit for defense of the Order with the aid of Indian neophytes; 4-5) two royal cedulas, May 26, 1609, and March 23, 1644, regarding the labor and general welfare of the Indians in New Spain; 6) certified copies of petitions, decrees, and related documents, ca. 1725, on disputes between Franciscans and the civil and ecclesiastical authorities regarding services of Indians in Tlaxcala and elsewhere; 7) order concerning the payment of tribute, November 16, 1741, at Toluca and Zinacantepec; 8) letter from Miguel Joseph Calderón, June 11, 1725, denying accusations of the Tlaxcalan Indians against the Nativitas monastery; 9) report from the governor of Chihuahua to Viceroy Fuenclara, September 1, 1744, regarding the royal program of Indian welfare; 10) apparently the closing portion of a circular, Mexico City, February 25, 1623, addressed to Franciscan monastery guardians, on the treatment of Indians, and other matters; 11) file on a suit, Mexico City, September–October, 1703, regarding a property dispute brought by the Indians, Juana Nicolasa and Miguel de los Angeles, against certain mulattoes; 12) certified copy of an order issued by Archbishop Payo Enríquez de Ribera, March 20, 1680, regarding collection of tribute at Santa María la Redonda, a Franciscan *doctrina*; 13) report of the Medical Board (Tribunal del Protomedicato) of Mexico City, January 8, 1773, apparently for the viceroy, on health conditions among the Indians and other underprivileged groups; 14-15) documents concerned with exaction of tribute and labor, 1693-1742, from the Indians of Santa María la Redonda, including a letter from Francisco Antonio de la Rosa y Figueroa, June 16, 1742, and other papers; 16) report on immorality of the Indians, Toluca, January 14, 1735, by Fray Martín Calderón; 17) correspondence between Francisco Jiménez Caro, Franciscan Vicar General for the Indians, and Fray Antonio de Arpide, December 2, 1752-March 23, 1753, regarding alleged neglect of the Indians, especially in education; 18) report of Fray Miguel Camacho Villavisencio, a Franciscan, to his Provincial, December 2, 1719, from Tlaltelulco, on parochial administration, with special reference to Indians; 19) papers relating to misconduct of Indian parishioners of Santa María la Redonda, 1742; 20-22) three printed items, 1683-ca. 1688, two to the king requesting aid on behalf of the Indians, and one to the Commissioner General for establishment of a Franciscan mission in Nicaragua; 23) hearings concerning parochial fees and perquisites, April 17, 1749, at the *doctrina* of San Miguel Tzinacantepec, province of Metepec, and an ecclesiastical edict of June 21, 1748, setting a scale of fees for parochial services; 24) a royal decree, Mexico City, May 15, 1703, reviewing royal and ecclesiastical orders regarding fees for parochial services at Santiago Tlaltelulco, a Franciscan *doctrina*; 25) file of documents, Mexico, 1672, on complaints of the Cuernavaca Indians against the Franciscans, and justification of the latter; 26) collection of documents from Mexico City and Tlaxcala province, 1629-1630, on complaints of Indians in three communities, attached to the Franciscan *doctrina* of Topoyango, and their plea for transference to Tlaxcala; 27) information on administration and parochial fees in the Franciscan *doctrina* of Santiago Tlaltelulco, April 24, 1749; 28) relates to a suit brought by the Nativitas Indians against their Franciscan monastery, Mexico City, June 15, 1745.

CHAVES, GABRIEL DE

Relacion de la prov.ª de Meztitlan. Meztitlán. October 1, 1579.
20 p. 33 cm. HHB [M-M 310]

Report on the town and district of Meztitlán, prepared by Chaves, the alcalde mayor, in compliance with an order from the Viceroy of New Spain. Covers briefly the early history of the region, the location of its various towns, its climate and natural products, and the rites and customs of the indigenous inhabitants.

CHIAPAS, MEXICO. MUNICIPAL COUNCIL

Libro de acuerdos ordinarios . . . . Chiapas. 1640-1649.
396 p. D.S. 31 cm. [M-M 1888]

Minutes and other records of the Cabildo of Chiapas, for the period November 26, 1640-November 4, 1649. Deals with public works; sales taxes and various fiscal matters; military defense; elections, appointments and commissions; repairs to public buildings; relations with the Real Audiencia de Guatemala, the Diocese of Chiapas, and local monasteries; a reported discovery of gold mines; and miscellaneous subjects.

CHIAPAS DIOCESE, MEXICO

Primer Libro de Visita del Yll.ᵐᵒ S.ᵒʳ D.ʳ Don Carlos Maria Colina. . . . Chiapas. 1855-1874.
227 p. 40 cm. [M-M 1742]

Copies of records of parish visits made by two bishops of Chiapas.

1. The general visit of Carlos María Colina y Rubio, 1855-1856, to the parishes of Tuxtla Chico, Tapachula, Escuintla, Tonalá, and Zintalapa.

2. The visits of Germán Ascensión Villalvaso y Rodríguez, 1871-1874, to Comitán, Tuxtla Chico, Tapachula, Escuintla, and Tonalá. Includes preliminary correspondence for Colina's visit, episcopal orders and edicts, and reports on local ecclesiastical administration and finance, marriages, baptisms, deaths, brotherhoods, and the establishment of a school in Comitán by Villalvaso. A loose sheet of notes on Pijijiapa Parish, 1873-1874, is laid in.

CHICKERING, ALLEN LAWRENCE, 1877-1958

Diary of a Trip to the San Pedro Martir Sierra. August-September, 1923.
20 p. (Typescript) D.S. 28 cm. [68/5m]

Excursion to Baja California, describing the flora and fauna of the area.

CHIHUAHUA, MEXICO

Documents and Correspondence. 1811-1844.
22 folders. 134 p. 10x26-33 cm. [M-M 1797]

Documents and official correspondence, mainly addressed to various governors of Chihuahua, relating to the civil and military administration of Chihuahua as a province of New Spain and, subsequently, as a state or department of Mexico. They include documents concerning appointments, taxes and government expenditures, Indian affairs, official addresses and proclamations, and military dispatches from Janos presidio.

CHILE
Documents concerning Relations between Chile and the United States. 1840-1887.
6 reels (On film) [z-d 124]
Diplomatic, consular, and commercial correspondence. Selections and notes made by Abraham P. Nasatir. A "key" to the collection is available.

CHILE. INDIANS
Documents concerning Fray Luis de Valdivia.
11 reels (On film) [z-d 114]
Microfilm of material relating to Valdivia, a Jesuit who sought to implement a policy of defensive war against the Araucanians in Chile in the 17th century. Selected for filming by Louis De Armond from the Sala Medina of the Biblioteca Nacional, Chile. Film of volumes 110-129; record prints are available for volumes 110-122.

CHILE. INDIANS
Documents concerning Fray Luis de Valdivia and the Defensive War against the Araucanians in Chile in the 17th Century.
163 exp. (On film) [z-d 115]
Microfilm of material selected by Louis De Armond from the Archivo de Jesuitas and the Archivo Vicuña Mackenna in Chile. Record prints also available.

CHIMALPOPOCATL GALICIA, FAUSTINO, *comp.* (fl. 1840's-1850's)
Náhuatl, Otomí, and other Manuscripts. [N.d.]
13 folders in portfolio. 22-33 cm. HHB [m-m 474]
Manuscripts either translated or transcribed by Chimalpopocatl. Folders 1-8 contain translations into Náhuatl of the following: "Coloquio de la invencion de la Santa Cruz por la virtuosa Santa Elena," by Manuel de los Santos y Salazar, a play dealing with the legend of the discovery of the true cross, 26 p.; "El evangelio segun San Mateo," 116 p.; "El evangelio segun San Marco," 47 p.; "Catecismo historico . . . ," by Claudio Fleury, 39 p.; "Elementa lógica . . . versa in idiomate Nahuatl . . . ," 58 p.; "Borradores, para la Virgen" (in Spanish, Latin, and Náhuatl), 4 p.; chapters from the Book of Ecclesiastes, articles 8 and 9 of *El Centavo de Nuestra Señora de Guadalupe*, and information on atole and the pomegranate tree, 8 p.; and "El catequista en el pueblo de Sta. Maria la Milpalta . . . ," 16 p.

Folders 9-13 contain the following, written in Chimalpopocatl's hand: notes in Spanish, Latin, Náhuatl and Italian, 8 p.; a manuscript in Náhuatl, 8 p.; a foreword, in Spanish, possibly written for "Esta colección de muchos dialectos indígenos," with translations also into Náhuatl and Latin, 5 p.; "Copia simple de una gramática de la lengua otomí, o mas bien breves noticias del tal idioma," incomplete, in Spanish, 13 p.; and miscellaneous notes on Aztec kings, religious drawings and genealogical information (?) on the Mendoza (?) family, 4 p.

CHIPMAN STONE & CO., and WILLIAM E. GRIFFIS
Memorandum of Agreement. September 10, 1873.
3 p. D.S. 31 cm. [z-z 100:73]
Concerning royalties for publication in English of Griffis' New Japan readers. With bill, July, 1874, for printing "Yokahama Guide."

CHOCOLATTE. [N.p., n.d.]
15 p. (Photocopy). 26 cm. [z-c 213]
Treatise on the origins, preparation, and medicinal values of chocolate. Original in the British Museum.

CICERO, MARCUS TULLIUS, 106-43 B.C.
Idea que se formò de un orador perfecto M[arco] Tulio Cicerón, expresada à Marco Caton en el lib. que le escribio intitulado El Orador: Traducido . . . al Castellaño. . . . 46 B.C.
308 p. 21 cm. HHB [M-M 64]
A translation (n. d.) of Cicero's *Ad M. Brutum Orator*, a treatise on the ideal orator, addressed to Brutus, by Manuel Gutiérrez Huesca, a student of the Real y Pontificio Colegio of Puebla. Prologue and summary by the translator. Prepared for the college's Academia de Letras Humanas.

CILLY, JOHN S
Civil War Diary. 1863-1864.
112 p. 15 cm. [z-z 140]
Pocket diary, accompanied by transcript of military record and clippings of poems and anecdotes.

CLARK, CHARLES UPSON, 1875-1960(?)
Notebooks. ca. 1929-1939.
1,557 exp. (On film) [z-n 7]
Notes on materials for the history of the Americas in the archives of Spain, made by Clark while resident investigator in Europe for the Smithsonian Institution

CLARKE,   1847-
Remarks on Mexico. [Mexico. 1883?]
37 p. 32 cm. HHB [M-M 348]
Statement dealing in part with the careers of the American journalist Clarke and his father, George W. Clarke, founder of the newspaper *The Two Republics*, but principally with public affairs in Mexico during the presidential terms of Juárez, Lerdo, Díaz, and González. Topics discussed include relations between the United States and Mexico, Mexican railroads, and internal political organization.

CLAYTON, JOHN MIDDLETON, 1796-1856
    Letter to Asbury Dickens [Dickins], Secretary of the U.S. Senate. April 25, 1850.
    2 p. A.L.S. 18 cm. [z-z 100:20]
    Requesting secrecy concerning treaty of April 19, 1850, with Great Britain.

CLAYTON, LLOYDINE DELLA (MARTIN)
    George Victor Collot. Berkeley and San Diego State College. ca. 1934.
    470 p. Ms. and typescript. 28 cm. [M-R 8]
    Notes and draft for reports on Collot, author and explorer who reconnoitered down the Ohio and Mississippi Rivers for the French in 1796.

CLEGERN, WAYNE McLAUCHLIN, *comp.*, 1929-
    A Calendar of Documents . . . pertaining to British Honduras, 1859-1902. 1957-1958.
    43 exp. (On film) [69/84z]
    Concerning a road between Guatemala and Belize, 1859-1900; boundary disputes between Guatemala, Mexico, and British Honduras; British arms trade with the Indians; punitive expeditions in British Honduras against the Indians, 1877-1878; and proposals for railway construction in British Honduras. From the Public Record Office, London.

CLEVELAND, DANIEL
    Across the Nicaragua Transit.
    177 p. A.D. 25 cm. HHB [M-M 65]
    Preface dated San Francisco, April 15, 1868. Narrative of trip by steamboat from Greytown up San Juan River to Lake Nicaragua, and thence overland to San Juan del Sur on the Pacific. Descriptions of towns, natives, and customs, with some information on the history of the country.

CLIONICO PANEGIRICO NUMEN. 1730-
    154 p. 20 cm. HHB [M-M 190]
    Collection of 18th-century Spanish and Latin verses, largely anonymous, including many anagrams, acrostics, and similar pieces, with a few prose sermons or addresses. They relate primarily to religious topics or to public events of special interest for the Diocese (later Archdiocese) of Puebla, notably the proposed beatification of the deceased Bishop Palafox y Mendoza. The verses cover the period from 1729 into the reign of Charles III.
    Entered by Bancroft and by Puttick and Simpson under "Palafox. . . ."

CODEX FERNÁNDEZ LEAL
    5.73 by 0.36 meters. [M-M 1884]
    A pre-Cortesian Mexican Indian picture-writing, in color, of early date (8th to 15th centuries?). It tells of the conquest and migration northward from the Guatemalan area of a tribe of Mixtecan-Zapotecan linguistic stock which finally settled in the area of Oaxaca. Made from a vegetable fibre, perhaps amatl. One of the oldest surviving documents of Indian America.
    See John Barr Tompkins, "Codex Fernández Leal," in *The Pacific Art Review*, Summer, 1942, pp. 39-59.

COFRADÍA DE SANTA MARÍA DE LA SOLEDAD
  Ordinances. Oaxaca, Mexico. December 23, 1619.
  26 p. D.S. 23 cm.   HHB   [M-M 461]
  A compilation of rules, written in Náhuatl and signed by Diego Marcos, apparently containing regulations for the government of the Cofradía and its hospital, situated near San Miguel Coatlán.

COFRADÍAS DEL SANTÍSIMO SACRAMENTO Y NUESTRA SEÑORA DE LA LIMPIA CONCEPCIÓN. LIBRO DE HAZ.to DE LOS HERM.os DE LA MUI ILL.tre COFRADIA DEL DIVINO S[AG]R[ADO] SACRAM.to FUNDADA EN LA IGL.a PARROCHIAL DE ESTA VILLA. . . . CUERNAVACA, MEXICO. 1776-1810.
  291 p. D.S. 30 cm.   [M-M 1760]
  Joint records of two Cuernavaca brotherhoods, containing minutes of meetings, annual accounts, including also those for the Chapel of the Virgin of Guadalupe, and related materials.

COIT, DANIEL WADSWORTH, 1787-1876
  Sixteen Letters to his Brother-in-law, Pelatiah Perit. 1821-1831.
  56 p. A.L.S. 25-31 cm.   [Z-Z 162]
  Concerning commercial transactions, primarily in South America. Written from Lima, Peru, various cities in Europe, and Norwich, Connecticut. With typed transcripts of a part of the collection.

COLECCIÓN DE DOCUMENTOS IMPRESOS Y MANUSCRITOS P.a LA HISTORIA DE LOS ESTADOS DEL NORTE DE MÉXICO. . . . MAY 23, 1816-FEBRUARY 8, 1846.
  2 vols. Ms. and printed. 21-34 cm.   HHB   [M-M 285-286]
  A collection of numbered documents and official communications, chiefly printed, relating for the most part to political and military developments in the northern states of Mexico. Volume I contains several Mss., among them a "Reglamento" for a commissariat of war, Mexico City, May 23, 1816; an Acta for the reinstatement of Francisco Iriarte as governor of Sonora, June 8, 1829; a letter of Ignacio de Bustamante, Arispe, November 3, 1821; papers of José Antonio de Echávarri, 1823, regarding a Congress; an exhortation of Gaspar de Ochoa, Durango, March 5, 1823, in support of Mexican independence; letter of Antonio Cordero, March 6, 1823, reporting his illness and inability to serve; letters of Antonio Campuzano, February 5 and 7, 1840, concerning affairs in Ures; Governor José María Gaxiola's statement, February 6, 1846, regarding matters at Ures; letter of March 16, 1823, of Pedro María de Allande of Chihuahua concerning the Plan de Casa Mata; another letter, February 8, 1846, of Antonio Campuzano protesting the appointment of Francisco Islas to a judicial post; letter of Ignacio de Pérez, commander at Janos, concerning a military matter; and a Ms., no 109, written in December, 1828, or January, 1829, by Governor Lorenzo de Zabala and General José María Lobato, exhorting the people to peace after the recent revolution.
  The remainder of these volumes, consisting of several hundred printed items, are analyzed in Bancroft Library's catalog under "Pinart Prints," and hence are not described here.

COLOMBIA
Documents for the History of. 1550-1652.
8 reels (On film) [z-d 121]

Residencia records and other documents selected and filmed by Miss Mary Ross in the Archivo Histórico Nacional and Biblioteca Nacional, Bogotá, Colombia.

COLOMBIA AND THE CARIBBEAN
Documents Pertaining to the History of. 1820-1940.
732 exp. (On film) [z-c 212]

Selected documents from the Consular Correspondence in the U.S. National Archives regarding Barranquilla, Bogotá, Cartagena, Sabanilla, and Santa Marta, 1823-1922; and items from Bogotá periodicals consisting of laws, contracts, censuses, etc., for Cartagena, Santa Marta, Barranquilla, and the lower Magdalena River area.

COLOQUIO ENTRE SOPHRONIO Y LEONIDO SOBRE MATERIAS POLITICAS, Y DE ESTADO. . . . MEXICO. 1775.
101 p. 17 cm. HHB [m-m 67]

Discussion of Spanish public affairs in the middle 18th century, including international policy, promotion of mining in New Spain, papal recognition of Our Lady of Guadalupe as Patroness of New Spain, and arrival and early administration of Viceroy Agustín de Ahumada.

COLUMPIO SILVER MINING COMPANY
Stock Certificate. San Francisco. [186-?]
1 p. 14x24 cm. HHB [m-m 1700:21]

Blank stock certificate for a mining company of Cosalá District, Sinaloa, Mexico, incorporated on January 6, 1864; in English.

COMISIÓN MEXICANA-AMERICANA PARA LA ERRADICACIÓN DE LA FIEBRE AFTOSA. DISTRITO DE HUAJUAPAM. SECTOR DE CHALCATONGO. [N.d.]
89 exp. (On film) [m-a 14]

Gives maps of Chalcatongo and nearby towns included in the survey, with lists of owners of cattle and hogs, and census of these animals. Filmed for the Library of Congress.

COMPAGNIE DE SONORE
Statuts de la Compagnie de Sonore. 1852.
38 p. 23 cm. HHB [m-m 230]

Statutes of the Compagnie de Sonore, founded by Raousset-Boulbon in San Francisco in 1852, by agreement with the Mexican Compañía Restauradora, to provide military aid in the exploration and development of lands, mines, and placers, in exchange for a share of the profits; membership roll of the Compagnie de Sonore, with relevant data; order of the day, recording chiefly appointments within the company and modification of its statutes; and tables of equipment required.

COMPAGNIE DES FILLES DE NOTRE-DAME
History of the Compagnie des Filles de Notre-Dame. 1698?-1710.
3 vols. 389, 404, 413 p. 28 cm. HHB [M-M 394]

Spanish translation, apparently prepared by the Jesuits José Escrig and Ignacio Bruno, with the assistance of Father Francisco Garau and others, of a French history of the Daughters of the Virgin Mary, an educational order founded in Bordeaux in 1606 by Jeanne de Lestonnac, widow of the Marquis Gaston de Montferrand and niece of Montaigne. Contains biographical accounts of the founder and certain members, as well as a history of the Order and of various chapters or communities. Composition of the history was initiated by Mother Clara de Madallán and continued by other Daughters.

COMPAÑÍA ANÓNIMA DE NAVEGACIÓN DEL LAGO DE CHAPALA Y RÍO GRANDE. 1866-1867
23 p. 32-36 cm. [M-M 1809]

Documents relating to the steamship company founded by Adolfo Emilio Cavaillon, with headquarters in Guadalajara. Included are a notary's statement and draft of statutes on formation of the company, 1866; a note concerning election of the company's board of directors, 1866; and a facsimile of an instrument granting certain authority, including power of attorney, to Cavaillon, 1866-1867.

CONDE Y OQUENDO, FRANCISCO JAVIER, 1733-1799
Disertacion Historica sobre la Aparicion de la Portentosa Imagen de Maria Santisima de Guadalupe de Mexico. Mexico. [N. d.]
2 vols. (576, 436 p.) 31 cm. HHB [M-M 71-72]

A history of the Virgin of Guadalupe prepared to counteract the irreligious implications of the account written by José Ignacio Bartolache, Mexico City, 1790. Contains a prologue, historical introduction, and nine chapters dealing with Cortés' devotion to Our Lady, the miraculous appearances of the Virgin of Guadalupe, characteristics of the painting, written and oral sources of the legend, and the recognition accorded to it in various countries.

Practically identical with the printed edition published in Mexico, 1852-1853, under the title given above.

[CONDE Y OQUENDO, FRANCISCO JAVIER], 1733-1799
Sermones y elogios varios. ca. 1772-ca. 1792.
598 p. Ms. and printed. 31 cm. HHB [M-M 223]

A collection of sermons and orations on religious and political topics—the Sacraments, lives of saints, the Council of the Indies, Philip V, et cetera—delivered in Havana, Madrid, Mexico City, and possibly other localities. Preceded by a dedication (n.p., n.d.) obviously intended for Revilla Gigedo the Younger. Entered by Bancroft under "Sermones Varios. . . ."

CONFEDERATE STATES OF AMERICA
Fifty Dollar Bill. Richmond, Virginia. February 17, 1864.
1 piece. D.S. 8x18 cm. [Z-Z 100:43]
With signatures for Register and Treasurer.

CONQUYSTA BERDADERA DEL PUEBLO DE TONALAN, Y MERYTOS DEL GOBERNADOR, DON SALBADOR ALBARADO, NOMBRADO MASCARON CHYTALPOPOCA. [16TH-19TH CENT.]
110 p. 32 cm. [M-M 1738]

File on land titles and other privileges granted to the Chucalco (Chicalco) Indians of Tonalá(n), Nueva Galicia, in recognition of their docile cooperation with the early conquerors and Franciscan fathers, and particularly the services rendered by their governor, Salvador Cortés Alvarado Mascarón Chitalpopoca, brother of Moctezuma, and by members of his family. Copied in part, according to the text, from the *Crónicas de Nueva España* of Fathers Juan Pastraño and Diego Solórzano. Contains petitions, reports from missionaries, royal grants from Charles V and his successors, requests for copies of the pertinent documents, and related material. Written primarily in Jalisco and Madrid. Certified at Guadalajara, July 3, 1848, with the signature of Mariano Hermoso, notary in charge of land-title archives.

CONVENTO DE SAN AGUSTÍN, GUADALAJARA. ca. 1570-1770.
1 box. (Photocopy) [M-A 9]

Controversy over the lands and property of this convent. From the Biblioteca Pública, Guadalajara, Mexico.

COOKE, ROSE (TERRY), 1827-1892
Untitled Poem. February 15, 1855.
2 p. A[?].D. 16 cm. [Z-Z 100:92]

COOLEY, TOM M
Letter. Potrerito, District of Sahuaripa, Sonora, Mexico. June 28, 1873.
3 p. A.L.S. 26 cm. HHB [M-M 1700:59]

Writes his brother, A. S. Cooley, in Plumas County, California, that he has a 1/5 interest in a promising silver mine that will be in operation by August.

COPIA DE CARTAS ESCRITAS POR EL P.ᵉ P.ᵒʳ FR. JUAN CRESPI, MISSIONERO APPOSTOLICO . . . SOBRE LAS EXPEDICIONES DE TIERRA . . . EN EL AÑO DE 1769 . . . [AND OTHER PAPERS, 1769-1772].
216 p. 34 cm. [M-M 1847]

Transcripts of letters and reports concerning the journeys of Franciscan missionaries, the missions of Alta and Baja California, Indians of the region, discovery of the Bay of Monterey, provisions of José de Gálvez affecting the missions. Addressed by Fathers Juan Crespí, Junípero Serra, Francisco Palóu, José Francisco Ortega, and Rafael José Verger (later Bishop of Nuevo León), to Fathers Juan Andrés and Palóu, Fiscal Manuel Lanz de Casafonda, Mother Antonia Valladolid, and probably other correspondents not specified.

Transcripts made at the British Museum in 1910 from *Manuscritos de Indias . . .* , Ms. Add. 13974, f. 231-293. There is a chronological list of the transcripts.

CORDERO, ANTONIO, 1753-1823
  Correspondence as Commandant General of the Western Provincias Internas (or *ad interim* Commandant General). 1819-1821.
  2 folders. 5 p. L.S. 21-22 cm. [M-M 1796]
  Letter from Trinidad Rodríguez to Cordero, requesting protection for the Indians in San Juan de Sultó, Huejotitán, March 22, 1819. Also letter of Cordero to Angel Pinilla for dispatch of requested documents, Los Alamos, February 21, 1820.

CÓRDOVA, JUAN DE
  Permit. Mexico City. September 1, 1860.
  1 p. D.S. 31 cm. [M-M 1883:2]
  Issued by the Provincial of the Dominican Province of Santiago to Fray Sebastián de Soto, giving him power to make financial arrangements at the Atzcapotzalco monastery.

CORONA, RAMÓN, 1837-1889
  Apuntes Biográficos. [N. p., 1885]
  229 p. 28 cm. HHB [M-M 372]
  Biography of the Mexican patriot, General Ramón Corona, hero of the Battle of La Mojonera (1873), covering the first 48 years of his life. A copy of his military record is appended.

CORREOSO, BUENAVENTURA, ca. 1831-
  Statement of General Buenaventura Correoso at H. H. Bancroft's Library. San Francisco. July 13, 1883.
  14 p. 31 cm. HHB [M-M 353]
  Statement by Correoso summarizing his personal career and reviewing events in Panama and Colombia during the period 1854-1883, with emphasis upon the struggle between Liberals and Conservatives and upon the Panamanian chiefs of state. Refers briefly to current work on the Panama Canal.

CORTÉS, HERNANDO, 1485-1547
  Ordenanzas. Mexico. March 20, 1524.
  6 exp. (On film) [M-M 1836]
  Basic ordinances for the administration and government of New Spain. Microfilm of original document at Tulane University.

COSTA RICA. CABILDO
  Relacion mui circunstanciada escrita al Rey de los sucesos de Juan Vasquez de Coronado en las provincias de Nueva Cartago, y Costa Rica en la pacificacion y descubrimiento de ellas. December 12, 1562.
  5 p. 33 cm. HHB [M-M 304]
  Report to the King of Spain from the Cabildo of Costa Rica, recording the aid received from Juan Vázquez de Coronado in the settlement and pacification of the province.

COSTANSÓ, MIGUEL, 1741-1814
>*70 p. (Typescript and manuscript) 23-36 cm.* [M-M 1849]
>Miscellaneous translations, excerpts, and notes of Costansó's diaries, relating to the 1769-1770 expeditions from San Diego northward in search of Monterey Bay.

COWLEY-BROWN, J S
>Letter to H. R. Momat. Chicago. January 26, 1903.
>*1 p. A.L.S. 28 cm.* [z-z 100:96]
>Concerning publication of the *Goose-Quill*, a literary magazine of which Cowley-Brown was the editor.

COZZENS, JOHN B
>Correspondence and Papers. 1846-1875.
>*70 exp. (On film)* [M-M 1726]
>Includes letters and papers in connection with his service as a sutler to the American forces in Mexico during 1846-1847, a challenge to a duel with Lt. Charles Deas, U.S.N., in 1848, and Cozzens' financial affairs.

CRANDALL, DANIEL M
>A Return of the Men, Arms, Ammunition and Accoutrements, of the Third Regiment of Militia . . . in the 3d Brigade in the State of Rhode-Island, commanded by Brigadier-General John S. Champlen. . . . Hopkinton [Rhode Island]. June 25, 1836.
>*2 p. D.S. 17x41 cm.* [z-z 100:51]
>Printed form, filled in and signed by Crandall.

[CREIGHTON, FRANK WHITTINGTON, bp., 1879-1948]
>The Bishop's Journal. Mexico (State). April 16-19, [1926?]
>*7 p. (Typescript) 28 cm.* [M-M 1729]
>A report on an evangelical episcopal tour through several towns and settlements near Toluca. Discusses ecclesiastical matters, describes local conditions and means of travel, contains information on the Protestant Montes de Oca family. Ascribed to Creighton, Protestant missionary bishop from 1926 to 1933.

CRESCENT CITY BANK, NEW ORLEANS
>Bank Note to George M. Branner, on the Bank of the Republic, New York. New Orleans. March 28, 186(?).
>*1 piece. D.S. 9x19 cm.* [z-z 100:55]

CRESPÍ, JUAN, 1721-1782
>Letter. Cádiz. December 24, 1749.
>*1 p. (Photocopy) 28 cm.* [M-M 1700:52]
>Informs Don Miguel Serre y Maure of his arrival at Cádiz, September 21, with other friars, and their plan to sail for Mexico on December 26. Includes English translation.

CRESPO, ANTONIO
  Lista del número total de Religiosos de la Provincia del Santo Evangelio de México. . . . August 27, 1804.
  13 p. 43x31 cm. [M-M 1887]
  List of friars in the Franciscan Provincia del Santo Evangelio, indicating native land and age of each friar, with additional data relating to his work in the Order. Prepared for Fray Pablo de Moya, Franciscan Commissioner General of the Indies.

CRIADO DE CASTILLA, ALONSO, d. 1611
  Papers Relating to the Port of Santo Tomás de Castilla. Guatemala. February 4, 1604-July 1, 1606.
  8 items. 33 cm. HHB [M-M 315]
  Official letters and reports, addressed for the most part by the Governor of Guatemala, Alonso Criado de Castilla, to the King of Spain. Relate to the exploration of Amatique Bay, the founding of the new port of Santo Tomás de Castilla, and the desirability of developing that port as superior to Puerto Caballos or any other in the vicinity.

CROIX, CARLOS FRANCISCO DE, MARQUÉS DE, 1699-1786
  Correspondence and Papers. 1768-1769.
  11 folders (29 p.) D. and D.S. 16-31 cm. [M-M 1870]
  Relate to the administration of Viceroy de Croix; concerned principally with disposition of former Jesuit property, and in most cases written to or by the Guadalajara factor, José de Trigo.

CROIX, CARLOS FRANCISCO DE, MARQUÉS DE, 1699-1786
  Papers. Mexico. 1769, 1771.
  2 items. D.S. [69/166m]
  Communications from Domingo Antonio López to Croix, reporting an alleged theft of a letter by mailman Antonio Gavino, with annotation by Croix; and a letter from Croix concerning a dispute between officials of Veracruz and the Jesuits over certain income or benefits of the latter.

CROIX, TEODORO DE, CABALLERO DE CROIX, 1730-1791
  Correspondence. 1777-1783.
  5 vols. (Transcripts) 28 cm. [Z-E 10]
  Typescripts of letters selected by Alfred B. Thomas from the Archivo General de Indias, Seville. A "key" to the collection is available in the Bancroft Library.

CROIX, TEODORO DE, CABALLERO DE CROIX, 1730-1791
  Letters and Documents. Mexico. 1778-1784.
  9 folders. 29-31 cm. [M-M 1789]
  Papers relating to the administration of the Provincias Internas (principally in Nueva Vizcaya and Coahuila) under Commandant General Croix, primarily

concerning Indian disturbances and finances. Includes information on many Lipan and Mescalero leaders.

Folder 1. Two letters, April 1 and 4, 1778, from Commandant-Inspector José F. Rubio, concerning negotiations with the Apaches and other matters, notably the pending trial of the apostate Indian Apodaca. 5 p.

Folder 2. File of official documents, 1778-1784, on the plan of Croix and a Chihuahua war council for payment of annual presidio allotments and costs of missionary synods in coins received by the local excise offices, with a view to facilitating circulation of new coinage and suppression of the old. 70 p. Copy.

Folder 3. Accounts of presidio and other funds, rendered to Croix by Manuel Antonio de Escorza, Treasurer of Chihuahua. 1779. 39 p. D.S.

Folder 4. Outline, by Croix, of a round-trip route and time-schedule for a new monthly mail service from Bahía del Espíritu Santo, Texas, to Arispe, Sonora. Followed by similar directions for the communications between certain Nueva Vizcaya presidios and others of the north. February 15, 1779. 9 p.

Folder 5. Letters addressed to Croix by Juan de Ugalde, Governor of Coahuila, concerning orders from the former on relations with the Lipan and Mescalero Indians. Also transmitting copies of papers received from Captain Rafael Martínez Pacheco, Commandant of the Valle de Santa Rosa garrison, relating to doubtful peace offers from the Mescaleros. 1779. 34 p. L.S.

Folder 6. Diary of Governor Juan de Ugalde of Coahuila, recording a campaign waged against the Mescalero Apaches. May 13-16, 1779. 28 p.

Folder 7. Two letters to Croix from Captain Domingo Díaz, June 9-12, 1779, concerning a campaign against the Lipans planned in conjunction with the Mescaleros. 13 p. A.L.S.

Folder 8. Letter to Croix from Governor Juan de Ugalde. With copies of six letters addressed to Ugalde from Monclova and Villa de San Fernando, concerning Lipan disturbances caused by the Nueva Vizcaya-Mescalero attack. July 14-17, 1779. 19 p. L.S.

Folder 9. Four letters to Croix from Governor Juan de Ugalde concerning apparently successful efforts to calm the Lipan disturbance. Enclosed are copies of two letters to Ugalde regarding Lipan disorders near San Juan Bautista, and other documents. July 19-29, 1779. 40 p. L.S.

CROIX, TEODORO DE, CABALLERO DE CROIX, 1730-1791
Ynstrucion formada por la Comandancia G.^{ral} de Provincias Ynternas para el establecimiento de nuebas poblaciones. . . . [Provincias Internas, 1783?]
11 p. 31 cm. [M-M 1790]

Instructions issued by the Commandant General of the Provincias Internas for the establishment of new settlements. Covers their classification, local government, provisions for Indian inhabitants, distribution of lands, agriculture and irrigation, and obligations and rights of settlers.

CROSMAN, GEORGE HAMPTON, 1798-1882
Letters. May 16-29, 1847.
3 items (7 p.) 25 cm. HHB [M-M 1700:31]

Letters addressed to Major Crosman, Quartermaster, by Colonel Robert T.

Paine, San Francisco, May 16; Depot Superintendent Arnold Angell, San Francisco, May 19; and W. S. Gregory Reynosa, Mexico, May 29, relating to the war with Mexico, particularly the movements of supply vessels and the transmittal of instructions.

CROSSMAN, A. W., THOMAS, J. L., AND PATTERSON, W. E.
Letter to Dr. Crouch in Lead, South Dakota. San Benito, Texas. October 15, 1916.
1 p. 26 cm.   HHB   [M-M 1700:56]
Covering letter sending the skull of a Mexican bandit shot in August, 1915, by the South Dakota Cavalry. Copy.

CRUILLAS, JOAQUÍN DE MONTSERRAT, MARQUÉS DE, 1700-1771
Document Relating to the Estate of Agustín de Vildosola, Former Governor of the Provinces of Sinaloa and Sonora. Mexico City. July 18, 1763.
8 p. D.S. 30 cm.   [M-M 1700:77]

CRUZ DE LA BANDERA, JUAN IGNACIO
Papers. Mexico. 1832-1833.
9 folders in portfolio. 25 p. Ms. and printed. 10-44 cm.   HHB   [M-M 496]
Letters and documents either addressed to Juan Ignacio Cruz de la Bandera (also known as "Juan Banderas," "Bandera de la Cruz," and "Juan Ignacio Jusacamea," and other variants), as well as documents relating to the disturbances fomented by him among the Yaqui Indians of Sonora. Includes a report signed by Governor Escalante y Arvizu on Bandera's circulation of propaganda predicting his own coronation and inciting revolt against the "Yoris," or white men, with a printed cartoon affixed. Written principally in an Indian language, presumably the Yaqui dialect of Cahita, but also partly in Spanish. Originating for the most part in Sonora.

CUADRO ESTADÍSTICO DE LA SIEMPRE FIEL ISLA DE CUBA CORRESPONDIENTE AL AÑO DE 1827. . . . HAVANA, CUBA. 1829
66 p. 34 cm.   [71/45M]
Copy of report on Cuba prepared by a commission headed by Francisco Dionisio Vives. Includes a brief history of the island, geographical description, information on the flora and fauna, minerals and other resources, climate, population, and agriculture.

CUEVAS, LUIS DE
Letters. Loreto, Baja California. April 26, 1832.
11 p. A.L.S. 25 cm.   HHB   [M-M 1700:29]
Three letters from the Commissariat of Baja California to the Administrator and the Auditor of Maritime Customs in Guaymas, concerning provisions and armament needed for the troops, in view of threatened frontier hostilities.

CURTIS, SAMUEL RYAN, 1805-1866
Diaries and Papers. 1846-ca. 1860.
3 vols. and 5 folders. 19-33 cm.   [M-M 1723]
Journals kept by Curtis during his command of the Third Ohio Infantry,

principally 1846-1847, while he was on occupation duty at Matamoros, Camargo, and Saltillo. Correspondence, including drafts of letters to President Polk and General Taylor, and clippings.

CUSHMAN, CHARLOTTE SAUNDERS, 1816-1876
Letter to Leon John Vincent. Philadelphia. April 8, 1875.
2 p. A.L.S. 13 cm. [z-z 100:58]
Requesting tickets for a performance.

CUSTER, FERDINAND V., *comp.*
Colonial Brazil, 1746-1774.
35 items. 33 cm. [z-d 125]
Copies of documents relating to Brazil in the mid-18th century treating such diverse subjects as agriculture, Jesuit administration of temporalities, multitude of native dialects, treaty of limits of 1757, rents, and finances. Most are from the Colecção Pombalina, Biblioteca Nacional, Lisbon, Portugal.

CUYUTLAN GOLD MINES COMPANY
Memoria de Raya por el mes de Diciembre de 1916. Rosamorada, Tepic.
32 p. 33 cm. HHB [m-m 1700:60]
Balance sheet, December, 1916. Gives names of men employed, their duties, wages, and other details; includes two receipts.

DAKIN, FRED H
Some Notes on Francisco Villa. [N.p.] December 8, 1933.
5 p. D.S. (Typescript) 33 cm. [m-m 1734]
Notes on a trip taken in June, 1933, to the Hacienda of Francisco Villa, at Canutillo, Durango, donated to Villa by the Mexican Government to provide him and his followers with peaceful employment. Contains a description of the estate, an estimate of Villa's character and career, and comments on his relations with the U.S. Government.

[DALL & DRÉGE CO.]
Letterbook. San Luis Potosí. 1833.
1 vol. and index [m-b 8]
Contemporary record of letters sent in the company's varied business transactions with clients in all parts of Mexico. They reflect the difficulties in the shipment of goods, funds, and messages, and in occasional outbreaks of cholera.

DANISH WEST INDIES
Documents Relating to. 1655-1852.
2 boxes (72 folders), and 1 volume (photocopy) HHB [z-a 1]
Originals and Pinart transcripts of correspondence and documents mainly relating to the Danish government's rule of the islands of St. Thomas, St. Croix, and St. John, with provisos for the regulation of Negroes and their conversion to Christianity, and the recording of various deeds in the island of St. Croix. There are a few documents from the British rule, 1807-1819,

chiefly passports. The one volume is a photocopy of the extremely fragile Philip Gardelin letterbook (folder 9).

Materials gathered for H. H. Bancroft by Alphonse Pinart. Arranged chronologically. A partial "key" to the collection is available in the Library.

DATOS SACADOS DE LOS LIBROS DE ALGUNAS MISIONES DE SONORA EN LA PIMERÍA ALTA, QUE ESTUVIERON PRIMERAMENTE Á CARGO DE LA COMP.ª DE JESUS, Y DESPUES AL DE LOS P. P. FRANCISCANOS DEL COLEGIO DE S.ta CRUZ DE QUERÉTARO. [SONORA, MEXICO] 1693-1838.
73 p. 32 cm.   HHB [M-M 423]

Data copied in 1879 from records of Sonora missions directed first by the Jesuits and later by the Franciscans. The material is arranged under the heads of individual mission areas and deals with the careers of specific friars and priests. It refers also to the character of the natives, episcopal visits, births, baptisms, burials, and related matters. Pinart collection.

DAVIDSON, NATHANIEL
Accounts. Paris and Mexico. 1863-1867.
5 items. 10x22 to 12x27 cm.   HHB [M-M 1700:68]
Drafts and bills of exchange; one receipt. Four in French, one in Spanish.

DÁVILA Y LUGO, FRANCISCO DE
Descripcion de las islas Guanajas. 1639.
8 p. 33 cm.   HHB [M-M 307]
Initial portion of a report on the Bay Islands and the advisability of their abandonment. Contains descriptions of the three principal islands, Guanaja, Guyama, and Utilla, and their inhabitants.

DEFENSA HECHA A NOMBRE DE LA SAGRADA PROV.ª DE N.ª S.ra DE LA MERCED . . . EN LA CAUSA CRIMINAL FORMADA AL P.e FR. JACINTO MIRANDA. . . . [MEXICO CITY. JANUARY 12(?), 1792]
224 p. 30 cm.   HHB [M-M 26]
Defense, on jurisdictional grounds, of the Mercedarian friar, Jacinto Miranda, accused of murdering Gregorio Corte, Provincial, and wounding Father José Alcalá; drawn up by Ubaldo Indalecio Bernal y Malo and Manuel Domingo Chavero, attorneys of the Real Audiencia; presented by the Order to Archbishop Núñez de Haro y Peralta.

Substantially identical with two items of "Disturbios de Frailes," M-M 85, Nos. 2 and 12; a printed version of this plea, *Alegato año de 1792* (Oaxaca, 1844) gives the date as December 14, 1792.

DENHARDT, ROBERT MOORMAN, 1912-
Reports on Agriculture in Brazil. 1942-1944.
12 folders (Typescript) 32 cm.   [Z-D 137]
Reports on climate, meat packing houses, and various phases of agriculture, chiefly in Rio Grande do Sul. Written as agricultural analyst, U.S. Consulate, Porto Alegre, Brazil.

DERROTERO PARA LA NAVEGACION DE LOS PUERTOS DE ESPAÑA Á LOS DE AMÉRICA. [N. p., n. d.]
332 p. 21x30 cm. HHB [M-M 76]
An atlas for navigators between Spanish ports and the New World, divided into two books: 1) a general discussion of the routes and sites involved; 2) pictorial maps of the islands, ports, bays, and similar features of the Canaries, the West Indies, and American, Spanish, and Portuguese coasts, with brief individual descriptions. Contains 115 maps, numbered through 118 (1-3 missing).

DESCRIPCION DE LA AMERICA MERIDIONAL Y SEPTENTRIONAL CON UN INFORME SECRETO D.¹ FISCAL SOBRE LA ADMINISTRACION D.¹ GOBIERNO DE LAS YNDIAS [MADRID. 1701-1710]
480 p. 30 cm. HHB [M-M 11]
Collection of documents (copies) dealing with the territorial subdivisions, commerce, and administration of the New World, including the Philippines, based largely on Pierre d'Avity's *Le Monde*; a confidential report, Madrid, September 3, 1709, from the Fiscal General to the king of Spain, deploring the growth of American commerce with foreign nations, especially France, and suggesting reforms; and a brief survey, Madrid, 1701, of Spanish dominions in the New World, with official comments prefixed.

DE SHIELDS, ALF
Reminiscences. Red Bluff, California. 1910.
9 p. (Typescript) 28 cm. [Z-C 206]
Account of his adventures in Nicaragua with the Walker Filibustering Expedition, 1856. Includes letter of presentation to Professor Henry Morse Stephens. Red Bluff, September 14, 1910.

DESTRADA, JUAN
Memorial de las advertencias i cosas que . . . D.ⁿ Phelipe Nuestro Señor i su R.¹ Consejo de Yndias manda hazer i de las cosas i particularidades destas provincias para ennoblecimiento dellas i las diligencias que zerca dello se han podido hazer en esta provincia i costa de Çapotitlan i Suchitepeques. 1579.
20 p. 33 cm. HHB [M-M 314]
General description of the Guatemalan province of Zapotitlán, including its government, mineral products, and commerce, primarily cacao, and Franciscan monasteries, prepared by order of García de Valverde, Governor of Guatemala. The original was signed by Destrada, Alcalde Mayor of the province, and Fernando Niebla, notary. The document is in the present-day Vol. 24 of the Muñoz Collection of the Real Academia de la Historia in Madrid.

DIARY. 1864
143 p. A.D. 14 cm. [Z-Z 158]
Pocket diary kept by an unidentified young woman who taught school near Canandaigua, New York.

DIARY. AUTHOR AND PLACE UNKNOWN. 1861-1864
    102 p. 20 cm. [z-z 100:79]
    Miscellaneous local and domestic details.

DIARY OF AN UNIDENTIFIED MECHANIC. ENGLAND. APRIL 27, 1849-DECEMBER 31, 1851
    158 p. A.D. 15 cm. [z-z 108]
    Noting unemployment, search for work, and other activities.

DIAS FERREIRA, GASPAR
    Letters. Amsterdam. 1645.
    7 p. (Photocopy) 34 cm. [z-d 101]
    Five letters to Johan Maurits, Count of Nassau-Siegen, concerning Brazil. From the Koninklijke Huisarchief at The Hague.

DÍAZ, JOSEPH TIRSO
    Papel sobre el verdadero modo de beneficiar a los Yndios en lo espiritual, y temporal con utilidad del Estado: impugnando un proiecto acerca de lo mismo. Mexico City. 1770.
    222 p. 21 cm. HHB [M-M 271]
    A treatise by a Mexico City priest on methods for promoting the spiritual and temporal welfare of the Indians. Consists of a detailed rejection of the proposal made by a Puebla priest for the sale of indulgences to release Indians from the prohibition against eating meat on certain days, and Díaz's own proposals to aid the natives and enhance their utility to the State by their establishment in towns, suppression of the *repartimiento* system, correction of abuses among government officials and landlords, and similar devices.

DÍAZ, PORFIRIO, 1830-1915
    Conversacion entre el Sr. G.^{ral} Porfirio Díaz y Mr. H. Bancroft. Mexico City. 1883-[1884]
    561 p. 32 cm. HHB [M-M 390]
    Transcripts of the notes taken by stenographers during conversations held by Díaz and Bancroft in Díaz's house, from December 26, 1883, through early January, 1884; partially in dialogue form, but chiefly a third-person paraphrase of information supplied by Díaz. Deals with the latter's career and his opinions on public questions, including incidental information on Benito Pablo Juárez and the State of Oaxaca.
    Appended (p. 513-560) are transcripts of information dictated to Bancroft in the house of Manuel Romero Rubio in January, 1884, regarding the lives of Romero, José María Iglesias, and Juan N. Méndez, followed by general information on the development of Mexico.

DÍAZ, PORFIRIO, 1830-1915
    Letter. Mexico. September 14, 1903.
    2 p. (Photocopy and typescript) 23 cm. HHB [M-M 1700:62]
    To Martin J. Bentley and Román Galán, granting them an audience.

DÍAZ, PORFIRIO, 1830-1915
    Letter to H. H. Bancroft. Mexico City. March 29, 1887.
    1 p. L.S. 27 cm.   HHB   [M-M 1700:63]
    Regrets Bancroft's departure, and states that he will support Mr. Urrea in obtaining historical information, especially after 1885.

DÍAZ, PORFIRIO, 1830-1915
    Letter to Messrs. Cox and Carmichael. Mexico City. August 6, 1901.
    1 p. L.S. 27 cm.   HHB   [M-M 1700:8]
    Letter of thanks for photographs taken on July 4, 1901.

DÍAZ, PORFIRIO, 1830-1915
    Miscellany. Mexico. 1881-1893.
    1 envelope and 15 folders in portfolio.   HHB   [M-M 392]
    Collection of material signed by, or relating to, Porfirio Díaz, made up chiefly of signed letters from Díaz to Bancroft and a list of detailed suggestions for alteration of Chapter XIX, Vol. VI, of Bancroft's *History of Mexico*. Includes a military commission issued to Lieutenant Enrique Marín, a copy of Domingo Laredo's oration in honor of Díaz, and some calling cards.

DISCURSO HISTORICO CRITICO S.re LA ORATORIA ESPAÑOLA Y AMERICANA. [MEXICO. ca. 1800]
    430 p. 31 cm.   HHB   [M-M 169]
    A treatise on oratory in three parts, dealing with the history and abuses of oratory, particularly in the Spanish tongue; Spanish-American oratory, with special reference to New Spain; and attempts to improve religious oratory in Europe and America, with precepts for so doing.
    Entered by Bancroft under "Oratoria Española y Americana, Discurso Histórico-Crítico."

DISTURBIOS DE FRAILES. 1621-1840
    2 vols. Ms. and printed. 32 cm.   HHB   [M-M 84-85]
    Collection of 72 items, relating to religious developments in the Indies, and primarily to internal history of the monastic orders in New Spain, Peru, and the Philippines, as affected by conflicts with ecclesiastical and civil authority.
    Volume I concerns the disputed election of Fray Alejandro Casquero as Provincial of the Franciscan Province of San José in Yucatán; the distribution of offices between Creoles and native Spaniards in religious orders in the New World; and verses by José Antonio de Alfaro y Ochoa, protesting his arrest by Bishop Francisco Gabriel Olivares y Benito.
    Volume II deals for the most part with jurisdictional questions, including two manuscripts (Nos. 2 and 12) substantially identical with the defense in the criminal case against Fray Jacinto Miranda. For the latter see "Defensa hecha a nombre de la Sagrada Prov^a . . ." (M-M 26).
    A more detailed analysis of these two volumes is given in their tables of contents.

DIX, JOHN ADAMS, 1798-1879
   Dispatch sent as Secretary of the Treasury. January 29, 1861.
   1 p. (Photocopy) A.L.S. 24 cm. [z-z 100:35]
   Ordering Lieutenant Caldwell to arrest Captain Breshwood, assume command of the revenue cutter *McClelland,* and protect the American flag.

DOBYNS, HENRY F   , 1925-
   Identifications and explanatory notes for various items in Alphonse L. Pinart's Colección de Pimería Alta. January-October, 1958.
   13 folders in portfolio. (Typescript) [M-M 1845]
   Notes on the mission records collected in Sonora, in 1848, by Pinart.

DOBYNS, HENRY F   , 1925-
   An analysis of one week's reporting of an incident of interracial violence in the Peruvian Andes by the Lima daily press. Lima. September 15, 1960.
   60 p. (Typescript) 28 cm. [z-D 126]
   Comments on press reports of an incident in which the Guardia Civil fired on a group of Indian workers on the Huapra estate, province of Carhuas.

DOCUMENTOS HISTORICOS MEXICANOS. 1838-1845
   264 p. Ms. and printed. 33 cm. HHB [M-M 86]
   Collection of 15 items relating to civil and ecclesiastical developments in the early years of the Mexican Republic.
   Includes account of a conspiracy by two Englishmen, Patrick Jordan and James White, and a Frenchman, Antoine Deloche, to assassinate General Santa Anna, 1844-1845; letter of Bishop Pedro Barajas regarding appointment of sacristans, Guadalajara, 1845; consecration of the Durango cathedral, 1844; report on the activities and finances of the Academia Nacional de San Carlos by Francisco Manuel Sánchez de Tagle, 1845; statement of Manuel Díez de Bonilla on negotiations for transferring the former Real Patronato to the Republic of Mexico, 1838; report on prison funds of Mexico City, 1844; file of papers on the formation of a Mexican Junta de Fomento de Artesanos, 1845; data on agricultural and industrial progress in the Departments of Durango, Zacatecas, and Veracruz, 1843; indemnification for destruction of the "Parián," a Mexico City market, 1843-1845; letter of Valentín Gómez Farías, May 4, 1845, to Bernardo González Angulo, and his reply, on the problem of Texas; and report by a committee of the Supreme Court on ceremonial respect to be shown to court representatives at public functions, 1844.

DOCUMENTOS INÉDITOS REFERENTES A MICHOACÁN ENCONTRADOS EN LA BIBLIOTECA SUTRO DE SAN FRANCISCO. [1553-1690]
   24 p. 28 cm. [M-M 1850]
   Typed transcripts of three manuscripts concerning the province of Michoacán. One grants a coat of arms and the title of "city" to Pátzcuaro, July 21, 1553-May 28, 1642; another deals with forced labor among the Pátzcuaro Indians, April 27-May 20, 1690; and the third concerns commercial exploitation of these people, October 28, 1668-March 23, 1682.

DOCUMENTOS ORIGINALES PARA LA HISTORIA DE BAJA CALIFORNIA Y SOBRE TODO DE LA COLONIA MILITAR DE LA FRONTERA. . . . [FEBRUARY 3, 1848-SEPTEMBER 20, 1859]
2 vols. Ms. and printed. 35 cm.   HHB [M-M 20-21]

Collection of papers (originals, drafts, and copies) relating to the establishment, administration, and foreign relations of the Colonia Militar de la Frontera in Lower California, under the command of Manuel Castro and successors. The collection includes correspondence of Castro, Rafael Espinosa (inspector-in-chief of the colony and political chief of Lower California), Lt. José Antonio Chaves, and many others; military registers, petitions for land and land grants; regulations, orders and proclamations from the central and local governments; lists of funds and equipment required, received or distributed; proceedings of cases tried in the colony; records of international incidents; payrolls and receipts; passports, permits, et cetera.

Noteworthy items: Vol. I, 1848-1850, a proclamation containing the July 19, 1848 regulations for establishment of the colony; Vol. II, chiefly 1851-1859, census list of July 25, 1851, letter from José R. Moreno, Washington and San Diego, August 11, 1850-May 10, 1851, regarding a plan for alliance of Lower California with a Southern Confederacy in the United States; proceedings of the Isaac Banes case, 1852; papers relating to the wreck of the steamer *Union*, 1851; and many items concerning the conflict between Castillo Negrete and the Castro party.

DOCUMENTOS ORIGINALES PARA LA HISTORIA DE CHIAPAS, VERAPAZ, CHICHEA [sic] ITZA, ETC. TOMO I [1548-1820]
208 p. 30-31 cm.   HHB [M-M 432]

A collection of reports, decrees, and related material, originals and copies, dealing with Guatemala, Yucatan, and the Dominican province of Chiapas which stresses the work of Dominican missionaries and the problems created by the unsubdued Indians. There are twelve major items:

1. Report of Francisco Xavier de Aguirre, former Alcalde Mayor of Verapaz Province, to the governing board of the Real Consulado of Guatemala, with a summary description of the area, topography, inhabitants, products, etc., with suggestions for development. Hacienda de los Llanos, Guatemala, February 3, 1803. 8 p., D.S.

2. A reproduction of the oral petition presented by the leading Indians of Cobán, Guatemala, to their parish priest, Rafael de Aguirre, requesting confirmation of their statements regarding the difficulty of paying taxes, with a confirmatory declaration by Aguirre. Cobán, September 4, 1807. 12 p.

3. Copies of reports and related material prepared by Dominican friars in various parts of Guatemala at the request of Archbishop Molina, on Verapaz mission conditions. Guatemala, October 23, 1819-December 6, 1820. 44 p.

4. Copy of a report by local authorities on the early development of San Marcos and neighboring territory. San Marcos (Alta Verapaz?), Guatemala, 1548. 3 p.

5. Report of Gabriel de Salazar, Prior of the Dominican Convent of Cobán,

Guatemala, on the Verapaz missions, prepared on behalf of his monastery and the entire province of San Vicente of Guatemala and of Chiapa, with requests for aid. Cobán, December 20, 1636. 9 p., D.S.

6. Copy of a letter from the Provincial of Santo Domingo Province to the Archbishop of Guatemala, praising the work of Dominican missionaries, particularly among the Chole-Lacandón Indians. Provincia de Santo Domingo de Guatemala, n.d. 4 p.

7. Report by the Dominican, José Delgado, on the settlements, inhabitants, and other features of the region between San Miguel Manche and the territory of the Ahiza [Itza?] Indians, based on his journey begun on June 7, 1677. Bacalar, Yucatan, September 26, 1677. 7 p.

8. An 8-page anonymous fragment of a report defending the conduct of the Chole Indians, and setting forth their grievances against Bartolomé Coz, one of the tribe members who had used an official commission to rob them.

9. Two copies of a royal decree, November 30, 1680, on provision of friars for the conversion and pacification of the Chole Indians, addressed respectively to Lope de Sierra Osorio, Acting Governor of Guatemala, and to Navas Quevedo, Bishop of Guatemala; and a copy of a letter, October 13, 1677, from the King to Sebastián de Olivera y Angulo, Alcalde Mayor of Verapaz, also relating to the work of pacification in that region. Spain, 1677-1680. 6 p.

10. Copy of a letter from the Dominican, José Delgado, to the Provincial of Santo Domingo province; and the original, signed by Delgado and Juan Serrano, of the proposal to be presented before the Provincial. Both items relate to the conduct of work among the Choles. Rancho de San Lucas, Chol Province, Guatemala, March 12-17, 1682. 6 p.

11. Notes on the work of the friars among the Indians of Guatemala and of neighboring territory, including considerable material on individual Dominicans and a few references to Franciscans, as well as to royal decrees on the pacification of the Indians; apparently based to a large extent on Remesal's *Historia de San Vicente de Chiapa y Guatemala*. Guatemala, ca. 1700. 83 p.

12. Two anonymous reports on experiences among the Ahiza [Itza?] Indians and those in the region of Bacalar, Yucatan. Includes mention of imprisonment by English pirates. Santa Cruz, Guatemala, October 20, 1703. 4 p.

This collection is in a bound volume bearing the bookplate of Alphonse Pinart. "Tomo II" for this group of documents has not been located, but there may have been a plan to assign that volume number to "Documents of Chiapas, Yucatán and Guatemala" (M-M 433).

DOCUMENTOS PARA LA HISTORIA DE BAJA CALIFORNIA. BAJA CALIFORNIA. 1847-1864
138 p. 33 cm.   HHB [M-M 260]

Correspondence, reports, proclamations, and other material relating to military and political developments in Baja California, its missions, economic and industrial problems, notably those deriving from the salt-mines contract with Rufus K. Porter, and legal questions such as the Criss case; with English notes, lists, and queries at end.

Compiled by Benjamin Hayes and presented by him to the Bancroft Library in 1877; written on pages of various sizes; signed originals, drafts, resumes, and copies.

DOCUMENTOS PARA LA HISTORIA ECLESIÁSTICA Y CIVIL DE LA NUEVA VIZCAYA. MEXICO. ca. 1595-ca. 1750
766 p. 33 cm.   HHB [M-M 166]
Collection of documents relating to the ecclesiastical and civil history of Nueva Vizcaya from 1595-1750. Consists of reports, correspondence, petitions, decrees, and other items concerned chiefly with the work of Jesuit and Franciscan missionaries, but also with governmental and military matters. Contains Martín Duarte's account of the Ávila-Santarén expedition. Substantially identical with Volumes 3 and 4 of *Documentos para la Historia de México, 4th ser.*, Mexico, 1857.

Entered by Bancroft under "Nueva Vizcaya, Documentos para la Historia."

DOCUMENTOS PARA LA HISTORIA ECLESIASTICA Y CIVIL DE LA PROVINCIA DE TEXAS. 1689-1789
726 p. 32 cm.   HHB [M-M 235]
Copy of a compilation made in 1852 of 74 items relating to the ecclesiastical and civil history of the Province of Texas and outlying regions, including Louisiana and Florida, prepared by an anonymous Franciscan to supplement the *Memorias* of Morfi. Copied from the "Historia" section in AGN., Vols. 27-28, and corresponding in large part to the closing portion of Brantz Mayer's "Manuscritos Mexicanos" (M-M 281, Nos. 19 *et seq.*).

Contains Bonilla's "Breve Compendio de la Historia de Texas" (1772); diaries of León (1689), Terán (1691-1692), Bruno (1692), Martínez (1691), Ramón (1716), and Solís (1767) on expeditions to Texas; letters, statements, and reports of Massanet, San Miguel de Aguayo, Margil, Ramón, etc., and documents concerning the journeys of Saint-Denis (1713-1715).

The volume includes also the diary of Peña, 1721-1722, on the Aguayo expedition to Texas; letters of Urrutia, Alcivia, Jiménez, Ripperdá, and Mézières, and many petitions and reports concerning Texas missions. For more detailed analysis, see Bolton's *Guide . . . ,* p. 28-31.

DOCUMENTOS RELATIVOS A LA RENTA DEL TABACO. 1751-1824
12 reels. (On film)   [M-A 18]
These documents concern the various phases of tobacco culture and manufacture, and especially its sale and taxation. Selected by Father Francis J. Sweeney from the Archivo General de la Nación, Archivo Histórico de Hacienda, Biblioteca Nacional, and Archivo del Ayuntamiento de Orizaba, Mexico.

DOCUMENTS CONCERNING CONDITION AND TREATMENT OF THE INDIANS, AND THE EMPLOYMENT OF SLAVE LABOR IN SPANISH POSSESSIONS. 1567-1568
412 exp. (On film)   [Z-G 14]
Original depositions, reports, and replies to interrogatories, taken for the most part on oath before Juan de Ovando. From the British Museum.

DOCUMENTS CONCERNING THE ADMINISTRATION AND DEFENSE OF SONORA AND SINALOA. MEXICO. 1749

3 folders. D.S. 31 cm. [M-M 1783]

Folder 1. A report to the first Viceroy Revilla Gigedo from the Auditor General for War, Juan Rodríguez de Albuerne, Marqués de Altamira, mainly concerning proposed measures for the pacification of the Seris, Guaymis, Upanguaymis, Pimas Bajos, Tiburones, and other Indians of the region. Deals also with financial problems, recognition of services by various leaders, plans for exploring Baja California, and appointment of an *ad interim* governor for Sinaloa and Sonora. Dated March 17-21, 1749. Appended is a document appointing Diego Ortiz Parrilla to serve as governor *ad interim*, March 21, 1749. 20 p.

Folder 2. An order from Viceroy Revilla Gigedo instructing the Royal Accounting Tribunal and Audiencia to transmit 15,000 pesos to the *ad interim* governor for completion of the Pitic and other projects. With appended statement recording execution of the order. Both dated March 26, 1749. 12 p.

Folder 3. Acceptance by Diego Ortiz Parrilla of his appointment, with certifications regarding relevant formalities and financial transactions. March-July, 1749. 2 p.

DOCUMENTS FOR THE HISTORY OF MEXICO. ca. 1524-1855.

12 cartons and 204 volumes. (Transcripts and photocopies) [M-A 1]

A great miscellany, from the time of Hernán Cortés through the exploration of the Pacific Coast and the occupation of Texas, the northern provinces, California, to the Gadsden Purchase. From the Archivo General de la Nación, Mexico. There is a "key" to the collection.

DOCUMENTS FOR THE HISTORY OF MEXICO. 1635-1812

294 exp. (On film) [Z-F 3]

Described by numbers 195, 295, 179, 119-148, 176, 84, 180, 174, 175, and 164 in Eugène Boban, *Documents pour servir a l'histoire du Mexique; catalogue raisonné de la collection de m. E.-Eugène Goupil* (Paris, 1891), volume 2. Microfilm of miscellaneous items selected by J. L. and Mildred Luna in the Bibliothèque Nationale, Paris.

DOCUMENTS FOR THE HISTORY OF MEXICO AND CALIFORNIA. 1556-1810

1 box. (Transcripts) 28-33 cm. [Z-E 7]

Documents selected by France V. Scholes and Francis S. Philbrick from Cartas de Indias and Papeles de Estado of the Archivo Histórico Nacional, Madrid. Subjects include ordinances governing the raising of livestock, exploration and foreign intrusions into the Californias, Lapérouse and the French in Spanish America.

DOCUMENTS FOR THE STUDY OF CUBAN RELATIONS WITH THE UNITED STATES. 1492-1910

2 cartons and 1 box. (Transcripts) [Z-E 6]

Documents selected by Francis S. Philbrick, primarily from the Archivo

Histórico Nacional, Madrid. A "key" to the collection is available in the Library.

DOCUMENTS OF CHIAPAS, YUCATAN, AND GUATEMALA. 1685–[ca. 1845]

132 p. 25-31 cm. HHB [M-M 433]

Collection of reports and notes, chiefly copies, concerned with Guatemala, including Chiapas and Yucatan, which relate primarily to Dominican and Franciscan missionaries or to native customs and traditions. There are seven principal items:

1. Copy of report, addressed by the Prior of the Dominican Convent in Cobán to Bishop Navas y Quevedo of Guatemala, defending the Dominican missionaries against the complaints presented to the King of Spain by Olivera y Angulo, former Alcalde Mayor of Verapaz. Cobán, Guatemala, February 8, 1685. 15 p. A collection of notes is appended on missionary expeditions and Indian disturbances. This 14-page addition was compiled, according to Brasseur de Bourbourg, by the Dominican Blas del Valle for use in revising and extending Remesal's *Historia*.

2. Blas del Valle's description of the province of Verapaz and its indigenous inhabitants. Guatemala, n.d. 3 p.

3. Copies, in Spanish and French, by Brasseur de Bourbourg of Ramón de Ordóñez y Aguiar's notes on various features of the towns of Chiapas and Palenque. Ciudad Real, Chiapas, n.d. 6 p.

4. Extract copied from letter addressed by Francisco Núñez de la Vega, Dominican Bishop of Chiapas, to the Captain General of Guatemala, requesting the destruction of certain Indian writings on the superstitious practices of *nagualismo*. Ciudad Real de Chiapas, ca. 1691. 2 p. This copy was made in 1859 by Brasseur de Bourbourg from an incomplete Ms. in the episcopal Archivo de San Cristóbal at Ciudad Real de Chiapas.

5. Copy of an excerpt of Francisco Vázquez's chronicle concerning the Franciscan "Provincia del Santísimo Nombre de Jesús de Guatemala" which contains some information on military conquest and the establishment of Guatemala City, but deals chiefly with missionary work. A list of the towns under the jurisdiction of the various monasteries and vicariates. This excerpt constitutes part of Chapter I and all of Chapter II, Volume I, of the *Chrónica* which was published in 1714. Guatemala, ca. 1700. 22 p.

6. Copy of an article by the Mexican jurist, Juan Pío Pérez, on the ancient calendar and chronological system of the Yucatan Indians. Taken from the "Registro Yucateco," Vol. 3. Mérida, Yucatan, ca. 1845. 28 p.

7. Eleven selections copied from the "Registro Yucateco," Vols. 3, 4, and possibly others, which describe the customs, legends, cities, and other features of Yucatan. Mérida, Yucatan, ca. 1845. 41 p.

The above seven items are in a bound volume bearing the bookplates of Brasseur de Bourbourg and Alphonse Pinart, with binder's title of "Documentos de Verapaz y Lancadón [sic]."

DOCUMENTS RELATING TO BAJA CALIFORNIA. 1795-1854
53 exp. (On film) [M-M 1839]
Materials on the Walker expedition and correspondence of Joaquín de Arrillaga.

DOCUMENTS RELATING TO CONGREGACIONES, TASACIONES, AND TRIBUTOS. MEXICO. 1578-1804
2 reels. (On film) [M-A 16]
Gives a lengthy "Indice de Congregaciones," with documents; "Documentación relativa a Tributos y Rentas de 1804." Also, "Huejotzingo, Puebla, Tributos y libros de comunidad, tasación y memoria de oficiales . . . 1578;" and "Testimonio de la Matrícula de los tributarios de la jurisdicción de San Cristóbal Ecatepec." From the Archivo General de la Nación, Mexico.

DOCUMENTS RELATING TO MAYAN CULTURE
223 exp. (On film) [M-M 1837]
Microfilm of materials from various sources, including a Mayan codex, hieroglyphics, and inscriptions.

DOCUMENTS RELATING TO SHIPPING BETWEEN HAMBURG AND MEDITERRANEAN PORTS. 1590-1626
3 reels. (On film) [Z-Z 156]
Microfilm of original documents in the Stadtsarchiv, Hamburg, Germany. Filmed through the courtesy of Engel Sluiter.

DOCUMENTS RELATING TO THE DEFENSE OF NUEVA VIZCAYA AGAINST THE SUMAS, APACHES, AND ALLIED INDIANS. MEXICO. 1754-1760
6 folders. D.S. 21-31 cm. [M-M 1786]
Folder 1 is a file on plans for the defense of the northern frontier, 1754-1755, including decrees of Viceroy Revilla Gigedo the Elder and Governor Mateo Antonio de Mendoza, and related documents concerning defense projects. 186 p.

Folder 2 consists of proposals for frontier defense, 1755-1757, with reference particularly to the Valle de San Buenaventura. Includes reports from Governor Mendoza, the Marqués de Aranda, and others. 82 p.

Folder 3 contains papers on a dispute between Governor Mendoza and Bernardo Antonio de Bustamante y Tagle, captain of the mobile unit based at Huejuquilla for the protection of Chihuahua and central Nueva Vizcaya. Includes petitions, letters, decrees, official opinions, annotations, certifications, and related materials, 1756-1761. 102 p.

Folder 4 has portions of a report prepared on behalf of the Captaincy General of Nueva Vizcaya in connection with a war council assembled to discuss establishment of new frontier presidios and other defense measures [1757?]. 44 p.

Folder 5 is a certified copy of a file, 1759-1760, on charges brought against

Captain Rubín de Celís for inefficiency, peculation, maltreatment of the Indians, and failure to execute orders. Contains depositions of witnesses, orders of Governor Mendoza, commissions, instructions, and related docudents. 270 p.

Folder 6 is a report, apparently addressed to the Viceroy by Governor Mendoza at the close of 1759 or the beginning of 1760, dealing with the deficiencies of Mendoza's three presidio captains, Rubín de Celís, on the Conchos, Santiago Ruiz at Janos, and Bustamante y Tagle at Huejuquilla, and measures for their replacement. 22 p.

DOCUMENTS RELATING TO THE PROVINCE OR STATE OF DURANGO. 1770-1827
4 folders. 7 p. D. and L.S. 21-30 cm. [M-M 1798]

Concern local appointments and the sending of deputies to the national Congress.

DOCUMENTS RELATING TO THE SEARCH FOR THE MYTHICAL CITY OF THE "CESARES" BY JOACHIN DE ESPINOSA. 1777-1778
6 reels. (On film) [Z-D 116]

Microfilm of materials selected by Louis De Armond from the Biblioteca Nacional, Chile.

DOMÍNGUEZ, JUAN
Parte Oficial de la Defensa de Jalapa. . . . Mexico. December, 1822.
32 p. L.S. 23 cm. HHB [M-M 87]

Letter from Colonel Domínguez to José María Calderón, Jalapa, December 21, reporting on the successful Imperialist defense of that town against Santa Anna; and a signed autograph letter, Mexico City, December 28, from Domínguez to his brother, referring to the same matter and to the general military situation.

DOMÍNGUEZ DE ZAMORA Y AZEVEDO, ANTONIO
Pruebas de nobleza de sangre y limpieza de D.ⁿ Antonio, D.ⁿ Manuel, y D.ⁿ Miguel Dominguez de Zamora y Azevedo, natibos de la ciudad de Mex.ᶜᵒ Fechas ante la Juzticia Ordinaria en 19 de Octubre de 1768 y en Castilla la Viexa año de 1675. Mexico City. 1768.
62 p. 30 cm. HHB [M-M 252]

A genealogical file containing copies of petitions, decrees, depositions, baptismal certificates, and related documents, originating in Mexico City, Jadraque (province of Guadalajara), and Guatemala City, 1655-1768, which establish the nobility and Christian descent of Antonio Domínguez de Zamora, resident of Mexico City, and his brothers and sisters in Mexico and Spain. Certified by Zambrano in Mexico City on November 22, 1768, with secondary certification of November 23, attesting Zambrano's competence.

Ornamental title page, folded genealogical table, and coats of arms for the Domínguez de Zamora and Azevedo families painted on vellum.

DOMINICAN MISSIONS AND MISSIONARIES OF LOWER CALIFORNIA.
ca. 1794-1798
4 p. 20-29 cm. [M-M 1764]

Two lists of Dominican missions and missionary fathers in Baja California. One, headed "Nómina" and undated, was evidently written before April, 1794, since it omits the Mission of San Pedro Mártir founded in that month, besides listing two missions suppressed in 1795. The other is dated in Loreto on December 31, 1798.

DOMINICANS. PROVINCE OF SAN SALVADOR, GUATEMALA
Tractado de la fundacion del Convento de la Ciudad de San Salvador de la provincia de Guathemala, y de las cosas notables, que desde ella han succedido en él, hasta estos tiempos. [San Salvador, 18th century]
28 p. 31 cm. HHB [M-M 443]

A brief history of the Dominican Convent of San Salvador, in the city of that name, formerly a part of the Captaincy General of Guatemala. It is divided into thirteen sections dealing with the history of the city, foundation and development of the monastery up to a date not earlier than 1708, the lives of outstanding members, work among the Indians, and related matters; written by an anonymous Dominican.

DOMINICANS. PROVINCIA DE SANTIAGO DE MÉXICO
Actas provinciales de la Provincia de Santiago de Mexico del Orden de Predicadores. Mexico. 1540-1590.
346 p. (Photocopy) 20 cm. HHB [M-M 142]

Minutes of chapter meetings held by the Province, chiefly in Latin, some signed; include lists of priests, with their stations, and administrators of the Province.

DOMINICANS. PROVINCIA DE SANTIAGO DE MÉXICO
Fundacion y progressos de La Prouincia de Santiago de Mexico del orden de Predicadores en sus principios. Con el catalogo de los Prelados que con titulo de Prouinciales la han gouernado, hasta este presente año de 1716. . . . Mexico. 1716-[1788?]
29 p. 22 cm. HHB [M M 102]

A history of the Dominican Province of Santiago. Includes a list of the Provincials from 1534 to 1788 and their dates of service; lists of Dominican popes, antipopes, and cardinals, with dates of election; a summary of the prophecies of Saint Malachy; a list of the governors and viceroys of New Spain to 1759; and a guide to the Freemasons' code.

DORVE, H (?)
Letter. London. June 9, 1894.
1 p. A.L.S. 18 cm. [z-z 100:34]

Acknowledging receipt of letter which he says he is unable to read because he has no command of English. In German script.

DRAFT OF A CERTIFICATE OF RECOGNITION OF THE SERVICES OF LUIS DE ECHAVARRÍA, TOBACCO FACTOR OF SANTIAGO. SANTIAGO DE CUBA. JANUARY 14, 1796
1 p. 31 cm. [z-a 200:1

DRYDEN, WILLIAM G
Papers relating to. 1839-1939.
2 vols. 76 p. (Typescripts) 20-31 cm. [m-m 1735]
Papers concerning the trial, imprisonment, and damage suit of Dryden, a citizen of the United States charged by the Mexican Government with complicity in the 1841 attempt of Texas to annex New Mexico through the armed "Santa Fe Expedition" organized by President Lamar of Texas.

Contains original correspondence, August 12-September, 1939, between W. E. Bard of Waco, Texas, and Herbert I. Priestley, dealing principally with Bard's research on the Dryden case, the loan of his notes, and translations. Also notes and transcribed material on the case from the National Archives of the United States, Records of the Department of State.

DUARTE, ALONSO
Relacion de lo que yo Alonso Duarte vecino de esta Ciudad de Santiago de Guatemala entendi y vide quando D.ⁿ Francisco de Valverde y Mercado vino a sondar los Puertos de Cavallos y el de Fonseca. . . . Guatemala City. May 22, 1605.
8 p. 33 cm. hhb [m-m 306]
Report by the notary, Duarte, at the command of Alonso Criado de Castilla, President of the Real Audiencia of Guatemala, concerning the expedition undertaken in 1590 by Francisco de Valverde y Mercado for the purpose of examining the ports of Caballos and Fonseca as possible substitutes for the ports of Nombre de Dios and Panama.

[DUARTE, MANUEL]
Pluma rica, nuevo Fenix de la America. [*Post* 1769]
100 p. 31 cm. hhb [m-m 297]
Portion of a treatise intended to prove, on the basis of traditions and citations, that St. Thomas preached the Gospel in America.

Entered by Bancroft under "Sigüenza y Góngora, Carlos, El Fénix de la América." For the probably incorrect attribution of this work to Sigüenza, *see* Beristáin, *Biblioteca Hispano Americana Septentrional*, 3rd ed., Vol. II, p. 208, Note 46 (Ramírez's note), and Vol. IV, p. 348, Note 112 (Adición).

DUBLÁN, MANUEL, 1830-1891
Biographical Sketch. [N.p., n.d.]
8 f. 26 cm. hhb [m-m 366]
Sketch of the career of Manuel Dublán, Mexican statesman closely associated with Benito Juárez. He was of French descent.

DUCATEL, PROF. (?)
Second Journal of an Expedition to the Volcano of Popocatepetl. November 10-13, 1827.
9 p. 33 cm. [M-M 1873]
Details of an ascent of Popocatepetl, including descriptions of various botanical and geological features.

DU FRECHON
Writ of Payment of Debt. Jacmel, Haiti. June 10-14, 1793.
2 p. 30 cm. HHB [Z-A 5:2]

DUMAS, ALEXANDRE, 1802-1870
La Tour de Nesle. Paris. 1832. Catherine Howard. Paris. 1835.
356 p. 23 cm. HHB [M-M 89]
"La Torre de Nesle," a Spanish translation of the historical drama by Dumas and Frédéric Gaillardet; with an anonymous Spanish adaptation (n. d.) of Dumas' "Catherine Howard."

DUNCAN FAMILY PAPERS. 1860-1865
8 p. (Typescript) 28 cm. [Z-Z 143]
Letters from friends in Elkton, Kentucky, describing the political climate and local events. Typed transcripts of originals in private possession.

DURÁN, DIEGO, 1538-1588
Historia antigua de la Nueva España, con noticias de los usos é costumbres de los Yndios y explicacion del calendario mexicano. [Mexico. 1579-1581]
15 p. 33 cm. HHB [M-M 123]
An outline summarizing by chapters Durán's three treatises on the history, religion, and calendar of the Mexican Indians. Probably prepared for H. H. Bancroft on the basis of a Ms. in the Library of Congress, Washington, D.C.

DURÁN, DIEGO, 1538-1588
Historia de las Indias de Nueva-España y Islas de Tierra Firme. Mexico. 1579-1581.
3 vols. 32 cm. HHB [M-M 90-92]
The title supplied above is taken from the Mexico City edition of 1867-1880; the binder's title, "Historia Antigua de la Nueva España," reappears in expanded form in another Bancroft Ms. (M-M 123) also by Diego Durán. The dates of composition given here are those inserted in the text (Treatises 1 and 3) by Durán, whereas the date assigned by Bancroft is 1585.
Three treatises by the Dominican, Fray Durán, dealing respectively with the history of Mexico from its origin through its conquest by Cortés; the gods and religious rites of the indigenous peoples; and their calendar.

DUTCH WEST INDIES
Documents relating to. 1685-1881.
2 boxes (175 folders). HHB [Z-A 2]
Originals, contemporary copies, and Alphonse Pinart transcripts, relating

mainly to the government of the islands of Curaçao, St. Martin, and St. Eustatius. The collection contains official correspondence, ordinances, appointments, and instructions for various officials, reflecting French and British dominion. The St. Martin documents also show the division of the island into the Dutch and French parts.

Box 1 contains the materials for Curaçao, box 2 those for St. Eustatius and St. Martin. Arrangement is chronological within each box. A partial "key" to the collection is available in the Library.

EBERLEIN, LOUIS A
Letter to his Mother. U.S.S. *Petrel,* Manila. May 8, 1898.
12 p. A.L.S. 21 cm. [z-p 120]
Describing the Battle of Manila.

EBERSTADT, EDWARD EMORY, 1883-1958
Correspondence with W. L. Mellon. Pittsburgh and New York. November 7-20, 1934.
5 p. L.S. 27-28 cm. [z-z 100:88]
Concerning acquisition of a copy of *Larimer Reminiscences.*

ECHAVE, JOSÉ MARÍA DE, AND OTHERS
Request for Forced Loan. Mexico City. February 25, 1822.
3 p. D.S. and Printed. 21 cm. HHB [M-M 1700:35]
Notification addressed to José Vicente Valdés and Pedro Garibay of amount to be contributed by them to a loan for the government, with the former property of the Inquisition and the Pious Fund of the Californias as security.

ECHEVELAR, JOAQUÍN DE, *comp.*
Questiones sobre la Regla de N. S. P. S. Francisco, sacadas de la Exposicion, que de ella hizo el P. Navarro. Por Fr. Joachín de Echevelar, religioso layco del Colegio de N. S.ra de Guadalupe de Zacatecas. [N. p., n. d.]
374 p. 16 cm. HHB [M-M 94]
Compilation prepared by Echevelar, lay brother of the Colegio de Nuestra Señora de Guadalupe de Zacatecas, containing excerpts from Father [Francisco?] Navarro's exposition of the Rule of Saint Francis in question-and-answer form, with table of contents at end; Latin and Spanish verses setting forth the Rule; and two items in Latin prose and verse by Saint Bonaventure, 13th century Minister General of the Friars Minor, each entitled "Alphabetum Religiosorum" and consisting of precepts for monastic conduct, so arranged that the initial letters form an alphabet.

ECONOMIC HISTORY OF MEXICO AND CENTRAL AMERICA. [1529?]-1795
1 box. (Photocopies) [z-e 13]
Documents selected by Sanford A. Mosk from various Spanish archives, including the Archivo General de Indias, Seville; and the Academia de la

Historia, the Biblioteca de El Escorial, and the Biblioteca de Palacio, in Madrid.

EDWARD (?)
Two Letters to his Wife, Janie. Buck Island, South Carolina. 1859-1860.
8 p. A.L.S. 20 cm. [z-z 100:97]
Describing his life as minister on the island.

EITEL, FREDERICK, 1846-
Reminiscences and Journal. 1876-1884.
305 p. A.D.S. 31 cm. [z-d 138]
Eitel's account of his boyhood; his years in Sacramento, California; and his travels in Peru, Ecuador, Panama, and Colombia, 1869-1884, prospecting, cutting rubber, and working on railroads.

ELEGÍAS QUE DEDICA MI AMOR. A SU DIGNO OBJETO.... [N.p., 1817]
9 p. 21 cm. HHB [M-M 1700:18]
Anonymous love poem, in four parts, preceded by quotation from Ovid, on the desirability of secrecy in love.

ELIZABETH I, QUEEN OF ENGLAND
Letters to the States General, The Netherlands. March 24, 1596, and September 21, 1597.
5 exp. (On film) [z-g 12]
Microfilm of originals, with the Queen's signature, in the Algemeen Rijksarchief, The Hague.

ELOGIO DE LOS SACERDOTES DIFUNTOS ... 14 DE ENERO DE 1800. ... MEXICO. 1800-1830
375 p. 23 cm. HHB [M-M 25]
Drafts and copies of sermons and eulogies, prose and verse, delivered or composed by José Mariano Beristáin de Souza, José Nicolás Maniau y Torquemada, Pablo de la Llave, José Demetrio Moreno, José de Soria, and possibly others; the will and epitaph of Beristáin, and an elegy on the death of José Joaquín Geredo.

ERB, GABRIEL S   , 1843-
Dictation. [ca. 1887]
6 p. 22 cm. HHB [M-M 526]
Hotel business in Illinois and Utah; trip to Baja California in 1887; construction of hotel at Punta Banda in agreement with the International Company of Mexico. Recorded for H. H. Bancroft.

[ESCOTO, BARTOLOMÉ DE, b. 1580(?), AND FAMILY]
Documents relating to the Province of Honduras, the Inquisition, and the Escoto Family. Guatemala, Captaincy General. 1634-1638.
9 items. D.S. 31-44 cm. HHB [M-M 511]
Papers relating to the career and genealogy of Bartolomé de Escoto, civil

official, Inquisition Chief Constable, and mining man, and to the career of his son, Juan Bautista de Mendoza Escoto, during the period when Honduras was a part of the Captaincy General of Guatemala. There are nine principal items:

1. Certified copy of a power of attorney conferred by Bartolomé de Escoto upon Inquisition Commissioner Felipe González de Dueñas, Tegucigalpa, October 27, 1634; appended annotation on delegation of González's powers to Eugenio de Saravia and others, April 27, 1635. 4 p. 31 cm.

2. Signed document appointing Bartolomé de Escoto as Chief Constable of the Inquisition in Tegucigalpa, May 11, 1635. An addendum of September 28, 1635, records delivery of the title and swearing in of Escoto. 2 p. 44 cm.

3. Signed document appointing Juan Bautista Escoto as a familiar of the Inquisition. Honduras, September 20, 1635. 1 p. 42 cm.

4. Petition presented to Inquisition Commissioner González de Dueñas by Bartolomé de Escoto, requesting a genealogical investigation with a view to establishing the status of his son as a familiar of the Tribunal, Tegucigalpa, October 3(?), 1635. Appended is an undated order granting this request. 3 p. 32 cm.

5. Certified copies of the file on investigation of the genealogy and activities of Capt. Baltasar de Mendoza, compiled at the request of Don Baltasar's son-in-law, Bartolomé de Escoto. It quotes background documents from various parts of Spain and New Spain dating back to the 16th century, and includes data indicating that Mendoza was related to the Marqués de Gelves, Viceroy of New Spain from 1621-1624. Tegucigalpa, 1635. 97 p. 31 cm.

6. Statement issued by Alcalde Mayor José de Orozco on May 5, 1637, prior to his departure on an expedition to pacify the Jicaque Indians, in which he certified that Bartolomé de Escoto and his son Juan Bautista had served the King meritoriously; evidently a preliminary to the appointment of Don Bartolomé as *justicia mayor* pending Orozco's return. Tegucigalpa. 1 p. 32 cm.

7. Signed document tentatively appointing Bartolomé de Escoto as Deputy Alcalde Mayor pending the return of Orozco from the above-mentioned expedition, and submitted by Orozco to Governor Alvaro Quiñones Osorio, Captain General of Guatemala, for confirmation. Tegucigalpa, December 18, 1637. 2 p. 44 cm.

8. Document issued by the Real Audiencia de Guatemala appointing Bartolomé de Escoto as *justicia mayor* of the Minas de Tegucigalpa (Honduras Province) for the duration of Orozco's excursion into Jicaque territory. Santiago de Guatemala, February 13, 1638. 2 p. 31 cm.

9. Letter from Bartolomé de Escoto to Eugenio de Saravia, Inquisition secretary in Mexico City, requesting confirmation of the writer's title of Chief Constable for that tribunal. Honduras, July 26(?), 1638. 2 p. 31 cm.

ESPEJO, PEDRO
Family Papers. 1856-1898.
1 box [M-B 11]
Contain certificates of baptism and confirmation of some of their children,

appointment to military posts under Emperor Maximilian, and numerous letters of the family from San Francisco, especially to Edward Espejo, after the fall of the Empire. Chiefly personal. A daguerrotype, pictures of Espejo family, and books of devotion.

ESPINOSA DE LOS MONTEROS, MANUEL
Ynterpretacion del Escudo y Tau, signos, estampados en . . . Tianquiztepetl en la Sierra de Metztitlan. . . . [Mexico. N. d.]
2 vols. 31 cm.　　　　　　　　　　　　　　　　　　　　　　HHB [M-M 96]

Two treatises interpreting the hieroglyphics inscribed on the peak of Tianguistepetl, a mountain of the Metztitlán range in the State of Hidalgo, as a shield that symbolizes conquest and subjugation of the Indians and a tau cross that symbolizes their eventual salvation and liberation. Authorities are cited to connect the two hieroglyphics with Biblical and other traditions.

The author was a former canon of the Colegiata de Santa María de Guadalupe. Internal evidence places the date of composition after the establishment of the Mexican republic.

ESPINOSA [VIDAURRE, JOSÉ IGNACIO DE]
Letter referring to Certificate of Appointment. Mexico City. July 6, 1831.
1 p. D.S. 30 cm.　　　　　　　　　　　　　　　　　　　HHB [M-M 1700:44]

Announcement by Espinosa of confirmation by the acting chief of state, Anastasio Bustamante, of a papal bull, appointing José Antonio Zubiría y Escalante as Bishop of Durango. Incomplete.

[ESPIRÍTU SANTO], BERNARDO [DEL], bp.
Letter. Culiacán, Mexico. November 29, 1824.
1 p. L.S. 21 cm.　　　　　　　　　　　　　　　　　　　HHB [M-M 1700:28]

Letter to Fray Pedro González, President of the Missions, concerning a requested marriage dispensation for Antonio José de la Rocha.

ESTRADA RÁVAGO, JUAN DE
Descripcion de las Provincias de Costa Rica, Guatemala, Honduras, Nicaragua y Tierra Firme, y Cartagena. . . . May 6, 1572.
11 p. 33 cm.　　　　　　　　　　　　　　　　　　　　　HHB [M-M 311]

Letter from the ecclesiastic, Estrada Rávago, to Father Diego Guillén, Commissioner of the Province of Cartago and Costa Rica, supplying information in regard to the province, stressing its potential riches, and urging governmental support for the colonization project undertaken by Estrada himself in collaboration with Juan de Cavallón.

EVERETT, EDWARD, 1794-1865
Letter to William J. Eve. Boston. May 24, 1858.
2 p. A.L.S. 19 cm.　　　　　　　　　　　　　　　　　　　　　[Z-Z 100:60]

Sending receipt and thanking him for hospitality. With three newspaper clippings about Everett.

EXPLORATION OF CALIFORNIA. 1769-1788
140 exp. (On film)   [z-g 18]
  Records concerning Domingo Elizondo's expedition to Sonora, 1769; an account of the port of Monterey, 1770; a report of Esteban José Martínez's voyage, 1788; description of a diary of the Portolá expedition, 1769; and maps and plans of a number of the frontier presidios of New Spain. From the British Museum, Add. Ms.

EXPLORATION OF NEW MEXICO, CALIFORNIA, AND NORTHWEST COAST; AND OTHER PAPERS. 1743-1798
765 p. 29 cm.   hhb [m-m 401]
  Thirty-three items, originals and copies, concerning exploration and development of the Northwest Coast, New Mexico, California, and other outlying regions of New Spain; military defense of California and Mexico; and irrigation and flood-prevention projects in New Spain.

  1. An incomplete copy of Nicolás de Lafora's inspection trip to Santa Fe, New Mexico, 1766, for mapping purposes, 85 p.

  2. Manuel Agustín Mascaró's diary of a reconnaissance from Chihuahua to Arispe, 1779, 10 p.

  3-5. Documents relating to exploration of the northern California coast by Juan Pérez and others, 1773-1791, including a compendium begun by Francisco Antonio Mourelle on February 15, 1791, with excerpts from the correspondence of de Lacy, Jerónimo Grimaldi, Julián de Arriaga, and Viceroy Bucareli; the latter's instructions, 1773, for the Pérez expedition; an anonymous diary on Pérez's voyage, 1774, aboard the *Santiago*, with notes and navigation tables, 70 p.

  6. Letter from engineer Costansó reporting to the viceroy on the garrisons of Upper California, 1794, 27 p.

  7. Description of the ten intendancies of New Spain, undated, with references to New Galicia and New Vizcaya, 16 p.

  8-12. Copies of documents on the Huehuetoca Canal and drainage of the Valley of Mexico, including report of Alberto de Córdoba, 1794, Joaquín Velásquez, 1774, Miguel Costansó and José Burgaleta, 1788, and review of the drainage of Lake Zumpango, ca. 1788, 103 p.

  13-15. Documents relating to a project for conducting water from the Jamapa River to Veracruz, ca. 1754-1795, 34 p.

  16-27. Papers concerning the defense of New Spain in the region of Veracruz, with emphasis on the fortress of San Juan de Ulúa, 1775, 191 p.

  28. Diary of Portolá's land journey to San Diego and Monterey, 1769, accompanied by Fathers Junípero Serra and Miguel Campa, 35 p.

  29. Portolá's council of war, October 4, 1769, in regard to the search for Monterey Bay, 6 p.

  30. Anonymous description of Culiacán, Sinaloa, Ostimuri, and Sonora, 1772, with suggestions for development of the territory, 30 p.

  31. Juan Francisco de la Bodega's account of the voyage of the *Favorita* on the 1779 Arteaga-Bodega expedition up the Pacific Coast, 51 p.

  32. Copy of diary kept on the first trip of Juan Bautista de Anza, 1774, from Tubac to San Gabriel Mission in California, and Anza's return, 12 p.

33. Report of July 13, 1795, by Costansó and others, advising the viceroy on aid for Alta California, 9 p.

Some parts bound out of order, and some missing. There is an index.

EXTRACTS ON ORIGIN OF THE INDIANS
189 p. 31 cm.   HHB [M-M 97]

Brief extracts from 42 different printed works on the Indians of the New World, their origin, linguistic, and racial background. These publications date from the early 17th century to the middle of the 19th.

FABREGAT, LINO JOSÉ, 1746-1797
Esplicazione delle figure geroglifice del Codice Borgiano Messicano. . . . [N. p., n. d.]
509 p. 33 cm.   HHB [M-M 98]

Copy of an Italian work by the Mexican Jesuit, Fabregat (written Fabrega in Spanish), describing and interpreting the *Codex Mexicanus Borgianus,* which is a pictorial representation of the Mexican calendar and related rites, preserved in the Borgia Museum (Congregation of Propaganda Fide, Rome) and reproduced in Kingsborough's *Mexican Antiquities,* London, 1831, Vol. III, No. 1.

The above copy was completed in 1852, with water-color reproductions of Mexican hieroglyphics on title page.

FABRY, JOSÉ ANTONIO
Segunda Demonst.^{on} Numerica de los crecidos adelantamientos, q.^{e} pudiera lograr la R.^{l} Haz.^{de} de S. M. mediante la rebaja en el precio de azogue. . . . [Mexico City. ca. 1743].
622 p. 21 cm.   HHB [M-M 99]

Two monographs from a series written by Fabry, Mexican treasury official and chief mining agent for the Crown, to prove that a reduction in the price of quicksilver would stimulate Mexican mining. Comprises a refutation of the opposing arguments of the Comptroller General, José de Villaseñor y Sánchez, and the mining expert, José Alejandro de Bustamante, and an analysis of the reports cited by them from Pachuca, Guanajuato, Zacatecas, and Guadalajara.

FARABEE, ETHEL
William Stuart Parrott, Businessman and Diplomat in Texas. 1944.
32 p. (Typescript) 28 cm.   [M-R 5]

Digest of Miss Farabee's M.A. thesis, University of Texas, prepared by Marion D. Mullins.

FERÉ, MARÍA DE LA, b. 1847
My Recollections of Maximillian. [N.p., ca. 1910].
29 p. 29 cm.   [M-M 1751]

Recollections of the reign of Emperor Maximilian and Empress Carlota in Mexico, written some 43 years after the events by a daughter of one of Carlota's ladies-in-waiting. Her account covers the period of preliminary negotiations and the election of Maximilian as emperor by the Council of Notables, his arrival at Veracruz, life at the court, some details on contemporary life in Mexico, revolts led by Juárez and Díaz, the departure of the Empress, and execution of the Emperor, with hearsay reports on the later life of Carlota. Includes nine illustrations.

FERNÁNDEZ DE HERRERA Y GÓMEZ, JOSÉ MARÍA
Crítica sobre las Cartas Americanas de Rinaldo. Querétaro, Mexico. September 20, 1820.
18 p. L.S. 25 cm. HHB [M-M 112]
A letter to the publishers of the "Semanario Político y Literario," submitting for publication Fernández's translation of the Cremona, 1781-1782, edition of Count Giovanni Rinaldo Carli's *Cartas Americanas,* reviewing the content of the *Cartas,* and praising them as an important contribution to the history of America.
For text of translation, see "Carli . . . Cartas Americanas . . ." (M-M 55-56).

FERNÁNDEZ DEL CASTILLO Y DE MIER, MANUEL
Business Papers. 1869-1914.
31 vols. [M-B 4]
Records of the estate, or Hacienda, of this family, of which Fernández del Castillo was the owner or patrón.
There are journals, ledgers, cash books, and other records which illustrate the management of a typical family estate of that time, including the care of impecunious relatives or workers and payments to the Church.

FERNÁNDEZ LEAL, MANUEL, 1831-
Biography. [N.p., n.d.]
4 p. 21 cm. HHB [M-M 370]
Biographical notes on the Mexican engineer and statesman, Manuel Fernández Leal.

FERRÉ
Journal. July, 1837-August, 1839.
594 p. A.D. 20-22 cm. [M-M 1903]
Experiences as ship surgeon aboard *La Gloire* during the "Pastry War" in Mexico. Includes descriptions of naval blockades and skirmishes, diplomatic negotiations, Mexican politics, the position of the French in Mexico, and a note which includes copies of letters by Charles Baudin in 1839 relating to Ferré's services. In French.

FERRÉ, b. 1777(?)
Letters to Henri Moulin and Others. 1838-1839.
21 letters. A.L.S. 20-27 cm. [M-M 1772]
Letters from the director of the health service for the French fleet that was sent to San Juan de Ulúa to enforce payment of reparations to French na-

tionals in Mexico. Two were written to Ferré's wife and daughters, the remainder addressed to his "son," Henri Moulin, a Parisian lawyer left in charge of the writer's domestic affairs and apparently the widower of one of Ferré's daughters. The papers deal in part with preparations for the naval expedition, seizure of San Juan de Ulúa, French-Mexican peace treaty, the civil war in Mexico, political conditions in Portugal, and Anglo-Mexican relations, but also contain much personal material. Sent from towns or harbors of France and the Gulf of Mexico.

FILIASIONES DE LOS SOLDADOS QUE SE ALISTARON PARA LAS YSLAS FILIPINAS. MEXICO CITY, CUERNAVACA, AND QUERÉTARO. 1700
34 p. D.S. 31 cm. [M-M 1700:82]
Documents relating to the recruiting of a company in Querétaro for service in Manila, including proclamation of the viceroy, Conde de Moctezuma, a list of soldiers in the company, and marching orders, with signature of the viceroy, and military officials and soldiers enlisted.

FILISOLA, VICENTE, 1785-1850
Letter to José Mariano Michelena. Toluca. March 26, 1845.
1 p. L.S. 28 cm. HHB [M-M 1700:58]
Supports Michelena's recommendation for promotion of Sr. Villegas.

FLORES, VICTOR MARIA
Estadistica de la Seccion Ec[clesiásti]ca de Tapalapa. . . . Tapalapa (Chiapas, Mexico). April 10, 1839.
24 p. A.D.S. 31 cm. HHB [M-M 447]
Statistical report on the ecclesiastical district of Tapalapa, in Chiapas, and its four principal settlements, Tapalapa, Pantepec, Ocotopec, and Coapilla. Includes a brief section on local geography and topography, a civil and sociological survey, emphasizing moral conditions and the state of agriculture and industry, and nine appended statistical tables showing baptisms, births, deaths, marriages, and developments in agriculture and industry, for the period 1784-1838 or shorter terms within that period.

FONT, PEDRO, d. 1781
Diario que forma el P. Fr. Pedro Font. . . . Ures, Sonora, Mexico. June, 1776.
79 p. A.D.S. 21 cm. [M-M 1724]
Records the second Anza expedition, September 29, 1775-June 5, 1776, from San Miguel de Horcasitas to San Francisco and back, conducted by order of Viceroy Bucareli for the settlement of Monterey and San Francisco. Written in Ures from notes made during the expedition, it contains valuable geographical and topographical information. The Spanish text, with an English translation, has been published in the Academy of Pacific Coast History, *Publications*, Volume III (Berkeley, 1913). Another translation was published by Herbert Eugene Bolton in *Anza's California Expeditions*, Vol. III (Berkeley, 1930).

FONT, PEDRO, d. 1781
    Plan Geografico Historico del Nuevo Descubrimiento de el Puerto de Monte Rey, S.ⁿ Francisco, y las tierras que se marcaron en el derrotero de el Teniente Coronel de Caballeria D.ⁿ Juan Bautista de Ansa. . . . Ures. 1776.
    43 p. 30 cm. [M-M 1725]
    Copy of Font's diary of the second Anza expedition, made by Antonio Martínez Velasco, in Querétaro, November 23, 1776. Corresponds substantially to Font, "Diario . . ." (M-M 1724) but includes copies of the ground plan of the Casa Grande de Moctezuma on the Gila River and a plan of the mouth of San Francisco harbor.

FONTANA, BERNARD LEE, 1931-
    Guía a los documentos del Archivo del Gobierno de la Mitra de Sonora. Hermosillo. 1782-1841.
    21 p. (Typescript) 28 cm. [M-A 24]
    Co-authors: Fray Luis Baldonado and Henry F. Dobyns.

FONTE Y HERNÁNDEZ DE MIRAVETE, PEDRO JOSÉ, abp., 1777-1839
    Documents and Correspondence. 1815-1834.
    81 folders. Ms. and printed.   HHB [M-M 382]
    A collection of papers, mostly originals or certified contemporary copies, relating to the installation and activites of Fonte as Archbishop of Mexico, the majority addressed to or written by him, in Spanish, Latin, and Italian.
    The first major portion of this collection consists of papal rescripts issued by or in the name of Pope Pius VII, with related material, September 4, 1815-March 15, 1816. Nos. 1-8 are rescripts addressed to Fonte and concerned with blessings or indulgences; Nos. 9-19 are summaries of petitions presented by Fonte to the Pope through various cardinals, with statements of the latter on the corresponding papal grants. Dated in Rome and Madrid in 1815 and 1816. Nos. 20-27 comprise seven papal bulls and one profession of faith to be made by the new archbishop, all dated in 1815, and relating to his election and installation.
    The second major part, Nos. 28-81, consists primarily of letters addressed to Fonte, or, in a few instances, to his secretaries, from 1815 to 1834, with drafts of his replies, two printed pastoral epistles, etc. Topics dealt with include Fonte's appointment, requests for financial and other assistance, Fonte's saint's day, his return to Spain, his support of a Spanish translation of Milton's "Paradise Lost," and his project for distribution of 100 copies of the Bible, in Latin and the vernacular, throughout Mexico.

FORREST, EDWIN, 1806-1872
    Letter to J[ames] E[dward] Murdock. New York, N.Y. May 19, 1841.
    2 p. L.S. 23 cm. [Z-Z 100:67]
    Enclosing check.

FORSYTH, JOHN, 1780-1841
    Letter to Sarah W. Wheeler. Washington, D.C. January 22, 1831.
    1 p. A.L.S. 21 cm. [Z-Z 100:63]
    Thanking her for gift and giving local news.

FORSYTH, JOHN, 1780-1841
  Letter to Senator Hugh L. White. U.S. Department of State. December 2, 1834.
  1 p. L.S. 33 cm. [zz 100:16]
  Written as Secretary of State, acknowledging letter recommending the appointment of F. S. Heiskell as Publisher of the Laws.

FORT CALHOUN [FORT WOOL], VIRGINIA
  Statement . . . of Funds expended. . . . April, 1825, to April 30, 1826.
  6 p. Contemporary copy. 50x40 cm. [z-z 104]
  Submitted by Lt. Col. Charles Gratiot to Major General Alexander Macomb.

FOULKE, GEORGE CLAYTON, 1856-1893
  Correspondence and Papers. ca. 1876-1889.
  460 items [z-z 148]
  Records of Foulke's naval career in the Far East, as diplomatic representative in Korea, in business and teaching in Japan. Chiefly correspondence, official Navy orders, a diary for 1884, photographs, and miscellaneous manuscript and printed items. Collected in Korea by Harold J. Noble.
  The Library has a "key" to the collection.

FOURTH MEXICAN PROVINCIAL COUNCIL. MEXICO CITY. 1771
  773 p. 32 cm. [M-M 1732]
  Copies of documents relating to the Fourth Mexican Provincial Council held under the presidency of Archbishop, later Cardinal, Francisco Antonio de Lorenzana.
  The first part, p. 1-149, consists of excerpts copied from the adverse comments on the work of the Council written by the Peruvian Fiscal, Don Pedro de Piña y Mazo. These excerpts are directed chiefly against the work prepared by Antonio Joaquín de Ribadeneyra y Barrientos, Asistente Real of the Council.
  The second part, p. 150 f., contains apparently the complete text of the five books of *Actas*, or Decrees, approved by the Council, and concerns the rules governing religious and moral life in Mexico. The majority of these rules are of a varied ecclesiastical nature, but Book II is devoted to legal matters, and Book IV deals with matrimony.
  The original document was signed in Mexico City on October 26, 1771, by Lorenzana and others.

FRAGMENTO HISTORICO DEL NAYARIT, TARAHUMARA, PIMERIA, É INDIOS SERIS . . . PROVINCIA DEL SANTO EVANGELIO. MEXICO. 1791.
  34 p. 33 cm. HHB [M-M 163]
  Compiled by an anonymous Franciscan friar from the manuscripts of various unnamed Jesuit missionaries in the provinces of Nayarit, Tarahumara, Chiripas, Sinaloa, and Sonora, 1686-1766; describes these provinces, their inhabitants, particularly the Pima and Seri Indians, the work of Father Kino and his successors, the 1751 rebellion, and other aspects of colonization.

FRANCE. CONSULAT GENERAL, KOREA
Documents. 1897-1910.
66 items. 14-39 cm. [z-z 149]
Correspondence with French consuls and ministers in China and Japan, the Korean Foreign Minister, the Japanese Minister and Resident at Seoul; and miscellaneous papers. The collection concerns the opening of the port of Mokpo to foreign commerce and the regulation of its international settlement.

FRANCISCANS. 1688-1707
9 p. 30-31 cm. HHB [M-M 427]
Two copies of documents written to or by Franciscan Commissioners General for the Indies: 1) petition addressed to Juan de Luzuriaga, Franciscan Commissioner General for the Indies, by Martín del Castillo, a Franciscan friar of the Mexican Provincia del Santo Evangelio, requesting information on eleven doubtful points relevant to a Provincial meeting scheduled for June, 1688, with appended citations corresponding to the queries; 2) the decision handed down by Álvarez de Toledo, Franciscan Commissioner General for the Indies, which absolves Manuel de Argüello, chronicler of the Order, from charges previously upheld by Commissioner Juan de la Cruz, and provides for the restoration of the accused to his former status in Mexico.

FRANCISCANS. PROVINCIA DEL SANTO EVANGELIO DE NUEVA ESPAÑA
[Códice Franciscano]. 1523-1810.
300 p. 30 cm. HHB [M-M 201]
A collection of documents, copies and originals, from Mexico and Spain, relating to the mendicant orders in New Spain and primarily to the Franciscan Provincia del Santo Evangelio in the 16th century. Somewhat arbitrarily divided into 24 items, most of which were reproduced in García Icazbalceta's, *Nueva Colección de Documentos Inéditos*, Mexico City, 1886-1889.

FRANCISCO, PRIOR OF VIANA
Relacion de la Provincia i tierra de la Vera Paz i de las cosas contenidas en ella . . . desde el año de 1544 hasta este de 1574. Convento de Santo Domingo de Cobán, Guatemala. December 7, 1574.
19 p. 33 cm. HHB [M-M 312]
Report of three Dominican friars, Francisco, prior of Viana, Lucas Gallego, and Guillén Cadena, describing the province of Verapaz, its topography, climate, products, churches, roads, leading settlements, and diminishing population, as well as the work done there by the Dominicans during the period 1554-1574.

FRANCO, JUAN
Breve noticia ò apuntes de los usos y constumbres [*sic*] de los habitantes del Ysthmo de Panamá, y de sus producciones para la expedicion de las Corvetas alreedor del Mundo. . . . [ca. 1792?]
375 p. 30 cm. HHB [M-M 451]
Notes on the indigenous inhabitants of Panama, particularly Panama City

and neighboring regions, with material on local flora and fauna, mineral curiosities, and a special section on fruits. Followed by a 76-page Spanish-Indian vocabulary of Durasque and three Guaymi dialects, which was begun by the priest Franco at the request of the naturalist, Antonio Pineda, before the death of the latter in 1792, and probably completed shortly thereafter.

[FRANCO Y ORTEGA, ALONSO]
Segunda Parte de la Historia de la provincia de Santiago de Mexico, Orden de predicadores en la Nueva España ... año de 1645.
378 p. 30 cm. HHB [M-M 75]
A compilation dealing with the history of the Dominican Province of Santiago, in Mexico, and especially with the lives of its outstanding figures, including Archbishop-Viceroy García Guerra, Bishop Juan Ramírez, Hernando Cortecero, Luis Gandullo, Sebastián Montaño, and many others. With the exception of a few opening and closing pages, the Ms. corresponds substantially to portions of the printed edition of Franco's work, issued in Mexico in 1900, under the title given above.

FRANKLIN, BENJAMIN, 1706-1790
Letter to Humphrey Marshall. London. April 22, 1771.
3 p. (Photocopy) A.L.S. 35 cm. [z-z 100:13]
Concerning development of manufactures in the colonies.

FREEMASONS. BAJA CALIFORNIA. LODGE 30
Apuntes mandados . . . al Sup[remo] Con[sejo]. . . . La Paz, Baja California. September 30-October 2, 1882.
57 p. and chart. D.S. 23-36 cm. [M-M 1871]
Reports of Lodge No. 30 of Baja California to the Masonic Supreme Council, with a history of the lodge, 1869-1871, lists of officers and members, and a financial statement.

FREEMASONS. IRELAND. GRAND LODGE
Certificate of Membership for Richard Irvine. Dublin. June 8, 1909.
1 p. D.S. 42 cm. [z-z 100:80]

FRELINGHUYSEN, FREDERICK THEODORE, 1817-1885
Letters. Washington, D.C. January 17, 1882 and January 19, 1885.
2 p. L.S. 20 cm. [z-z 100:14]
Two letters, one referring to the election of President Arthur, and the other, addressed "to the President," concerning approval of Senate Bill No. 1820.

FRISBIE, JOHN B , 1823-1909
Reminiscences. [N.p., n.d.]
40 p. 32 cm. HHB [M-M 351]
Statement concerning Frisbie's early life, Stevenson's Regiment, the war between Mexico and the United States, California and the Gold Rush, United

States' relations with Mexico, particularly in the 1870's, mining interests in Mexico, railroads, and the economic conditions and resources of Mexico and California.

FUNDACION DE LA CAPILLA DE NUESTRA S.ª DE LA CONSEP.ᵒⁿ QUE HIZO EL CAP.ⁿ XPSTOVAL DE ZULETA EN EL COMB.ᵗᵒ de S.ʳ S.ⁿ FRAN.ᶜᵒ DE ESTA CIUDAD Y DOS CAPELLANIAS. . . . MEXICO CITY. JANUARY 1-APRIL 11, 1628
46 p. 31 cm. [M-M 1802]
Establishment of a chapel, family burial site, and two chaplaincies at the Franciscan monastery in Mexico City, with details of provisions for perpetual masses and other arrangements and agreements for carrying out the donor's wishes.

GABILONDO, HILARIO SANTIAGO
Diario de lo ocurrido desde el arribo de los Filibusteros á Caborca. . . .
Caborca, Mexico. April 7-20, 1857.
19 p. D.S., A.L.S., and printed. 29-35 cm. and 58x43 cm. [M-M 1881]
Gabilondo's account of the defeat of Henry Alexander Crabb's filibustering expedition to Sonora, Mexico, and execution of the prisoners. With related papers.

GALLARDO, LUCIANO J
Diario de. Recuerdos y Amor. Guadalajara, San Luis Potosí, etc. 1864-1869.
11 vols. (No. 8 missing) [M-B 13]
These diaries reveal Gallardo's long courtship of Carlota Gil, and the exchange of letters between them. Very little mention of political or national affairs. Some parts signed. Index in each volume.

GÁLVEZ, JOSÉ DE, MARQUÉS DE SONORA, 1720-1787
Materials on the Life and Career of. 1691.
1 box. (Transcripts) [Z-E 4]
Church records, royal orders, cédulas, and other sources on Gálvez collected from parochial archives, various Spanish archives, and the British Museum, by Laurence P. Briggs. See Herbert I. Priestley, *José de Gálvez, Visitor-General of New Spain* (University of California Press, 1916). A "key" to the collection is available in the Library.

GÁLVEZ, JOSÉ DE, MARQUÉS DE SONORA, 1720-1787
Ynforme de el Visitador de este Reyno al Ex.ᵐᵒ S.ᵒʳ Virrey Marques de Croix.
Mexico City. December 25, 1767.
164 p. 21 cm. HHB [M-M 273]
Copy of the report addressed by Gálvez, as Visitador General, to the viceroy, Marqués de Croix. Gives an account of the steps taken by Gálvez to Croix to facilitate execution of the royal order for expulsion of the Jesuits, the subsequent disturbances in outlying provinces, and measures adopted to restore peace.

GÁLVEZ, JOSÉ DE, MARQUÉS DE SONORA, 1720-1787
Yntendencias. Ynforme y plan de Yntendencias, que conviene establecer en las Provincias de este Reyno de Nueva España. Mexico City. January 15, 1768.
16 p. (Typescript) 34 cm. [M-M 1848]
Report drawn up at the request of the King and the Viceroy concerning the feasibility of remodeling the government of New Spain to accord with the Spanish intendancy system. Excerpt from "Informe sobre el estado de México, California, Sonora y Provincias remotas de Nueva España, 1768-1778," a manuscript in the Ayer Collection of the Newberry Library, Chicago.

GÁLVEZ, MATÍAS DE, 1717-1784
License to Manuel Ramón Pérez of Querétaro. Mexico City. November 10, 1783.
5 p. D.S. 31 cm. [M-M 1700:84]
Permission to slaughter unproductive goats and sheep.

GAMBOA, FRANCISCO JAVIER, 1717-1794
Representacion Juridica que haze Don Antonio de Arrieta en el pleito que trahe con Dn. Manuel de Sn. Juan Santa Cruz . . . sobre restitucion de sus Minas en el Rl. de Sta. Eulalia. . . . Mexico. January 14, 1743.
44 p. 31 cm. HHB [M-M 529]
Defendant's brief in suit of Antonio de Arrieta against Manuel de San Juan Santa Cruz concerning the restitution of his mines in the Real de Santa Eulalia.

GAMIO, MANUEL, 1883-1960
Notes and Papers on Mexican Immigration. 1926-1928.
1 carton [Z-R 5]
Interview, case histories, notes, folklore material, and samples of Mexican newspapers published in the United States, gathered for his study, *Mexican Immigration to the United States.* . . . , for the Social Science Research Council, and published by the University of Chicago Press, 1930.

GARCÍA, NICOLÁS ANTONIO
Scrupulus Theologicus, sive Compendiosus de Dominica Incarnatione. . . . [Mexico City] October 18, 1744.
18 p. D.S. 22 cm. [M-M 1878]
Scholastic treatise in Latin by the Instructor in Theology of the Franciscan Convent of San Francisco in Mexico City, concerning the doctrine of the "Word made flesh." Note in Spanish at end, signed by García, certifying that Brother José Otón has completed a course in this subject.

GARCÍA, PEDRO MARCELINO
Informe sobre la sublevación de los Zendales. . . . 1714-1741.
158 p. 31 cm. HHB [M-M 435]
Reports and miscellaneous documents relating chiefly to the 1712-1713 uprising of the Tzental Indians in Chiapas, and to the Dominicans in that region, then a part of Guatemala. There are eight main items:

1. Copy of file compiled by order of Bishop Olivera of Chiapas and circulated by him, concerning the four Dominican friars, Manuel Mariscal, Juan Gómez, Nicolás de Colindres, and Marcos Lamburu, who were murdered in 1712 by Tzental Indians. Includes petitions addressed to the Bishop by García, Vicar of the Dominican Provincia de San Vicente de Chiapas; the commission entrusting García and Diego de Cuenca with investigation of the case, episcopal orders, and the testimony of witnesses. Chiapas, September 20, 1715-June 5, 1716. 43 p.

2. Incomplete copy of García's report on the origin, events, and suppression of the Tzental uprising, prepared for Bishop Olivera. Chiapas, June 5, 1716. 86 p.

3. Certified copy of deed contracting for payment of annual ground rent by Diego José de Rojas and his wife to the Dominican monastery of Chiapas. Chiapas, 1714. 6 p.

4. Order of Francisco Rodríguez de Rivas, Governor of Guatemala, granting a petition presented by Captain Juan Antonio de Uncilla, procurator of the royal audiencia, on behalf of the towns of Acala, Chiapillas, and Ostuta in Chiapas, relating to the agricultural damage caused by the sugar mill of Juan del Solar and to the employment of Indians in sugar mills. Santiago de Guatemala, January 5, 1716. 4 p.

5. Copy of power of attorney conferred upon Captain Uncilla by the three towns named above. Ciudad Real de Chiapas, June 15, 1716. 4 p.

6. Two certified documents signed by Antonio de Zuazua y Múxica concerning the election and functions of municipal officials and municipal regulations in Chiapas, January 13, 1740, and January 12, 1741. Both documents include lists of elected officials. The concluding portion of the second document is mistakenly bound in the volume listed under "Memorias sobre limites territoriales . . . ," (M-M 434, No. 4). Chiapas, 1740-1741. 4 p. D.S.

7. Certified copy of the sentence passed by the Marqués de Torre-Campo against certain Indians who assisted in the escape of María Candelaria, heroine of the Tzental rebellion. (Certification signed by Pedro Pereira.) Santiago de Guatemala, August 26, 1716. 3 p.

8. Certified copy of a Latin circular sent by Antonino Cloche to Dominican authorities and friars, requesting aid in the preparation of a history of the Dominican Order and giving instructions for participation. Rome, May 30, 1714. 4 p. (Certification signed by Pedro Marcelino at the Convento de Santo Domingo de Ciudad Real, Chiapas, October 12, 1715.)

GARCÍA CANTARINES, FRANCISCO
Vexamen que para cerrar el curso de Artes dió á sus disipulos. . . . Seminario Palafoxiano. Puebla, Mexico. January 14, 1795.
88 p. 23 cm.　　　　　　　　　　　　　　　　　　　　　　　HHB [M-M 103]

Address of García, professor of the Puebla seminary, to his students in the graduating class of the Letters and Arts course. Consists of a verse introduction, the customary satirical allegory (*vejamen*) in which each student is assigned a part, personifying, in this case, some feature of a dance; a list of graduates in the order of scholastic merit; an appeal for patronage of their careers; and closing words of advice.

GARCÍA CONDE, ALEJO, 1797-1861
    Papers relating to his Administration as Commandant General of the Western Provincias Internas. Durango. 1820.
    2 folders. 3 p. 21, 61x44 cm. [M-M 1795]
    Letter to the Ayuntamiento of San Buenaventura, August 29, 1820, and proclamation, September 9, 1820, of a royal decree dated April 22, 1820, concerning rights and privileges of the Indians.

GARCÍA CONDE, ALEXO, AND LORENZO CANCIO BONADARES
    Correspondencia oficial de Sonora. 1766-1770.
    7 vols. (Photocopy) [M-A 4:3]
    Correspondence relating to Sonora, including Governors Juan de Pineda, Enrique de Grimarest, letters of Juan Bautista de Anza, José de Gálvez, and others. Collected by Sherburne F. Cook. From the Biblioteca Nacional, Mexico. There is a "key" to the collection.

GARCÍA DE HERMOSILLA, JUAN
    Memorial presented by Juan García de Hermosilla . . . in favor of changing the navigation and route of the Fleets of Spain, from Nombre de Dios and Panama to the Ports of Honduras . . . Valladolid, Spain. 1556.
    37 p. 32-34 cm. HHB [M-M 321]
    English translation of a portion of García de Hermosilla's "Memorial . . ." (M-M 319, item 3), recommending navigation from Spain to Peru via Honduran rather than Panamanian ports. The translation extends to f. 39 of the Spanish transcript.

GARCÍA DE HERMOSILLA, JUAN
    Memorial que dió . . . para que se mudase la Navegacion y derrota de las flotas á los Puertos de Honduras, en lugar de la que se hazia al Nombre de Dios. . . . Valladolid, Spain. 1556.
    3 items. 33 cm. HHB [M-M 319]
    Comprises a royal cedula of October 17, 1556, calling for opinions on the recommendation of García de Hermosilla that the ports of Trujillo and Caballos in Honduras and Realejo in Nicaragua be substituted for those of Nombre de Dios in Panama and Panama City; and his Memorial, setting forth the reasons for this view.

GARCÍA VALLECILLOS Y RUIZ, GABRIEL ANTONIO, b. 1779(?)
    Report on the Merits and Services of. 1803-1820.
    60 p. D. and printed. 21-32 cm. [M-M 1770]
    Documents relating to the career of Dr. García Vallecillos, native of Algeciras, Spain, attorney and judge of the Real Audiencia, Alcalde Mayor of Sololá Province, Guatemala, and defender of the Spanish régime in the closing days of the Viceroyalty of New Granada. Written in Spain (Madrid, Cádiz), Guatemala (Guatemala City, Sololá, Quezaltenango, Panajachel, Santa Catalina, Ixtahuacán, Santa Cruz del Quiché), and Colombia (Santa Fé [de Bogotá], Cartagena). Originals, certified copies, and printed.

GARVISO, VICENTE
Account Book. Mexico City. 1814-1834.
560 p. D.S. 36 cm. [M-M 1745]
Records of legal and documentary services in civil and criminal cases rendered by Licentiate Garviso, one-time Administrative Director of the Mexico City Hostel for the Poor, to individuals, governmental and religious bodies, business firms, and other organizations in Mexico or, in a few instances, Spain. Clients included Dr. Martín Gil y Garcés, Dean of Valladolid Cathedral; Lt. Col. Gabriel de Iturbe y Iraeta, Mexico City assemblyman; Buenaventura Arturo Short, Consul General of His Britannic Majesty in Mexico City; William Tailor, U.S. Consul in Alvarado and Veracruz; Angel del Toro, Governor of Tabasco Province; and several noblemen. With an alphabetical index of clients' names at beginning, and a list of contributors to a fund handled by Garviso for the relief of epidemic victims.

GASTAÑETA, JOSÉ VICENTE DE
Mexico. 1811-1813.
2 folders. 14 p. 21-31 cm. [M-M 1801]
Documents relating to Gastañeta's career, including expediente concerning trial to clear him of charges of collaboration with Hidalgo's insurgents, April 8-June 22, 1811, and army commission, January 6, 1813.

GATY, SAMUEL
Documents concerning Property in St. Louis, Missouri. 1868-1873.
11 p. D. and A.L.S. 25-31 cm. [Z-Z 141]
Leases of land by Samuel Latham Mitchill Barlow to William Wells, executed by Gaty, agent; letter to Gaty from John Maguire; and statement in unidentified hand relating to St. Louis property.

GAVARRETE, JUAN, *comp.*
Letters, Papers and Maps relative to the History of Guatemala. 1534-1846.
58 p. 21-31 cm. HHB [M-M 436]
Papers compiled by the Curator of the Guatemalan National Archives, with five principal items:
1. Excerpts from Part I of Francisco Antonio de Fuentes y Guzmán's *Recordación Florida*, a history of Guatemala, first published in its entirety in Guatemala City in 1932. Includes portions dealing with the entry of Pedro de Alvarado into Soconusco, Indian uprisings, customs and superstitions of the Guatemalan Indians, the city of Tecpán, the conquest of Mixco, the names of Alvarado's companions, et cetera. An analysis of the whole of Part I, an "appendix" on the disturbances caused by the visiting inspector Orduña, and a table of contents for this item are also included. Guatemala, 1690-1699 (?). 36 p.
2. Copies and summaries of letters, addressed primarily to the municipal authorities in Guatemala City, by prelates and civil or military officials, and relating chiefly to needed financial aid for missionary and administrative activities, and to the pacification of the Indians. (Copied from the "secret"

Municipal Archives of Guatemala City.) Written from various places in present-day Guatemala and Honduras, 1534-1691. 10 p.

3. Incomplete fragment copied from a Franciscan manuscript which describes the principal towns of Guatemala and reviews the indigenous history of the region. N.p., n.d. 6 p.

4. Copy of the epitaph of Pedro de Alvarado, in verse. N.p., 1541? 1 p. Followed by an apparently unrelated historical note regarding a dispute between Bishop Navas Quevedo and the President of the Real Audiencia of Guatemala. Madrid, March 13, 1690. 1 p.

5. Gavarrete's map, dated 1846, of the old Kingdom of Guatemala, a topographical map of the region around Guatemala City, and Gavarrete's copy of Rivera's 1834 plan of the environs of Tecpán, Guatemala, ancient capital of the Cackchiquels.

GEOGRAPHY. [MEXICO. ca. 1910?]
22 p. 34 cm. HHB [M-M 1700:39]
Notes on world geography, with emphasis on North America. Source unknown.

GIFFORD, HENRY F
Letter to his Cousin, Warren B. Ewer. January 24, 1834.
3 p. A.L.S. 32 cm. [z-z 100:11]
Written from the whaling ship *Uncas*, at sea, describing the voyage. With typed transcript.

GOLSON, B
Letters and Documents concerning Border Relations between the United States and Mexico. El Paso, Texas. May 2-11, 1916.
18 p. (Photocopies) D.S. 33 cm. [M-M 1759]
Letters and reports relating to meetings at El Paso, attended by Major Generals Frederick Funston and Hugh Lennox Scott, and the Mexican representatives, Álvaro Obregón, Minister of War and Marine, and J. N. Amador, Undersecretary of Foreign Affairs, and others, together with the text of a tentative agreement on withdrawal of U.S. troops from Mexico and prevention by the Mexican government of further incidents.

GÓMEZ, JOSÉ, 18th cont.
Anales de México . . . [Mexico City. 1776-1798]
730 p. Ms. and printed. 24 cm. HHB [M-M 105]
Copy (Mexico City, December, 1839) of the diary kept by Gómez, a corporal of halberdiers, covering the period August, 1776-May, 1798, and providing intimate glimpses of social, political, and juridical life in Mexico; refers to the Corte-Miranda murder case. Introductory and closing material, titles, and alterations have been supplied by the editor, Carlos María de Bustamante, and additional data inserted by him concerning the murder of Joaquín Dongo in 1789.

This work, which has been printed and reprinted, is also known as *Diario*

Curioso de México and as *Diario del Alabardero*. It appears in *Documentos para la historia de México*, Series I, Tomo VII (Mexico, 1854).

GÓMEZ, JUSTO
   Bill to Señor de Navarro for Hat Emblem. Madrid. November 1, 1866.
   1 p. 21 cm. [z-z 100:95]

GÓMEZ DE CERVANTES, NICOLÁS CARLOS, bp., 1665-1734
   Hecho del Litigio. . . . ca. 1696.
   49 p. D.S. 31 cm. HHB [M-M 241]
   Exposition of the arguments favoring the claims of Joseph Gómez de Cervantes as opposed to those of Leonel Cervantes Cassaus, in a legal dispute over succession to an endowed chaplaincy founded in 1574 by Francisco de Velasco and his wife, Beatriz de Andrada. Signed by Nicolás Carlos Gómez de Cervantes, subsequently Bishop of Guadalajara.
   To this is appended the unsigned draft of a petition, Mexico City, May 3, 1696, evidently addressed to the King of Spain, protesting undue civil interference in the management of funds for benefices and pious works.
   Entered by Bancroft under "Velasco, Francisco . . . ."

GONZÁLEZ, J   M   , 1854-
   Dictation. . . . [N.p.] May 18, 1887.
   4 p. 28 cm. HHB [M-M 377]
   Information dictated by J. M. González, a native of California and longtime resident of Mexico, regarding his personal career in Lower California, the potentialities of that region, and the attitude of native Mexicans toward the International Company of Mexico and its projects.

GONZÁLEZ, MANUEL, 1833-1893
   Decree. Mexico. May 26, 1882.
   5 p. D.S. 35 cm. [67/151M]
   Creating a bureau of statistics for the purpose of compiling, classifying, and publishing data concerning the population, real property, industry, commerce, finance, etc., of the country. Signed by President González.

GONZÁLEZ DÁVILA, GIL, d. 1543
   Documents. 1519-1524.
   49 p. 33 cm. HHB [M-M 300]
   Record relating to the transfer of the remainder of Balboa's fleet to González Dávila; royal agreement with the pilot, Andrés Niño, for discoveries in the Pacific; and González Dávila's report of March 6, 1524, on his discoveries in Nicaragua.

GONZÁLEZ DEL CAMPILLO, MANUEL IGNACIO, bp., ca. 1740-1813, *comp.*
   Papeles Varios Compuestos por el Exmo É Yll.^{mo} Sor Campillo [1542-1804]
   3 vols. 22 cm. [M-M 1737]
   Copies of letters, reports, decrees, and miscellaneous papers relating prin-

cipally to ecclesiastical affairs, compiled by González del Campillo, including material composed by him either as Bishop of Puebla or in an earlier subordinate capacity. Written for the most part in Spanish, with a few items in Latin, in the diocese of Puebla (Mexico), Mexico City, Spain, and Rome.

Not arranged in chronological order. Many items are undated.

Vol. I. 652 p. [1776-1804] Unsigned letters or reports, probably from González del Campillo, or, in a few instances, from Bishop Victoriano López Gonzalo, addressed to the King, Viceroy Mayorga, or Bishop López Gonzalo, concerning the obligation of restitution, ecclesiastical jurisdiction, appointment of American-born Spaniards to ecclesiastical posts in the Indies, reform of religious orders, benefices, and similar matters; two royal decrees—on benefice funds (1776) and an ecclesiastical appointment; a sermon (1804) delivered by the compiler; an episcopal edict on gambling; a legal file on the bequest of Juan Francisco López de Solís to a religious community; an anonymous laudatory oration; and notes.

Vol. II. 693 p. [1722-1800] Episcopal edict of López Gonzalo on marriage; letters, reports, and other papers, including many probably written by López Gonzalo or González del Campillo, and several addressed to the King, on marriage, ecclesiastical jurisdiction, ex-Jesuit communities in Puebla, administration of the Order of Bethlehemites, complaints of certain nuns, financial administration of religious funds such as the bequest of José de Arria (p. 585 ff.), religious asylum, and a flour shortage caused by governmental restrictions. The name "Manuel Ignacio Gonz.^{z} d.^{1} Campillo," on p. 376, may be an original signature. Many papers in the collection are in this same handwriting.

Vol. III. 773 p. [1542-1786] Anonymous treatises on the ecclesiastical and political history of Spain, with a last will and "testament of Spain" in her decadence; opinions of fiscals on politico-ecclesiastical questions in Spain; anonymous discussions, and appended papal pronouncements (1542-1560) of Paul III, Julius III, and Pius IV on various matters, notably, taxation of the clergy and administration of benefices; opinion of the Augustinian, Juan de Mazurriaga, on ecclesiastical vacancies in the Indies; pleas (1786) addressed to the King and to Archbishop Núñez de Haro by the Puebla Dean and Chapter, protesting the transfer of Bishop López Gonzalo; and plea of 1777 to the King from the University of Mexico for more favor to American-born Spaniards in ecclesiastical appointments.

GONZÁLEZ ORTEGA, JESÚS, 1824-1881
Correspondence and Papers. 1884, 1864-1866.
1 box [M-B 7]

Concern the efforts of General González Ortega to recruit men and obtain munitions in the United States to oppose Emperor Maximilian in Mexico.

There is correspondence with Colonel William H. Allen, General James Henry Carleton, and Duff Green; agreements between General Gaspar Sánchez Ochoa and John C. Frémont for the construction and operation of a railroad between Guaymas and the United States, for transit across the Isthmus of

Tehauntepec, and for establishing mints in Matamoros and Mazatlán. There are also letters from volunteers, mainly addressed to Colonel Allen, seeking information on immigration to Mexico; and offers from various firms to supply the volunteers with equipment and weapons.

GOODSPEED, THOMAS HARPER, 1887-1966
Plant Hunters in the Andes . . . . [1961?]
542 p. (Typescript) 28 cm. [z-d 133]
Account of Goodspeed's association with the Botany Department of the University of California, Berkeley, and of his six expeditions to the Andes. Printer's copy for second edition.

GOROSPE, MANUEL IGNACIO DE
Exposition concerning Episcopal Authority. Durango. ca. 1757
91 p. D.S. 30-31 cm. [m-m 1860]
Addressed to the Jesuit Father Provincial in view of a proposed visit of inspection to the Durango Jesuit missions by an episcopal representative. Questions the authority of bishops over missionaries of the regular orders, discusses similar incidents in other parts of America, and reviews Jesuit history in Nueva Vizcaya.

GOVERNMENT AFFAIRS IN MEXICO
Documents concerning. 1535-1597.
8 folders. (Photocopies and typescript) [m-a 5:2]
Miscellaneous papers relating to Indians, regulation and prohibition of pulque, church affairs, shipping from Mexican ports, government of New Spain, measurement of land, and making of beer. The last five folders contain copies, made for Francisco Paso y Troncoso, of documents in various sections of the Archivo General de Indias, Seville.
From the Museo Nacional, **Mexico.**

GOYA, JESÚS MARÍA, *comp.*
Prontuario Curioso de Derecho Práctico, arreglado á leyes recopiladas, de Partidas, de Indias y de Venezuela. 1845.
360 p. 22 cm. [z-d 112]
Lists of laws and statutes, with an index of cases by subject.

GRANDEZA Y EXCELENCIAS DE LOS SIETE PRINCIPES DE LOS ANGELES ASSISTENTES AL THRONO DE DIOS, Y VTILIDAD DE SU DEVOCION. [MEXICO. N. d.]
152 p. 21 cm. HHB [m-m 106]
Anonymous treatise, possibly by a Jesuit author, consisting of two books: 1) 25 general chapters on the seven archangels, dealing with sources of information regarding them, their names and attributes, reasons for devotional homage to them, and their special favors to the Jesuit Order; 2) prologue and 10 chapters eulogizing the individual archangels, followed by prayers in prose and verse to be offered to them on different occasions. Final portion of volume missing.

GRANT, ULYSSES SIMPSON, 1822-1885
Letter to Robert Edward Lee. Appomattox, Virginia. April 9, 1865.
2 p. (Photocopy) A.L.S. 26 cm. [z-z 100:38]
Concerning terms of surrender.

GREAT BRITAIN. ADMIRALTY OFFICE
Letters and Reports relating to California and Central America from Rear Admiral Sir George F. Seymour and Others of the Pacific Squadron. 1846-1847.
120 exp. (On film) [z-g 8]
From the Public Record Office, London.

GREAT BRITAIN. ADMIRALTY OFFICE
Logs of Various Ships on Voyages to the Northwest Coast of America. ca. 1790-1795.
3 reels. (On film) [z-g 22]
Primarily logs of the sloop *Discovery*, but also included are records of the *Chatham, Daphne, Dorset,* and *Dover*. From the Public Record Office, London.

GREAT BRITAIN. COLONIAL OFFICE
Records of the Governor and Company of Adventurers of Old Providence Island. 1630-1650.
371 exp. (On film) [z-g 6]
Records of the colony off the Mosquito Coast, British Honduras, sponsored by the Earl of Warwick. Book of entries, 1630-1641; journal, 1630-1650. Filmed in the Public Record Office, London.

GREAT BRITAIN. FOREIGN OFFICE
The Mosquito Territory. London, Madrid, Bogotá, Guatemala, etc. 1847-1848.
149 p. (Transcript) 32 cm. HHB [z-g 5]
Correspondence between Lord Palmerston of the British Foreign Office, Frederick Chatfield from Guatemala, and others, respecting the boundaries of the Mosquito Territory, especially with respect to the line dividing it from New Granada and the states of Central America. With copies of royal orders from the King of Spain from 1720.

GREAT BRITAIN. HIGH COURT OF ADMIRALTY
"Examinations." 1555-1605.
15 reels. (On film) [z-g 9]
Depositions in cases of ships (Spanish, Dutch, Portuguese, etc.) captured by English privateers on the high seas, to determine legitimacy of "prizes." Many relate to American trade.
Microfilmed in the Public Record Office, London. A "key" to the collection is available in the Library.

GREEN, GEORGE M, b. 1836-
Statement of his Recollections of Life in Mexico, 1853 to 1855. 1879.
25 p. 31 cm. HHB [M-M 276]
A statement dictated for the Bancroft Library by Colonel Green, summar-

izing his experiences as a peripatetic photographer in Mexico, chiefly in or near Durango, including various encounters with savage Indians and armed robbers as well as an abortive gold-mining venture.

GREENE, WILLIAM CORNELL, 1851-1911
Report on Disorders at the Greene Consolidated Copper Company. Cananea, Sonora, Mexico. June 11, 1906.
5 p. (Photocopies) 28 cm.   HHB [M-M 1700:37]
Brief resume of recent disorders in Cananea, June 1, 1906, with explanatory letter of Leavenworth (Lem) Porter Sperry of September 30, 1957.

GREGORY I, THE GREAT, Saint, Pope. 540-604
Moralia. Libri XXXV. ca. 590. [A 14th century copy?]
434 p. 33 cm.   HHB [M-M 107]
Copy of St. Gregory's exposition on the Book of Job, begun in Constantinople during his ambassadorial service there, 579-ca. 586, and generally held to have been completed in Rome during the first year of his pontificate, 590, although internal evidence points to revision at least as late as 596.

Contains three preliminary items, an account, customarily prefixed to Spanish copies, of the miraculous discovery of the closing portion of the *Moralia* by Bishop Samuel Tajón of Zaragoza, a eulogy by Saint Isidore of Seville, and a discussion of methods employed in expounding Holy Writ; Gregory's dedicatory epistle to Bishop Leander of Seville, brother of Isidore; the author's preface; 35 books expounding the Book of Job, verse by verse, historically, allegorically, and morally; and a copious index.

GRIMM, HANS, 1875-1959
A Nation without Room (*Volk ohne Raum*, Published by A. Langen, Munich, 1927).
2 vols. (Typescript) 28 cm.   [Z-Z 165]
Translation by Henry Safford King. German political novel.

GROSO, ÁNGEL
Statement on Mexican Photographs. [N.p., n.d.]
32 p. 32 cm.   HHB [M-M 350]
Statement to accompany a collection of 46 photographs depicting typical Mexican figures, institutions, customs, and objects. There is an explanation of each photograph, with incidental comments on socio-economic conditions in Mexico.

GUADALAJARA, MEXICO. ROYAL TREASURY
Account Books. 1622-1738.
3 vols. D.S. 30-31 cm.   [M-M 1832]
Annual accounts for the Guadalajara branch of the Royal Treasury. Volume 1 is for April, 1622, to March, 1623; Volume 2, for the year 1714; Volume 3, for 1738.

GUADALCÁZAR, DIEGO FERNÁNDEZ DE CÓRDOVA, MARQUÉS DE
Decree. Mexico City. September 15, 1620.
2 p. D.S. 31 cm. [M-M 1819]
Viceregal order restricting for two years the sojourn and mercantile activities of transients, whether foreigners or newly arrived Spaniards, in mining regions, to prevent collusion and defrauding the Crown of its tax, "the royal fifth."

GUADALUPE HIDALGO, TREATY OF
Papers Relating to . . . . February 2, 1848.
5 p. (Typescript) 28x32 cm. HHB [M-M 1700:55]
Copy of articles 8, 9, 21, and 23 of the above treaty, and notes from Robert Glass Cleland's *The Mexican Yearbook*, 1922.

GUANAJUATO, MEXICO. COMISIÓN DE OBRAS PÚBLICAS
Cuenta de la Fabrica de la nueva Alondiga de Granaditas. Guanajuato. 1797-1810.
24 p. D.S. 33 cm. HHB [M-M 108]
A collection of accounts and related documents concerning the new Guanajuato Alhóndiga, or public granary, now famous for its use as a fortress in 1810. Includes receipts and expense statements for construction, 1797-1809, acknowledgments and orders for transmittal signed by members of the Town Council, January 12-March 14, 1810; and a letter to the Council, November 21, 1809, transmitting several volumes of accounts and vouchers, with appended note.

GUATEMALA
Biographies. 1885-1886.
13 folders. 32 cm. HHB [M-M 517]
1. Manuel Lisandro Barillas, farmer and soldier, rose from the ranks to become president of the republic, 1885-1890. Summary of his life. N.p., n.d. 4 p.
2. Statement of the career of Fernando Cruz of Guatemala (b. 1845), Ministro de Gobernación and other official posts. N.p., n.d. 1 p.
3. Lisandro Letona, b. September 17, 1838, in Salvador, migrated to Guatemala and entered the military; served in Costa Rica as commander at Punta Arenas; returned to Salvador in 1876 and placed in charge of its eastern departments; maintained peace between Guatemala and Honduras. N.p., ca. 1885. 3 p.
4. Career of Juan J. Rodríguez, b. 1840, lawyer, student of flora and zoology; founded zoological museum; member of the constituent assembly from the department of Sacatepequez. N.p., ca. 1886. 6 p.
5. Manuel Eliseo Sánchez, b. 1828, distinguished lawyer, held various government posts. N.p., ca. 1885. 2 p.
6. Ricardo Casanova y Estrada, b. 1844. Lawyer and public official; took holy orders, 1875, and in 1886 was named Archbishop of Guatemala. N.p., ca. 1886. 3 p.

7. Manuel Echeverría, b. 1817, lawyer, public official. N.p., ca. 1885. 3 p.

8. Oton Bleuler, b. in Zurich, 1843; migrated to Guatemala in 1868. Businessman. N.p., ca. 1885. 2 p.

9. Antonio Aguirre, b. 1850. Businessman and civic leader. N.p., ca. 1885. 1 p.

10. Dr. Manuel Joaquín Dardón, b. 1821. Lawyer, judge, and public leader. N.p., ca. 1885. 3 p.

11. Manuel Cárdenas, b. 1844, merchant and government official. N.p., ca. 1885. 1 p.

12. Salvador Falla, b. 1845, professor, cabinet minister and public servant. N.p., ca. 1886. 4 p.

13. Justo Rufino Barrios, president of the republic. Personal description; method of government. N.p., ca. 1886. 8 p.

GUATEMALA
Documents pertaining to the History of. 1534-1549.
52 exp. (On film) [z-c 210]
Filmed by Lesley B. Simpson from the Manuscripts Collection of Don Ricardo Vázquez, Colombian Minister to Guatemala.

GUATEMALA
Documents pertaining to the History of. 1607-1788.
89 exp. (On film) [z-c 211]
Selected items. Includes also letters of José María Chacón, Tapachula, 1846.

GUATEMALA
Documents relating to the History of. 1524-1880.
4 reels (On film) [z-c 216]
Documents from various Guatemalan archives, selected for filming by Lesley B. Simpson.

GUATEMALA
Documents relating to the History of. 1745-1768.
148 p. (Photocopy) 26 cm. [z-c 214]
Materials, chiefly related to expenditures in the conquest of the Jicaque Indians, selected for filming by V. W. Von Hagen.

GUATEMALA (CITY). SANTO COLEGIO DE CRISTO SEÑOR NUESTRO CRUCIFICADO
Constituciones municipales de este Santo Colegio . . . de Guathemala. . . . [1686-1778].
292 p. 22 cm. HHB [M-M 109]
A collection of documents relating primarily to the Franciscan order in America and comprising copies of the Constituciones of the above Colegio, March 1, 1756, revised from the 1702 text; briefs of Pope Innocent XI, May 11 and October 16, 1686, concerning Franciscan seminaries in Spain and the Indies; life and miracles of Saint Theresa, based on the biography of Diego

de Yepes; a circular letter from the Franciscan commissioner general for the Indies, transmitting a decree of the Propaganda Fide in Rome, January 26, 1778; pastoral letter of Pascual de Avaricio, August 19, 1768, written on the occasion of the commissioner general's election; and some pronouncements on morals and behavior.

GUIZOT
Letter. December 13, 1854.
2 p. A.L.S. 13 cm. [z-z 100:68]
Sending tickets.

GUTIÉRREZ Y ULLOA, ANTONIO
Ensayo Historico-Politico del Rno. de la Nueva Galicia con Notas Politicas y Estadisticas de la Provincia de Guadalaxara. 1816.
125 p. 29 cm. [71/46m]
History of Nueva Galicia to about 1656. With description of the component provinces, the Indians, government, development of the missions, discovery of mines, and the growth of towns.

GUZMÁN, JOSÉ MARÍA
Letter. Mexico City. January 26, 1832.
1 p. 21 cm. HHB [M-M 1700:51]
Covering letter to the Junta del Banco de Avío forwarding the answers of the missionaries in Alta California to a questionnaire Fray José María had sent them.

HABBERTON, JOHN, 1842-1921
Letter to Mr. May. Westwood. November 2, 1907.
1 p. A.L.S. 23 cm. [z-z 100:59]
Regretting that they cannot meet.

HABIG, MARION A, comp.
Selected Documents on the Missions of Sonora and Southern Arizona. 1729-1842.
5 folders. (Typescripts and photocopies) 25-28 cm. [M-A 25]
Includes a "Relación" made at the College of the Holy Cross at Querétaro and sent to Rome, 1729 (30 p.); an "Informe" by Fray Manuel de Urcullu of San José de Guatemala, 1758-1764 (49 p.); "Cartas de Sonora" and other documents, 1813-1831, from the College at Querétaro (137 p.), and from 1769-1842 (171 p.); mission, ecclesiastical, and governmental affairs, 1821-1833 (97 p.).

HACIENDA DEL CARRIZAL, NUEVO LEÓN
Documents relating to Valle de San Juan Bautista de Pesquería, Mexico. 1798-1809.
6 p. D.S. 30 cm. [M-M 1700:70]
Contemporary copy of deposition made by Ignacio Elizondo to Juan Cristóbal de la Garza. Relates to the leasing of the hacienda.

[HACK, WILLIAM ?]
   An appendix to Sharps South Sea Waggoner, translated out off the originall Spanish manuscript. ca. 1685.
   303 p. 32 cm.   HHB [M-M 224]
   Atlas, probably made in the workshop of William Hack, based upon a Spanish *derrotero* captured by Bartholomew Sharpe in 1680. Text contains instructions for sailing from Callao to Panama, from Panama to Peru and to Acapulco, from Acapulco to California, and from Callao to Chiloe. Includes 75 maps. With note in Dutch by Nicolaas Witsen, dated 1692.

HALE, EDWARD EVERETT, 1822-1909
   Papers. 1871-1902.
   15 p. L.S. and A.L.S. 20-32 cm.   [Z-Z 151]
   Letters from Hale, mainly relating to his duties as magazine editor. With a few clippings and photographs of Hale.

HAMILTON, J   B
   Three Letters [to his First Wife's Mother?]. Neenah and Oshkosh, Wisconsin. 1865-1869.
   12 p. A.L.S. 20 cm.   [Z-Z 100:100]
   Concerning his life and business.

HARDING, GEORGE LABAN, 1893-
   Notes on Alphonse L. Pinart and Zelia Nuttall. ca. 1933.
   7 folders. 7-28 cm.   [Z-R 12]
   Biographical and bibliographical information obtained from the Library of Congress and the California State Library.

HAVANA, CUBA
   Miscellaneous papers. 1788-1887.
   17 p. D. S. and A.L.S. 27-32 cm.   HHB [M-M 516]
   1. Passport issued to Agustín Ronda, July 12, 1788. D.S. 1 p.
   2. Proclamation by Archbishop Felipe José de Tres Palacios y Verdeja concerning abuse of bell-ringing and proper funeral ceremonies. January 9, 1792. D.S. 12 p.
   3. Passport issued to José Francisco de la Madrid, March 31, 1792. D.S. 2 p.
   4. Request by Miguel Farón for information concerning Lieutenant Dionisio Boloña. March 17, 1835. L.S. 1 p.
   5. Request by Federico G. Paez of Ricla to the Contador General de Hacienda for a certificate from the contador. September 2, 1887. A.L.S. 1 p.

HAYA FERNÁNDEZ, DIEGO DE LA, fl. 1718-1722
   Informe dirijido al Rey . . . sobre el estado en que se halla [la] . . . provincia [de Costa Rica] y medios de proveer á su seguridad y adelanto. Cartago, Costa Rica, March 15, 1709 [1719]
   24 p. 28 cm.   HHB [M-M 438]
   Copy of a report addressed to the King of Spain by Diego de la Haya, Governor of Costa Rica, describing the topography, towns and cities, inhabitants, products, commerce, and other features of the province, and stressing its

military and other needs, particularly with reference to the annexation of Talamanca.

The correction of the date "1709," at the beginning and end of the Ms., is based upon internal evidence and the fact that Haya did not become Governor until 1718.

HEIZER, ROBERT FLEMING, 1915-
Papers on Identification of Anza's Remains. 1962-1967.
2 boxes. [67/179M]
Material relating to the discovery of the burial site of Juan Bautista de Anza, and identification of his remains and their reburial, in Arizpe, Mexico, 1963-1964. Correspondence, notes, clippings, photographs, artifacts, manuscripts and galley proofs of Heizer's book, *Anza and the Northwest Frontier of New Spain* (1967). Included are some papers of the book's co-author, Jacob N. Bowman. "Key" to arrangement available.

HENDERSON, SIMEON REDDICK, *comp.*
Civil War Letters. February and April, 1863.
3 p. A.L.S. 24-25 cm. [z-z 132]
Letter from Willis Arnold Gorman (1814-1876), and letter from E. A. Hall to Joseph A. Sanders, enclosing samples for jackets for Company F, 24th Indiana Volunteers.

HENRÍQUEZ, JOSEPH ANDRÉS
Questión Escolástica Canónica Moral. Zacapulas, Guatemala. October 11, 1792.
152 p. D.S. 21 cm. [71/35M]
Justification of his actions in the legal questions raised in the marriage of Francisco de Vera, who lacked proof of baptism. Illustrated frontispiece.

HEREDIA Y SARMIENTO, JOSÉ IGNACIO, fl. 1800
Sermon Panegyryco de la Gloryosa Aparycyon de Nuestra Señora de Guadalupe . . . *and* Resumen Hystoryco de las Pryncypales Nacyones que poblaron el Pays de Anahuac, o vyrreynato de Nueva España. Mexico. 1801-1803.
141 p. 31 cm. HHD [M-M 110]
Copies of two works by Heredia, professor of the royal and pontifical seminary of Mexico: a sermon delivered on the anniversary of the apparition of the Virgin of Guadalupe, December 12, 1801; and a brief account of the principal indigenous tribes of New Spain, intended for publication with the sermon and based upon the work of Clavijero.

HERIZE, IGNACIO DE
Platicas, ó Collaciones Espirituales, que se accostumbran en el Collegio App.co de N. S. de Guadalupe de Zacatecas. . . . Zacatecas, Mexico. September 20, 1725-[April 25, 1736?]
320 p. A.D.S. 22 cm. HHB [M-M 111]
Collection of informal sermons or talks by the Franciscan, Herize. There

are 16 discourses in two numbered series, delivered during his two three-year terms as Guardian of the above-mentioned Colegio, and seven unnumbered items which conclude with an Easter sermon, apparently delivered in 1736.

HERMOSILLO, SONORA
Selected Papers. 1777-1848.
5 folders. (Typescripts) [M-A 19:1]
The documents relate to Philip Nolan in Texas, 1797-1800; a party of American fur traders hunting beaver on the Rio Gila, 1826; report of another group doing the same on the Rio Colorado in 1828; defense of Guaymas against a possible American invasion, 1847; an excerpt, 1853, concerning foreign expeditions in Sonora. From the Archivo del Estado, Hermosillo.

HERNÁEZ, FRANCISCO JAVIER, 1816-1876
Extract from *Colección de bulas, breves y otros documentos relativos a la Iglesia de América y Filipinas* .... Brussels. 1879.
9 f. 24x33 cm. HHB [M-M 361]
List of Bishops of Panama, with biographical data and a few comments on the history of the See, ca. 1514-1871. Taken from Vol. II, p. 133-136 of Hernáez's printed work.

HERNÁNDEZ, JUAN
Processo criminal contra. Mexico and other cities. 1617-1621.
159 p. A.D.S., D.S. 32 cm. [67/140M]
Proceedings against Juan Hernández, a mulatto, for bigamy, with depositions, copies of marriage records, interrogations, sentence, and annulment of marriage. Includes signatures of Fathers Diego Muñoz, Ambrosio Carrillo, and other Inquisition officials.

HERRERA Y MONTEMAYOR, JUAN
Viage ... de Mexico al Reyno del Piru, y ciudad de Lima .... Lima, Peru. October, 1618.
212 p. (Photocopy) 25 cm. [71/82M]
Report on voyage from Acapulco to Peru in 1617. From the Biblioteca Nacional, Mexico.

HERVAS, SANTOS
Letter to Manuel Herrera. Madrid. June 10, 1873.
1 p. A.L.S. 20 cm. [Z-Z 100:31]
Challenge to a duel.

HILDEBRAND, MILTON, 1918-
Letters to his Family. El Salvador. 1941-1942.
105 p. (Typescript) 28 cm. [Z-C 221]
Description of experiences of the University of California expedition to El Salvador to collect specimens of mammals, fossils, and plants.

HILL, ROSCOE R   , 1880-1960
   Papers.
   30 cartons.   [z-z 159]
   Personal correspondence, together with papers and items copied in various foreign archives. Materials accumulated during Hill's long career as Latin American historian, teacher, and archivist.

HINCHMAN,
   [Mexican Railroads. N.p., 1883?]
   8 p. 32 cm.   HHB [M-M 345]
   A summary review of Mexican railway lines, particularly the Mexican National System, of which Hinchman was President. Entered by Bancroft under "Hinchman," from whom the data was presumably obtained.

HISTORY OF A HOUSE AND LOT IN MEXICO CITY. MEXICO CITY. 1612-1815
   262 p. D.S. and Ms. 31 cm.   [M-M 1739]
   Originals and certified contemporary copies of documents tracing the history from 1675 to 1815 of a house and lot variously described as situated in the "Hornillo" or "Santa Cruz" ward of Mexico City or "by the Manzanares Bridge," and eventually bequeathed by María Teresa Gómez Galván for charitable purposes under the administration of the Congregación del Santísimo Cristo de Burgos. Includes records of transfer through direct sale, auction, and inheritance, as well as evaluations, petitions, judicial decisions, certifications, and a floor plan of the house, and background material dating from as early as 1612.

HOLMER, NILS MAGNUS, 1904-
   Letter to Frank G. Speck, University of Pennsylvania. San Blas, Island of Ustuppu, Panama. May 1, 1947.
   2 p. A.L.S. 27 cm.   HHB [M-M 1700:54]
   Tells of his linguistic studies among the Cuna Indians, plans for publication, and for further research among American Indian groups.

HOVEY, CHARLES MASON, 1810-1887
   Correspondence and Papers. 1844-1880.
   17 p. D.S. and A.L.S. 17-41 cm.   [z-z 113]
   Passport, 1844, signed by Edward Everett, U.S. Ambassador to Great Britain; and correspondence, chiefly concerning horticulture.

HOWARD, THOMAS
   Indenture. Ottawa, Canada. April 8, 1902.
   6 p. Copy, printed and typed. 33 cm.   [z-z 100:72]
   For mining property in the Yukon Territory.

HUANTAJAYA, MINE, TARAPACÁ, PERU
  Documents relating to Indian Labor. 1757-1767.
  118 p. D.S. 32 cm. [z-d 135]
  Petition, grants, and supporting documents for a location of Indians to enforced labor in the silver mines of Joseph Basilio de la Fuente y Aro. With typed transcript, 56 p., and explanatory note, 1878, by George R. Ghiselin.

HUEJUQUILLA, NUEVA VIZCAYA
  Legal documents regarding Assignment of Lands for the Presidio and Town of Santa María de las Caldas de Guajuquilla [Huejuquilla]. Mexico and Spain. 1749-1779.
  166 p. 31 cm. [m-m 1785]
  Contains royal and viceregal decrees, gubernatorial orders, judicial pronouncements, petitions, surveyors' reports, summonses, certifications, data about presidio reform, documents concerning land-tribunal magistrates, and related material.

HUGO DE OMERICK, IGNACIO JOSEPH DE
  Conversaciones familiares de vn Cura â sus Feligreses Yndios, formadas sobre las reglas de felicidad espiritual, y temporal, que dirigio por veredas el Yll.^{mo} Sor Dn Francisco Antonio Lorenzana. . . . Tepecuacuilco, Mexico. 1769.
  146 p. 22 cm. HHB [m-m 113]
  Four essays by the parish priest of Tepecuacuilco, an Inquisition official, designed to guide other priests in expounding the bases of spiritual and temporal felicity to the Indians in accordance with instructions circulated by Archbishop Lorenzana in 1768; preceded by the author's prologue and followed by a brief exposition of basic Christian doctrines.

HUMBOLDT, ALEXANDER, FREIHERR VON, 1769–1859
  Tablas Estatisticas del Reyno de N. España en el Año de 1803. [Mexico. 1803]
  70 p. 21 cm. HHB [m-m 114]
  Copy of a statistical report on the geography, population, economy, and military strength of New Spain in 1803, including the Provincias Internas and both Californias.
  Almost wholly identical in content with Humboldt's, "Tablas Geografico-Politicas . . ." (m-m 115).

HUMBOLDT, ALEXANDER, FREIHERR VON, 1769–1859
  Tablas Geografico-Politicas del R.^{no} de N. E. que manifiestan su superficie y poblacion, fabricas, comercio, minas, rentas, y fuerza militar. [Mexico. 1803]
  116 p. Ms. and printed. 22 cm. HHB [m-m 115]
  Copy of a statistical report upon the intendancies and provinces of New Spain in 1803, prepared for presentation to the Viceroy. Substantially identical with Humboldt's "Tablas Estatisticas . . ." (m-m 114), except for an added table and other minor variations.

HUNTER, DARD, 1883–
    Letter to Wolfgang von Hagen. Chillicothe, Ohio. July 18, 1938.
    1 p. L.S. 28 cm. [z-z 100:2]
    Concerning paper-making and a paper museum.

HYDE, ALBERT A
    A short account of my prison life during the Civil War, 1861-1865. North Haven, Connecticut. November 25, 1909.
    8 p. (Typescript) 28 cm. [z-z 100:39]
    Account of the author's experiences from May 1864 to 1865 in Andersonville and other Confederate prisons.

IBÁÑEZ, JOSÉ MANUEL DE, *comp.*
    Coleccion de Poesias escogidas, asi manuscritas, como impresas de los mejores Autores Españoles y Americanos. Querétaro, Mexico. 1802.
    422 p. 22 cm. HHB [M-M 116]
    An anthology containing selections from major and minor Spanish or Latin American poets, drawn from published and unpublished sources, including translations and adaptations from other languages as well as some Latin verses; citations and explanatory notes by the compiler. Gaps in the original pagination indicate that p. 1-176, 217-224, 227-232, and 301-308 are missing.

IGLESIAS, JOSÉ MARÍA, 1823-1891
    Biographical Data. Mexico City. 1873–[1885?]
    3 folders in portfolio. 33–34 cm. HHB [M-M 389]
    Material relating to the life of José María Iglesias, president of the Mexican Supreme Court. The three folders contain 1) an extract copied from Mexico City's *El Federalista*, May 17, 1873, and written under the pseudonym, "Orfeo," with an appended copy of a portion of letter 439 from *Foreign Relations of the United States*, regarding Iglesias' tendered resignation from the Supreme Court (6 p.); 2) a copy of the official record of Iglesias' life from 1823 to 1885 (7 p.); 3) a copy of biographical data eulogizing Iglesias, written by Manuel Payno y Flores (3 p., n.p., n.d.).

IGLESIAS, JOSÉ MARÍA, 1823-1891
    Recuerdos Políticos [N.p., ca. 1877]
    89 p. A.D. 22 cm. HHB [M-M 342]
    A condensation of Iglesias' *La Cuestión Presidencial en 1876* . . . , written in New York, May–September, 1877, and published in Mexico City in 1892.

ILLARREGUI, MIGUEL FRANCISCO DE
    Calculo Astronomico . . . para el año del S.^{r} de 1750 y meridiano de d.^{ha} ciudad. [Puebla, Mexico. 1749]
    24 p. A.D.S.(?) 25 cm. HHB [M-M 117]
    Astrological forecast for the year 1750, prepared by the pilot and mathematician, Illarregui, a resident of Puebla; dedication signed by him and addressed to Guipuzcoans in the New World.

ILLANES, MARIO
    Social Problems on the Farm in Chile.
    7 p. (Photocopy) 26 cm. [z-d 113:2]
    Talk given by Mr. Illanes, Chilean consul in San Francisco, before a class conducted by Mme. Labarca.

INDIAN AFFAIRS, MICHOACÁN
    7 folders. (Photocopies) 25 cm. [m-a 8]
    Indian complaints over payment of tribute, and related matters, 1566–1573. From the Archivo del Tribunal, and from the Ayuntamiento, Pátzcuaro.

INDIAN AFFAIRS, MORELIA. 1544–1608
    18 folders. (Photocopies) 25 cm. [m-a 7]
    Reflecting relations of Indians and Spaniards over tribute, wool mills, treatment of the natives, and government regulations.

INDIANS OF TEXAS, 1785–1789
    22 p. D.S. 31 cm. [m-m 1858]
    Documents relating to the purchase and delivery of annual gifts for Indians in Texas friendly to the Spanish government. Written in Texas and Mexico City.

INQUISITION. MEXICO
    Documents relating to the Inquisition in Mexico. 1608–1771.
    9 folders in box. Ms. and printed. hhb [m-m 398]
    A collection (originals and copies) of genealogical records, criminal proceedings, and edicts of the Inquisition, originating in New Spain, Spain, or Peru, relating to residents of Mexico. Includes genealogical material, 44 p., about Fray Luis de Solórzano, applicant for Inquisition qualificator in Mexico City (1608–1609); Bartolomé de Escoto, a Sevillian resident of Honduras (1611–1617), 22 p.; and Jerónimo Gutiérrez Montealegre, candidate for Inquisition counsellor, and Montealegre's Peruvian wife, Micaela de Solier (1613–1620), 131 p. Also contains 124 folios of documents (1617–1621) covering the Mexican Inquisition's trial of Alonso de Torres, a Negro slave charged with fraudulence and soothsaying; and certified copies of Inquisition edicts (1713–1771) on abuse of the confessional, prohibited reading matter, heresy, and superstition.

INQUISITION. MEXICO
    Proceedings against Fray Nicolás Montero. Mexico. 1772–1773.
    60 p. D.S. 31 cm. [m-m 1827]
    Collection of documents from Antequera, Oaxaca, and Mexico City, on Inquisition proceedings against the Mercedarian friar and Bethlehemite chaplain, Nicolás Montero, for misconduct with women and failure to make confession.

INQUISITION. MEXICO
   Processo contra Joan Vizcayno, llamado Joanes de Galarraga, natural de Urrieta. . . . 1571–1583.
   108 p. D.S. 31 cm. [M-M 1826]
   Documents from the Archdiocese of Guadalajara, Mexico City, and Guipúzcoa, Spain, on proceedings of the Mexican Inquisition against the blacksmith, Juan Galárraga, charged with bigamy.

INQUISITION. PHILIPPINE ISLANDS
   Causa criminal por deposicion de Ana Pandan . . . contra Ysalbeltia e Ysabel Ylag Indias babailanas, y el sarxento Antonio de Roxas. . . . Iloilo, Philippine Islands. February 7, 1646.
   2 items (204 and 128 p.) D.S. 31 cm. [Z-P 1]
   Inquiry into accusation, made by Ana Pandan, of two native women for being priestesses and of Sargento Antonio de Rojas and his family for being accomplices. Original; and copy dated June 16, 1654.

INTER-AMERICAN HIGHWAY
   Papers relating to. ca. 1929–1955.
   792 exp. (On film) [Z-Z 152]
   Illustrated monographs on the history, construction, and maintenance of the Alaska Highway, and reports loaned by the Library of the Office of Chief Engineer, U.S. War Department. Materials collected by George R. Stewart.

INTERNATIONAL COMPANY OF MEXICO
   Biographical Notes. ca. 1887?
   3 folders. 27 cm. HHB [M-M 367]
   Biographical sketches of Captain George C. Cheape, Captain Francis Pavy, and Edgar T. Welles, evidently officials of the International Company of Mexico; with stress on their qualifications.

ISABEL I, LA CATÓLICA, QUEEN OF SPAIN, 1451-1504
   Letter to Cristóbal Colón. Granada. April 13, 1492.
   7 p. 23 and 33 cm. [Z-A 203]
   Purported letter on imitation vellum, with simulated seal. With typed transcript of a brief biography of Columbus from an unidentified printed source.

ISUNZA, FRANCISCO J
   Conversacion . . . *and* Viage al Paiz de las Ciencias. . . . [Mexico] 1769–[1787?]
   91, 131 p. 22 cm. [M-M 1740]
   Two items (copies), ascribed to "F.J.Y.," i.e., "Francisco Isunza."
   1. Conversacion joco-seria, críticio-apologética, satirico-moral . . . sobre un Fárrago que ha salido cuyo título es: Carta â una Religiosa . . . , Puebla, 1769-[1774?]
   A satire in prose and verse, in the form of dialogues between the fictitious

Justo Calzurrias, sacristan of a Carmelite convent, and Santiago Chapulín, porter of another convent. In two parts: the first, 1769, directed against the "Carta â una Religiosa Para su Desengaño y Dirección" of "Jorge Mastheophoro," i.e., José Ortega Moro, which severely criticized certain Puebla convents; the second, [1774?] discussing a proclamation of Viceroy Bucareli based on a royal order of 1774 which forbade perusal of the "Carta," and ordering all copies destroyed, but left open the way for circulation of a new and expurgated edition, likewise condemned by Calzurrias and Chapulín. Contains laudatory references to Bishop Palafox and other Puebla personages.

According to Beristáin, *Biblioteca Hispano Americana Septentrional*, Vol. IV, p. 56, Ortega's "Carta" was not published until 1772. Possibly Ms. copies were circulated as early as 1769.

2. Viage al Paiz de las Ciencias. Bejamen que se diò a los cursantes de Philosophía de Francisco Isunza. [1787?]

A *vejamen*, or academic allegory in prose and verse, delivered by Ysunza as professor of philosophy in the Real y Tridentino Colegio Seminario (of Puebla?) at the graduation ceremonies of his students from a tripartite course begun in 1784; lists the graduates in order of scholarship; includes details of the author's student life in Mexico City; and mentions in a footnote an incident that occurred in 1786.

ITINERARY OF TRIP FROM LAGOS TO GUADALAJARA. [N.p., n.d.]
1 p. 22 cm. HHB [M-M 1700:14]

ITURBIDE, AGUSTÍN DE, 1783-1824
Letter to Colonel Domingo Claverino. Salvatierra [Guanajuato]. March 5, 1816.
3 p. L.S. 21 cm. HHB [M-M 1700:42]
Refers to comments of Lieutenant Manuel de la Madrid regarding military accounts presented by Claverino.

ITURRIGARAY, JOSÉ DE, 1742-1815
Commission of Martínez de la Vega. Mexico City. March 10–18, 1806.
2 p. D.S., 31 cm. HHB [M-M 1731]
Commission appointing Cadet Martínez de la Vega, of the Santa Barbara Presidio, as *alférez* of the San Diego Company of New California, to replace José Luján. Printed text with Ms. insertions and signatures.

ITURRIGARAY, JOSÉ DE, 1742-1815
Documents. Mexico. 1804-1808.
2 items (17 p.) D.S., L.S. 20-30 cm. [70/59M]
Documents signed as Viceroy of Mexico: one concerning the ownership of Rancho Bejarano near Horcasitas (1804); and a letter of Juan Francisco Domínguez requesting a copy of laws regulating the sale of liquor on feast days, with draft of Domínguez's reply (1808).

IXTLILXOCHITL, FERNANDO DE ALBA, 1568(?)-1648

Sumaria Relacion de todas las cosas que an sucedido en la Nueva España, y de muchas cosas que los Tultecas alcanzaron y supieron desde la creacion del Mundo hasta su destruccion, y venida de los terceros pobladores y Chichimecas, hasta la venida de los Españoles, sacada de la original Historia de esta Nueva España.... [Mexico, 1622]

774 p. 31 cm.　　　　　　　　　　　　　　　　　　　　　HHB [M-M 426]

Also known as "Relaciones varias e importantes sobre todas las cosas que han sucedido en la Nueva España . . ." (J. M. Beristáin de Souza, *Biblioteca Hispano Americana Septentrional*, 3rd ed., Mexico, 1947, Vol. I, p. 126, note by Osorio, and as "Relaciones" or "Relaciones Históricas" in Lord Kingsborough, *Antiquities of Mexico*, London, 1848, Vol. IX, p. 321 *et seq.*).

Copy of a group of historical treatises on Mexico covering the period from antiquity to the early years of the Spanish conquest; based on native sources and compiled by Ixtlilxochitl from his own history of New Spain at the request of the viceroy, Marquis of Gelves. Consists of five main parts and three additional items.

1. Five numbered sections, or "relaciones," dealing with the creation of the world and Toltec history, 98 p.

2. Twelve sections on the coming of the Chichimecas and the reigns of their various rulers, through that of Negual Coyotzin, 338 p.

3. Additional data on Mexican history, geography, and customs, including a section on the arrival of the Spaniards, 56 p.

4. Supplementary historical data, relating primarily to the Toltecs and the Chichimecas, 54 p., in part reproduced by Kingsborough.

5. An account of Mexican history from the earliest times to that of Cortés, not expressly ascribed in the Ms. to Ixtlilxochitl, but generally accepted as his work, 76 p.

The appended items, tentatively attributed to Ixtlilxochitl in the above-cited Osorio note, are not his work but were perhaps copied by him for the original version of the present collection. They are:

6. Copies of Audiencia records covering the investigation of Guzmán's conduct in executing Caltzontzín, ruler of Michoacán, and confiscating his property; including inquiries as to the confiscated property due the royal treasury, the text of the Queen's orders (Spain, 1531) for the investigation, and the testimony of witnesses, 25 p.

7. Copies of the decision handed down by the Council of the Indies in response to a second appeal presented by María de Cano [Moctezuma] regarding a property dispute among the heirs of Isabel, eldest daughter of Moctezuma II, and revoking earlier decisions of the Audiencia of New Spain, with supplementary material (Mexico, 1579) on implementation of the Council's decision.

8. Pedro Vázquez's Spanish translation (Mexico City, October 21, 1641) of a journal on the 1541 expedition against the Chichimecas undertaken by Francisco de Sandoval Acazitli in the service of Viceroy Mendoza. Originally written in an Indian language by Gabriel de Castañeda, in compliance with orders from Sandoval, and sometimes erroneously ascribed to the latter. Substantially

identical with Juan Agustín Morfi, Colección de Documentos . . . , No. 5 (M-M 162) and Mota Padilla, "Historia de la Conquista de la Nueva Galicia."

IZAGUIRRE, PEDRO DE
Relacion de los sitios y calidades de los Puertos de Caballos, y el nuevo de Santo Tomás de Castillo en la Provincia de Honduras. . . . ca. 1606.
6 p. 33 cm.   HHB [M-M 305]
Report by the naval officer, Izaguirre, on the port of Caballos in Honduras and the new Honduran port of Santo Tomás del Castillo, describing the site and other characteristics of both, and stressing the superiority of the latter.

JACKSON, ANDREW, PRESIDENT, 1767-1845
Patent to John Hayden, Jr., for Land in Wayne County, Michigan. Washington, D.C. October 14, 1835.
1 p. D.S. (by deputy). 25 cm.   [Z-Z 100:86]

JACKSON, ROBERT HOUGHWOUT, 1892-
Letter to Fulmer Mood. Washington, D.C. December 3, 1941.
1 p. L.S. 20 cm.   [Z-Z 100:3]
Conveying thanks for information.

JACKSON & COMPANY
Market Report. Ningpo, China. October 24, 1865.
4 p. Ms. and printed. 25-27 cm.   [Z-Z 150]
Printed price lists of imports and exports, with comments.

JACOBS, E   1822-
Dictation of E. Jacobs, Banker. Shreveport, Louisiana. September 12, 1887.
4 p. 18-29 cm.   HHB [Z-B 5:1]
Notes on Jacobs' life and information about Shreveport, recorded by one of Bancroft's interviewers.

JAILLANDIER, P[ÈRE?]
Extrait d'une lettre . . . dattée de Pondichera, au mois de Fevrier 1711, et inserée dans l'onzieme Recueil des Lettres edifiantes. . . . 1711-1732.
30 p. 26 cm.   HHB [M-M 119]
A collection of five items, extracts, translations, and notes, in French, relating to New Spain, and including: 1) Jaillandier, Extrait d'une lettre . . . Pondicherry, February, 1711, describing a trip from Buena Vista to Acapulco; 2) Extrait d'une Lettre . . . Campeche, December 5, 1731, published in June, 1732, in the *Gazette de Hollande*, concerning conflict between the Spaniards and the English in Yucatán; 3) [Campagne d'Ursúa. n. p., n. d.], A description of Governor Ursúa's campaign, ca. 1697, against the Itza Indians, which resulted in opening a highway between Yucatán and Guatemala; 4) Observations

Astronomiques, made by Joseph Harris, Veracruz, January–March, 1728, and João Baptista Carbone, Lisbon, 1726, apparently translated from "Transactions filosofiques," January, February, and March, 1728; 5) Chemin de la Vera Cruz a Guaxaca [n. p., n. d.] a list of sites on the Veracruz–Oaxaca road, with explanatory annotations.

Entered by Bancroft under "Jaillandier, P."; the initial is presumably the abbreviation for "Père."

JALISCO, STATE OF. JUNTA DIRECTORA DE ESTUDIOS
Copiador de las comunicaciones dirijidas por la Ynspeccion g[ene]ral de instruccion primaria, á la Junta Directora de Estudios del Estado. Guadalajara, Mexico. December 20, 1849.
71 p. 29 cm. HHB [M-M 507]
Letterbook containing copies of reports and tabular data on primary education in the State of Jalisco from September 23, 1848, to December 20, 1849.

JAMIESON, STUART
Notes. 1941-1943.
1 carton and 1 box (28 folders) [Z-R 2]
Field notes, papers, and printed material used in preparing doctoral dissertation, *Labor Unionism in American Agriculture*. List of contents in carton.

JANSSENS, JAN
Certificate. Culiacán, Mexico. November 25, 1848.
1 p. D.S. 22 cm. HHB [M-M 1700:32]
Letter stating that the claim of Casimir De Galand against Vega Frères is just. Countersigned with a cross by Ysdoer De Praet, whose name was evidently signed for him by Janssens. In French.

JESÚS ARCE, JOSÉ IGNACIO DE
Confirmation of Title to Property. Veracruz. December 31, 1859.
2 p. D.S. (Photocopy) 33 cm. HHB [M-M 1700:9]
Confirmation of title transferring land in Baja California to Jesús Arce as of January 15, 1834. Signed by Benito Juárez and José de Emparán.

JEWITT, H   J
Letter to Emily(?). Edinburgh, Scotland. February 18-27, 1849.
4 p. (Copy.) 31 cm. [Z-Z 100:33]
Description of a European trip.

JONES, JOHN R
Receipt to William A. Newell. Utica [New York] September 8, 1845.
2 p. D.S. 10 cm. [Z-Z 100:49]
Issued for payment on property.

JONES, MOSES Z
    Letter to E. B. Jones. Lafayette, Indiana. June 11, 1860.
    4 p. A.L.S. 20 cm. [z-z 100:82]
    Civil War letter.

JUNKER VON LANGEGG, FERDINAND ADALBERT, 1828-
    El Dorado, History of the Exploratory Expeditions to the Land of gold . . . in the 16th and 17th Centuries. Leipzig. 1888.
    327 p. (Typescript) 28 cm. [68/147z]
    Copy of a translation from the German by Walter Rink, 1940, prepared under a WPA project.

JUNTA DE AGUAS DE LA ZANJA MADRE DEL RÍO DE QUERÉTARO
    Bill for irrigation water. Querétaro. December 20, 1946.
    1 p. D.S. 13 cm. [M-M 1700:88]
    Printed form, filled in. Signed by the treasurer.

JUZGADO DE INDIOS, MEXICO
    Documents relating to. 1580-1820.
    26 boxes. (Photocopies) [M-A 3]
    Selected from the *ramos* in *Civil, Criminal,* and *Historia* of the Archivo General de la Nación, Mexico. There is a "key" to the collection.

KAUTZ, ALBERT, 1839-1907
    The story of a Yankee prisoner of war. How he was captured, his prison experience, and how he was exchanged.
    42 p. (Typescript) 26 cm. [z-z 111]
    An account of Kautz's capture by the Confederate steamer *Winslow,* his treatment as a prisoner, and his parole to Washington to effect an exchange of prisoners. Covers the period June–October, 1861. Photocopy available.

KERR, CLARK, 1911-
    Notes and Papers concerning Self-help and Consumer Cooperatives in the United States. 1930-1938.
    3 cartons (23 envelopes). [z-R 3]
    Field notes, questionnaires, reports, printed matter, and clippings used in preparation of his doctoral dissertation, *Productive Enterprises among the Unemployed, 1931–1938.*

KEWEN, EDWARD JOHN CAGE, 1825-
    Nicaragua and Walker. In Two Parts. Part First. Historical Retrospect of the Isthmian States. 1879.
    85 f. A.D.S. 32 cm. HHB [M-M 340]
    The first part of a projected work on Nicaragua and Walker, containing only background material which traces the history of Central America through the period of Spanish domination, the struggle for independence, union with Mexico, and the rise and fall of the Central American Federation, to the eve of William Walker's arrival in Nicaragua in 1855. Includes letter of transmittal to H. H. Bancroft, San Francisco, February 28, 1879, signed "E. J. C. Kewen."

KIDDER, D G
    Report on Expedition Prospecting for Copper in Sonora. [N.p., n.d.]
    21 p. (Typescript) 28 cm. [M-M 1862]
    Report on an expedition undertaken "just after the close of World War I" to examine a copper deposit allegedly discovered in the eastern part of the Sonora desert by Rafael Tello.

KINNAIRD, LAWRENCE, 1893-, *comp.*
    Miscellaneous Photocopies, Translations, Printed Works, and Students' Dissertations on Various Subjects.
    1 box (12 items). 19-30 cm. [Z-D 127]

KINO, EUSEBIO FRANCISCO, 1644-1711
    Reports. Mission Nuestra Señora de los Dolores. 1698-1703.
    25 p. D.S. and A.L.S. 22-23 cm. [M-M 1854]
    Two reports from the Jesuit missionary, dated May 3–November 4, 1698, and February 5, 1703. The first describes Apache hostilities and aid rendered against them by the Pima-Sobaipuri Indians, and stresses the need for governmental assistance in the conversion and protection of these allies. The second, addressed to the viceroy, reports on the history of existing missions and on plans for future missions in Pimería Alta and Alta California.

KLEIN, JOHN C
    Letters and Papers. 1889.
    7 items (11 p.) and 2 clippings. 18-54 cm. [Z-C 205]
    Materials concerning the Panama Canal and the French Canal Company. Include letters from General Victor Vifquain, U.S. Consul at Colón, and newspaper clippings of two articles by Klein.

KLEINSCHMIDT, HEINRICH
    Letters. 1851-1853.
    13 p. A.L.S. 25-28 cm. [Z-Z 164]
    Correspondence with members of the family in Germany, advising them on preparations for a journey to St. Louis, Missouri. With typed translation of one letter.

KUNSTMANN, FRIEDRICH
    The Discovery of America; from the oldest sources historically represented. [Munich. 1859]
    155 p. 32 cm. HHB [M-M 121]
    A translation of *Die Entdeckung Amerikas nach den Aeltesten Quellen Geschichtlich Dargestellt,* made by Albert Goldschmidt in 1873.

KUYKENDALL, RALPH SIMPSON, 1885-1963
    Notes relating to the History of Mexico.
    2 boxes [M-R 7]
    Notes and transcripts of documents in the Archivo General de Indias concerning Mexico, ca. 1773-1796.

LA SOCIEDAD DE AMIGOS DE AGUAS CALIENTES
  Estatutos de. Aguas Calientes, Mexico. March 18, 1827.
  18 p. D.S. 20 cm. [67/66M]
  By-laws of a society devoted to promote the welfare of the state.

LACANDÓN INDIANS, GUATEMALA
  Documents relating to. Guatemala and San Lorenzo, Spain. 1789-1799.
  64 p. D.S. 30-31 cm. [M-M 1853]
  Correspondence of civil and religious authorities concerning the attempted pacification and Christianization of the Lacandón Indians in the vicinity of Palenque.

LACAYO, MARCO H
  Letter to N. W. Peake on Gathering Material for H. H. Bancroft. With Memorandum on Archeological Items. Granada, Nicaragua. February 4, 1887.
  5 p. A.L.S. 26 cm. HHB [Z-C 7]
  Information on the first Indians who once inhabited the islands of Zapatera and Ometepe.

LANSING, ROBERT, 1864-1928
  Correspondence and Papers. 1915-1922.
  699 exp. (On film) [Z-Z 155]
  Confidential memoranda and character sketches, together with notes mainly concerning European diplomacy. Microfilm of manuscripts in the Library of Congress.

LAPÉROUSE, JEAN FRANÇOIS DE GALAUP, COMTE DE, 1741-1788
  Letters. 1778 and 1783.
  6 p. A.L.S. and typescripts. 20-28 cm. [Z-Z 126]
  Letter to his sister, January 19, 1778; and transcript of letter concerning money due him, July 3, 1783. With transcripts and translations.

LATORRE, CARLOS, 1799-1851
  Noticias sobre el arte de ejecutar las tragedias. [N. p.] 1832.
  45 p. 21 cm. HHB [M-M 124]
  A monograph or address by the Spanish actor, Carlos Latorre, giving advice on the art of declamation, or acting, with special reference to tragedy; written in the year when the author received the title of "Master of Declamation."

LAZO, J   S
  Honduras sketches. 1854.
  29 p. 7-18 cm. [68/133M]
  Pencil drawings of buildings and scenes. Small notebook and nine sketches. Note inside cover of notebook: "John L. Eckley to J. C. Tucker."

LEFEBVRE, ALFRED
   Business Papers of the Maison de Mexique and the Maison de Paris. Mexico and Paris. 1858-1898.
   113 vols. and 1 box. [M-B 3]
   Papers concerning the wholesale business in Mexico and Paris of Alfred Lefebvre, a French exporter and importer who traded with firms in France, Germany, Switzerland, Great Britain, the United States, and many places in Mexico. Principal exports from Mexico were agricultural products, furs, and India rubber. The papers give an excellent picture of business methods and practices of the time and the problems of operation in the absence of banking firms.

LEGAL PAPERS. 17TH-18TH(?) CENT.
   25 folders. Ms. and printed. 23-31 cm. HHB [M-M 406]
   A compilation of legal documents, originals and copies, relating principally to collection of debts, taxes, property disputes, or criminal cases, and other miscellaneous legal papers of lay and ecclesiastical tribunals.

   1. Certified copies of documents relating to a suit for payment of tithes, brought against certain religious orders by the representative of the Crown and the ecclesiastical officials of New Spain and Peru, ca. 1664.

   2. File on the suit brought by Francisco de la Cruz, Martín Lázaro, and others, natives of Chontalcuatlán near Mexico City against Juan de Santiago and Pedro Joseph, natives of the same town, for theft of mules and other animals, Mexico, June–July, 1675; written partly in an Indian language.

   3. Petition of November 29, 1690, for confirmation of a sentence absolving Magdalena de Fonseca, widow of Alonso Fernández Rincón, from a debt incurred by her son, Juan Rincón, for which suit had been brought against her by Alonso Martínez de Piña.

   4. Appeal from a sentence, Cuernavaca (?), ca. 1705, against Miguel de Villalobos, for charges of rape and related crimes.

   5. Documents originating in Madrid and Mexico City relating to collection, through the Real Acuerdo, of funds owed to the Merchants' Board of Seville by the Board's agents in Mexico, Miguel de Ubilla and Captain Lucas de Careaga, 1709.

   6. Dispute over a governmental gunpowder concession claimed by both Colonel Francisco Aguirre y Gomendio and his debtor, Juan Miguel de Vertiz, Mexico, ca. 1715.

   7. Appeal of Juan de Salinas and Antonio de Córdoba, attorneys of the Audiencia of Mexico, from a sentence passed against them and other persons for collusion with an English company to defraud the Spanish crown of taxes due on a shipment of silver, Mexico, ca. 1727.

   8. Letter of Miguel Pacheco Solís, Mexico, February 15, 1783, dealing principally with a lawsuit on distribution of quicksilver.

   9. Opinion, Mexico, April 20, 1728, regarding the obligations of Antonio Lucio of Zacatecas, with respect to his niece Manuela.

   10. Brief of Salvador de Zúñiga y Barrios, Guadalajara, March 24, 1730, on

the right of retraction in regard to property in the Sierra de Pinos, sold by Antonio Anselmo de Quijar, which his relative, Manuel Morquecho, wishes to reclaim.

11. Two petitions, Mexico, 1736, of Francisco Antonio de Echávarri, a judge of the Audiencia of Mexico, for recognition of his claims in a dispute on precedence with another member of that body, Domingo Valcárcel y Formento.

12. Document of Canon Juan de Castro, Mexico, ca. 1738, on evaluation of an estate purchased from the Conde del Fresno by Manuel de la Peña and later seized by Peña's creditors, arguing that the appraisal of the ecclesiastical tribunal was too high.

13. File of papers written in Durango and Mexico, May 3–November 8(?), 1748, on the imprisonment and trial of Sisimble Indians charged with murder and robbery in the vicinity of Mapimí, New Vizcaya.

14. Brief for the defense, Mexico, July 30, 1757, of Salvador Clavel in the suit of Josefa de Florencia, widow of Manuel de Villate, for payment of a debt owed to Villate by Juan Bautista Clavel, deceased brother of the defendant.

15. Incomplete file from San Miguel de Horcasitas and Sahuaripa, February 4–March 7, 1768, concerning collection of a debt owed by the Sahuaripa mission.

16. An incomplete record, Mexico, 1769, of the case of Juliana María, an Indian accused of sorcery in San Miguel Acatlán, jurisdiction of Tulancingo, Hidalgo, including correspondence between the acting ecclesiastical judge, José Tamariz, and officials of the archdiocese.

17. File on the trial of the Indian, Santiago Antonio, Mexico, 1774-1776, charged with superstitious medical practices, including records of ecclesiastical courts in the jurisdiction of Tulancingo and those of the Mexico City Tribunal for Indians and Chinese.

18. File of documents and correspondence sent principally to or from the Alcalde Mayor of San Luis de la Paz, 1784-1785, on restoration of property rights to the exiled Jesuits, with the royal instructions of 1783-1784 on pertinent legal measures.

19. Document recording power of attorney, Puebla, November 13, 1792, by Esteban Munuera to Antonio Monteagudo, assistant secretary of Archbishop Núñez de Haro y Peralta.

20. Plea on behalf of Toribio Fernández de Ribera's client, Ignacio de Echeverría, sargento mayor of Puebla (18th cent.?), asking that the authority of the latter over the Commercial Company of Puebla be upheld.

21. Brief on behalf of María Teresa de Medina by Salvador Zúñiga y Barrios (Mexico, 18th cent.?), in her suit for recovery of three sites owned by her and appropriated by Juan Ignacio Larrañaga for the pasturage of animals used in mining projects, with some information on mining legislation.

22. Brief prepared by El Doctor Machado, Mexico, n.d., in proceedings instituted against Francisco de Negrete by his creditors, chief of whom was Baltasar de los Ríos.

23. Plea addressed to the Papal delegate in Puebla by former members of the Franciscan Third Order in Toluca, n.d., protesting their expulsion and requesting reinstatement.

24. Fragment from a report, n.p., n.d., in defense of an unnamed provincial

and other members of a religious order who refused to acknowledge their excommunication by a bishop, and citing authorities to exalt the status of monastic administrators in relation to that of bishops.

25. Plea presented by Martín de Pinedo y Alarcón, Mexico, n.d., on behalf of a restored Carmelite convent, in its suit against the Royal Fiscal for revocation of a decree passed by the Audiencia of Mexico declaring it to be a new establishment, and for recognition as a continuing old establishment.

LEGARÉ, HUGH SWINTON, 1797-1843
   Letter to W. C. Preston. Charleston. July 18, 1840.
   2 p. A.L.S. 25 cm.   [z-z 100:15]
   Forwarding a letter and commenting on current issues.

LENCH, PATRICIO
   Relacion puntual de toda la Costa del Mar del Norte desde Portovelo hasta el Puerto de Omoa. León [Nicaragua?]. May 27, 1757.
   19 p. 31 cm.   HHB [M-M 134]
   Description of the Caribbean coast from Porto Bello, Panama, to Omoa and Puerto Cortés, Honduras, written by Lench, a pilot of Irish extraction, in accordance with orders from Acting Governor Melchor Vidal de Lorca y Villena of Nicaragua; note appended relating to the Colorado and San Juan rivers.
   Listed by Bancroft under "Lynch."

LEÓN, J   J
   Order to Captain Hidalgo. Guaymas. August 1, 1863.
   2 p. A.D.S. 16 cm.   [M-M 1700:85]
   Concerning agreement about sailors' wages.

LEÓN Y GAMA, ANTONIO DE, 1735-1802
   Carta que sobre las observaciones critico-apologeticas . . . escribia à un Amigo D. Antonio de Leon y Gama. [Mexico. 1783-1822]
   378 p. 24 cm.   HHB [M-M 125]
   Miscellany of six main items, *i.e.*, León y Gama's reply to an anonymous friend regarding his treatise on medical experiments involving lizards, Mexico, October, 1783; tables and formulas relating to taxation on silver mining and minting; formulas for the reduction of pesos to smaller silver and copper currency; notes and corrections for Mariano Veytia's *Baluartes de México*, concerned chiefly with the image of Nuestra Señora de los Remedios near Mexico City; some theological essays of José Honorato Melero y Fernández; and a collection of verses of José Joaquín Fernández Lizardi, written about 1822.

LEONARD, HENRY P
   Commonplace Books. Sheffield, Massachusetts. 1815-1816.
   2 vols. 30-32 cm.   [z-z 130]
   Newspaper clippings of poetry, stories, articles, etc., selected and assembled by Leonard.

[LETTER FROM AN UNIDENTIFIED WOMAN TO HER HUSBAND]. "MIDWAY." NOVEMBER 14, 1848
  2 p. A.L.S. 25 cm. [z-z 100:77]
  Signed "Martha." Gives family news.

LETTER TO WILLIAM ?, BROTHER OF THE WRITER. CAMP WOOD, HART COUNTY, KENTUCKY. DECEMBER 29, 1861
  2 p. A.L. 24 cm. [z-z 100:53]
  Civil War letter describing military actions.

LIBRO NOTICIOSO QUE CONTIENE ALGUNOS APUNTES PARTICULARES, ACAESIDOS EN ESTA VILLA DE ORIZAVA Y OTRAS NOTICIAS Q.ᵉ AN YEGADO AQUI DE SUJETOS FIDEDIGNOS. ORIZABA, MEXICO. 1812-1821
  165 p. 22 cm. HHB [M-M 178]
  Anonymous diary relating chiefly to events of the Mexican Wars of Independence in the vicinity of Orizaba, March 5, 1812–May 12, 1821.
  Entered by Bancroft under "Orizava, Libro curioso que contiene algunos puntos particulares...," as the word "Noticioso" is superimposed on another word, evidently, "Curioso." The flyleaf bears a deleted alternative title: "Diario de Ocurrencias en Orizaba entre los años 1812 y 1821."

LIMA. ARCHIVO ARZOBISPAL
  Selected Documents. Province of Huarochiri, Peru. 1660-1701.
  128 p. (Typescript) 28 cm. [z-d 105]
  Concern idolatry in various towns of the province of Huarochiri. Selected by Nancy Gilmer.

LIMA, PERU. REAL SALA DEL CRIMEN
  Rebelion de Tupac Amaro. Tomo I. Testimonio de los autos seguidos contra Mariano Tupac Amaro y Andrés Mendigure sobre atribuirseles la reincidencia en la revelión. Lima. 1782-1798.
  386 exp. (On film) [z-d 108]

LINCK, WENCESLAUS, 1736-1790(?)
  Diario del Viage, que se hizo en la Prov.ª de California al Norte de esta Peninsula.... Vellicatá (?). February 20–April 18, 1766.
  39 p. D.S. 22 cm. [M-M 1855]
  Journal of the trip made by the Jesuit Linck, head of the frontier mission of San Francisco de Borja, in search of mission sites and the Colorado River, with an armed escort commanded by Blas Fernández y Somera.

LINCOLN, JACKSON STEWARD
  An Ethnological Study of the Ixil Indians of the Guatemalan Highlands.
  306 exp. (On film) [z-c 204]
  Microfilm of typescript from the University of Chicago Microfilm Collection of Manuscripts on Middle American Cultural Anthropology.

LIST OF PHOTOCOPIES OF MATERIAL IN THE LIBRARY OF CONGRESS FROM PAPELES DE CUBA IN THE ARCHIVO GENERAL DE INDIAS, SEVILLE
83 exp. (On film) [z-e 14]

LISTA DE LA GENTE QUE SE BA LEBANTANDO EN ESTA CIUDAD DE QUERETARO. . . . MEXICO CITY AND QUERÉTARO. JANUARY 10–FEBRUARY 10, 1705
47 p. D.S. 31 cm. [70/80m]
Documents relating to recruiting soldiers at Querétaro for service in Manila, including viceregal orders signed by the Duke of Alburquerque, and rolls of men enlisted, with information on wages paid them.

LIVINGSTON, EDWARD, 1764-1836
Letter to his Brother, Robert R. Livingston. New Orleans. May 18, 1812.
3 p. L.S. 8-25 cm. [z-z 100:19]
Enclosing bill of exchange for one thousand dollars.

LIZANA Y BEAUMONT, FRANCISCO JAVIER DE, 1750-1811
Letters to Andres Cochrane Johnstone. Mexico. 1809.
13 p. L.S. 21-30 cm. [m-m 1901]
The archbishop-viceroy requests that Cochrane transport certain funds from Veracruz to Cádiz, and also that he take two French prisoners, General Octaviano de Alvimar, and a Mr. Champantier, still awaiting passage due to refusal of Spanish captains to take them on board.

LOGBOOKS. [1779-1782?]
2 folders. 26 p. 30-31 cm. [m-m 1803]
Fragments, probably copies, of logbooks recording two voyages along the California coast in conjunction with the frigate *Favorita*. The first is evidently from the frigate *Princesa*, which sailed from San Blas to San Francisco and back, February 11–November 21, 1779, under the command of Ignacio Arteaga. The second is perhaps also from the *Princesa*, which sailed from San Blas under Esteban José Martínez, on March 6, 1782, bound for Santa Barbara and other California settlements.

LÓPEZ, FRANCISCO
Documents concerning Title of Property. Mexico. 1503-1728.
374 p. D.S. 32 cm. [70/41m]
Collection of documents (originals and contemporary copies) relating to the title to the Haciendas of Hueyapam, Rocaferro, and Isclaguacán, near Tulancingo.

LÓPEZ, GREGORIO, 1542-1596
Declar.ᵒⁿ del appocalipsi [Hospital de Huaxtepec, Oaxaca (?), Mexico. ca. 1583]
116 p. 30 cm. hhb [m-m 279]
An exposition of the Revelation of St. John the Divine, written by the hermit,

Gregorio López, at the request of the Dominican, Juan Cobo (?).

Printed in Madrid, in 1678, under the title *Tratado del Apocalypsi*, and in various editions thereafter.

LÓPEZ, PATRICIO ANTONIO

Mercurio Yndiano. Poema historico. . . . [and other manuscripts]. 1690-1754.
100 p. A.D.S. (?) 22 cm.   HHB [M-M 131]

Four manuscripts relating to the merits and needs of the Indians: 1) a 220-stanza poem on the history and contemporary status of the Zapotec Indians, by the Zapotec interpreter, López, with a signed dedication, dated at Jalapa in July, 1740; 2) letter of Fray Bernardo Inga, or Inca, January 10, 1690, concerning the genealogy of certain Spanish descendants of the Incas; 3) royal decree of March 26, 1697, providing for better treatment of the Indians; and 4) an unfinished treatise of Patricio Antonio López in defense of the Indians of New Spain and Peru.

LÓPEZ DE HARO, GONZALO, d. 1823

Diario de Navegacion que con el Aucilio Divino y proteccion, de nuestra Señora del Carmen Espera haser . . . con destino . . . de Explorar la Costa Septentrional de la California. . . . 1788.
217 p. (Photocopy) 37x48 cm.   [M-M 1771]

Diary kept by López de Haro, captain of the packetboat *San Carlos* (alias the *Filipino*), recording a voyage from San Blas northward and back, taken in company with the frigate *Princesa* and under the command of the latter's captain, Esteban José Martínez, for the purpose of exploring the northern coast of California. Entries cover the period from March 8 to October 22, 1788. With nautical tables and photographed signature of López de Haro.

Photostat from the copy in the Henry E. Huntington Library.

LÓPEZ MATOSO, ANTONIO IGNACIO, DEFENDANT

Extracto cuasi à la letra de la causa criminal formada por la sala del crimen de Mejico a . . . Antonio Ygnacio Lopez Matoso . . . la cual comenzò en 28 de febrero de 1815. Mexico City. October 15, 1810–April 4, 1816.
293 p. Ms. and printed. 21 cm.   HHB [M-M 132]

Excerpts from the proceedings conducted by the Mexico City criminal court, with Juan Antonio de la Riva and others as judges, Ramón Osés as fiscal, and Vicente Guido as rapporteur, against López Matoso, rapporteur of the civil court, on charges of conspiracy to promote civil strife, initiated by the Audiencia of Guatemala in 1813.

LÓPEZ PORTILLO, ANTONIO, b. 1730

Manifiesto legàl del d.r d.n Antonio Lopez Portillo, hecho al Rey N.ro S.or en su Real Camara de las Yndias. Sobre haver el Yll.mo S.or Arzobispo de Mexico suspendidole la colacion de una Racion. . . . [Spain? ca. 1761]
143 p. 21 cm.   HHB [M-M 133]

Copy of a legal plea submitted to the King of Spain in 1761 or shortly thereafter by the Guadalajaran, López Portillo, apparently a resident of Spain at the time, complaining that a prebend allotted him in Mexico City by royal authority had been withheld by the Archbishop of Mexico on the false pretext of López's illegitimacy, through the influence of Francisco Arén, secretary of the archdiocese; and requesting immediate bestowal of the prebend, with payment of costs and damages.

LÓPEZ RAYÓN, IGNACIO, 1773-1832
Asedio y defensa de Mexico, ò sucesos del 13 de Agosto al 15 de Setiem.ᵉ de 1847. Mexico City. 1847.
342 p. Ms. and printed. 22 cm. HHB [M-M 204]
An account of the defense of Mexico against the United States during the period from August 13 to September 15, 1847, with special attention to the battles of Padierna, Churubusco, Molino del Rey, and Chapultepec. Appended are copies of relevant documents, August 20–September 14, 1847, including the official reports of Generals Manuel Rincón and Nicolás Bravo and various communications exchanged by General Winfield Scott, General Santa Anna, and others. Includes four battle maps.

LÓPEZ URAGA, JOSÉ, 1814-1885
Correspondence and Papers. ca. 1840-1882.
3 boxes. [71/94M]
Materials relating to the career of López Uraga, diplomat and soldier, in Mexico, Guatemala, and California. A promoter of Benito Juárez in the early 1860's, he later became a loyal supporter of Maximilian and Carlota. Under the presidency of Sebastián Lerdo de Tejada he again served the Mexican government, in Guatemala, and when Porfirio Díaz became president he went into exile in San Francisco. Collection includes letters from Maximilian, Porfirio Díaz, Benito Juárez, one from Zelia Nuttall Pinart, and others. With clippings and many pictures.

LOS ANGELES, CALIFORNIA
Proclamation. Mexico City. May 23, 1835.
1 p. D.S. and printed. 30 cm. HHB [M-M 1700:30]
Circular containing the decree proclaiming Los Angeles the capital of Alta California and granting it the new status of "city."

LOS PASTORES. CHIHUAHUA, MEXICO
2 typescripts, 32 and 63 p., and copy of a letter, 2 p. 28 cm. [M-M 1761]
Text of traditional Christmas pageant, or pastorela, given in Ocampo and Pueblo Sacramento. Two typescripts of the play, one of them made in the field from the pageant director's copy, which he in turn had copied from a very old notebook in Ocampo.

LOUDON, DE WITT CLINTON
Diaries and Papers. 1846-1886.
15 items in 3 portfolios. [M-B 15]
Diaries of service in the Mexican War, June 1, 1846–February 19, 1847

(written in notebook of his father, 1836-1843, as member of the Ohio Legislature), and June 15, 1847–August 2, 1848, while serving with the First Ohio Infantry in Mexico and later as a student. Includes letters to his family during this period, one from General Wm. T. Sherman of 1886, and newspaper articles of the 1860 election campaign and the Civil War.

LOUISIANA

Documents for the History of. 1741-1783.
704 exp. (On film). [Z-F 5]
Selected materials from the Bibliothèque Nationale, the Archives du Ministère des Affaires Étrangères, and the Archives Nationales, Paris.

LOUISIANA PAPERS, 1767-1816

5 boxes and 16 vols. Many sizes, mostly 25 to 32 cm.
(Originals, copies and photostats) HHB [M-M 508]

This vast collection of papers consists of correspondence, reports, printed pamphlets, and broadsides relating to Louisiana after its occupation by Spain. The Louisiana territory comprised the Lower Mississippi River Valley, upstream to St. Louis and the Illinois country, as well as West Florida and the Texas and Arkansas area.

Much of the correspondence is that of the Spanish governors or lieutenant governors with their superiors in Spain, as well as with local commandants of remote trading posts, Indian agents, squaw-men, untutored men of the border, or Indians (speaking through interpreters). The manuscripts reflect the trilingual character of the inhabitants—Spanish, French, and English—and the international conflict for possession of the lower Mississippi Valley, i.e., French Louisiana. As New Orleans was the capital of the province, most of the letters and reports are dated there, but others came from agents and correspondents throughout the entire region.

Many of the documents through 1794 have been published in transcribed or translated form in Lawrence Kinnaird's *Spain in the Mississippi Valley, 1765-1794*, volumes 1–3 (U.S. Government Printing Office, Washington, D.C., 1949).

The papers are arranged for the most part according to administrations of the governors.

Antonio de Ulloa was the first Spanish governor of Louisiana, 1766 to 1768. His papers, which begin in 1767 and end with his expulsion by the French settlers the following year, are contained in Folders 1 to 4.

Alexander O'Reilly effectively restored Spanish authority as a special commissioner. His papers are in Folders 5 and 6, limited to the year 1770.

Luis de Unzaga y Amezaga governed from 1770–1776, with a lieutenant governor in each of the chief subdistricts: Pedro Piernas at St. Louis, Baltazar de Villiers at the Arkansas Post, and Athanase de Mézières at Natchitoches. Folders 7-30, dated 1770-1777, cover this period.

Bernardo de Gálvez, governor from 1777 to 1781, popular and successful, reconquered West Florida. Folders 31 to 84, dated 1777–1782, contain material on his administration.

Estéban Miró, acting governor and then governor, was much occupied with disturbances in West Florida, especially Indian affairs and the encroachment of American settlers. His term of office extended from 1782 to December 20, 1791. Folders 85 to 224 relate to this disturbed period.

François Hector Carondelet, or Baron de Carondelet, became governor of Louisiana and West Florida on December 31, 1791, and held office until August 5, 1797. His papers detail his vast problems with the Indians, encroaching American settlers, and matters of trade. They may be found in Folders 225 to 493.

Manuel Gayoso de Lemos, a military officer, followed Carondelet as governor. He was chiefly occupied with opposition to the advance of American settlers and with the problem of providing for defense against them while encouraging commerce with them. His term of office extended from August 5, 1797, until his death in July, 1799. Folders 494 to 527 contain material on his administration.

The second Marqués de Casa Calvo, Sebastián Calvo de la Puerta y O'Farrill, was named ad interim governor from Gayoso's death until the arrival of Manuel Juan de Salcedo in 1801, and later served as commissioner. Folders 528 to 544 and 557 to 570 relate to the period from 1799 to 1806, and contain Calvo's correspondence and papers.

Manuel Juan de Salcedo governed from his arrival in June, 1801, until Spain's flag was lowered in November, 1803. His papers for this period may be found in Folders 545 to 556.

Folders 571 and 572 contain miscellaneous material for 1810 and 1816. Folder 573 has four Alphonse Pinart transcripts from the Arzobispado de Cuba, 1772–1805.

Among the correspondents of the Spanish governors of Louisiana were such men as the following:

Moses Austin	Charles Howard
William Blount	Alexander McGillivray
Francisco Bouligny	Pedro de Nava
Pedro Chouteau	Manuel Pérez
William C. C. Claiborne	Tomás Portell
Jacques Clamorgan	Baron de Ripperdá
Teodoro de Croix	Joseph M. Robidoux
(Caballero de Croix)	Félix and Zenón Trudeau
Francisco Cruzat	Jean Louis Farault de la Villebeuvre,
Louis Charles de Blanc	Chevalier de Garrois
Jacobo DuBreuil	Gil Ybarbo
Carlos de Grand-Pré	Enrique White

The printed documents—including many rare pamphlets and broadsides—originally a part of this collection of Louisiana papers, have been removed from it and catalogued separately. There is a list of them in the "key" to this collection which is available in the Bancroft Library.

LOVATT, WILLIAM NELSON
Papers. 1853–1905.
1 carton. [z-z 154]

Journals, 1853–1868 and 1890; photograph albums; clippings; and miscellaneous items. Mainly relating to experiences in China.

LOWERY, WOODBURY, 1853-1906
   Transcripts from Spanish Archives relating to the Franciscan Missions of Florida, 1599-1705.
   388 exp. (On film) [Z-B 502]
   Microfilm of selected items from volumes 4 and 6-9 of the Lowery transcripts in the Library of Congress. With chronological card index.

LOWRIE, MRS. JOHN R
   Tombstone Inscriptions of the St. Martinville, Louisiana, Cemetery. St. Martin Parish, Louisiana. November, 1956.
   41 p. (Typescript) 28 cm. [Z-B 503]
   Tombstone inscriptions and information about the cemetery compiled by Attakapas Chapter, D.A.R.

LUDLOW, VOLNEY P   , AND OTHERS
   Family Correspondence. 1834-1874.
   21 p. A.L.S. 21-32 cm. [Z-Z 101]
   Eight letters, four of them concerning the Mexican War, 1847-1848.

[LUNA, FELIPE S.]
   Vocabulario de la lengua oputo [sic], 1876.
   58 p. 19 cm. HHB [M-M 476]
   Opata vocabulary and phrase book (copy ?); in several handwritings. The name of Luna, evidently as compiler or user, is on the cover and elsewhere.

LUYANDO Y GUERRERO, MANUEL MONRROY DE
   Mexico City and Querétaro. 1791.
   22 p. 31 cm. [M-M 1800]
   Expediente on the petition submitted to Viceroy Revilla Gigedo the Younger by the numerous creditors of Luyando, a regidor of Mexico City. Certified copy of December 2, 1791.

MACDONALD, CHARLES J., vs. CORNELIUS K. GARRISON AND CHARLES MORGAN
   Papers relating to the Lawsuit of Macdonald vs. Garrison and Morgan. Court of Common Pleas. New York. 1855-1860.
   11 folders. D.S., A.L.S. 25-33 cm. [69/44z]
   The case involved an action brought by Macdonald to recover from the defendants for services by him as their agent in Nicaragua, October, 1855–September, 1856, to secure transportation privileges from William Walker.
   Included are copies of legal documents, transcripts of testimony, papers used in evidence, correspondence relating to progress of the trial, letters from John T. Doyle, Macdonald's San Francisco attorney, and clippings concerning the trial and William Walker.

MACDONOUGH, [THOMAS], 1783-1825
   Letter to Joseph Hull, Navy Agent. Middletown, [Connecticut]. March 6, 1810.
   2 p. A.L.S. 25 cm. [Z-Z 100:65]
   Concerning work done on gunboats.

MACKENZIE, ROBERT SHELTON, 1809-1880
    Letter to Samuel Jenks Smith. Liverpool. July 8, 1835.
    4 p. A.L.S. 19 cm. [z-z 100:66]
    Thanking him for copies of the *Sunday News*.

MADISON, JAMES, 1751-1836
    Presidential Appointment of E[rasmus] Watkins as Midshipman in the United States Navy. Washington, D.C. June 6, 1815.
    2 p. D.S. 21 cm. [z-z 100:46]

MADRID, MANUEL J
    Letters. 1849-1884.
    15 p. A.L.S. 20-27 cm. [M-M 1911]
    Letters to Madrid from Jean Baptiste Jecker and others, concerning business transactions in Mexico.

MAGALLANES, JOSÉ YRINEO
    Family Papers. 1776-1901.
    57 folders. D.S., L.S., A.D.S. [M-B 20]
    Papers of José Yrineo Magallanes and his sons, Mariano, Francisco and Juan, relating to the sale, inheritance, or transfer of lands and estates mainly in Tlaltenango and Jérez, province of Zacatecas, Mexico.

MALDONADO, SIMÓN
    Asuntos Políticos de Panamá. [N.p., n.d.]
    26 f. 32 cm. HHB [M-M 361]
    Account of political developments in Panama, 1848-1868. Stresses the population increase caused by the California Gold Rush, diminution of ecclesiastical civil power, relations between foreigners and Panamanians, whites and Negroes, and the Conservative-Liberal conflict.
    Typescript available.

MANERO, VICENTE E
    Desagüe del Valle de Mexico. 1866-1877.
    1 vol. Ms. and printed. 34 cm. HHB [M-M 528]
    Scrapbook containing clippings, chiefly from newspapers, of articles by Manero and others relating to drainage projects in the Valley of Mexico, maps and charts, printed copy of statement by engineer Miguel Iglesias, 1866, printed decree of President Manuel González, and notes by Manero.

MANERO, VICENTE E
    Relación. Mexico City. October 26, 1883.
    4 p. A.D.S. 30x21 cm. HHB [M-M 352]
    Statement regarding events in Mexico during the 1861-1867 invasion by European powers, with special attention to the gallant part played by Porfirio Díaz and to the fate of Maximilian.

MANGE, JUAN MATEO, fl. 1670-1735+
History of Discoveries in America. 1720 [1721?].
215, 46 p. (Photocopies) 21-27 cm. [M-M 1721]
　　Libro I. Luz de Tiera Incognita, en la america Septentrional o Indias Orientales de la Nueva España. . . . 1720. Manuscript copy in the Biblioteca Nacional of Mexico.
　　Libro II. Noticias y descubrimientos en la Sonora p.ʳ los Jesuitas, y el Capitan Mánge. [1721?] Manuscript copy in the Lancaster-Jones papers of the Museo Nacional de Antropología, Mexico.
　　A general history of discoveries in America, with special attention to the places visited by Mange, Libro I; followed by diaries recording his own expeditions and Jesuit participation in them, Libro II. Chapters IX and XI of Libro II have been ascribed by some authorities to the Jesuit, Luis Velarde. Published in Volume X of the *Publicaciones del Archivo General de la Nación* (Mexico, 1926).

MANGIN, ANTIDE
Nociones Matematicas de Chimia, y de Medicina ó Theoria del Fuego, en que se demuestra p.ʳ las causas la luz, los colores, el sonido, la fiebre, nuestros males, et cetera.
419 p. 15 cm. HHB [M-M 136]
　　A Spanish translation of Mangin's French treatise, *Notions mathématiques de Chymie et de Médecine* . . . , Paris, 1800, on chemistry, physics, astronomy, medicine, etc. Translation or transcription was made by "J.(?) M.V." and was completed in Mexico City on January 6, 1816.

MANIAU Y TORQUEMADA, JOSÉ NICOLÁS, 1775-
Panegirico de San Juan Nepomuceno, Patron de los Estudios. . . . Mexico City. 1832.
14 p. 23 cm. HHB [M-M 137]
　　Eulogy of Saint Jan of Nepomuk, patron saint of studies, and exhortation to emulate his virtues; delivered at a ceremony held in his honor on his feast day, at the University of Mexico.

MANILA, PHILIPPINE ISLANDS. AYUNTAMIENTO
Actos de cabildo. 1770-1771.
226 p. D.S. 30 cm. [Z-P 107]
　　Records of pleas, petitions, trials, complaints, etc., heard or received by the cabildo.

MANILA, PHILIPPINE ISLANDS. AYUNTAMIENTO
Documents concerning Municipal Government of Manila. ca. 1775.
154 and 49 p. 32 cm. [Z-P 108]
　　Two documents, bound together. The first is a book of ceremonies for public occasions drawn up by the Regidor, Andrés Joseph Roxo, and dated June 30, 1775. The second, undated but after 1755, contains ordinances for governing the city of Manila, including rules for elections, procedures, and duties of officials.

MAÑOZCA, LUCAS DE
Expediente regarding Hereditary Benefits of Pedro de Chávez. Manila. December 31, 1611.
2 items (224 and 224 p.) D. S. 31 cm. [z-p 2]
Documents relating to petition of Lucas de Mañozca to participate in hereditary benefits granted by royal decree to his father-in-law, Pedro de Chávez, as grandson of Captain Gutiérrez de Badajoz.

MANSO Y ZÚÑIGA, FRANCISCO, abp. 1587-
Appointment of Marán Gallegos as Chaplain for the Chapel of the Hospital of the Virgin. Mexico City. October 14, 1628.
1 p. D.S. 31 cm. [m-m 1700:73]

MANUEL DE LOS ANGELES, FRAY
Letter. Mexico City. September 18, 1798.
2 p. A.L.S. 31 cm. [m-m 1700:79]
Petition of Carmelite monk regarding taxes, with reply by José Ignacio Pinto concerning the request, and note that the Contaduría has been informed.

MANUSCRITS RELATING TO LINGUISTIC STUDIES, CHIEFLY IN NÁHUATL. [Mexico. 1793?-1844?]
54 p. 23 cm. HHB [m-m 466]
1. Letters in Spanish, apparently models for social and business usage, possibly compiled for Indian students of Spanish. Written in Coyotepec (Cuautitlán) and Mexico City, from 1793-1814. 14 p.
2. A Spanish-Náhuatl vocabulary with a concluding note signed by Martín José, possibly the compiler, on August 12, 1812. 26 p.
3. A manuscript written in alternating Náhuatl and Spanish phrases, dealing with the Mexican calendar and the early Mexican tribes; evidently an exercise in translation. N.d. 5 p.
4. Definitions of a few Náhuatl terms. N.d. 2 p.
5. Bibliography of works on various Indian languages, ranging in date from 1555 to 1844. N.d. 2 p.
6. A Náhuatl-Spanish vocabulary. N.d. 2 p.

MAPS OF THE BATTLEFIELDS OF MONTERREY AND BUENA VISTA
2 sketch maps. 21x26 cm. HHB [m-m 506]
Accompanied by envelope addressed to H. H. Bancroft, with a note on it in his hand.

MARÍA MAGDALENA, MOTHER, d. 1636
Vida Manuscripta de la Madre Sor Maria Magd.ª Relig.ˢᵃ del Monasterio de S. Gerón.º de Mexico y florecio azia los años de 1600 y murio el de 1636. ca. 1636.
158 p. 20 cm. HHB [m-m 180]
Autobiography of Mother María Magdalena, a nun in the Conceptionist Convent of San Jerónimo, Mexico City, now famous as the convent of her successor, Sor Juana Inés de la Cruz. Includes a note recording approval of

the work by two Jesuit fathers, as well as the circumstances of the narrator's death, and a closing invocation in Latin signed by Lucas Fernández de Ortega.

MARQUINA, FÉLIX BERENGUER DE, 1738-1826
Order. Mexico City. November 26, 1801.
2 p. D.S. 31 cm. [M-M 1700:81]
Order to the magistrate of Querétaro to publish a proclamation concerning a fair to be held for the sale of cargo of the warship *Montañés*, recently arrived in Acapulco from the Philippines.

MARTIN BEHAIM'S GLOBE AND HUMBOLDT'S ESSAY ON THE OLDEST MAPS OF AMERICA. . . . NÜRNBERG. 1852.
56 p. 32 cm. HHB [M-M 24]
Translations of F. W. Ghillany's preface to his *Geschichte des Seefahrers Ritter Martin Behaim* . . . , Nürnberg, 1853, and of the essay by A. von Humboldt contained therein; includes a facsimile, with transcript, of Columbus' letter dated Seville, December 20, 1504, four engraved portraits, and facsimile signatures of Ferdinand and Isabella, Hernán Cortés, and Francisco Pizarro.

MARTÍNEZ, ESTEBAN JOSÉ, fl. 1789
Diary of the voyage which I, Ensign of the Royal Navy, Don Estevan Josef Martínez, am going to make to the port of San Lorenzo de Nuca . . . . Aboard the *Princesa*, 1789.
2 vols. (496 p., Typescript) 28 cm. [M-M 1885]
Two typed English translations, prepared by Herbert Ingram Priestley, of Martínez's journal recording his expedition of February 17–December 5, 1789, from San Blas and back, in command of the frigate *Princesa* and the packet-boat *San Carlos*. With related materials, including vocabularies of the Nootka and Sandwich Islands languages.
See "Selected items on maritime discovery . . ." (Z-E 2), Pt. II, box 3:19 for typed transcript of original manuscript, which is in the Museo Naval, Madrid.

MARTÍNEZ, MANUEL
Commission for Collection of Tribute. Mexico City. August 11, 1779.
3 p. D.S. 31 cm. HHB [M-M 1700:4]
Commission empowering Manuel Martínez, Alcalde Mayor of Teziutlán and Atempa to collect taxes from the natives for the salaries of special defenders of the Indians. Signed by Juan de la Riva Agüero, an official of the Mexico City accounting office.

MATAMOROS, MEXICO
Documents concerning Tamaulipas and Texas. 1811-1859.
68 vols. (Photocopies) [M-A 11:1]
Records from the municipal archive covering the entire scope of local affairs, together with reports on the entry of foreign vessels and their seizure, colonists from the United States, reports of the American consul, files of local news-

papers, government decrees (local and national), passports, naturalization of foreigners, appointments to office.

For the first twelve volumes there is a list of the documents, by volume, giving date, author, and subject. In addition, there is available a chronological list of all the documents, by date, subject, and volume. There is a "key" to the collection.

MATEO, LUCAS
Catecismo Hispano-Mexicano. . . . [Mexico]. August 19, 1714.
48 p. 23 cm. HHB [M-M 465]
A catechism of Christian doctrine for the instruction of children and young people, with Spanish and Náhuatl texts in parallel colums. Transcribed by Faustino Chimalpopocatl Galicia.

MATHERS, ALONZO M
Letters. Mexico. 1897-1899.
17 exp. (On film) [M-M 1867]
Letters to Ulric L. Music concerning agricultural and other economic opportunities in Chihuahua. Accompanied by explanatory notes and clippings.

MATRIMONIAL MATTERS. MEXICO. 1666-1863
25 folders. Ms. and printed. 15-31 cm. HHB [M-M 407]
Compilation on marriage and related matters. Written in Mexico City, Puebla, Hidalgo, Sonora, and other parts of Mexico. Contains the following:

1. Documents on the proposed marriage of Juan de Santander of Real del Monte, Hidalgo, and Ana Morán with a prohibition against the union, 1666.

2. Opinion on a suit for annulment of the marriage of Luis de Matienzo and María Pestaño with claim for alimony, (n.p.), May 14, 1684.

3. Brief prepared by José de Torres y Vergara for Juana Meléndez in her suit for annulment of her forced marriage to Manuel de Cifuentes, (n.d.).

4. Documents concerning the dispensation granted Montano José de Arezorena y Oisa, former alcalde mayor and present treasury agent, permitting him to marry María Gertrudis Enríquez without publication of banns, February-March, 1777.

5. File on the request of Captain José Navarro of the Spanish Regiment of Dragoons for permission to marry Ana María Sánchez of Puebla, January-February, 1778.

6. Documents on the proposed marriage of Squadron Leader Juan Ignacio Díaz of the Mexican Regiment of Dragoons to Josefa Bufanos of Puebla, April 9-22, 1778.

7. Letter from Father Francisco Moyano of the Oquitoa mission to Father Narciso Gutiérrez of the Tumacácori mission requesting the publication of marriage banns of two Indians, with reply, February 3-23, 1800.

8. Documents concerning the petition of Miguel García Rozales and Josefa Trujillo Casta, his mulatto mistress, for a dispensation permitting them to marry, with the text of the dispensation, granted by Archbishop Francisco Javier Lizana, September-November, 1805.

9. Documents regarding a dispensation for the marriage of José Vicente Sánchez and Joaquina Leiva with subsequent order from Archbishop Lizana granting it, November, 1805.

10. File concerning the exoneration from bigamy charges of Juan Nepomuceno Ximénez, 1813-1818.

11. Documents relating to a matrimonial dispensation for Vicente Guzmán and María Juana Hoyos, with a conditional grant from Archbishop-elect Bergosa y Jordán, July 26-29, 1814.

12. Documents relating to a dispensation for the marriage of Cristóbal Martínez and Micaela Resendes, 1814.

13. Petition of María Gertrudis López against Juan Manuel Domínguez, parish priest, for the support of her three illegitimate daughters, December 18, 1816.

14. File on the marriage of José Tomás and Juana María Gertrudis, May–June, 1827.

15. Letter requesting publication of banns for the marriage of Bernardo Vélez to Juana Isidra Ramírez, with later notation of her father's objections, March–April, 1829.

16. File on the marriage of Valentín Fuentes and María Juana Eufracia of Tlaltizapán, April 7-22, 1829.

17. File on the marriage of José de Luz Peralta and María Concepción Ignacio of Tlaltizapán, June 6-13, 1829.

18. Letter from Gabriel de Sautier to Buenaventura Pérez regarding an intended marriage, June 29, 1838.

19. Record of measures to secure a dispensation for the marriage of Gregorio Figueroa and Susana Castro of Sonora, 1862-1863.

20. Licenses issued by Vicar General José Osorio de Córdova for permission for marriage of Diego de Herrera, Pachuca merchant, and Isabel de Vargas, of Puebla, December 1, 1676.

21. File on the proposed marriage of Miguel López and Teresa de la Cruz, residents of Pachuca, February 25–March 3, 1677.

22. File on the proposed marriage of Mateo de la Cruz and Luisa Benítez, residents of Pachuca, July 27–August 13, 1678.

23. File on the proposed marriage of Domingo de Garay and Inés de Vargas of Pachuca, February 19-23, 1682.

24. License from Archbishop Francisco de Aguiar authorizing partial dispensation of banns for the marriage of Pedro de Inclán and María de la Cruz, residents of Pachuca, May 21, 1684.

25. Document written by vicar Juan de Molina Betancurt authorizing the marriage of Pedro González and Juana de Quijosa, residents of Pachuca, November 19, 1684.

MATTHEWS FAMILY CORRESPONDENCE
Letters to Robert L. Matthews. 1865, 1868.
8 p. A.L.S. (Photocopy) 25 cm. [z-z 131]
From his brother, Samuel, and from his nephew, Robert J(?) W., concerning the family during and after the Civil War.

MATZAHUA MANUSCRIPTS. [MEXICO. N.d.]
50 p. 23 cm.   HHB   [M-M 473]
A group of manuscripts, largely in the Mazahua language, an Otomí dialect, with some passages in Spanish and Latin. It includes two sermons, a Mazahua catechism with Spanish headings, a Spanish-Mazahua vocabulary with the Mazahua columns only partially filled, and several fragments of a religious nature.

MAXIMILIAN, FERNANDO, EMPEROR OF MEXICO, 1832-1867
Contract. Cuernavaca, Mexico. January 28, 1866.
4 p. D.S. 39 cm.   [M-M 1743]
Contract signed by the Emperor Maximilian on the basis of advice received from his Minister of Development, authorizing Jorge L. Hammeken to undertake a canalization project in the Valley of Mexico, subject to specified conditions.

MAXIMILIAN, FERNANDO, EMPEROR OF MEXICO, 1832-1867
Documents and Letters relating to the Empire of. 1863-1866.
2 vols. 22 p. D.S. and photocopies. 18-28 cm.   [M-M 1806]
Volume I is a diploma, signed by Maximilian and Empress Carlota, awarding the Cross of the Imperial Order of San Carlos to Doña Concepción Troncoso de Duarte. Mexico City, December 1, 1865.

Volume II contains photocopies of a draft of a constitution for the empire, in the handwriting of the Empress, 1863; letters to Madame Dolores Quesada de Almonte (?) from the Baron de Pont and from Maximilian, 1863; and various official appointments, signed by Maximilian, 1864-1866.

MAYER, BRANTZ, 1809-1879, comp.
Manuscritos Mexicanos. [1715-1842]
30 numbered items. 36 cm.   HHB   [M-M 281]
Transcripts, made chiefly in 1850 from archives in Mexico, of various documents relating to California, Texas, Louisiana, Canada, and Mexico, largely in the handwriting of Robert Greenhow, although a portion is in that of his wife, Rose. Contains table of contents.

Documents 1-8 relate to the Provincias Internas, 1786-1812, including letters from the Spanish Court to Viceroys of New Spain; instructions from José de Gálvez to Ugarte y Loyola; and correspondence referring to relations with the United States.

Nos. 9 and 10 give a resume of the history of New Spain from the time of Cortés to 1821, with a list of viceroys and governors.

Nos. 11, 14-18a, and 22 relate to the missions of New Spain, 1716-1842. They consist of reports drawn up by Revilla Gigedo the Younger and Father Palóu and Mangino, orders for division of the California mission field between Franciscans and Dominicans, and Domingo Ramón's account of his 1716 expedition to Texas for the encouragement of missions.

Nos. 12, 12a, and 13 deal with exploration of the northwest coast of America, i.e., accounts of the 1774 Pérez voyage and of the 1775 Hezeta-Bodega-Ayala expedition (first portion), with Bodega's account of the 1779 Arteaga-Bodega expedition—from which the final paragraphs are omitted.

Nos. 19-21 and 23-30 bear upon Hispano-Franco-Anglo-American disputes in the New World, and the disputed territories, 1689-1824, i.e.: diaries of Domingo Ramón and Juan Antonio de la Peña on the 1716 and 1720-1722 expeditions to Texas; diary on Alonso de León's 1689 expedition to Espíritu Santo Bay; excerpts from de La Harpe's diary on journeys of St. Denis, with related documents; letters from Athanase de Mézières and Ripperdá to Teodoro de Croix, and from Claiborne to Secretary of State Madison; and miscellaneous reports and summaries involving conflicting colonial claims.

MAZATEVE ALVARADO FAMILY GENEALOGY. CUATRO VILLAS DE LA COSTA, SPAIN. 1586-1616

74 p. 31 cm. HHB [M-M 425]

Copy of file establishing the legitimacy and the Christian and noble lineage of the brothers Pedro, Luis and José de Mazateve Alvarado, natives of the district of Cuatro Villas de la Costa, located in present-day Santander. Includes a colored coat-of-arms and the petition of Pedro for genealogical investigations, September 27, 1586, and that of his brothers, June 18, 1615, for application of the 1586 records to their own testimony of witnesses, and pertinent orders.

MEDRANO Y PEÑALOZA, MANUEL

Alegoria sobre los Meteoros, ó Vexamen con que concluyó su curso el P.ᵉ D.ⁿ Manuel Medrano y Peñaloza en el R.¹ Colegio de Guanaxuato. Guanajuato, Mexico. June 17, 1782.

64 p. 21 cm. HHB [M-M 138]

Address delivered by Father Medrano at the close of his course in the Colegio. Consists of the customary satirical allegory in which each student is assigned a part, a list of students in order of scholastic merit, and verses of eulogy and farewell.

MEJÍA, IGNACIO, 1813-1906

Letters to René Bonnin. New York and Mexico. 1864-1868.

17 letters (61 p.) A.L.S. 13-21 cm. [M-M 1904]

Concern the fall of Oaxaca and Chihuahua to the French, Mejía's meeting with Benito Juárez, the recapture of Chihuahua, and Mejía's appointment as Minister of War.

MEMOIRE SUR LA LOUISIANN. APRIL 19, 1717

15 p. 33 cm. [Z-B 500]

A report on trade and organization of the colony, prepared during the liquidation of the monopoly of Antoine Crozat and the formation of La Compagnie d'Occident.

MEMORANDUM CONCERNING HEIRS AND ESTATE OF ASA RICKETSON, DECEASED. [1849?]

2 p. 32 cm. [Z-Z 100:23]

Endorsed "Page v. E. B. Smith &c."

MEMORIAS DE MEXICO. VARIAS PIEZAS DEL ORDEN REAL. MEMORIAS PIADOSAS DE LA NACION INDIANA. . . .
3 vols. in one, 32 cm. HHB [M-M 240]

In this copy, Part I is called "Varias piezas del Orden Real," Part II, "Memorias de Mexico," and Part III, "Memorias Piadosas de la Nacion Indiana."

Part I contains Sigüenza y Góngora's treatise on princely virtues (1680), Motolinía's story of three Tlaxcalan child martyrs (1791), and Father Zárate Salmerón's essay on the history of New Mexico and other regions, 1538-1626, "Relación de todas las cosas que en el Nuevo Megico se han visto," followed by a letter (1778) from Father Vélez de Escalante to Morfi on the same subject.

Part II, ca. 1654 to 1764, consists of reports and papers of Baltasar de Medina, Andrés de Rivas, Isidro Sariñana, Julián Gutiérrez Dávila, and others, relating primarily to the work of various religious orders in New Spain and the Philippines, and to drainage of the Mexico City area, with two maps of the City, one in color, ca. 1618.

Part III deals with the Indians of New Spain, particularly from the religious standpoint, gives biographies of some outstanding Indians and accounts of miraculous apparitions seen by natives, such as the Virgin of Guadalupe. Compiled in 1782 by José Díaz de la Vega, a Franciscan.

MEMORIAS PARA LA HISTORIA DE LA PROVINCIA DE SINALOA. [MEXICO. N.d.]
992 p. 30 cm. HHB [M-M 227]

An account of the Jesuit missions in Sinaloa and neighboring localities, covering the period 1593-1629 and including information on the early history of the region, its inhabitants and its natural characteristics, and its conquest and pacification under Spanish rule. Composed chiefly of an introduction, transcripts or summaries from annual reports addressed to the Jesuit Provincial or from letters of Jesuit missionaries such as Martín Pérez, Juan Bautista Velasco, Nicolás de Arnaya, and others, and a copy of Martín Duarte's "Testimonio Jurídico" (1600) on the Avila-Santarén expedition.

MEMORIAS SOBRE LIMITES TERRITORIALES CON RESPECTO Á LA AUTORIDAD ECCLESIASTICA, ENTRE CHIAPAS Y YUCATAN [Y GUATEMALA], POR LO QUE TOCA À TABASCO. . . . MEXICO. 1681-1767.
138 p. 30-31 cm. HHB [M-M 434]

Documents relating primarily to problems of religious jurisdiction, affecting different monastic orders as well as the Sees of Chiapas, Yucatan, and Guatemala, in the geographical province of Tabasco. There are six main items:

1. Copies of petitions, viceregal orders, opinions of the Fiscal, letters, certifications, etc., relating to the conversion of the Indian pueblo of Tacotalpa, hitherto served by Dominican missionaries, into a Spanish *villa* with an ecclesiastical curate. Written by Spanish and native civil officials and by Dominican friars in Tacotalpa and other parts of Tabasco or in Mexico City. Includes Spanish translations of Indian documents. Mexico, 1681-1682. 27 p.

2. Copies of petitions, decrees, certifications, etc., from Tabasco and Mexico

City, relating to the appointment of Antonio de Arcos as curate for the Spaniards of Villahermosa, Tacotalpa, and Jalapa, and the use of the Indians' church and equipment for his services. Mexico, 1683-1685. 20 p.

3. Copies of orders, petitions, certifications, etc., from Mérida in Yucatan, Tacotalpa, and Jalapa, which relate to the appointment of Antonio de Arcos by the episcopal authorities of Yucatan, the difficulty of finding a church for him, and the protests of Dominicans, notably Fray Martín de Torquemada, and of the Indian communities affected. Mexico, 1682-1685. 60 p.

4. Concluding portion of a document signed by Antonio de Zuazua y Múxica, setting forth municipal regulations for Chiapas. Mistakenly bound in this volume instead of the volume listed under "García, Pedro Marcelino" (M-M 435, #6). Chiapas, January 12, 1741. 3 p.

5. Report from Manuel Francisco Pimentel, Guardian of the Recollect Monastery in Ciudad Real, Chiapas, addressed to the Franciscan Commissioner General, defending the rights of friars of his order in the province of Tabasco, particularly in regard to collection of alms. Ciudad Real, Chiapas, n.d. 17 p. A.D.S.

6. Certified copy of the decision of the Franciscan Commissioner General, Manuel de Nájera, and other members of his tribunal awarding jurisdiction over the geographical province of Tabasco to the monastic Provincia del Nombre de Jesús of Guatemala, in the dispute between the latter and the Provincia de San Joseph of Yucatan. Mexico City, February 3, 1767. 2 p.

MERCEDES, POSESIONES, Y TITULOS DE AMOLADERAS Y ALBERCAS. ... MEXICO. 1610-1657
302 p. 30 cm. [M-M 1709]

Collection of land grants, deeds of purchase and sale, decrees, petitions, declarations, appointments, certifications, and other documents relating to distribution and ownership of lands in the vicinity of the Amoladeras and Albercas valleys, situated in or near the present State of Querétaro. Deals primarily with possessions of the Galván family and those of the Jesuit college in Tepozotlán. Quotes royal decrees of 1591 as background documents, and contains viceregal grants of Luis Velasco the Younger, the Marqués de Guadalcázar, and the Conde de Salvatierra; with list of early grants prefixed.

METODO FACIL Y BREVE PARA APRENDER EL YDIOMA MEXICANO. [MEXICO. N.d.]
18 p. 22 cm. HHB [M-M 139]

A primer for Spanish students of the Aztec language in Mexico, explaining pronunciation, parts of speech, conjugation of verbs, and other fundamental points.

MÉTODO QUE SE OBSERVA CONSTANTEMENTE EN MÉXICO, ACAPULCO Y MANILA PARA RECIBIR Y DESPACHAR TODOS LOS AÑOS EL GALEON DE FILIPINAS. CÁDIZ, SPAIN. 1763
2 vols. 21 cm. and 29 cm. HHB [M-M 140-140A]

Compilation of data on procedure for the annual commerce carried on between Mexico and the Philippines. Contains an explanatory note from the Acapulco accounting headquarters (Real Caja), models of viceregal orders for the reception and dispatch of expeditions, copies of petitions to the viceroy for enforcement of procedural requisites, a copy of a royal decree, April 8, 1734, on Mexico-Philippine trade, and pertinent excerpts from the New Laws of the Indies.

MEXÍA, JOSÉ ANTONIO, et al. d. 1839
Mexía Family Papers. 1694-1951.
5 boxes, 2 cartons, portfolios. [M-B 1]
Extensive collection of papers representing three generations of the Mexía family: José Antonio Mexía, a Cuban who came to Mexico in 1823, became a general, and was eventually captured and shot by Santa Anna's forces in 1839; Enrique Guillermo Antonio Mexía, 1829-1896, son of José Antonio, who fought in the war against the United States, on the liberal side in the War of the Reform, 1857-1860, against the French invasion under Maximilian, and for Benito Juárez, as well as occupying himself with business and politics in his later years; and finally Ynez, daughter of Enrique, who became an eminent botanist, collecting specimens and research materials in Mexico, Central and South America, and Alaska for the University of California and the Smithsonian Institution.

The Mexía Collection is a cross section of Mexican life, business, politics, and relations with the United States for a period of more than a century, and includes correspondence with many high level officials.

MEXÍA, YNÉS, 1870-1938
Correspondence and Papers. 1910-1938.
2 cartons, 11 boxes, 1 volume. [68/130M]
Papers of Ynés Mexía, the granddaughter of José Antonio Mexía, and a noted woman botanist, explorer, and lecturer. They include letters to and from Mrs. Mexía; biographical data on the Mexía family; and materials, assembled by Mrs. H. P. Bracelin, concerning and describing the Mexía botanical collections from South America and Mexico.

MEXICAN COMPANY, THE
The Deed of Constitution of.... London. 1825.
1 vol. D.S. 44 cm. [67/63M]
A British company, capitalized at one million pounds, to work mines in Mexico and adjacent countries. Gives signatures of shareholders.

MEXICO. 1531-1805
10 folders. (Photocopies) [M-A 4:2]
Miscellaneous documents relating chiefly to northern Mexico in the 18th century, but containing one on Juan Alonso de Sosa, treasurer of Mexico, 1531, and another on Peru, 1617. From the Biblioteca Nacional, Mexico. There is a "key" to the collection.

MEXICO
> Complete List of Presidents, from Victoria to Juárez. 1824-1867. . . . [ca. 1876]
> *20 p. 32 cm.*   HHB   [M-M 373]
>
> List of Mexican chiefs of state during the period 1824-1867, allegedly based on Manuel Rivera's history of Jalapa, but probably compiled from Volume II of his work on *Los Gobernantes de México,* Mexico City, 1873. Gives dates of each president's term and, in some cases, additional data regarding his political career.

MEXICO
> Documents for the History of.
> *1 box, and 37 exp. on film.*   [M-R 6]
>
> Typescripts of interviews and other materials, assembled about 1918, concerning various aspects of republican Mexico, including local government, revenues, public health, mining, foreign trade, race, labor, and land reform; and a microfilmed list of documents relating to Cortés, land titles, and the Inquisition, 1533-1652.

MEXICO
> Miscellany. 1644-1816.
> *6 folders. 22-32 cm.*   HHB   [M-M 395]
>
> An order from Bartolomé Rey y Alarcón and Juan de Aranda requesting Captain Rivera y Alarcón to account for a consignment of arms delivered to him in 1635, with his reply and receipt (3 p.), Mexico City, May 10-June 22, 1644; letter (2 p.) to the Assistant Deputy Superintendent General of the Royal Treasury sending requested documents and signed by Felipe de Hierro and José de la Riva, officials of the General Directive Bureau of Tobacco, Mexico City, August 6, 1787; a balance sheet (5 p.) on the sale of merchandise contracted for in Jalapa, May 23–June 6, 1786, and signed by Manuel Benito de Barros and Manuel José Herrera, Mexico City, January 15, 1788, and a statement of accounts signed by Angel María Merelo, covering his stewardship during May–June, 1790; copies of documents (17 p.) relating to the genealogy and personal qualifications of Ignacio de la Barrera y Andonaegui, royal notary, and his wife, María Francisca Troncoso, Mexico City, 1802; an eight-page file regarding request for sick leave by Don Francisco Grau, a guard employed by the Tobacco Revenue Office, Orizaba, February 9-10, 1810; a fragment of 3 p. from a collection of essays on epistolary style, edited by José del Valle, Guatemala City, June 1, 1816.

MEXICO
> Miscellany. [ca. 1826-1851]
> *7 folders. L. S., D. S., A.L.S. 22-32 cm.*   HHB   [M-M 497]
>
> Letters and documents relating to Mexico, probably from the collection of autographs compiled by William Henry Knight.
>
> 1. Esteva, José Ignacio. Signed letter (n.p., n.d.) from the Mexican Minister of Finance to David Porter, United States Secretary of the Navy, asking for

a boat and a guard to escort the writer to a French frigate. 1 p.

2. Facio, José Antonio. Mexico, March 31, 1830. L. S. from the Mexican Minister of War and Marine Affairs to Francisco Pizarro Martínez in New Orleans, concerning Pizarro's forthcoming visit to Veracruz, and private matters. 2 p.

3. Castillo [y Lanzas], Joaquín María de, 1781-1878. Philadelphia, December 10, 1835. Presents the compliments of the Mexican Chargé d'Affaires in the United States to James H. Caustin [Causten], requesting transmittal of an enclosure [not present] to the President of the United States. 1 p.

4. Passport. Veracruz, November 16, 1842. D. S. Issued to Mr. Cochran, an Englishman, for passage to New York on the American packetboat, *Ann Louisa*, signed by José de Emparán, later an official of the Benito Juárez administration. 2 p.

5. Cadena, Elías (?). San Buenaventura, Mexico, August 12, 1846. L. S. Letter to Colonel Cristóbal Ramírez, requesting information concerning the movements of General Taylor's troops. 2 p.

6. Landero, José Juan. Veracruz, October 8, 1846. D. S. Request for duplicate of a report of a mutiny in the fortress [San Juan de Ulúa?]. 1 p.

7. Javero, José María. April 7, 1851. A.L.S. Letter to "Minister" Manuel Carvallo, regarding financial matters. 2 p.

MEXICO

Miscellany. Mexico. 1822-1892(?)

8 folders. 15-48 cm. HHB [M-M 396]

Contains the following:

1. A document of 1 p. addressed to Rafael Pérez Maldonado, minister of finance, May 10, 1822, regarding a voluntary gift and loan fund.

2. Letter of 1 p. to Fray Pablo Vivar, February 1, 1823.

3. File, 1829-1830, concerning compensation for emancipation of two slaves, in accordance with a national decree of 1829. 5 p.

4. Copies of two letters from the Bishop of Durango, January, 1834, 8 p., regarding appointment of curates and suppression of some ecclesiastical posts.

5. Copy of an item from *La Voz de México*, 1 p., September 30, 1871, announcing the betrothal of Gisela to Prince Salvador de Iturbide.

6. Copies of weekly newspaper, *El Pinolillo*, Vol. 1, Nos. 1-7, April 11–June 12, 1880.

7. Biographical notes, 1892 (8 p.), on Cecilio Agustín Robelo, Mexican statesman descended from Moctezuma, active in the development of the state of Morelos; record of expenditures, 15 p., apparently for a trip by cart in Mexico, April 3(?)–May 26 (n.p., n.d.); summary report, 2 p., on the state of Oaxaca (n.p., n.d.).

MEXICO

Resources and Development. 1890(?)-1892.

23 folders in portfolio. D.S. and printed. Mostly 33 cm. HHB [M-M 386]

Compiled for H. H. Bancroft, largely under the auspices of the Mexican

Government, in preparation for his *Resources and Development of Mexico* (San Francisco, 1893). The contents relate primarily to economic and agricultural progress, construction work, and educational institutions in Mexico. There is a questionnaire by David F. Watkins seeking information on the above; reports on conditions in Michoacán, Sinaloa, Guerrero, Morelos, Veracruz, Durango, and Yucatan; a report on Mexican rivers; and the plan of a hospital in Nuevo León.

MEXICO. ARCHIVO GENERAL DE LA NACIÓN
Documentos históricos manuscritos que existen en este Archivo General. [Mexico City. 1877]
83 p. 32 cm.   HHB [M-M 393]
A descriptive list of manuscripts in the Mexican National Archives, section on "History," Vols. 1-162, prepared at Bancroft's request. Includes a covering note, Sonoma, December 28, 1877, initialed by Mariano Guadalupe Vallejo.

MEXICO (ECCLESIASTICAL PROVINCE) COUNCIL, 1771
Cathecismo echo por el S.^{to} Conc.° Mexicano 4.° provinc.[1] Mexico City. 1771.
204 p. D.S. 30 cm.   HHB [M-M 68]
The Third Mexican Provincial Council, 1585, enacted a code of Church discipline, framed a new catechism, and adopted regulations for contacts between civil and ecclesiastical powers; revised and approved by the Fourth Council, 1771.

MEXICO (ECCLESIASTICAL PROVINCE) COUNCIL, 1771
Cathecismo y suma de la Doctrina Christiana con declaracion de ella, ordenado y aprobado por el III Concilio Provincial Mexicano. . . . Revisto, aprobado y dado á luz por el IV Concilio. . . . Mexico City. [N. d.]
314 p. 23 cm.   HHB [M-M 59]
A copy of doctrinal material which was approved by the Third Mexican Provincial Council, 1585, and revised and published by the Fourth Council, 1771. From the Fourth Council's printed edition—Biblioteca Mexicana del Lic. Josef de Jáuregui, Mexico City. [N. d.]

MEXICO (ECCLESIASTICAL PROVINCE) COUNCIL, 1771
Documentos relativos al Cuarto Concilio Provincial Mexicano.
2 vols. 30 cm.   HHB [M-M 69-70]
Call of the Council by the king, other decrees and notices of convocation, journal of its sessions from January 13 through November 9, 1771, reports and analyses of the meetings by the viceregal proxy, Antonio Joaquín de Rivadeneira, and the Peruvian fiscal, Pedro de Piña y Mazo. See also Fourth Mexican Provincial Council, *Actas* (M-M 1732).

MEXICO. JUNTA DE FOMENTO Y ADMINISTRACIÓN DE MINERÍA
Libro 3.° de Actas de la Junta de Minería desde 2 de Abril de 1846 hasta 30 de Junio de 1847. 1846-1847.
336 p. 34 cm.   HHB [M-M 141]
Certified copy of minutes of the Mexican board for the administration of

mining, covering the period above indicated; concerned chiefly with financial matters, including the budget of the Colegio de Minería.

MEXICO. MINISTRY OF FOREIGN RELATIONS
Miscellaneous Documents. 1764-1921.
2 boxes. (Typescripts and originals) D.S., L.S., A.L.S. [M-A 26]

A very miscellaneous collection, from tax matters (the Media Anata, 1764-1766), to events of Mexican history throughout the 19th century, especially the independence period, the Benito Juárez-Maximilian contretemps, and more recent events.

There is a "key" to the collection.

MEXICO, REPUBLIC
German Diplomatic Service in. 1822-1941.
8 boxes, 1 portfolio. (Ms. and printed) [M-B 12]

Box 1: Correspondence and papers of Mexican officials with the consuls in Mexico City of Frankfurt, Bremen, and various German towns. Box 2: Outgoing correspondence of Etienne Benecke, consul of Prussia and later of Germany, 1850-1876, and other papers, 1838-1871, mainly certificates of appointments and decorations. Box 3: Incoming correspondence for Etienne Benecke, 1850-1876. Box 4: Papers of the German consulate in Mexico City, 1893-1906, especially concerning F. C. Rieloff's appointment as consul in 1906; and also from the consulates in Oaxaca, Puebla, Zacatecas, and Guadalajara. Box 5: Outgoing correspondence of German ministers in Mexico, 1846-1918, namely, F. Seiffart, 1846-1850; E. K. H. Richthofen, 1851-1856; E. Wagner, 1859-1862; A. von Magnus, 1866-1867; K. von Schlözer, 1869-1871; E. von Winckler, 1893-1895; H. von Wangenheim, 1904-1905; P. von Hintze, 1912; H. von Eckhardt, 1917-1918. Boxes 6-7: Letters to the German Legation in Mexico, 1851-1941, also miscellaneous papers and clippings, 1861-1918. Box 8: Papers relating to liquidation of the debts of Maximilian's Empire, 1867-1868, including lists of individuals, accounts, repatriation of Belgian and other subjects.

The portfolio contains passports, appointment papers, models of consular flags and other insignia, some in color, and instructions for officials in the foreign service, ca. 1840-1868.

MEXICO. SECRETARÍA DE LA DEFENSA NACIONAL 1706-1857
1 carton, 1 box, 10 vols. (Typescripts and photocopies) [M-A 17]

Documents relating to the filibustering activities of Raousset-Boulbon (1852-1853); Henry A. Crabb (1857); defense of Veracruz and the Gulf Coast against English attack (18th century); administrative and foreign affairs of Upper California, 1830-1846. Many of these documents are described in Bolton's *Guide* (1913), at which time they were in the Secretaría de Guerra y Marina of the Archivo General de la Nación. Now they are deposited in the Archivo Histórico Militar de México. See the published *Guía* (Mexico, 1948). There is a "key" to the collection in the Bancroft Library.

MEXICO. UNIVERSIDAD NACIONAL
Acto Literario con que la R.¹ y Pontificia Universidad de Mexico recibio ã su Ex.ᵐᵒ Vice-Patrono el Señor Don José Manuel de Iturrigarai . . . Virrey . . . de esta Nueba España . . . el dia 24 de Julio de 1803.
64 p. 37 cm.   HHB [M-M 237]
A record of the ceremonial function held under the auspices of the University of Mexico on July 24, 1803, in honor of the first visit paid the University by Viceroy Iturrigaray and his wife, Doña María Inés Jáuregui y Aróstegui. Contains a description of the arrangements for the ceremony, the Latin texts and Spanish translations of the dedicatory tribute to Iturrigaray, an outline of the debate on the main agenda topic, i.e., monarchical government, the laudatory orations of González Lastiri, monitor of the debate, and Chairman Juan Nicolás de Larraguiti, and a Spanish ode honoring Doña María Inés.

Most of this material was printed in a publication of the Instituto de Investigaciones Estéticas of the University of Mexico in 1943. It describes the present item as the original report.

Entered by Bancroft under "Yturrigarai, J. M. Acta Literario."

MEXICO. VICEROYALTY
Acuerdos de la Junta Superior de Real Hacienda de Nueva España. Archivo de Conde del Valle. Libro 7.º Mexico City. 1794.
282 p. 31 cm.   HHB [M-M 284]
A record of the decisions taken by the Junta Superior de Real Hacienda, January 3–December 19, 1794, on matters relating to royal revenue and expenditures in various parts of New Spain. The approximately weekly reports on these decisions include the text of relevant background documents. Each report is signed and certified by Félix Sandoval, operating under the direction of the Conde del Valle [de Orizaba], with the exception of the records for June 14–July 2, which bear the signature of Lic. Miguel Domínguez as certifier.

MEXICO. VICEROYALTY
Decretos de Parte. Decisiones del Virey en México en pleitos de particulares. January 19, 1801–August 14, 1811.
412 p. 31 cm.   HHB [M-M 270]
A collection of petitions, viceregal decrees, *fiscal's* statements, and related documents from Mexico, and a few from the Philippines, recording *ex parte* proceedings in cases which were brought before the Viceroy of New Spain during the period 1801-1811 and which involved a wide variety of subjects, such as taxation and tithes, land ownership and exploitation, conduct of public officials, ecclesiastical expenses, treatment of Indians, construction projects, execution of wills and contracts, et cetera.

MEXICO. VICEROYALTY
Documents relating to the Administration of Royal Monopolies. Mexico. July 16–November 26, 1643.
82 p. 31 cm.   HHB [M-M 277]
A collection of documents relating to the administration of royal monopolies,

particularly playing cards, in Guatemala and Mexico. Consists chiefly of viceregal orders issued in Mexico City by the Conde de Salvatierra, or royal decrees promulgated through the Viceroy, to confirm the decisions of Maestre de Campo Antonio Urrutia de Vergara regarding the administration of such monopolies. First portion missing.

MEXICO. VICEROYALTY
Instructions of the Viceroy, Duke of Linares, and Others, to their Successors. 1716-1797.
230 p. 21 cm. HHB [M-M 128]
Reports and instructions prepared by retiring viceroys for their successors, with related documents: report of Fernando de Alencastre, Duke of Linares, to his successor, Baltasar de Zúñiga, Marquis of Valero, 1716; letters of the archbishop-viceroy, Juan Antonio de Vizarrón Eguiarreta, to the king, on his services, 1740; instructions of Viceroy Agustín de Ahumada, Marquis of las Amarillas, 1760, given by his secretary; instruction of Viceroy Manuel Antonio Flores, 1789; and report of Miguel de la Grúa Talamanca y Branciforte, Marquis of Branciforte, to his successor, 1797.

MEXICO. VICEROYALTY
Providencias sobre Azogues. 1670-1673.
88 p. 32 cm. HHB [M-M 294]
Copies of viceregal orders, reports, etc., relating to the Government monopoly of quicksilver in New Spain, and primarily to the assignment of specified amounts of quicksilver to individual petitioners.

MEXICO. VICEROYALTY
Sobre fuga de siete religiosos coristas y un laico del Convento de la Merced de esta Capital. April 24, 1792–November 13, 1800.
250 p. D.S. 32 cm. HHB [M-M 293]
A collection of letters, viceregal orders, depositions, petitions, reports and related documents concerning the flight of seven Mercedarian novices and one lay brother from their monastery to others in Mexico City, their capture and punishment, the resultant inspection of the Mercedarian monastery, and the proceedings against Jerónimo Pulgar, an attorney of the Real Audiencia, for his presentation of the fugitives' case. With letters from Knight Commander Francisco Dávila to Pulgar, Mexico City and Guadalajara, 1792-1800, submitted by the latter to attest his services to the Mercedarian Order.

MEXICO. VICEROYALTY
Testimonio de la causa de infidencia formada contra Ignacio Adalid y socios. Mexico. 1813-1815.
3 vols. (339, 324, 101 p.) 24 cm. HHB [M-M 1-3]
Proceedings of the viceroyalty against alleged members of the insurgent Guadalupe band, in 13 sections (*cuadernos*), as follows: vol. I, sections 1-5, relating to the case against Manuel Cortazar, Ignacio Adalid, Juan Vargas Machuca, and others; vols. II and III, sections 6-13, relating primarily to Adalid.

MEXICO. VICEROYALTY
Yndize comprehensibo de todos los Goviernos corregimientos y Alcaldías mayores que contiene la Governacion del virreynato de Mexico.... 177-.
107 exp. (On film) [69/83M]
Listing and description of government offices in New Spain, Guatemala, Peru, and Chile. Microfilm of original in the New York Public Library.

MEXICO (VICEROYALTY), REAL HACIENDA
Record Book of the Royal Treasury in Mexico City. Mexico City. 1658-1659, 1807.
360 p. D.S. 40-52 cm. [M-M 1886]
Account book of the Royal Treasury, arranged according to types of income or outgo, such as ecclesiastical tithes, royal fifths, sales taxes, fees for episcopal appointments, revenue from monopolies, donations and fines; payments of salaries, payments to conquistadors, quicksilver payments, interest to monasteries, military and naval expenses, payments for papal bulls, and other items. Relates to New Spain and the Philippines. Includes title page and index of a Treasury account book, 1807, and an undated sheet referring to the Mexico City mint, bearing the royal coat of arms.

MEXICO. VICEROYALTY. TRIBUNAL Y REAL AUDIENCIA DE CUENTAS
Certification de las mercedes, limosnas, consignaciones de missiones, pensiones, y ayudas de costa, que estan situadas y se pagan annualmente de la R.¹ Haz.ª de todas las cajas de la jurisd.ⁿ del Virreynato de Nueva España. Mexico City. 1758-1763.
214 p. D.S. 29 cm. HHB [M-M 399]
Detailed statement of the gifts, alms, mission allotments, pensions, and other expenditures paid out annually by the royal treasury in New Spain, the Philippines, and various Pacific islands; certified in Mexico City on December 22, 1763.
Preceded by a viceregal order of November 23, 1758, calling for preparation of the statement in compliance with Chapter XIV of certain royal instructions dated May 1, 1758, and by preliminary documents of the responsible tribunal; followed by a table summing up the annual expenses of branch treasuries in various parts of New Spain.

MEXICO CITY. AYUNTAMIENTO
Libro de Cabildo. Copia de la mayor parte, y más ... importante y util del libro primero q.ᵉ comienza en ocho de Marzo de 1524 y finaliza en 10 de Junio de 1529, en que se asentaron todos los cabildos y juntas ... en dicho tiempo. [Mexico City. March 8, 1524–June 7, 1529]
260 p. 32 cm. HHB [M-M 127]
Copy of the records of municipal councils in Mexico City, here designated as "Temextitan" and "Tenustitan," corruptions of "Tenochtitlán," extending only through June 7, 1529; with notes at end describing the volume copied and its preservation by Carlos de Sigüenza y Góngora from the 1692 conflagration and riot.

Substantially identical in context with item 2 of José Fernando Ramírez..., "Monumentos Históricos y Políticos de la Administración Colonial" (M-M 158).

MEXICO CITY. AYUNTAMIENTO
Representacion umilde que hace la ymperial novilisima y muy leal ciudad de Mexico en favor de sus naturales a su amado soberano el Señor Don Carlos 3.º ... Mexico City. May 2, 1771.
96 p. 22 cm. HHB [M-M 154]
Copy of a petition from the Municipal Council of Mexico City to Charles III of Spain, requesting him to ignore a statement reputedly submitted to him on the unfitness of American-born Spaniards for high posts in the Indies; and arguing that, on the contrary, public posts in the Indies should be reserved almost exclusively for American Spaniards.

MEXICO CITY. AYUNTAMIENTO
Representacion umilde que hace la ymperial novilisima y mui leal ciudad de Mexico, en favor de sus naturales, a su amado soberano el Señor Don Carlos 3.º ... Mexico City. May 2, 1771.
165 p. 21 cm. HHB [M-M 155]
Substantially identical in title and context with M-M 154.

MEXICO (CITY) AYUNTAMIENTO. RAMO ARQUITECTOS
Miscellaneous Papers. ca. 1559-1855.
2 reels. (On film) [M-M 1909]
Materials relating to appointments, licensing, examinations, and salaries of architects; repairs on buildings damaged by earthquakes and floods; construction and maintenance of the Church of San Hipólito; programs for public buildings and for the demolition and repair of ruined buildings.
Filmed from originals in the Municipal Archives of Mexico City.

MEXICO CITY. CABILDO
Autos formados á pedim.to de esta nobilissima ciu.d para [que] se ampare en la posezion de [sus] ejidos. Y la dio el S.r D. Pedro de la Vastida, oydor de la R.l Aud.a de Nueva España el año de 1691. [Mexico City. 1608-1709]
346 p. 31 cm. HHB [M-M 272]
A collection of decrees, land deeds, petitions, declarations, reports, notifications, etc., relating to the establishment and implementation of the rights claimed by Mexico City over its public lands. Primary attention is given to the 1690 proceedings conducted by the Real Audiencia through Pedro de la Bastida, a judge of that body, at the instigation of the Municipal Council, but the compilation also includes material on similar measures taken in 1608 as well as a few 18th century documents concerned with municipal lands.
Entered by Bancroft under "Ejidos de México, Autos."

MEXICO CITY. CONVENT OF SAN FRANCISCO
Libro de entradas y profesiones de novicios de este Convento de Padre S. Fran.co de México. Mexico City. 1562-1680. [Title varies.]
3 vols. 21 cm. HHB [M-M 216-218]
A collection of novices' applications and related records preserved in the

Convent of San Francisco. Comprises signed statements and summary entries, divided as follows: Vol. 1, a contemporary record covering the period 1562-1584, items numbered 15-241; Vol. 2, also a contemporary record, covers the period 1585-1597, items 242-369; and Vol. 3, evidently a late compilation, including one explanation written in 1756, consists of original records and copied entries for the period 1597-1680, items 370-1214.

MEXICO CITY. MESA DE PROPIOS Y RENTAS
Records for 1736. Mexico City. January 2, 1736–November 15, 1737.
534 p. D.S. 22-31 cm. [M-M 1715]
Records of the Mexico City Board of Municipal Real Estate and Revenue for transactions of 1736, with a few belated receipts signed in 1737. Contains orders and receipts for payment of salaries and other expenses, such as bills for building, paving, water-pipes, maintenance of religious and charitable institutions, and religious celebrations; itemized lists of certain expenditures and apportionments; rental records; petitions; certifications; and related documents signed by Gabriel de Mendieta Rebollo, Chief Notary of the City Council, and many others.

MEXICO (CITY) SECRETARÍA DE SALUBRIDAD Y ASISTENCIA
Archives. 1569-1838.
19 reels. (On film) [M-M 1910]
Materials relating primarily to religious institutions and their hospitals, especially the Royal Convent of Jesús María and the Church of San Pedro with its affiliated hospital, confraternity, and school, and including accounts of expenditures and architectural records.
Filmed from originals in the Mexico City Department of Health and Welfare. A calendar of documents on the film is available in the Bancroft Library.

MIDDLETOWN, CONNECTICUT. CITY COURT. CLERK
Certificate of Declaration for Naturalization of Daniel Graham. April 25, 1853.
2 p. D.S. 26 cm. [z-z 100:5]

MILATOVICH, ANTONIO, *et al.*
Papers relating to Land Development in Baja California. 1841-1886.
2 boxes. D.S., A.L.S. [67/77M]
Documents, originals and contemporary copies, concerning land transactions in Baja California, near the Colorado River and Sebastián Vizcaíno Bay. They include petitions, grants to Milatovich and others, deeds, receipts, diseños, and similar material. Some pertain to Gochicoa y Compañía, a colonizing venture near the Colorado River.

MILITARY ACCOUNTS. [N.p., n.d.]
7 p. 30 cm. HHB [M-M 1700:12]
Model blank forms drawn up for the financial records of the Cuarta Compañía Volante (Fourth Mobile Company).

MILLER, WILLIAM, 1795-1861
  Papers. 1821.
  3 p. A.L.S. and D.S. 22-23 cm. [z-z 145]
  Letters and documents as colonel in the Peruvian Army.

MINE AND HACIENDA PAYROLLS. [N.p.] 1882
  2 p. 46x58 cm. HHB [M-M 1700:38]
  Chart, in English, showing numbers of men employed on specified tasks for a mine in Mexico (?).

MIRAMÓN, JOAQUÍN, 1828-1867
  Miramón Family Papers. 1844-1882.
  1 portfolio (38 folders) A.L.S., D.S. [M-B 17]
  Letters and documents relating to the career of General Joaquín Miramón, native of Puebla, who rose through the ranks from second lieutenant to General during the troublous period before the Mexican War with the United States and the French invasion, 1864-1867, in support of Emperor Maximilian. He was shot by order of General Treviño on February 8, 1867. His brother Miguel was shot with Generals Mejía and the Emperor, June 19, 1867.
  Numerous letters of Joaquín to his wife, several of his brother Miguel, correspondence of Joaquín's widow, Concha, including a letter of condolence from Maximilian, military commissions; and other letters and papers.
  There is a "key" to the collection.

MIRANDA, FRANCISCO JAVIER, 1816-1864
  La Vida ó la Muerte, ó la Primera Comunion. Lecciones y egercicios devotos para disponerse á recibir la Sagrada Eucaristia, precedidos de una instruccion relativa al Sacramento de la Penitencia. . . . Puebla. 1857.
  204 p. D.S. 32 cm. HHB [M-M 156]
  Instructions regarding the sacraments of Penance and the Eucharist, composed by the parish priest of Puebla and addressed particularly to children preparing for their first communion; includes prayers and other spiritual exercises for a preparatory novena as well as for the day of communion.

MISCELLANEOUS. 1603-1771
  908 p. 23 cm. HHB [M-M 199]
  A collection, chiefly copies, of 44 numbered items (1-45, No. 40 omitted), comprising essays, letters, satires, addresses, and one-act plays, in prose and verse (Spanish and Latin), which originated in New Spain, Spain, Italy, and France; composed principally of anonymous pieces written under pseudonyms and dealing with religious, political, social, and academic questions connected with 18th-century Mexico.
  Entered in the Andrade catalogue under the title of the first item, "Derecho de las Yglesias. . . ."
  Notable items are 1) "Derecho de las Yglesias Metropolitanas y Cathedrales de las Indias p.ª la prelacion de los Capitulares, i naturales de ellas . . ." (n.p.,

n.d.), a plea for ecclesiastical preferment of native-born Americans; 5) "Papel de Lugares . . ." (Puebla, 1731), an academic satire addressed by the Jesuit poet Arriola to his graduating pupils; 19) "Romance Chistoso" (ca. 1767), verses written in exile by the Jesuit José Francisco de Isla; 24) "El Perfecto Religioso Menor . . . ," marked "1760," a verse exposition of the Franciscan Rule, by Diego Pardo; 29-30) a satirical plea and related matter in defense of certain apothecaries attacked by Pedro de Vargas, physician to Archbishop Rubio; 32) correspondence between Pope Clement XIII and Charles III of Spain, Rome and Aranjuez, Spain, May 16-27, 1767, on the expulsion of the Jesuits; 35-36) Latin and Spanish versions of the address, Mexico City, January 14, 1771, delivered by the King's representative, Rivadeneira, at the inaugural session of the Fourth Mexican Provincial Council; 37) Spanish translation of address, Paris, December 24, 1603, delivered by Henry IV of France in defense of the Jesuits, and related material.

MISCELLANY. MILITARY. MEXICO. 1790-1896
8 folders. Ms. and printed. 14–34 cm.   HHB   [M-M 363]

Miscellaneous papers of a military nature, several very local. Comprises a letter of 1790 for use of a pasture for military training purposes; enlistment papers, 1804, for four soldiers; letters of three men, 1814-1815, regarding military service; others of 1847, 1856, 1861 (report of a victory in which Col. Porfirio Díaz took part), 1890 (Governor Jesús H. Preciado of Morelos), and one of 1896.

MISIÓN DE LA PAZ, BAJA CALIFORNIA
Informe de la Mission de N.ra Señora del Pilar de la Paz. [N.d.]
8 p. 21 cm.   [M-M 1899]

Description of the mission from its founding in 1721.

MISSION NUESTRA SEÑORA DEL REFUGIO
Records. 1807-1828.
103 p. (Photocopy)   [M-A 11:2]

Book of baptisms of the mission, April 21, 1807–February 21, 1828; book of burials, May 16, 1807–November 18, 1825. From the Archivo de la Iglesia Parroquial, Matamoros. There is a "key" to the collection. Cf. also Bolton's *Guide,* p. 447.

MISSIONS. MEXICO
Register of Baptisms. Mexico. July, 1597–December, 1610.
48 p. 23 cm.   HHB   [M-M 452]

A baptismal register written in Náhuatl, with the signatures of officiating missionaries, apparently incomplete at beginning and end.

Signatures include those of Sebastián de Aguilar, Diego de Almonte, Antonio de la Cruz, Juan García, Francisco de Haro, Baltasar de Morales, Francisco de Ortiz, Melchor de los Reyes, Alonso de Ribadeneira, Juan de Salazar, Francisco Tamayo, and Juan de Vargas.

MISSIONS OF BAJA CALIFORNIA. 1700-1724
113 exp. (On film) [M-M 1840]

Includes letters from Juan de Ugarte, Joseph Sarmiento, and others. From original documents in the Library of Congress.

MISSIONS OF NEW SPAIN. MEXICO. 1781-1790
519 p. 30-31 cm. HHB [M-M 431]

Collection of manuscripts, signed originals and certified copies, relating to the missions of New Spain in the provinces of Nuevo León, Coahuila (Nueva Estremadura), Nuevo Santander, Nuevas Filipinas (Texas), Nueva Galicia, Nueva Vizcaya, and Alta and Baja California. Also contains correspondence of viceroys, ecclesiastical officials, and Franciscan or Dominican missionaries regarding the royal decree of January 31, 1784, which requested comparative information on conditions in the Jesuit missions at the time of the expulsion of the Jesuits and thereafter. There are several charts and a map of the Province of Nayarit in Nuevo León. Binder's title is "Documentos para la Historia de México."

MISSIONS OF TEXAS
Documents relating to. 1730-1762.
58 p. D. and D.S. 31-32 cm. [M-M 1877]

Included are an expediente concerning transfer of three Texas missions, Nuestra Señora de la Purísima Concepción, San Francisco de los Neches, and San José de los Nazonis, to more suitable sites; a report on the Amarillas Presidio and on the potentialities of the province and character of its natives; and a copy of the report on Texas missions prepared by Fray Simón del Hierro, Guardian of the Franciscan Colegio de Guadalupe de Zacatecas.

MISSIONS OF THE CALIFORNIAS
Documents relating to. 1768-1802.
123 folders. (Typescripts and photocopies) [M-A 5:1]

1. Lancaster-Jones Collection. 1767-1797. Letters of Joseph de Gálvez, Fray Francisco Palóu, Fray Junípero Serra, Fray Fermín Francisco de Lasuén, Fray Juan Crespí, members of the College of San Fernando in Mexico City, and others, concerning arrangements for the expeditions to occupy and support Alta California in 1769 and the years following. Papers from the estate of Alfonso Lancaster-Jones, formerly Mexican representative in England. 118 folders.

2. Papeles del Padre Fischer. 1770-1773. Miscellaneous papers concerning the missions of the Californias and northern New Spain. Compiled by Fray Francisco Xavier Castro of the College of San Fernando, under Fray Rafael Verger. From the library of Fray Agustín Fischer. 5 folders.

Now in the Museo Nacional de Antropología, Mexico.

MÖBIUS, PAUL
Postcard to Hermann Möbius. August 19, 1918.
2 p. A.L.S. 9 cm. [Z-Z 100:30]

Postcard taken from German prisoner.

MOE, ALFRED KEANE, 1874-
Letters and Papers. 1898-1910.
3 vols. (920 p.) 25-52 cm. [z-c 208]
Letterpress copybooks kept by Moe while U.S. Consul in Tegucigalpa, Honduras, 1902-1904, containing some reports on political situations; miscellaneous papers and printed circulars pertaining mainly to Moe's consular activities in Dublin and Bordeaux, 1904-1910. Originals and copies.

MOLINA, ALONSO DE, d. 1585
Ordenanzas para los Hospitales. 1552.
30 exp. (On film) [m-m 1838]
Microfilm of original documents in the Chapultepec Library.

MOLINA, ALONSO DE, d. 1585
Ordinançaz para proverchar los Cofradías a llos que an de servir en estas Ospitalles. [Mexico]. September 3, 1552.
54 p. 23 cm. HHB [m-m 455]
A set of rules in Náhuatl drawn up by the Franciscan, Molina, for the guidance of members of brotherhoods serving in certain hospitals.

MOLINA, CRISTÓBAL DE
Relación de las fabulas y ritos de los Ingas. . . . Cuzco. 16th century.
103 p. 32 cm. [z-d 122]
Copy of document relating to Inca fables and religious rites. Original in the Biblioteca Nacional, Lima, Peru. From collection of Alphonse L. Pinart.

MONCADA, RAMÓN DE
Record of Rents Paid in El Zerrito each August, 1734-1745, by Moncada.
2 p. 31 cm. HHB [m-m 1700:13]

MONTERO, SIMÓN
Naturaleza de las Indias para . . . . Madrid. June 19, 1631.
2 p. D.S. 42 cm. [m-m 1820]
Naturalization certificate conferred on Montero, Portuguese resident of Seville, enabling him to carry on business in the Indies and other parts of the Spanish realm, on an equal basis with native Spaniards.

MONTERO DE MIRANDA, FRANCISCO
Memoria sobre la Provincia de Vera Paz. Verapaz, Guatemala. 1575?
25 p. 33 cm. HHB [m-m 313]
Report on the Province of Verapaz, addressed to Palacio, a judge of the Real Audiencia of Guatemala. Deals with the name, location, climate, vegetation, fauna, rivers, mineral products, and natives of the province.

MONTERREY, GASPAR DE ZÚÑIGA Y ACEVEDO, CONDE DE, 1548-1606
Liçençia a Elvira Gomes de Moscoso . . . . Mexico City. November 26, 1602.
2 p. D.S. 30 cm. [M-M 1818]
Viceregal permit granting to Elvira Gómez de Moscoso, widow of Garci Martínez and resident of Colima, license to install a sugar mill for domestic use, subject to certain conditions.

MONTES, FRANCISCO
Note. Sauceda, Zacatecas, Mexico. November 16, 1868.
1 p. A.D.S. 33 cm. HHB [M-M 1700:16]
Promissory note for the delivery, to Julián Rodríguez, of 16 fanegas of corn purchased from Hipólito Díaz.

MONTEVERDE, MANUEL, 1824-1889
Memoria sobre el Departamento de Sonora. . . . ca. 1847.
132 p. 35 cm. HHB [M-M 157]
A report on the Department of Sonora, covering geography, population, territorial divisions, principal towns, military posts, products, natural resources, and finances, during a period of invasion by United States' forces, and suggestions for strengthening the Department through colonizing, military, financial, educational, and political measures; dedicated to President Santa Anna by Monteverde, a native Sonoran.

[MOORE, NATHAN]
[Geological Sketch]
41 p. 32 cm. HHB [M-M 160]
Discussion of origin of rocks, the action of the forces of fire and water on the surface of the world, elements in the composition of rocks, et cetera.

MORÁN, PEDRO, FRAY
Bocabulario de solo los nombres de la lengua Pokoman. . . . [N.p., n.d.]
240 p. 30 cm. HHB [M-M 444]
Vocabulary of the language of the Pokoman Indians of Guatemala, for letters A-N only. 220 pages. This major section is followed by a vocabulary of parts of the human body, 11 p., and a vocabulary of Latin adverbs, prepositions, and conjunctions with their Indian translations. 8 p.

MORÁN Y DEL VILLAR, JOSÉ, MARQUÉS DE VIVANCO, 1774-1841
Cédula de retiro . . . p.ª Juan Morga. . . . Mexico City. November 19, 1825.
2 p. D.S. 30 cm. [M-M 1700:71]
Retirement certificate for a member of the Compañía de la Bahía del Espíritu Santo, with additional note by Mateo Ahumada, December 16, 1825. Printed form, filled in.

MORAZÁN, FRANCISCO, 1792-1842, AND RAFAEL CARRERA, 1814-1865
Documents relating to the Political History of Central America. 1829-1846.
53 p. Ms. and printed. 21-33 cm. HHB [Z-C 9]

MORELL DE SANTA CRUZ, PEDRO AGUSTÍN, bp., 1694-1768
Visita Apostólica, Topográfica, Histórica y Estadística de todos los Pueblos de Nicaragua y Costa-Rica, hecha por el . . . Obispo de la Diócesis en 1751; y elevada al conocimiento de . . . Fernando VI, en 8 de S.^{bre} de 1752. Santiago de León, Nicaragua. September 8, 1752.
208 p. 34 cm. HHB [M-M 161]
Certified copy, 1874, of the topographical, historical, and statistical report addressed by Morell, Bishop of León de Nicaragua, to the King of Spain, based upon the Bishop's 1751 trips of inspection in the diocese, with special attention to the provinces of Costa Rica and Nicaragua, and cursory references to the province of Nicoya; includes copies of correspondence between Morell and José Vásquez Prieto, President of Guatemala, regarding improvement of local conditions.

MORETE, JOSÉ DE JESÚS
Reports on Troops at the Río Grande Presidio, Coahuila. Río Grande Presidio. August 1, 1824.
2 p. D.S. 22 cm. [M-M 1700:72]
Printed form, filled in.

MORFI, JUAN AGUSTÍN, d. 1783. *comp.*
Collection of Documents relating to New Spain. 1541-1772.
642 p. 30 cm. HHB [M-M 162]
Contains 1) an annotated list of vessels engaged in the quicksilver trade through the port of Veracruz, 1581-1772; 2) some royal expenditures in the Caribbean, 1730-1750; 3) instructions for the Conde de Salvatierra, viceroy of New Spain, by his predecessor, Bishop Juan de Palafox y Mendoza, 1642; 4) a "Brief and Summary Report" by Alonso de Zurita, 1554 to ca. 1565, regarding taxation and government of the Indians as compared with earlier, native, procedures; 5) journal of an expedition against the Chichimecas by Francisco de Sandoval Acazitli in the service of Viceroy Mendoza, 1541; 6) reports by or concerning the royal cosmographer, Carlos de Sigüenza y Góngora, 1689-1699, on the importance of Pensacola, request for information on the fortifications of San Juan de Ulúa, and a dispute between Sigüenza and Andrés de Arriola on the mapping of Pensacola Bay; 7) Martín de la Torre's letter on the nature of comets and that of 1680-1681 in particular; 8) five letters of Juan María de Salvatierra, 1697-1699, on the conquest and conversion of Lower California; and 9) records dating from 1646 to 1769 relating to the Congregación de la Purísima Concepción de María Santísima, a semi-secular organization founded in Mexico City under Jesuit auspices in 1641.

MORFI, JUAN AGUSTÍN, d. 1783
Memorias para la historia de Texas . . . . [ca. 1781]
926 p. 30 cm. HHB [M-M 428]
A copy made by Manuel de Vega in 1792 of a collection of data which were the basis for Morfi's *Historia de Texas*. This material is divided into twelve

books. The first presents a physical description of the province of Texas; the second describes the various tribes of Indians; and the remaining ten provide a chronological account of the history of Texas from 1672-1778. Detailed information is presented on the French and Spanish exploration of the Mississippi River, Louisiana, and Texas; Spanish occupancy of Texas; conflicts with the French and with the Indian tribes; and the establishment of the missions and their tribulations.

MORGAN, PHILIP HICKY, 1825-1900
Remarks of Philip H. Morgan, American Ambassador to Mexico, on the Attitude of the United States, Past and Present, toward Mexico. 1883.
9 f. 31 cm. HHB [M-M 344]
Remarks made by Ambassador Morgan on the unfriendliness of the Mexicans toward visitors from the United States, his own successful intervention between Mexico and Guatemala, possible acquisition of Mexican territory by the United States, relations between the railroads and the Mexican Government, and the unsatisfactory financial and administrative status of that government. Interspersed with critical comments by Bancroft.

MORIANA, CONDE DE
Papers concerning the Bread Riot in Madrid. April 28, 1699.
6 p. 30 cm. HHB [z-z 20:1]
Two accounts of a Madrid riot on April 28, 1699, caused by the high price of bread and terminated by the King's appointment of the popular candidate, Francisco Ronquillo, to replace councilman Francisco de Vargas. Also notes on a play and a political sonnet.

MORRIS, JAMES
Papers as Sheriff. New York, N.Y. 1799.
4 p. D. and D.S. 31-32 cm. [z-z 127]
List of convictions in the February Sessions, and a statement of disbursements made for the city jail.

MORRIS, WILLIAM ALFRED, 1875-1946
Papers. 1901-1946.
2 cartons. [z z 134]
Miscellaneous clippings concerning Oregon, war and peace, English government, poetry, and correspondence, 1930-1946. Morris was professor of English History at the University of California, Berkeley.

MORSHEAD, OWEN F
Letter. Cambridge, England. February 17, 1922.
1 p. A.L.S. 18 cm. [z-z 100:27]
Written as Librarian, Magdalene College, Cambridge, concerning inquiry about landing places of Sir Francis Drake on the American coast.

MOTA PADILLA, MATÍAS ÁNGEL DE LA, 1688-1766
Historia de la Conquista de la Nueva Galicia. Guadalajara. 1742.
xxii, 832 p. and 26 unnumbered p. 33 cm.   HHB [M-M 189]

A history of New Galicia extending to 1742. Includes accounts of its aborigines, its conquest and colonization by the Spaniards, founding of the capital city, and the work of religious orders, with brief descriptions of other regions which lay within the jurisdiction of the same audiencia or diocese. Contains a foreword by the transcriber, Mexico City, February 1, 1848, which explains the omission of a map contained in the original and the inclusion of new material, and also copies of pertinent contemporary documents, such as a royal letter of 1747 requesting a copy of the Historia, statements approving the work, the author's preface, et cetera.

Appended is a copy of the "Diario de la expedición de los Chichimecas de Don Francisco Sandoval Acazitli... en compañía de... Antonio de Mendoza," a translation of Gabriel de Castañeda's journal, substantially identical in content with item 5 of Morfi (M-M 162), and with the last item of "Ixtlilxochitl... Sumaria Relacion..." (M-M 426).

The text is in two different hands, with table of contents and three pages of colored drawings representing the coats of arms of Guadalajara, Durango, and the conquistadores, Francisco de Mota and Cristóbal Romero. The work was printed in Mexico in 1856 and 1870.

MOTOLINÍA, TORIBIO, d. 1568
La Vida, y Muerte de tres niños de Tlaxcala que murieron por la confession de la Fee... traducida al Mexicano.... [Mexico. 16th century]
67 p. 22 cm.   HHB [M-M 456]

The story of the Tlaxcalan child martyrs, Cristóbal, Antonio, and Juan, as written in Spanish by the missionary Motolinía in the 16th century, and translated into Náhuatl by the Franciscan Juan Bautista in 1601. This copy, in Náhuatl, was made from the original Bautista Ms. in 1859 by Chimalpopocatl Galicia, at the request of J. F. Ramírez, and under his supervision.

MOTT, TALBOT AND COMPANY
Account Book. San José del Cabo, Baja California. 1847-1849.
156 p. 32 cm.   [M-M 1869]

MUNGUÍA, MARIANA
Affidavit. Los Angeles. November, 1882.
4 p. D.S. 32 cm.   HHB [M-M 1700:61]

Swears that she has never signed any paper or document relating to her rights to the Hacienda de Santa María, in the Magdalena district, Sonora, Mexico, nor authorized anyone else to do so.

MUÑOZ, JUAN BAUTISTA, 1745-1799
Central America. Extracts. 1545-1555.
149 p. 33 cm.   HHB [M-M 320]

Excerpts from Volumes 66, 67, and 69 (new numbering) of the Muñoz Collection, Academia Real de la Historia, Madrid. These are transcripts and summaries of letters and documents addressed chiefly to Emperor Charles I of Spain or to the Council of the Indies by officials, friars, and Indians of the provinces subject to the Audiencia de los Confines, namely, Guatemala, Honduras, Nicaragua, Yucatan, and Chiapa. They relate to the civil and ecclesiastical administration of these provinces, particularly to treatment of Indians, abolition of the encomienda system, the work of Dominican and Franciscan friars, administration of Alonso de Zurita, the expeditions of Pedro de la Gasca, activities of Francisco Pizarro in Peru, and the survey conducted by Diego Ramírez.

MURRAY, JOHN, d. 1919(?)
Papers. ca. 1898-1920.
12 boxes and 1 carton. [z-z 133]
Manuscripts, clippings, scrapbooks, pictures, and some correspondence, reflecting Murray's career as labor leader and journalist. Include material concerning miners' strikes in the West, the Mexican Revolution, and the Pan American Federation of Labor.

MÚSICAS TÍPICAS PANAMEÑAS. [N.d.]
1 p. (Typescript) 28 cm. [z-c 207]
Words of popular songs of Panama prepared for the consul-general in San Francisco.

NÁHUATL CODICES ON LAND DISTRIBUTION. MEXICO. 16TH CENT.
3 items. HHB [M-M 468-470]
Náhuatl documents, apparently land titles, written in the Spanish alphabet on maguey fibre. Dated in the 16th century, but apparently all forming part of the so-called "Techialoyan group," classified by Donald Robertson in *Mexican Manuscript Painting...*, Yale University Press, 1959, p. 190-195, as forgeries. Pictorial peculiarities and similarity of writing in the same group were explained by Federico Gómez de Orozco in *Anales del Instituto de Investigaciones Estéticas*, vol. IV, no. 16, p. 57-68, as the result of the scribes' training in Pedro de Gante's Franciscan school of San José de Belén; the documents were accepted by him and other authorities as genuine.

1. [Codex A] San Pedro Tlahuac (Xochimilco). 20 p. 23 cm.
Primarily a description of lands, buildings, and topography in the vicinity of Tlahuac, at one time a lake settlement some 26 km. southeast of Mexico City. Two conflicting 16th-century dates of the Mexican calendar appear in the opening lines, the second and more acceptable being interpreted by Chimalpopoca Galicia as 1571.

Bearing the signature of the scribe, "Ton Lucax te Xantiaco" (Don Lucas de Santiago), preceded by six other names, i.e., in modernized spelling: Don Juan Miguel, alcalde; Don Miguel de los Angeles, alcalde; Don Mateo de San Mateo; Don Pedro Miguel; Don Joaquín; and Don Nicolás Lorenzo. Concludes with an annotation or certification signed by the same scribe. Pictorial maps on cover and former reverse of cover, now p. 3. Similar in appearance to item 3, *infra*, though not found listed in accounts of the Techialoyan group.

Called "Codex A" by Robert H. Barlow. Copies and a translation of this

Ms. are thought to be in the possession of the Mexican Museo Nacional.

2. [Codex B] San Pedro Tlahuac (Xochimilco). 10 p. 27 cm.

Apparently a series of civic documents relating to land boundaries in the vicinity of Tlahuac. Contains references to "San Martín" and "San Sebastián;" dates at the end of several documents are based partly on the Christian calendar, and suggest "July 4, 1524," but their reading is doubtful.

With identical lists of six names at the close of two documents, in modernized spelling: Don Pedro Miguel, Don Ignacio de Santiago, Don Alonso Martín de San Juan, Don Diego Miguel, Don Feliciano de Santiago, and Don Sebastián Bartolomé. Several are followed by official titles. A phrase referring to the scribe appears opposite the name of Alonso Martín de San Juan. Pictorial map on loose sheet, probably the cover; incomplete. Similar in appearance to item 3, *infra*, though not found listed in accounts of the Techialoyan group. Called "Codex B" by R. H. Barlow.

3. [Codex C] Valley of Mexico. 32 p. 27 cm.

Sometimes called "Codex M" of the Techialoyan group, but a different Ms. has also been listed with this title by R. H. Barlow (in *Anales del Instituto de Investigaciones Estéticas, op. cit.*, Vol. IV, p. 66).

Fragments of paintings and texts, relating to land boundaries in San Bartolomé Tepanohuayan and other towns of the Acolhuas. Contains references to the Chichimec chieftain Xolotl, his son Nopaltzin, Viceroy Mendoza, and various historical figures; written in the Acolhua region of the Valley of Mexico. Internally dated "1504," which is obviously inaccurate in view of the allusion to Mendoza.

NANNE, HENRY F W 1830-
Dictation.

4 p. 27 cm.　　　　　　　　　　　　　　　　　　　　　　HHB [M-M 519]

Concerns his activity as a businessman and railroad builder in Costa Rica. John C. Frémont, Minor C. Keith, Henry Meiggs, and Colonel Louis Schlessinger also participated in these ventures.

NAVA, PEDRO DE
Documents Issued by or Addressed to Nava as Commandant General of the Provincias Internas. Chihuahua. 1796.

2 folders. D.S. 31 cm.　　　　　　　　　　　　　　　　　　　　[M-M 1791]

1. Plea for justice by Doroteo García de Bustamante, in a property dispute with Tomás Malo. Chihuahua, March 31 and April 13, 1796. 4 p.

2. Circular communicating the decision of the Commandant General to grant the plea of the Indians in Pagüichique against their removal to Basiseachic. Chihuahua, May 13, 1796. 2 p.

NEIRA Y QUIROGA, JOSÉ DE
Obligazion a fauor de su mag[esta]d . . . del capp.ⁿ Domingo de Apreza difunto. . . . San José del Parral, Nueva Vizcaya. August 29, 1697.

3 p. D.S. 31 cm.　　　　　　　　　　　　　　　　　　　HHB [M-M 1700:1]

Receipt and promissory note to the Royal Treasury for four quintals of quicksilver; signed by Neira as executor and co-heir of Captain Domingo de Apreza Falcón, deceased former official in charge of the local quicksilver concession.

Typed transcript in modernized spelling in same folder.

NENTVIG, JUAN BAUTISTA, 1713-1768
   Letters. 1764-1767.
   26 exp. (On film) [M-M 1816]
   Letters from Nentuig to Father Provincial Francisco Zeballos, Salvador de la Gándara, or the Marqués de Croix, from Opata, Ures and Guásavas.

NEW GRANADA
   Collection of Documents on the Negro Slave Trade and Slavery, especially in Colombia and Venezuela. 1565-1817.
   3 cartons. (Photocopy) [Z-D 118]
   Documents on the Negro slave trade and the institution of slavery in the mines and plantations, free Negroes, and colonial administration in the 17th and 18th centuries. From the Archivo Nacional at Bogotá, Colombia. Selected by James F. King, 1938.

NEW MEXICO AND THE SOUTHWEST
   Documents relating to. 1605-1720.
   7 boxes. (Photocopies) [M-A 4:1]
   Relate chiefly to the missions of New Mexico in the 17th and early 18th centuries. Assembled as Legajos 1-6 by France V. Scholes in the Biblioteca Nacional, Mexico. There is a "key" to the collection.

NEW SPAIN
   Rulers. [N.p., n.d.]
   15 p. 32 cm. HHB [M-M 374]
   A numbered list of the viceroys and other chiefs of state in New Spain, from 1535 to 1816, with brief comments on each.

NEW SPAIN
   Selected Items relating to.
   35 cartons. (Transcripts and prints) [Z-E 1]
   Topics dealt with emphasize Spanish exploration and settlement on the frontiers north from Mexico City, including the Provincias Internas, the Californias, New Mexico, and Texas; and maritime explorations and foreign intrusions into Spain's Pacific waters.
   These copies were made for individual scholars, mostly by hand or typewriter, in the Archivo General de Indias. A "key" to contents is available in the Library.

NEW YORK. COURT OF COMMON PLEAS
   Certificate of Citizenship for Leopold R. Gostorfs. New York, N.Y. October 21, 1850.
   1 p. D.S. 28 cm. [Z-Z 100:85]

NICARAGUA
Documents pertaining to. 1842-1848.
171 p. (Typescript) 32 cm.   HHB   [Z-C 4:3-7]
Relate to a dispute with the British government over San Juan del Norte (1842), the Mosquito coast (1847), the little Island of Cuba in Lake Nicaragua (1848), and the Bluefields area. Partially in handwriting of A. Pinart. Copies of imprints.

NICARAGUA MISCELLANY. 1851-1858
28 items (93 p.) 25-36 cm.   [Z-C 201]
Papers concerning affairs in Nicaragua, especially the filibustering activities of William Walker. The file includes letters and documents from William Walker, Bruno von Natzmer, Francisco de Castellón, Trinidad Cabañas, Máximo Jerez, and others; a petition from citizens of Granada in 1855 that General Ponciano Corral's death sentence be commuted; certification of John T. Doyle as agent for Vanderbilt's Accessory Transit Co.; and copies of patriotic songs. Originals and contemporary copies.

NICHOLSON, ROBERT, [ca. 1787]-1845
Correspondence and Papers. 1811-1873.
28 items.   [Z-Z 109]
Includes last will and testament, diplomas from Transylvania University, Kentucky, business correspondence, and letters to his daughter Ann (Mrs. William Anderson Scott). With notes and correspondence of William Anderson Scott concerning the Nicholson family and property in Ireland.

NOBLE, HAROLD JOYCE, 1903-1953
Papers. ca. 1930-1947.
1 carton and 1 box.   [Z-Z 147]
1. Manuscript and typescript notes gathered from Korean archives and secondary sources for Noble's doctoral dissertation, *Korea and her relations with the United States before 1895* (U.C. 1931). Roughly arranged by subject and date.
2. Correspondence relating to the Institute of Pacific Relations, 1944-1947; reports by Noble on Korea; reports by the Army and Navy boards of inquiry on Pearl Harbor; and miscellaneous printed items. Included are letters from Edward C. Carter, Harold Henry Fisher, Alfred Kohlberg, and others.
There is a "key" to the collection.

NORTON, CHARLES ELIOT, 1827-1908
Letters to Henry W. Haynes. Massachusetts. June 12, 1879–May 17, 1892.
35 items (77 p.) A.L.S. 18 cm.   [M-M 1828]
Letters from Norton, a founding member of the Archeological Institute of America, to Henry Williamson Haynes of the Institute's Executive Committee, primarily concerning Institute affairs, notably sponsorship of Adolph Bandelier's projects at Mitla, Cholula, and other Mexican sites.

NOTICIA TOPOGRAFICA DE LAS PROVINCIAS Y PUEBLOS DE LAS COM-
PREHENSIONES DE GUADALAXARA, ZACATECAS, DURANGO, SO-
NORA, SINALOA, NUEBO MEXICO, Y PERTENENCIAS DE LA DE SAN
LUIS, Á LA AUDIENCIA TERRITORIAL DE NUEBA GALICIA. [N.p.,
n.d.]
33 p. 12-22 cm. [M-M 1895]
Table of distances between various communities and along certain mail or
marching routes.

NUEVA GALICIA
Genealogical Records. 1537-1777.
360 p. 31 cm. [M-M 1714]
Collection of genealogical documents (originals and certified copies) con-
cerning interrelated families of Nueva Galicia—notably the Flores, de la Torre,
Alvarado, Contreras, Angulo, Figueroa, Padilla, Bañuelos, and Oñate families.
Composed principally of files on genealogical inquiries conducted by the
Audiencia of Guadalajara or lesser local tribunals at the request of petitioners
José and Nicolás Flores de la Torre, Archdean Diego Flores de Latorre, Presbyter Luis Gómez de Alvarado, and others, who claimed kinship with such noted
conquistadors as Pedro de Alvarado, Hernán Flores, Diego Pérez de la Torre
(successor of Nuño de Guzmán), and Francisco de Figueroa. With two appended genealogical reports, one prepared by the Precentor of the Guadalajara Cathedral on certain Juchipila families and the other on the Flores, de la
Torre, and González families, compiled by the Inquisition and a university
official, Dr. Vicente Ignacio Peña Brizuela, at the request of Vicente Flores
de la Torre y González. Contains petitions, questionnaires, testimony, texts
of royal decrees, viceregal or judicial orders, powers of attorney, certifications,
related material, and two colored coats of arms.

NUEVA GALICIA
Miscellaneous Legal Papers from San Miguel, Nombre de Dios, and Valle de
la Poana. 1664-1704.
16 p. D. and D.S. 31-32 cm. [M-M 1907]
Fragments of documents relating to sale of land and estate settlements.

NUEVA VIZCAYA. REAL JUSTICIA
De oficio de la Real Justicia q[ontr]a Sebastian de la Cruz negro esclauo del
Capp.ⁿ Manuel de Coy &c s[obr]e hurto que se hizo a Juan Lopez mercader.
San José del Parral, Nueva Vizcaya. September 7–October 8, 1657.
42 p. D.S. 31 cm. [M-M 1774]
File concerning the trial of Sebastián de la Cruz, Negro slave of Captain
Manuel de Coy, on charges of robbing the merchant, Juan López. Contains
orders, notifications, testimony of the accused and of witnesses, appointments,
questionnaire for defense witnesses, briefs of attorneys, decision absolving
Cruz, statement of costs, and related documents.

NÚÑEZ DE HARO Y PERALTA, ALONSO, abp. 1729-1800
   Letter to the "Juez de Bebidas Prohibidas." Mexico City. July 3, 1787.
   2 p. L.S. 30 cm. [M-M 1700:74]
   Requesting a file on the case of Daniel de Cruelle.

NÚÑEZ DE HARO Y PERALTA, ALONSO, abp. 1729-1800
   Letter to Viceroy Miguel José de Azanza. Tacubaya, Mexico. April 21, 1800.
   1 p. L.S. 21 cm. HHB [M-M 1700:57]
   Acknowledges receipt of letter, stating that the new viceroy, Félix Berenguer de Marquina, will enter the city on the 29th.

NÚÑEZ DE HARO Y PERALTA, ALONSO, abp. 1729-1800
   Papers. Mexico. March 19, 1777–April 2, 1796
   2 folders. D. and A.L.S. 20-31 cm. HHB [M-M 502]
   Letters addressed or transmitted to the Archbishop, and copy of a document issued in his name, as follows:
   1. Letter, dated March 19, 1777, by José Francisco de Rivas y Solar, priest of San Juan Evangelista Xochitepec (Puebla, Mexico), to the Archbishop concerning steps taken to prevent Indians on the Hacienda de Temisco from working on feast days. Enclosed is a holograph letter to Rivas from Francisco de Zorlado y de Haro, manager of the Temisco estate, accepting Rivas' instructions but questioning their validity. 6 p.
   2. Certified copy, dated April 2, 1796, of Núñez's pronouncement approving the accounts and related documents of the Convento de la Concepción (Mexico City), for the year 1794, as submitted to him by Antonio Rodríguez. 5 p.

NUTTALL, ZELIA MAGDALENA, 1858-1933, *comp.*
   Materials relating to Sir Francis Drake.
   1 vol. (52 p.) and 24 pieces. 4-34 cm. [Z-R 14]
   Transcripts of documents in the Public Record Office, London, and captions for an exhibit.

OAXACA, MEXICO
   Selected Documents relating to Civil and Criminal Affairs in the Municipality of Teposcolula (San Pedro y San Pablo Teposcolula), State of Oaxaca. 1560-1906.
   37 reels. (On film) [M-A 13]
   Part I: El Archivo del Juzgado de Teposcolula, 1688-1843.
   Part II: From officials of Coixtlahuaca, Tlajiaco, and other towns (1830's).

OBERNDORFER, LEONORA (LEVY)
   Scrapbooks. ca. 1880-1900.
   2 vols. and 1 envelope. 21 cm. [Z-Z 119]
   Miscellaneous newspaper and magazine clippings—poetry, news, short stories, and other items of special interest to the author.

OBJECCIONES HECHAS POR UN OFICIAL IMPARCIAL DE EL EGERCITO SOBRE EL NUEBO MÉTODO DE CAMPAÑA, PRACTICADO POR D.ⁿ PEDRO CEBALLOS EN LA AMERICA MERIDIONAL. 1777.
71 p. 31 cm. [71/84m]
Critical commentary on activities of Pedro Ceballos during a campaign for the island of Santa Catalina off the coast of Uruguay. With this, copies of correspondence of Pedro Ceballos with Pedro Martín Cermeño and the Marqués de Casa-Tilly concerning the battle, and extract of report on the operations of Casa-Tilly's squadron during the expedition to South America, 1776-1778.

OBRAS DEL R.ˡ PALACIO. . . . COMPOSICION DE LA CAÑERÍA DE LA FUENTE DEL JARDIN Y DE LA ESCALERA PRIVADA. MEXICO CITY. JUNE 30-AUGUST 8, 1795.
17 p. D.S. 30-31 cm. [M-M 1822]
Documents concerning cost, extent, and nature of repairs to the Viceregal Palace. Includes letters from Viceroy Marqués de Branciforte.

OBREGÓN, BALTASAR DE, 1544-
Historia de los descubrimientos antiguos y modernos de la Nueva España. Mexico. March 17, 1584.
243 p. D.S. (Photocopy) 23 cm. [71/47m]
A history of 16th century exploration in New Spain, including contemporary information on the exploration of New Mexico, especially by the expeditions of Francisco Sánchez Chamuscado (1581-1582) and Antonio de Espejo (1582-1583), both accompanied by friars.
Printed as *Historia de los Descubrimientos Antiguos y Modernos de la Nueva España*, (Mexico, 1924), edited by Mariano Cuevas; English translation by George P. Hammond and Agapito Rey (Los Angeles, 1928).

O'BRIEN, JOSEPH J
Correspondence and Papers. 1911.
166 p. Ms. and printed. 13-35 cm. [Z-C 202]
Relate mainly to efforts to secure San Francisco as the site for the exposition commemorating the completion of the Panama Canal, and the role California played in its development.

OCHOA Y AAÑA, ANASTASIO MARIA DE, 1783-1833
Don Alfonso. Tragedia en cinco actos . . . . 1672-ca. 1820.
729 p. 23 cm. HHB [M-M 168]
A collection of eleven dramatic works, originals and translations, by Ochoa and other authors, evidently prepared for presentation in Mexican theatres. Authors named are: A. M. de Ochoa y Aaña, 1783-1833; Jean Baptiste Racine, 1639-1699; Vittorio Alfieri, 1749-1803; Andrés Friz, 1711-1790; Pierre-Augustin Caron de Beaumarchais, 1732-1799; Juan Ignacio González del Castillo, 1763-1800.

O'CONOR, HUGO DE, d. 1779
   Diaries. 1772-1776.
   3 folders. 21 cm. [M-M 1788]
   Diaries recording three reconnoitering and punitive expeditions undertaken by Colonel O'Conor, Commandant General of the Nueva Vizcaya frontier and formerly *ad interim* Governor of Coahuila.
   Folder 1. Fragments of a diary, 1772-1773, on an expedition, ordered by Viceroy Bucareli and a war council of April 2, 1772, to examine possible presidio sites and check Indian hostilities. Includes copies of letters exchanged by O'Conor and Jacobo Ugarte y Loyola, then Governor of Coahuila, regarding the Lipan Indians. 10 p.
   Folder 2. Diary recording the expedition undertaken by O'Conor as Commandant-Inspector of the Internal Presidios of New Spain, in order to find and punish the hostile Indians in the sierras of Alamo Hueco, La Hacha, Boquilla, and Corral de Piedras. 1774-1775. 38 p.
   Folder 3. Diary of the march of a force from El Carrizal to find and punish hostile Indians in the Mescalero region near the Janos Presidio. May-July, 1776. 51 p.

O'GORMAN, CHARLES THADDEUS, AND ANA MARÍA NORIEGA DE VICARIO DILIGENCIAS MATRIMONIALES DEL SR. DN. CARLOS TADEO O'GORMAN, . . . Y DE DOÑA ANA MA. NORIEGA DE VICARIO. [1789]-1825
   55 p. 18-32 cm. [M-M 1703]
   File of documents compiled in Mexico City in 1825 preliminary to the marriage of O'Gorman, Consul General of Great Britain in Mexico City, and Señorita Noriega y Vicario, a minor. Includes baptismal records, petitions, maternal permission, order for publications of banns, etc. Originals and certified copies written in Mexico City, Guadalajara, Tepic, San Cosme, and London.

OLIVES Y SINTES, SEBASTIÁN
   Escritura de debitorio . . . . Manila. April 18, 1885.
   9 p. D.S. 31 cm. [70/35z]
   Contemporary copy of instrument recording loan transaction between Olives y Sintes and Adolfo Roensch.

OLLIFFE, H
   Letter to Mr. Nevall. [Paris]. March 14, 1853.
   1 p. A.L.S. 18 cm. [Z-Z 100:71]
   Introducing his brother, Charles Olliffe.

OLMOS, ANDRÉS DE, ca. 1491-1571
   Arte para aprender la lengua mexicana . . . . [Mexico. 1547?-1563?]
   182 p. 22 cm. HHB [M-M 454]
   A collection of copies, including an incomplete Spanish grammar of the Náhuatl language (1547?); a Náhuatl treatise (1563?) on the Ten Command-

ments, designed for Indian neophytes and containing a Spanish prologue which refers to the author's earlier work on the subject; a Náhuatl treatise and dialogue (1563) on preparation for the Sacrament of the Eucharist, also with a prologue mentioning an earlier, similar work; a monologue in Náhuatl, representing spiritual advice from an Indian father to his son; and two pages in Spanish containing a cosmographical chart with Spanish explanations.

ORDENAÇION. [MEXICO. JUNE, 1629?]
48 p. D.S. 23 cm.   HHB [M-M 467]
An incomplete document in Náhuatl, apparently an ordinance on the administration, primarily judicial, of Mexico City and neighboring regions, based upon a decree issued by Philip I in 1500. An appended notation, dated June, 1629, bears several signatures, evidently of Indian municipal officials.

ORDENANÇAS DE SU MAGESTAD. [MEXICO. 16TH CENTURY]
10 p. 21 cm.   HHB [M-M 460]
A digest, in Náhuatl, of Spanish laws for the government of Mexico. Issued during the reign of Philip II.

ORDINANCES CONCERNING TREATMENT OF THE INDIANS. VALLADOLID. JUNE 23, 1513
28 p. (Photocopy) 23 cm.   [Z-E 12]
Photostats of a copy of the "Laws of Burgos" in the Archivo General de Indias, Seville. A contemporary copy, made for the Governor of Puerto Rico, of the code drafted for the government of Española.
With a translation and notes by Lesley B. Simpson.

ORDÓÑEZ Y AGUIAR, RAMÓN DE, d. ca. 1840
Historia de la Creacion del Cielo y de la Tierra conforme al Systema de la Gentilidad Americana, Theologia de los Culebras ... Diluvio Universal ... Verdadero origen de los Indios ... Principio de Su Imperio, Fundacion, y destruccion, de ... Ciudad de Palenque ... Supersticioso Culto, con que los antiguos Palencanos adoraron al verdadero Dios ... [Chiapa and Guatemala, 1796]
701 p. 31 cm.   HHB [M-M 177]
The major portion of this volume, f. 24-326, is a treatise in eleven chapters on the cosmogony, origin, history, and culture of the American Indians, with particular reference to the Tzendal nation and the ancient court of Palenque, comprising extracts from indigenous records of Chiapas and Guatemala, and explanatory notes by Ordóñez.

ORIGEN DE LOS MEXICANOS [AND OTHER MANUSCRIPTS RELATING TO EARLY INDIAN TRIBES IN MEXICO]
42 p. 33 cm.   HHB [M-M 448]
Three manuscripts, primarily Franciscan, relating to the origins, theogony, and history of the early inhabitants of Mexico:
 1. Origen de los Mexicanos. [Mexico, 16th cent.] Copy of a fragment from

a report on the first tribes to inhabit Mexico, prepared by anonymous Franciscan friars at the request of Juan Cano. 4 p.

2. Historia de los Mexicanos por sus pinturas. [Mexico, 16th cent.] Copy of a treatise by Toribio de Motolinía dealing with Indian accounts of the creation of the world and succeeding developments, including the arrival in Mexico of its early inhabitants, based upon Indian painted and oral records. There are 20 chapters and an appended table of events from 1351 to 1519. 19 p.

3. Notes in French on the theogony, mythology, and ancient history of Mexico, followed by a genealogical report in Spanish on early Indian rulers. The latter section is probably copied from material compiled by Franciscan Archbishop Zumárraga at the request of Juan Cano. 19 p.

OROZCO CERVANTES, MANUEL, d. 1687
Documents relating to Estate of. [Mexico. ca. 1736]
2 folders. 30 cm. HHB [M-M 283]
Legal papers in the lawsuit on the estate of Manuel Orozco Cervantes (d. 1687) brought by his son-in-law, Pedro Alonso Dávalos y Braçamonte, Count of Miravalle, against Juan and Carlos Osorio. They include the plea of Miravalle for recovery of the inheritance of his deceased wife, Francisca Orozco de Dávalos, only child of Don Manuel, based upon judgments handed down in 1720 and 1736. And a statement of the case of Juan and Carlos Osorio, heirs and executors of Antonio Osorio, deceased executor of Lorenzo Osorio, who had served as executor for Francisco Orozco, brother of Don Manuel and custodian of the latter's estate. Signed, and presented to the Real Audiencia by the attorney, Joseph Hidalgo, in refutation of the claims advanced by Miravalle.

ORRANTIA, JUAN DE [NUEVA VIZCAYA. 1737?]
4 p. 30 cm. [M-M 1780]
Fragment dealing with the questionable election of Juan de Orrantia as alcalde [of San Felipe el Real?], and the calling of a new election which gave the disputed post to Matías del Solar.

ORTEGA, FRANCISCO DE
Descripcion y Demarcacion de las Yslas Californias. . . . Mexico. 1633-1636.
48 p. 31 cm. HHB [M-M 179]
Three files containing copies of documents relating to Ortega's 1632, 1633-1634, and 1636 expeditions along the California coast in search of pearl fisheries, aboard the *Madre Luisa de la Ascención*, including reports presented by Ortega, viceregal orders of the Marqués de Cerralvo, authorizing the expeditions, and the pertinent royal decree of August 2, 1628.

ORTIGOSA, VICENTE
Correspondence and Documents. Mexico. 1864-1873.
33 folders (125 p.) D. and L.S. 12-39 cm. [M-M 1812]
Collection of papers, originals and copies, relating to the career of Vicente

Ortigosa. Deals primarily with his posts in Maximilian's empire as Councilor of State; as Inspector of Roads and Bridges, and of the Mexico City–Chalco and other railways; as plenipotentiary for negotiations with the Hanseatic League; and as engineer on the Mexico Valley drainage project. Includes a number of signed letters from members of Maximilian's cabinet.

ORTIZ PARRILLA, DIEGO
Ynforme general de Sonora. . . . San Miguel de Ures (Sonora, Mexico). October 22, 1753.
70 p. 31 cm.   HHB [M-M 500]
Copy of report on the geography, topography, products, population, etc., of Sonora and Sinaloa. Prepared by the former Governor and Captain General of these provinces for his successor, Pablo de Arce y Arroyo.

OSSORIO, BUENAVENTURA FRANCISCO DE, 1714-
Q.^{no} 2º de los papeles mas utiles que se encontraron por del difunto Bachiller Dn Buena Ventura Ossorio, Clerigo Presbítero . . . . 1714-1783.
49 p. D.S. 15-31 cm.   [M-M 1897]
Collection of personal and family papers, including an expediente concerning his right to be designated an Indian cacique, permission to say Mass and hear confessions, and miscellaneous financial records. Assembled by the General Probate Court, Mexico, 1784.

OTERO, MARIANO, 1817-1850
Obras del Señor Licenciado Don Mariano Otero. Mexico. January 16, 1839-May 25, 1850.
7 vols. 21 cm.   HHB [M-M 181-187]
This series of seven volumes is divided into two parts. The first, 1842, is entitled, "Ensayo sobre el verdadero estado de la cuestion social y politica que se agita en la Republica Megicana." It is a treatise on the contemporary economic, social, and political problems of Mexico, with suggestions for their solution.

The second, 1839-1850, consists of legal allegations, reports and related material presented by Otero before the Supreme Court, the Federal Congress, and other authorities in Mexico City, Guadalajara, and Querétaro. It deals with civil and criminal suits, i.e., execution of wills, taxation, property rights, legal procedure, armed robbery, homicide, et cetera, including a conspiracy charge on which the author had been imprisoned. Edited by the author's son, Ignacio Otero.

OTOMÍ MANUSCRIPT. [N.p., n.d.]
4 p. 22 cm.   HHB [M-M 477]
Unidentified Ms., written in Otomí, according to Dr. Wigberto Jiménez Moreno, historian and ethnographer at the Instituto Nacional de Antropología e Historia, Mexico City.

OYARVIDE Y HEREDIA, ANTONIO DE

Diario de Navegacion, que desde el puerto de Cartajena de Yndias haze en la Balandra S.ⁿ Juan Nepomuceno el Th.ᵉ de Navio . . . Antonio de Oyarvide y Heredia . . . . 1763-1764.

28 p. D.S. 30 cm.   HHB [M-M 188]

Diary of a voyage made by Naval Lieutenant Oyarvide aboard the sloop *San Juan Nepomuceno*, from Cartagena in Colombia to Omoa in Honduras via various West Indian ports, at the bidding of the Viceroy of New Granada and for the purpose of checking on English settlements along the Honduran coast. Entries in the diary proper cover the period October 1-December 29, 1763.

PACHUCA. MEXICO. 1633-1821

9 folders. 30-31 cm.   HHB [M-M 524]

Documents relating to the town or district of Pachuca, in the present state of Hidalgo, arranged chronologically.

1. Pachuca, Mexico. Real Caja. Certified copy of receipt and of promise to pay, from Antón de Soto and his guarantor Yáñez, for six quintals of quicksilver delivered to Soto by Juan de Arrieta, alcalde mayor and quicksilver administrator of the Pachuca mines, in accordance with a viceregal order. Sets forth terms of payment. 4 p.

2. Moreno de Ocío, Antonio. Mexico, October 12-16, 1702. File on the appointment and installation of Moreno as deputy assayer and weightmaster for the Royal Treasury in Pachuca mines. Contains viceregal confirmation of the appointment made on August 25 by Captain Francisco Brito, Pachuca assayer and weightmaster, in view of the death of Antonio de Salas, Moreno's predecessor; and documents relating to Moreno's oath of office and installation. Written in Mexico City and Pachuca. Bears the signatures of Archbishop-Viceroy Juan de Ortega (y) Montañés and others. 5 p.

3-5. Mines of Santa Gertrudis y de San José. Real y Minas de Pachuca, 1715-1716. Certified copies of declarations on the acquisition, by Toribio García Pumarino, of portions of the Santa Gertrudis Mine and the contiguous San José Mine, either purchased by him, November 27, 1715, and June 22, 1716, from Martín Navarijo and Andrés de Vicuña, or transferred by Miguel de Castilla, December 5, 1715, in exchange for García's assumption of financial responsibility for operating the portion retained by Castilla. 12 p.

6. Mexico City, April 9, 1742. Order from the Real Audiencia governing New Spain in the interim between viceroys, instructing the Pachuca officials to remit local treasury funds to the central treasury in advance of the usual date, owing to urgent requirements for the defense of Veracruz. 3 p.

7. Iturria, María Amo(?) Extracto del Padron de esta Ciudad . . . de la Asumpción, Real y Minas de Pachuca, y sus anexos . . . . Asunción, Mexico, 1792. Data extracted from the census records of Nuestra Señora de la Asunción, giving figures under the heads of total population, families, racial groups, marital status, etc., for the town of Pachuca and dependent settlements; arranged by the Asunción priest and ecclesiastical judge, Iturria. 4 p.

8. Ordóñez, Juan. Mexico City. August 1, 1794. Report from Ordóñez, an official of the Central Reappraisement Office, apparently addressed to the Viceroy, concerning collection of Pachuca treasury agents from the districts

of Yahualica and Xochicoatlán, in Hidalgo, of additional taxes, April, 1793, because of the retroactive new tax roll issued in March, 1794; preceded by an explanatory financial statement prepared for the debtor governments; cites other documents evidently once included in this file. 5 p. Copies certified on October 4, 1794, signed by the Conde del Valle de Orizaba, an official of the Royal Treasury.

9. [Pachuca], 1821. Census table showing the number of families, and the location in relation to the parish center of the town of Pachuca itself and each of the other towns, estates, and farms of Pachuca parish; also a note on the Colegio Apostólico de Nuestro Padre San Francisco and the Convento Hospital de Nuestro Padre San Juan de Dios, both located in the Real de Pachuca. 1 p.

PACIFIC MAIL STEAMSHIP COMPANY
Journal and Logbook. 1883-1885.
242 p. 25-26 cm. [M-M 1829]

Journal kept by an agent of the company of a trip from New York to Mazatlán by way of the Isthmus of Panama, and up the Gulf of California, to assess business opportunities, including purchase of the ship *Sonora*. Written aboard the *Colima* at Mazatlán and the *Sonora* at various points on the Gulf. January 14-February 4, 1883.

Logbook, with navigational computations, of the S.S. *Colón*, for voyages between New York and Colón, Panama. August 11, 1884-July 29, 1885.

PALACIOS, CRISTÓBAL
Commission. Mexico City. February 26, 1846.
4 p. D.S. 43 cm. HHB [M-M 1700:46]

Commission appointing Palacios an "aspirante," or cadet, of the Army Medical Corps. Signed by the interim president, Mariano Paredes y Arrillaga and José María Tornel.

PALAFOX Y MENDOZA, JUAN DE, bp., 1600-1659
Documents relating to the Career of Palafox, Bishop of Puebla, Archbishop-elect of Mexico, Visitor General of New Spain, and 18th Viceroy.
2 folders. (Copies) 31 cm. HHB [M-M 503]

1. Royal appointment of Palafox, then Bishop of Tlaxcala, i.e., Puebla, as Archbishop of Mexico; refers to the death of his predecessor, Feliciano de [la] Vega, and urges acceptance of the promotion, which he subsequently rejected. Madrid, February 10, 1642. 1 p.

2. Portion of a pronouncement denouncing Palafox and dealing with his revocation of licenses needed for the functioning of religious orders; presumably connected with the dispute on tithes between Palafox and the Jesuits which was adjudged in 1647. Incomplete. N.p., n.d. 4 p.

PALMER, WALTER WILLIAM
Memo on Fresnillo, Veta Grande, Real del Monte y Pachuca & Bolaños. May 4, 1866.
16 p. D.S. 25 cm. [M-M 1891]

Report primarily concerned with the mines of Real del Monte y Pachuca, including a history of the mines, 1739-1865. With brief notes on Fresnillo, Veta Grande, and Bolaños.

PALOMAR Y VIZCARRA, MIGUEL, 1880-1968
The Conflict between Church and State in Mexico. Mexico City. 1954-1962.
14 p. (Photocopy) 28 cm. [M-M 1868]

Four typescript items written by or concerning Palomar, leader of the Catholic "Cristeros" who revolted in 1926-1929 against the Mexican government and the anti-Catholic provisions of the 1917 Constitution.

PALOMAR Y VIZCARRA, MIGUEL, 1880-1968
The Cristero Rebellion. 1926-1929.
62 reels. (On film) [M-B 16]

Selection of materials from a collection on the Cristero Rebellion. Palomar assembled and maintained this archive, which contains letters, newspaper clippings, pamphlets and other records on the rise of the rebellion, organization of La Liga Nacional Defensora de la Libertad Religiosa, course of the revolt, and the aftermath of defeat. The Cristero Rebellion, rural based, had its intellectual inspiration and leadership from the city. Palomar reflects the city view in contrast to the peasant leaders who did the fighting. The Palomar group carried on a bitter debate with other lay Catholics and the hierarchy during the 1930's and 1940's concerning these events; this debate is included in the collection.

The original Palomar collection, of which the above 62 reels is a part, is now maintained at the Archivo Histórico of the National University of Mexico in Mexico City. Cf. Wilkie, James W. and Edna Monzón de. *México Visto en el Siglo XX.* (Mexico, 1969). Pp. 411-490.

PANAMA
Baptisms, Marriages, et cetera. 1683-1827.
8 folders. 29-32 cm. HHB [M-M 512]

1. Fragment, signed by Manuel, Bishop of Panama, with part of another document, concerning abuses introduced by priests of the town of Penonomé. N.d. 2 p.

2. Book of marriages. City of Panama, March-December, 1710. 2 p.

3. Book of baptisms. Town of Nata, 1683, 1684, and May, 1755. 6 p.

4. Book of baptisms. Town of San Juan de Pen.ᵉ [Penonomé?], 1771. 2 p.

5. Fragment, part of letter from Bishop of Panama, José de Umerez. San Miguel de Atalaya, 1782. 2 p.

6. Book of Marriages. Town of San Francisco Xavier de Cañazas, 1794-1797. 8 p.

7. Book of baptisms. San Buenaventura de las Palmas, 1800. 4 p.

8. Letter of Pedro Adames and Luciano Adames concerning cattle belonging to the church. San Marcel de la Mera, December 3, 1827. 4 p.

PANAMA
Documents for the History of. 1513-1885.
101 reels (On film) [Z-C 219]

Microfilm made by UNESCO from printed and manuscript documents in the Archivo Nacional de Panamá, Biblioteca Nacional de Panamá, and Biblioteca de la Universidad de Panamá. A partial "key" to contents of the film is available in the Library.

PANAMA AND COLOMBIA, 1677-1897
3 boxes (239 folders). Mostly 30-32 cm.
Originals and copies. D.S., A.L.S.   HHB [M-M 510]

This collection of documents and letters includes official correspondence addressed primarily to the governors of the provinces of Veraguas and of Chiriquí. Veraguas, a province of Panama, was created in 1719 as a part of the Viceroyalty of New Granada. From 1819 to 1855 it was a province of Colombia, during which time it was divided, in 1849, and a part of Veraguas became known as the province of Chiriquí. From 1855 to Panama's declaration of independence in 1903 these two provinces were part of the state and later department of Panama in Colombia. Included are various decrees, ordinances and proposals of the legislative chambers of Veraguas and Chiriquí, with some census information, letters and documents relating to land development in these provinces, descriptions of the region, and diverse legal papers of Veraguas, relating chiefly to inheritance problems.

The bulk of these papers is from the second and third quarters of the 19th century, a period marked by strife, political disorders, and precarious economic conditions. Some indication of this turmoil may be seen in the number of constitutions promulgated in Colombia during the 19th century—1811, 1821, 1830, 1832, 1843, 1853, 1858, 1861, 1863, and 1886.

The correspondence includes letters from the following:

James Agnew
Juan José Argote
Blas Arosemena
Mariano Arosemena
Pablo Arosemena
Manuel de Ayala
Joaquín María Barriga
F. Boyd
Juan José Cabarcas
José María Carreño
Francisco Esquivel
Francisco de Fábrega
José de Fábrega
Miguel Figueredo
Diego García
Manuel Gregorio Gonzales
Ignacio Jurado
Edward Kennedy
Pedro Laza
Robert McDowall
Jerónimo Montealto
A. Montoya
Theodore Moore
G. A. Morel
Tomás Cipriano de Mosquera
Manuel Muñoz
Rafael Núñez
Domingo de Obaldía
Pedro de Obarrio
Victorio de D. Paredes
Ricardo de la Parra
Anselmo Pineda
Lino de Pombo
José Santos de Prados
Antonio del Rio
Francisco de P. Santander
José Sardá
Francisco Soto
Ambrose W. Thompson
Antonio Rodríguez Torino
José María Urrutia Añino
John Whiting

The folders in Box 1 (1-158) are arranged by place of origin, chronologically within each section, 1804-1859. Box 2 (folders 159-190) contains Chiriquí documents, primarily official governmental messages, decrees and ordinances, from the inception of the province in 1849 to 1855. Box 3 (folders 191-239) holds Veraguas documents, including many decrees, ordinances, and messages from the governors for the period, 1821-1855, and 27 folders on judicial matters, 1677-1828, relating primarily to the probate of estates.

Many of the above items were gathered by Alphonse Louis Pinart and were used, together with other material in this collection, by H. H. Bancroft in his *History of Central America.*

This large collection has been arranged with a "key" which is available at the Bancroft Library.

PANES [Y AVELLÁN], DIEGO GARCÍA
Extension interesante de la Plaza de Veracruz. Manifiesto sobre el estado presente de la Plaza de Veracruz . . . Necesidad que hay de su extension . . . . Veracruz. August 13, 1800.
280 p. D.S. 28 cm. HHB [M-M 243]

A proposal for the extension and improvement of Veracruz to meet the needs of its garrison and its residents. The text includes a brief account of the founding of the city; a detailed description of its buildings, streets, military and hospital facilities, actual and proposed; an explanation of two accompanying diagrams or plans, one of the proposed new garrison, and the other—now missing—of the Veracruz plaza; an estimate of the costs involved in the suggested improvements; and an appendix on roads leading from Veracruz.

PAPELES FRANCISCANOS. PRIMERA SERIE. 1562-1810
2 vols. Ms. and printed. 32 cm. HHB [M-M 191-192]

A collection of registers, reports, petitions, letters, and other materials from New Spain, the Philippines, Spain, and Italy relating to Franciscan administration and activities in the Indies, notably the beatification and canonization of Antonio Margil de Jesús, the life and martyrdom of San Felipe de Jesús, the disputed transfer of Fray José Torrubia, and the apportionment of offices among Spanish-born and native friars.

The volumes contain originals and copies drawn chiefly from the archives of Franciscan provinces in New Spain and the Philippines. They bear seals of the said provinces, the Franciscan Commissioner General, and the Archdiocese of Mexico, written in Spanish, Latin, and Italian. There are a few engraved or penwork decorations and illustrations.

PAPELES VARIOS, MANUSCRIPTS
564 p. 22 cm. [M-M 1755]

Miscellany dealing for the most part with court life, history, and politics in Spain during the 17th and 18th centuries, or with the Jesuits in the New World. Contains 33 principal items.

1. Instructions, based upon those of Juan de Vega, given by the Conde de Portalegre to his son for the latter's conduct at court and in warfare.

2-4, 9. Papers relating to the Jesuits, 1649-1757. Include letters from Bishop Palafox, 1649, from José de Barreda, Jesuit Provincial of Paraguay, 1753, and from Alvaro Cienfuegos, Jesuit cardinal, 1721, as well as a file containing a report, 1757, on a reputed plan to establish a Jesuit republic in Paraguay.

5, 6, 10, 13-15. Papers issued by or relating to the Conde-Duque de Olivares, until 1643 a powerful favorite at the court of Philip IV. They include warnings to the king about Olivares by the Conde de Osuma and others, and letters and instructions of Olivares to Fernando de Guzmán, to his secretaries, and to his son-in-law.

7. Satirical essay, in the form of an astrological prophecy, on conditions under Charles II of Spain. [1684]

8. Proclamation of Juan Alfonso Enríquez, Admiral of Castile, that he will tilt at the ring in honor of Doña María Coutiño. 1623.

11. Rules formulated for his own conduct by Matheo Vázquez, [royal?] secretary. [N.p., n.d.]

12. Anonymous condolences addressed to Philip III on the death of his consort, Margaret of Austria. [1611]

16. Anonymous history and analysis of the Royal and Supreme Council of Castile, with incidental information on the Tribunal of the Inquisition and the Council of Religious Orders. Madrid, May 14, 1627.

17. A defense of the Duque de Montemar, Commander of the Spanish army in Italy, [1742]. With supporting documents, including correspondence of 1742 between Montemar and José del Campillo, Minister of State.

18-20. Collections of verses, anecdotes, and miscellaneous jottings, principally about or by Rodrigo de Calderón. No. 20 is a compilation of anecdotes involving Pope Sixtus V.

21. A biography of Anacreon, compiled from various sources, with translations and paraphrases of his poems. Madrid, September 21, 1761.

22. A collection of letters and essays in epistolary form, 15th to 17th centuries, including a satire by Fernando de Guzmán, and letters of Diego Hurtado de Mendoza, of Guillén II, Lord of Ariza, to Ferdinand the Catholic, and of Pope Sixtus V to Philip II.

23-25, 28. Accounts, printed and manuscript, of French and Spanish military or naval victories, 1714-1747, such as the Battle of Lowfeld (1747), the Count of Montemar's expedition against Orán (1744), Franco-Spanish naval victory over the English fleet off the coast of Provence (1744), and Spanish victory at Barcelona (1714).

26, 27. Political material relating to the court of Charles II of Spain, including a letter to María Luisa de Borbón, consort of Charles, and a fragment of a political verse play.

29. Comedia famosa, la verdad y el tiempo . . . . An allegorical play in verse, satirizing Spanish subservience to French ideas. Possibly written during the reign of Charles II.

30. Nueva Relacion, y Curioso Romance . . . . Valladolid, 1714. A religious legend in *romance* verse form. Printed.

31. Amante . . . . [N.p., n.d.] A love poem in *romance* verse form.

32. Anonymous notes on literature, particularly the Spanish drama, and the studies necessary for a humanist. [N.p., n.d.]

33. Varias Notas, y observaciones a los . . . modernos . . . . [Spain, ca. 1780] A criticism of new methods of scholarship introduced by the French encyclopedists, and a plea for caution in reform of the universities. Apparently written after publication of the index to the *Encyclopédie, ou Dictionnaire raisonné* . . .

PAPELES VARIOS, MANUSCRIPTS

9 folders (10 items) in portfolios. Copies and originals.
21-33 cm. HHB [M-M 385]

Manuscripts removed from the printed volumes known as *Papeles Varios*, forming part of the original H. H. Bancroft collection, and dealing with a wide variety of topics.

1. Letter of José Espinosa, Mexico City, April, 1836, to the president of Mexico, proposing a plan for improving the condition of the national treasury; 8 p. L.S. 26 cm.

2. Letter of José María Covarrubias, Mexico City, February 1, 1846, on behalf of the Cathedral Chapter of the Archdiocese of Mexico, to certain clerics who had supported the stand against confiscation of ecclesiastical property; 2 p. 22 cm.

3. Letter of Tiburcio Cuenca to a high official who had attended a function celebrating the establishment of a municipal council for Papalotla, and a speech in reply; Papalotla, n.d. 8 p. A.L.S. 21 cm.

4. Proposal for establishment of a government tobacco monopoly (Mexico, 1835?); 6 p. 29 cm.

5. Proposal relating primarily to government support and control of tobacco growers after establishment of a government tobacco monopoly; Mexico City, October 18, 1835. 4 p. 31 cm.

6. "El Romano" (*pseud.*) A speech in which Hannibal is represented as slaying his son to prevent the latter's capture by the Romans, and terminating in Hannibal's suicide—evidently part of a verse drama; 16 p. 22 cm.

7. Speech of thanks by Manuel Gutiérrez (n.p., n.d.) to Fernando José Mangino for his contributions to the progress of the Real Academia de San Carlos, followed by verses in his honor; 24 p. 21 cm.

8. Collection of Spanish and Latin verses (n.p., n.d.) in praise of Bishop Juan de Palafox, including a brief eulogy by Francisco Javier Clavigero, and an anonymous 5-canto poem based on Palafox's autobiographical *Vida Interior*—with a portrait of Palafox.

9. Copy of a report of November 7, 1733, by Manuel de la Gándara on the mining town of San Luis Potosí, summarizing its history and describing current conditions, both in the town and neighboring settlements; San Luis Potosí, November 7, 1733. Certified copy, November 13, 1793.

10. Printed form, filled in, giving number of prisoners currently in jail. Mexico City, July 1, 1868.

PARDO, DIEGO
Metrica Exposicion de la Regla Serafica . . . dedicada a nuestro P.ᵉ S.ⁿ Francisco. . . . [1760?]
254 p. 16 cm.   HHB [M-M 194]

An exposition of the Rule of St. Francis, in various verse forms, principally *décimas*, composed by a Franciscan friar of the Mexican Province of San Diego, with three short religious poems appended.

The principal poem is substantially identical in content with "El Perfecto Religioso Menor," in Miscellaneous (M-M 199), No. 24, where the title page bears the date "1760;" but Beristáin, in *Biblioteca Hispanoamericana* . . . , Vol. IV, p. 100-101, mentions two Pardo verse Mss. on this subject, one of them printed in 1729. Possibly M-M 194 and M-M 199, No. 24, are later, revised versions of the same poem, or poems; alternatively, "1760" may be simply the date of transcription.

PAREJO, FRANCISCO, d. 1628
Cathecismo y examen para los que comulgan en lengua Castellana y Timuquana. Mexico. 1627.
550 p. 33 cm.   HHB [Z-B 2]

A catechism for the Timucuan Indians of Florida. Manuscript copy of a published work in the British Museum. Acquired by Alphonse Pinart.

PARISH RECORDS FROM NUESTRA SEÑORA DE GUADALUPE DE REINOSA. NUEVO LEÓN, MEXICO. 1781-1831
5 folders. 21-31 cm.   [M-M 1758:1-5]

1. Ocho Diligencias Matrimoniales q.ᵉ se practicaron en este Juzg.ᵈᵒ Ecc.ᶜᵒ de la Villa de N.ᵗʳᵃ S.ª de Guadalupe de Reynosa siendo Ministro el Reverendo Padre Predicador General Fray Francisco Antonio Rochel . . . . Nuevo León, January 5–November 19, 1781. 52 p. D.S. 31 cm.

Marriage records of the Reinosa Ecclesiastical Tribunal for eight couples. Contains petitions for investigation of fitness; testimony of witnesses; ecclesiastical orders; statements on publication of banns and marriage ceremonies; and, in the case of the incomplete Fernández-Contreras file, only the cover and the documents relating to a dispensation granted by Antonio Bustamante Bustillo y Pablo, Administrator (*Gobernador*) of the diocese.

2. Libro Segundo de Bauptismos para los Yndios Pertenecientes â esta Mission . . . , agregados â esta Villa . . . . Reinosa, 1790-1831. 88 p. D.S. 30-31 cm.

Baptismal register for the Franciscan mission of San Joaquín of the parish of Reinosa, July 1, 1790–August 31, 1831; with apparent gaps for 1812-1815 and 1816-1831; probably incomplete. Includes statements of Visiting Inspectors Gaspar González de Candamo, July 20, 1791, administrator of the diocese, and Primo Feliciano Marín de Porras, January 28, 1805, Bishop of Nuevo León.

3. Three letters relating to the parish. Nuevo León, 1795-1814. 7 p. 21-28 cm.

Concern restoration of the parish church, June 23, 1795; contributions of Nicolás Balli and his brothers to the parish, ca. 1807; interest of the Felipe

Antonio Abarca family in the Brotherhood of Nuestra Señora de la Soledad, April 1, 1814, and the desire of the family for a tomb in the chapel.

4. Record of the founding of the Cofradía de Nuestra Santísima Madre de la Soledad.... Reinosa. 1811-1823. *7 p. 31 cm.*

Founding of the *Cofradía*, a burial guild, April 26, 1811, with lists of various classes of members, 1811-1823.

5. Cuaderno con varios asuntos o papeles diversos. [N.p., n.d.] Cover only, for items 1-4, with faded inscription.

PARKE, JOHN GRUBB, 1827-1900

Letter to Major [James Lyman?] Van Buren. [ca. 1862?]
1 p. A.L.S. 20 cm. [z-z 100:24]

Requesting permit for Thomas Austin to visit George P. [Steiner?], confined on Johnson's Island under sentence of execution.

PARKMAN, SAMUEL PAUL (PABLO), 1804-1873

Family Papers. 1807-1961.
1 box. [M-B 10]

Samuel Paul "Pablo" Parkman, an American, was the founder of this Mexican family. From his birthplace in New York, the family moved westward until, in 1829, Samuel went to the Rocky Mountains with William L. Sublette as a trapper. After his return the next year, he became associated with Jedediah S. Smith, and in the spring of 1831, as clerk, accompanied Smith on the journey to Santa Fe on which the latter was killed.

Parkman entered into an association at Santa Fe with Smith's younger brother, Peter, and in the fall of 1832, went down into old Mexico. He settled at Guanajuato, famous mining town, and was soon connected with various mining enterprises. There he married Antonia de Vega and became a Mexican citizen. His descendants have continued to live in the country.

The papers include a first draft of Jedediah Smith's will, 1831; Parkman's diary of his journey to Mexico in November, 1832; a letter of Augustus Storrs, 1836; diary of Robert Watson Noble's journey from Chihuahua to California in 1849; reports of mining activities; family and genealogical papers; letters from President Porfirio Díaz to Parkman; and other correspondence. (Six of Parkman's letters from Mexico in 1833-1835 are preserved in the Library's Peter Smith papers [P-W 44].)

There is a "key" to the collection.

PARKS, C   E

Letter to Nat(?). Berwick, Illinois. December 14, 1867.
2 p. A.L.S. 20 cm. [z-z 100:69]

Asking him to write.

PARRA, FRANCISCO

Conquista de la Provincia de Xalisco, Nuevo Reyno de Galicia y fundacion de su capital, Guadalaxara. Narracion Poetico-sencilla distribuida en XXXI Cantos. 1805-1810.
800 p. 22 cm. HHB [M-M 195]

An epic in 31 cantos of 10 octaves each by a member of the Dominican

Convent of Rosario in Guadalajara, describing the Spanish conquest of Jalisco and also the founding and development of Guadalajara, during the period 1530-1547. There are notes following the majority of the cantos and three appended prose summaries listing respectively the presidents of the province through 1805, the bishops of the See to the time of Ruiz de Cabañas, and the cities and towns of the Intendancy.

Copy of the original Ms. rescued by José Fernando Ramírez during the 1861 disturbance from the Dominican library in Mexico City and deposited by him in the library of the Museo Nacional. A foreword, apparently in the hand of Ramírez, describes the original and states that two preliminary pages were lost.

PARROTT, JOHN, 1811-1884
Notes on. San Francisco. December 10, 1886.
19 p. 35 cm. HHB [M-M 378]
Biographical notes on John Parrott, businessman and United States Consul at Mazatlán from 1837-1846 and 1848-1850. Appended are extracts from several letters in 1846 regarding the war between the United States and Mexico, presumably by James R. Bolton, later Vice Consul at Mazatlán, to Parrott, Commodore John D. Sloat, and others.

PARVA DIALECTICA. . . . 1698
462 p. 16 cm. HHB [M-M 198]
A Latin treatise on logic, followed by two general philosophical accounts concerning the origin, end, and nature of matter and spirit.

PASIG, PHILIPPINE ISLANDS
Libro de Casamientos. April, 1894-1899.
174 p. D.S. 30 cm. [70/164z]
Book recording marriages in the parish of Pasig, archbishopric of Manila. Signed by various parish priests.

PATIÑO, PEDRO PABLO (?), fl. 1801
Synopciis de varios decretos de la S[agrada] C[ongregación] de R[itos]. . . . Sacole á luz el P. Fr. Pedro Pablo Patiño. . . . Coleccionados por Fr. Ygnacio Guadalupe Cerbantes. . . . Valladolid, Mexico. 1810.
244 p. Ms. and printed. 21 cm. HHB [M-M 63]
Summaries of regulations governing the celebration of Masses and other Church ceremonies; drawn primarily from decrees of the Congregation of Rites, for the instruction of clerics; explanatory notes, and leaflet on burials and prayers for the dead.

Entered by Bancroft under "Cerbantes, Ygnacio Guadalupe." The wording of the title page is ambiguous, but Patiño, a Franciscan, is known to have written works of this type and it seems probable that Cerbantes was the compiler.

PATIÑO DE ÁVILA, ÁLVARO
Descriçion de la ciudad de la Veracruz y su comarca . . . . Veracruz. March 15 and November 7, 1580.
41 p. D.S. (Photocopy) 32 cm. [M-M 1882]
Description of the city of Veracruz and the area in its jurisdiction, prepared

under the supervision of Patiño, the alcalde mayor, for Viceroy Martín Enríquez de Almansa. With a letter from Patiño to the Viceroy, and two maps.

Original in the University of Texas Library. For printed text, see Joaquín Ramírez Cabañas, *La Ciudad de Veracruz en el Siglo XVI* (Mexico City, 1943).

PAXSON, FREDERIC LOGAN, 1877-1948
  Notes and Papers. 46-39 B.C.–1948 A.D.
  Two cartons and numerous card file boxes [z-r 1]
  A card file of historical notes arranged chronologically, records of graduate students, lecture notes, class grades, book reviews, and speeches.

PAZ, IRENEO, 1836-1924
  Biography. . . . [ca. 1884-1885?]
  3 items. 21 cm. HHB [M-M 371]
  Biographical sketch of Ireneo Paz, Mexican newspaperman, together with some printed material on the Associated Press of Mexico, and other items.

PAZ, PEDRO DE
  Documents relating to the Estate of Don Pedro de Paz. 1738?-1740.
  118 p. 29 cm. HHB [M-M 197]
  Documents setting forth, in the name of Colonel Nicolás Benítez, a plea for implementation of the judgment passed by the Real Audiencia on April 3, 1737, regarding restoration of Paz's entailed estate to his descendant, María Josefa de Paz Cortés y Monroy, the plaintiff's wife, together with the fruits accruing from its illegal retention by the present possessor, Antonio Tamaris, and his ancestors. Consists chiefly of a clause copied from the will of Paz, and a statement drawn up for Benítez by the attorney, José Antonio Flores de Rivera, and an appeal, 1740, drawn up in the name of Antonio Tamaris and signed by the attorney, Pedro de Vargas Machuca, denying that the estate was entailed and contesting the jurisdiction of the Real Audiencia over the case.

PAZ BARAONA, MIGUEL, PRESIDENT OF HONDURAS, 1925-1929
  Título del terreno "Montaña de la Flor," Municipio de Orica, Dept.º de Tegucigalpa, concedido en calidad de ejidos a la Tribu de Jicaques que la ocupa. Tegucigalpa. January 25, 1929.
  41 p. D.S. (Photocopy) 25 cm. [M-M 1906]
  Patent for land granted to the Jicaque tribe. Contains information relating to the Indians.

PEARSON, NORMAN HOLMES, 1909-
  Letter to Dixon ———, and Book Review. [New Haven, Connecticut]. December 29, 1941.
  9 p. L.S. and typescript. 28 cm. [z-z 100:91]
  Sending review of *American Renaissance* by F. O. Matthiessen.

PEASE, ISAAC D
   A Journal of ower entended voiage . . . on bord of the good sloop called the
   Rebeca . . . . December, 1772–May, 1773.
   96 p. A.D. 33 cm.   [z-a 206]
   Account of a whaling expedition from Nantucket, Massachusetts, to the
   West Indies. Also included is a log for a whaling trip to Guiana on board the
   sloop *Hope*, September, 1773–April, 1774. With partial transcript and related
   correspondence.

PEIRCE, SILAS
   Letter to Silas Peirce & Co. Philadelphia. March 20, 1850.
   2 p. A.L.S. 25 cm.   [z-z 100:83]
   Sending bill of lading to Boston office and discussing other business.

PENNSYLVANIA
   Legal Documents. 1774-1816.
   11 p. D.S. and A.L.S. 17-36 cm.   [z-z 167]
   Miscellaneous papers concerning land transactions, and two letters from
   William Clark, 1816, relating to the proposed building of an arsenal in Meadville.

PEREA, ESTEVAN DE
   Tratado de las turbaciones desta nueva yglesia. . . . Mexico. 1626.
   303 p. (Photocopy) 35 cm.   [z-e 15]
   Original in the Biblioteca Universitaria de Oviedo, Spain.

PÉREZ, ANTONIO, 1534-1611
   Advertencia al Duque de Lerma, Ministro de Phelipe 4,° [and other papers].
   Copies.
   6 items (443 p.) 20 cm.   HHB [m-m 1908]
   1. Admonition to the Duke of Lerma, minister of Philip IV, by his secretary,
   Antonio Pérez, then in exile in France, advising him to continue in office, for
   the benefit of the people. [N.p., n.d.] 312 p.
   2. The Bishop of Puebla informs the king of the damage done by permitting
   long vacancies of canonships and prebendaries in the Church, and tells of this
   situation in the Cathedral of Los Angeles in Puebla. Dated Angeles [Puebla],
   April 15, 1662. 7 p.
   3. Rozas, Luis de. Letter from the governor of New Mexico to the Visitador,
   informing him of conditions in that province, and of the steps that should be
   taken to remedy them. Santa Fe, September 29, 1641. 56 p.
   4. Letter from Pope Clement XIII to Charles III, asking aid for the Catholics
   in Poland. Rome, April 27, 1767. 3 p.
   5. Freyre de Andrade, Gómez. Letter to the caciques and leaders of towns
   in rebellion, warning them to submit. Written at Campo del Rio Vardo, July
   18, 1754. Relates to conditions in Uruguay. 10 p.
   6. A 1767 file of papers relating to the expulsion of the Jesuits from Spain and
   her possessions, including two letters from the King of Spain to the Pope,

March 31 and May 2; the Pope's reply, April 16; and a "Consulta" or special report of the Council of Castile, Madrid, April 30, 1767, signed by the Count of Aranda and other members. 51 p.

PÉREZ, FRANCISCO
Receipts. Guadalajara. May, 1849.
2 items. 20x26 cm. HHB [M-M 1700:48]
Acknowledgment of receipt of coins for delivery to Barron, Forbes & Company.

PÉREZ ADAMDICOSIO Y CAUTO, JOSÉ MARÍA ALEJO DE
El Jacobinismo de Méjico. . . . Mexico. 1833.
125 p. A.D.S. 24 cm. HHB [M-M 4]
Political pamphlet defending the Constitution of 1824 and combating the reactionary Plans of Cuernavaca and Orizaba.

PERRY, OLIVER HAZZARD, 1821-1901
Diary and Papers. 1847-1849, 1964.
3 items (142 p.) A.D. 25-26 cm. [M-M 1896]
Perry's diary of his experiences in the Massachusetts Volunteers during the Mexican War, 1847-1848; a Spanish exercise book in his handwriting, 1849; and a written statement, 1964, by his grandson, Perry Patton, giving biographical details of his grandfather.

PERU. CASA DE MONEDA, POTOSÍ
Libro real g.^{ral} de compras de metales que se hazen de cuenta de S. M. en esta su R.^{1} Caza de Moneda . . . . 1772-1787.
2 vols. 48 cm. [Z-D 130]
Accounts of silver and gold coined.

PERU, COLONIAL
2 boxes (1441 p.) (Typescript) 28 cm. [Z-D 107]
Transcripts of selected documents from various archives.
1. Documents from the Archivo General de Indias, Seville, concerning José Antonio de Areche, Visitador General del Peru from 1777 to 1782, and Viceroy Manuel Guirior. 1781-1795.
2. Memorias relativas a la sublevación del Casique de Tunga-Saca José Gabriel Tupac-Amaro . . . . 1780-1789. From various archives in Lima.
3. Relación de los hechos mas notables acaecidos en la sublevación general fraguada en los Reynos del Perú, por el Yndio José Gabriel Tupac-Amaru . . . . [1786] Original in the Biblioteca Nacional, Lima.
4. Documentos reservados en los Autos Criminales contra Mariano Tupac Amaro y Andres Mendigure . . . . Bound in volume entitled "Rebelión de Tupac Amaru, Tomo II." Contains documents and letters covering negotiations for the surrender of Diego Cristóbal Tupac Amaru, 1781-1782. Original in the Biblioteca Nacional and Archivo Nacional, Lima.

PERU, INDIANS
Documents relating to. 17th century.
83 p. 33 cm. [Z-D 123]
Selected documents on early Peru, with description of character of the Indians, the provinces in which they lived, nature of matrimonial customs, haciendas, tribute, and some population figures. Copied from the Additional MSS Series, British Museum, for Alphonse L. Pinart. "Key" available.

PERU. INDIANS
Documents relating to . ca. 1730-1815.
3 reels (On film) [Z-D 106]
Selected materials from the New York Public and Yale University Libraries, filmed for John H. Rowe.

PESA Y CASAS, JOSÉ MARIANO DE LA
Expediente concerning Town and District of Apam, Hidalgo. January 9–February 27, 1789.
27 p. D. and D.S. 30-31 cm. [M-M 1821]
Two reports from the local alcalde mayor and subdelegate, Pesa y Casas, addressed to Intendant General Bernardo Bonavía; and copy of a letter from Bonavía to Pesa y Casas. The reports describe the location, climate, soil, natural resources, civil and clerical administration, churches, population, and other features of the district's rural estates and four towns—Apam, Almoloyán, Tepeapulco, and Tlanalapa.

PESQUERA, FELIPE
Cuadernos de órdenes . . . . Guadalajara, Mexico. 1838-1844.
2 vols. D.S. 31-32 cm. [M-M 1750]
Volumes I and III of records relating to the Departmental Revenue Guard for Guadalajara under Captain Felipe Pesquera.
Vol. 1. Cuaderno de Ordenes para el resguardo de rentas . . . á espensas del Capitan Felipe Pesquera. Guadalajara, August 1, 1838–February 18, 1840. 591 p. Orders of the day, with personnel lists and monthly payrolls. Also includes notes on visits of inspection, appointments, and similar matters.
Vol. 2. Cuaderno de Ordenes para el arreglo del resguardo de esta Capital . . . . Guadalajara, June 1, 1842–July 9, 1844. 592 p. Orders of the day, with personnel lists for June and July only, and miscellaneous notes.

PHILBRICK, FRANCIS SAMUEL, 1876-
Papers. ca. 1909-1912.
6 cartons and 7 boxes. [Z-E 8]
Correspondence, notes, and outlines on research in various Spanish archives for material relating to Cuba.

PHILIP V, 1683-1746
Decree of the King of Spain. [N.p.] 1731.
2 p. 31 cm. HHB [M-M 1700:49]
Relates to a residencia in New Spain. Incomplete.

PHILIPPINE ISLANDS
> The British capture of Manila. Manila. 1762-ca. 1765.
> *24 p. D. and L.S. 30-33 cm.* [z-p 106]
> An account of incidents in the siege and capture of Manila, correspondence, and a copy of the surrender terms.

PHILIPPINE ISLANDS
> British Expedition against the Philippines. 1762-1767.
> *15 vols. (Transcripts)* [z-p 104]
> Copies of correspondence and official records of proceedings of the agents of the East India Company at Manila, including official documents relating to the government at Manila and the Philippine Islands. Originals, entitled "Manila Records," in the Record Office at Egmore, Madras, India.

PHILIPPINE ISLANDS
> Documents relating to the Spanish Army in the Philippines. 1823-1863.
> *26 folders. D.S. and L.S. 11-32 cm.* [z-p 114]
> Miscellaneous official army papers, including correspondence, applications and petitions, complaints, appointments, and lists of personnel.

PHILIPPINE ISLANDS
> Miscellaneous Documents. 1803-1898.
> *8 folders. D.S. 31-33 cm.* [z-p 111]
> Records of trials and inquiries, certificates of good conduct, and letters of application for positions in the Spanish navy.

PHILIPPINE ISLANDS
> Miscellaneous Documents. 1842-1899.
> *18 p. D.S. 16-32 cm.* [70/166z]
> Primarily burial certificates; and documents relating to the transfer of cattle. From various villages of central Luzon.

PHILIPPINE ISLANDS
> Noticia de las cantidades invertidas en las atentaciones de la Marina de estas Islas desde 1.º de Enero hasta fin de Agosto del presente año. Cavite, Luzon. October 13, 1836.
> *3 p. 30 cm.* [z-p 115]

PHILIPPINE ISLANDS
> Ordenanzas para corregidores y alcaldes mayores. Manila. 1739-1764.
> *135 exp. (On film)* [z-p 102]
> From the Edwin Grabhorn Collection.

PHILIPPINE ISLANDS
> Papers relating to. 1886-1898.
> *9 p. 7-46 cm.* [z-p 119]
> Receipt from the Juez de Paz of Macati; papers of the parish of San Pedro Macati, Manila; Y.M.C.A. card and stationery; and a printed government proclamation, in Arabic, to the inhabitants of Mindanao.

PHILIPPINE ISLANDS
2.ª Pieza Del Expediente formado en punto de la Irrupcion Anglicana cōque procedió à el Acedio de esta Ciudad de Manila. Manila. August 6, 1763.
438 p. D.S. 31 cm. [z-p 105]
Certified copy of a report of the British capture of Manila in 1762.

PHILIPPINE ISLANDS
Reales Cédulas. 1575-1677.
4 vols. 30 cm. [z-p 100]
Copies of royal decrees relating to the Philippine Islands. A "key" to the collection is available in the Library.

PHILIPPINE ISLANDS
Selected Documents concerning the British Expedition against Manila. 1761-1766.
132 folders. (Transcripts) 32 cm. [z-p 103]
Copies of documents from the Public Record Office, London, and the Ayer Collection in the Newberry Library, Chicago. A calendar of the collection is available in Karl Clayton Leebrick, *The English Expedition to Manila in 1762, and the Government of the Philippine Islands by the East India Company* (University of California, Ph. D. Thesis, 1917).

PHILIPPINE ISLANDS. MINISTERIO Y CONTADURÍA GENERAL DE MARINA
Lista de varios oficiales de Guerra . . . . Cavite, Luzón. 1802-1805.
23 p. 29 cm. [z-p 110]

PILCHER, THOMAS, d. 1788
Last Will and Testament. Cheriton, Kent. June 19, 1788.
4 p. 39 cm. [z-z 100:8]
Copy extracted from the Registry of the Archdeacon's Court of Canterbury. With note of probate, July 14, 1788.

PINART, ALPHONSE LOUIS, 1852-1911, *comp.*
Documents for the History of Chihuahua. Extracts from Mss. & printed matter in the collection of Mons. Alphonse Pinart. 1786-1823.
2 vols. in one. 31 cm. HHB [m-m 287]
Notes, largely in English, on material collected by Alphonse Pinart relating to events in the Provincias Internas, particularly Chihuahua, during the period 1786-1823.

PINART, ALPHONSE LOUIS, 1852-1911, *comp.*
Documents for the History of Sonora. Extracts from Mss. & printed matter in the Collection of Mons. Alphonse Pinart. 1784-1877.
7 vols. in 5. 32 cm. HHB [m-m 288-292]
English notes on material collected by Alphonse Pinart (cf. Pinart . . . "Colección de manuscritos . . . ," m-m 379-381), relating to events in Sonora from 1784 to 1877. Vols. I-II cover the periods 1784-1833 and 1830-1841; Vol.

III, 1842-1846; Vol. IV, 1847-1851; Vol. V, 1852-1856; and Vols. VI-VII deal with the periods 1857-1863 and 1864-1877.

PINART, ALPHONSE LOUIS, 1852-1911, *comp.*
Documents relating to Northern Mexico. Series I. [ca. 1768-1833?]
106 items. 22-44 cm. HHB [M-M 379]

Letters and documents, originals and copies, relating to affairs in northern Mexico toward the close of the Colonial period and during the early years of independence, with emphasis upon frontier defense, the Iturbide Empire, mission administration, and mining.

The material may be divided into several classifications, namely, items relating to the Marqués de Rubí and frontier defense, 1768-1772, item 1; work to be done by Simón Elías González in his report on military posts and frontier defense from Sonora to New Mexico, ca. 1814, items 42-44; papers concerning Ignacio Pérez's overdue debt for cattle bought for the armed forces from a number of missions, correspondence with their priests, and Pérez's relations with the local authorities in the politico-military turmoil in the year 1823, notably Echávarri's Plan de Casa Mata and his correspondence with Colonel Alberto Máynez and the Chihuahua Town Council, items 49, 56-58, 60-62, 71-75, 77, 82-83, 92-109; Iturbide's rise to power in 1823, items 69, 70, 81; letters and proclamations of Governor Ignacio de Bustamante of Sonora, 1821, relating to convocation of a national constituent congress, items 65-68; letters of Pedro María de Allande concerning the Plan de Casa Mata, 1823, items 90 and 91; letters and proclamations of Gaspar de Ochoa, 1823, dealing with the Plan de Casa Mata, items 80, 85, 86, and 89; letters of Colonel Antonio Cordero, 1821-1823, regarding an order against judicial extortion of property from the natives, and his own refusal to resume official duties on the grounds of illness, items 59 and 87; a miscellany of papers on military and political affairs, ca. 1791-1823, items 5, 10, 46, 48, 64, and 84.

The collection contains also papers relating to diocesan or ecclesiastical matters, particularly in Durango, 1777-1794, items 2, 3, 6-8, and 13; papers of or about Fray Faustino González and problems among the Indians on the Sonora frontier, 1821-1833, items 51-55, 63, and 88; documents concerning mining affairs in Sonora, 1796-1803, items 14-16, 20, 23-24, 30-32, and 34; circulars and letters of José Tomás de Zuza relative to mining, items 17-18, 20-22, and 25-28; a miscellany on the mines of the Cieneguilla area, 1800-1831, items 19, 29, 37, 40, and 50; material relating to wills and inheritances, 1762-1818, in Sonora and Sinaloa, items 12, 33 and 41; on the distribution of lands, 1807-1817, items 4, 9, 11, 36, 38-39, and 47.

Although the documents are actually numbered 1-109, this collection consists of 106 items. Several numbers are missing, and others are used for more than one item.

PINART, ALPHONSE LOUIS, 1852-1911, *comp.*
Documents relating to Northern Mexico. Series II. Mexico. January 16, 1824–October 22, 1841.
68 items. 12-32 cm. HHB [M-M 380]

Letters and documents, originals and copies, relating to affairs in northern

Mexico, principally Sonora, with emphasis on mission administration, Indian questions, and political unrest.

Several items relate especially to mission affairs, including letters from Fray Faustino González, president of the Pimería Alta missions, to officials at the presidio of Altar, 1824-1828, items 2, 6, 22, 25, 28, 30 and 40; letters of Father Miguel Montés, 1827, to the alcalde at Altar, items 31-35; conflict of the friars with temporal authorities, 1827-1828, items 29, 39, and 41; letters of Fray Juan Vaño, 1827, concerning complaints against the alcalde of Altar, items 11 and 18; inventories of mission property at Tumacácori and San Ignacio Caburi, 1829-1841, items 46 and 65.

As to material relating especially to the Indians, there are letters from the Pima Chieftain, Captain Enrique Tejeda, 1826, items 20 and 26; others, concerning Indian threats in Sonora, from officials in Altar, Caborca, Horcasitas, Santa Cruz, Cieneguilla, and Arispe, 1824-1835, items 1, 13-14, 21, 24, 27, 36, 38, 54-55, 57-58, 62, 64, and 67.

Administrative questions are reflected in letters of Mariano de Urrea, 1824, concerning settlement of a dispute between Sonora and New Vizcaya, items 3-5; letters from Governor José María Gaxiola of Sonora, 1821, regarding establishment of a mail route from Altar to the Californias, and the arrest of some American intruders, items 42-44; rebellion aimed at removing Gaxiola as governor in favor of Francisco Iriarte, 1829, items 47 and 50-53; a tariff schedule of 1827 drawn up by Pedro de la Serna, at Cieneguilla, Sonora, items 37 and 59; miscellaneous items relating to the policies of government in the administration of affairs in northern Mexico, especially Sonora, 1825-1844, e.g., maintenance of public order, frontier defense, and local administrative problems, items 9, 10, 12, 15, 17, 49, 56, 60-61, 63, 66, and 68.

Other documents concern military matters primarily, with a report of Governor Simón Elías González and other papers, 1824-1826, regarding various garrisons, Apache threats, and lands, items 7, 16, and 19; report of a victory won by Captain Ramón Mier, and an exhortation by José Figueroa to maintain order, 1826-1829, items 23 and 48; and miscellaneous military affairs, 1824-1828, items 8 and 45.

PINART ALPHONSE LOUIS, 1852-1911, *comp.*
Documents relating to Northern Mexico. Series III. Mexico, October 26, 1842–December 27, 1861.
312 items. 21-35 cm.   HHB [M-M 381]

Letters and documents, originals and copies, relating almost entirely to military or politico-military affairs in Sonora, such as conflicts with Indians, revolutionary unrest, and Mexico–United States relations, but including a few Mss. on religious matters and land problems.

A major classification is politico-military affairs, under which the chief items are: a report from the acting commandant at Tubac, Roque Ibarra, 1842-1843, concerning a campaign against the Apaches, statistical tables on the infantry forces there, and events at Tubac during February, 1843, items 1, 37, 39, 43, 45-46, 51-53, 56, 58, and 60.

Further information on the infantry company at Tubac is recorded by Jerónimo Herrán, 1842-1843, in items 2 and 61. A record of outgoing letters, memoranda, and accounts, written mostly in Ures or Satebuchi, in the campaign against the Apaches, November, 1842, items 3-36.

The commandant at Tucson wrote reports and letters, 1842-1846, to José María Elías González, concerning relations with the Pápago, Apache, and other Indians, needs of the presidio, and seditious activities of Manuel María Gándara, items 38, 40-42, 47-50, 59, 64, 66, 70, 82, and 84-86.

Two documents over the signature of Francisco Narbona, 1843 and 1845, concern military activities against the Apaches, items 54 and 115.

A group of miscellaneous documents, 1843-1856, relate to hostilities with the Apaches and other Indians in the Sonora area, items 55, 111-113, 148, 157, and 312.

The Tubac commander, Andrés B. Centeno, made a series of reports, for the most part to Governor Gándara, on population data for Tubac, needs of the presidio, relations with the Apaches, and the lack of cooperation of officials at Tucson. See items 57, 118-126, 131-132, 136-139, and 149.

Reports and correspondence of military and civil officials resulting from an inquiry instituted by José María Elías González in 1844 concerning damage done in Sonora, as well as in Chihuahua, by the Janos Indians, items 63, 65, 67-69, and 71-79.

Reports from and to Elías González on frontier conditions, defense against the Indians, needs of the Tubac colony, and a petition from Antonio Culo Azul for clemency to Indian deserters; includes letters from other officials on the same topics, 1846-1853. See items 80-81, 83, 110, 114, and 116-117.

Letters of Antonio Campuzano, 1846-1857, concerning unrest ascribed to Francisco Islas, revolutionary activities of Rafael Andrade, and Guaymas affairs. Includes a letter of José María Vélez Escalante relating to Andrade; items 87, 89-93, 96, 98-99, and 212.

Ten letters from Governor José María Gaxiola of Sonora, 1846, dealing with problems of local unrest, a campaign against the Seris, financial problems, etc., and a communication from the Departmental Assembly urging the return of the governing authorities to Ures; items 88, 94-95, 101, and 103-109.

Letters from Francisco Islas and Juan Esteban Milla relating to Campuzano's conduct, especially in the Andrade-Madrigal case, 1846; items 97 and 102.

Notes of 1853 regarding the disability of a soldier, Agustín Escalante, and return of a deserter, 1855; items 127 and 150.

Circulars and an order relating to Centeno's command and the defense of the frontier posts at Tucson, Tubac, Santa Cruz, Fronteras, and Bavispe, in 1853; items 128, 133-135.

Records of outgoing correspondence, 1854-1861, ascribed to Manuel E. Elías Pro, dealing with United States filibusterers, frontier defense, Mexico–United States relations, and related topics; items 140, 159-208, 210, and 213-310.

Letters from Domingo Ramírez de Arellano, governor of Sonora, concerning the Pápago Indians and the United States–Mexico boundary, 1855; items 141 and 142.

Events at the presidio of Tucson in August, 1855; items 151-154.

Two official communications, 1857, relating to United States intrusions on Mexican territory by B. T. Davis; items 209 and 211.

Miscellaneous military matters in Sonora, 1844-1857, such as grain supplies, charges against Gándara, etc.; items 130, 155, and 158.

Four inventories of sacred vessels and various objects in chapels at Tucson, San Javier del Bac, and Tumacácori; items 143-147.

A report of 1844 on the Indians of the towns attached to the presidios of Caborca, Tubutama, and San Ignacio; item 62.

Dispositions compiled by José María Mendoza, 1843, in regard to the validity of land claims, with other documents of the same nature, 1853-1856; items 44, 129, and 156.

PINART, ALPHONSE LOUIS, 1852-1911, *comp.*
[Informes sobre parroquias y pueblos. San Luis Potosí, Mexico]. 1865-1870.
4 folders. 34 cm.   HHB [M-M 274]

Summary reports, in Pinart's handwriting, on various parishes, towns, and settlements situated entirely or for the most part in San Luis Potosí, and within the ecclesiastical jurisdiction of Tulancingo. They deal with population, indigenous languages, products, industries, locations, areas, climate, etc. Apparently prepared by the respective parish priests in response to requests from ecclesiastical superiors.

PINART, ALPHONSE LOUIS, 1852-1911, *comp.*
La Purísima Concepción de Caborca Mission. 1764-1822.
3 folders in portfolio. D.S. 29 cm.   HHB [M-M 421]

Record of baptisms, 1764-1769, 10 p.; burials and marriages, 1790-1803, 14 p.; baptisms, 1820-1822, 6 p.

PINART, ALPHONSE LOUIS, 1852-1911
Letters to Albert Samuel Gatschet. 1879-1889.
1 box. A.L.S.   [68/51z]

The letters were written from San Francisco, New York, Paris, and various places in Mexico and Central America, and deal primarily with linguistics of the original peoples of Mexico and Central America. There is a copy of Fray Pedro de Llisa's "Confesionario en Idioma del Choconate, Paya, Tapaliza, etc.," and bibliographic and linguistic information. A bound volume contains notes, word lists, and clippings (perhaps collected by Gatschet), 1878-1893, relating largely to North American Indian dialects, customs and legends.

PINART, ALPHONSE LOUIS, 1852-1911, *comp.*
Linguistic Material relating to the Indians of Central America. 1882-1883.
250 p. 21-28 cm.   HHB [Z-C 8]

Includes vocabularies and catechisms in various Indian languages. With typed list of contents.

PINART, ALPHONSE LOUIS, 1852-1911, *comp.*
Linguistic Material relating to the Indians of Mexico.
17 vols. 16-32 cm.   HHB [M-M 478-494]

[Ara, Domingo de]. Bocabulario de lengua tzeldal según el orden de Copanabastla [1571]
304 p. 21 cm.   HHB [M-M 478]

Tzental vocabulary, notes on grammar, and prayers, copied in 1616 from a 1571 original, with numerous additions and annotations of uncertain date. Contains the signature of Fray Alonso de Guzmán, to whom the volume was at one time assigned.

[Ara, Domingo de]. Bocabulario en Lengua Tzeldal. [N.d.]
325 p. 21 cm.   HHB [M-M 479]

Tzental-Spanish vocabulary with prayers and names of pueblos translated into Tzental; also some pages of prayers and other material translated into Tzotzil.

Temporal, Bartolomé. Libro de comparaciones, y de moral cristiana en lengua tzendal. . . . [N.d.]
342 p., A?D.S. 23 cm.   HHB [M-M 480]

A religious work translated into Tzental, with a table of contents. The Abbé Brasseur de Bourbourg dates this volume as the end of 16th or early 17th cent.

[González, Fray Luis]. Arte Breve en Lengua Tzoque, conforme se habla en Tecpatlan. . . . [ca. 1652]
86 p. 23 cm.   HHB [M-M 481]

A grammar on the language of the Zoque Indians, preceded by a catechism translated into the same language; originally part of a larger work which included a vocabulary. Attributed by the Abbé Brasseur de Bourbourg to Fray Luis.

Moyano, Francisco. Sermons in the Pima language.
61 p. 16 cm.   HHB [M-M 482]

Ascribed by José Miranda to the end of the 16th, or early 17th cent. Incomplete.

[Barbastro, Francisco Antonio] ca. 1725-1800. Religious materials in the Opata language.
438 p. A?Ms. 21 cm.   HHB [M-M 483]

A vocabulary and religious topics in the Opata language prepared for use in the Aconchi mission. Contains sermons, a brief confessionary litany, a catechism, and prayers. Attributed to Fray Francisco in a note by Pinart. Incomplete.

Náhuatl manuscript.
3 p. 16 cm.   HHB [M-M 484]

Unidentified Ms. in Náhuatl; ascribed by Dr. Wigberto Jiménez Moreno to the early 17th cent.

Balbastro, Pablo, *comp.* Vocabulario de la lengua Opata—dialecto Tehuima.
87 p. 32 cm. HHB [M-M 485]
Vocabulary of the Tehuima dialect of the Opata language. Title page written and signed by Pinart, February 22, 1879, at Aconchi, with some of the Ms. in his handwriting.

Pinart, Alphonse Louis. Vocabulario del dialecto Hehúe de la lengua Opata. December 11-21, 1878.
15 p. A.D.S. 32 cm. HHB [M-M 486]
Copy of an Opata-Spanish vocabulary, based upon information supplied orally to Pinart by an unidentified person, possibly Antonio Ruiz, through the Indian interpreter Rosa Tecla.

Pinart, Alphonse Louis. Vocabulario de la lengua Papaga. Pitiquito, Río del Altar. March 4, 1879.
29 p. A.D.S. 27-32 cm. HHB [M-M 487]
Pápago vocabulary compiled by Pinart with the aid of the interpreters, Trinidad González and Matías Parras.

Pinart, Alphonse Louis. Vocabulario de la lengua Seri. Pueblo de Seris. April 4, 1879.
24 p. A.D.S. 32 cm. HHB [M-M 488]
Vocabulary of the language of the Seri Indians compiled by Pinart with the aid of Seri interpreters.

[Pinart, Alphonse Louis?] Fragmentary notes in French on the Seri language.
9 p. A.D. 32 cm. HHB [M-M 489]

Christian doctrine translated into the Matlatzinca language. [1634-?]
2 vols. (192 p., 150 p.) 17 cm. HHB [M-M 490]
Copies in the handwriting of Pinart of a guide for instructors of Indians in Christian doctrine and conduct, written in the Matlatzinca language (a branch of the Otomí language), Spanish and Latin. Also includes bilingual religious texts, translations of Biblical passages, a translation into Matlatzincan based upon the dialogue of Father M. Gilberti and prepared in 1634 by order of Father Miguel de Guevara, and some miscellaneous material of a bibliographical nature relating principally to work of Father Francisco de Alvarado and other Dominicans.

Roldán, Bartolomé. Cartilla y Doctrina Christiana, breve y compendiosa, para enseñar los ninos; y ciertas preguntas tocantes a la dicha doctrina, por manera de Dialogo .... 1580.
164 p. 19 cm. HHB [M-M 491]
Texts for religious instruction, including material in dialogue form, compiled and translated into the language of the Choco Indians by the Dominican Roldán.

Nájera Yanguas, Diego de, 1580-1635. Doctrina y enseñança en la lengua Maçahua de cosas muy utiles y provechosas para los ministros de doctrina y para los naturales.... Mexico City. 1637.
8 p. 19 cm. HHB [M-M 492]

The preliminary matter of a doctrinal work written by Nájera Yanguas, an Inquisition official, for use among the Mazahua Indians. Copied by Pinart from a published work.

Aztec pictographs. Valle de Toluca. [N.d.]
112 p. 17 cm. HHB [M-M 493]

Five pictographic Aztec catechisms. Copied by Pinart, in 1881, from Mss. in the library of Joaquín García Icazbalceta.

Soriano, Juan Guadalupe. Arte del Idioma Pame *and* Prologo Historial. [July 15, 1567?]
2 vols. (148 p., 23 p.) 21-34 cm. HHB [M-M 494]

Volume I contains material on the grammar and vocabulary of the Pame dialect, a divergent branch of the language group of the Otomí Indians. Volume II, the "Historical Prologue," is a treatise on the history of the Pame nation and missionary work among the Pame Indians. Copied by Pinart from Mss. in the collection of Joaquín García Icazbalceta in December, 1879.

PINART, ALPHONSE LOUIS, 1852-1911, *comp.*
Real de San Ildefonso de la Cieneguilla Mission. 1771-1773.
1 folder in portfolio. 14 p. D.S. 29 cm. HHB [M-M 416]

Marriage register for above years.

PINART, ALPHONSE LOUIS, 1852-1911, *comp.*
San Antonio de Oquitoa Mission. 1757-1845.
1 folder in portfolio. 124 p. D.S. 29 cm. HHB [M-M 417]

Baptismal record kept from January 27, 1757, to January 26, 1845. Also includes records of episcopal visitations by Bernardo del Espíritu Santo, Bishop of Sonora, on January 30, 1821, and October 28, 1845; and a notation of the visit of the Commissary Prefect for the Pimería Alta missions on March 23, 1822.

PINART, ALPHONSE LOUIS, 1852-1911, *comp.*
San Francisco del Ati Mission. 1757-1827.
85 p. D.S. 29 cm. HHB [M-M 418]

Baptismal register of above mission, but including some from San Antonio de Oquitoa and Tubutama.

PINART, ALPHONSE LOUIS, 1852-1911, *comp.*
San Ignacio de Caburica Mission. 1697-1812.
6 folders in 3 portfolios. 454 p. D.S. HHB [M-M 413]

Portfolio 1 contains two folders of baptismal registers, 1720-1812, with records of episcopal visitations of Benito Crespo, 1725, and Martín de Elizacochea, 1737. Portfolio 2 contains two folders of burial records, 1697-1788. Portfolio

3 contains two folders, marriage records, 1713-1737, and fragment of a census report, 1768.

PINART, ALPHONSE LOUIS, 1852-1911, *comp.*
San Ignacio de Tubac Mission. 1806-1848.
3 folders in portfolio. 48 p. 30 cm. HHB [M-M 411]
Cover (only) for Mission register, 1806; record of marriages and burials, 1814-1824, and burials, 1848.

PINART, ALPHONSE LOUIS, 1852-1911, *comp.*
San Pedro y San Pablo de Tubutama Mission. 1768-1806.
1 folder in portfolio. 49 p. D.S. 29 cm. HHB [M-M 419]
Baptismal register of the mission and its dependent *visita*, Santa Teresa.

PINART, ALPHONSE LOUIS, 1852-1911, *comp.*
Santa Ana Pueblo. 1778-1795.
2 folders in portfolio. 30 p. D.S. 29 cm. HHB [M-M 415]
Records of baptisms, 1778-1780, and marriages, 1778-1795.

PINART, ALPHONSE LOUIS, 1852-1911, *comp.*
Santa María Magdalena Mission. 1698-1825.
7 folders in 2 portfolios. 213 p. D.S. 29 cm. HHB [M-M 414]
Portfolio 1 contains four folders of baptismal registers, 1698-1824. Portfolio 2 contains three folders of marriage and burial registers, 1702-1825, and includes records of the deaths of Fathers Manuel González, 1702, Ignacio Iturmendi, 1702, and Eusebio Francisco Kino, 1711. Also includes descriptions of the Seri raids at San Lorenzo, 1757, and at Magdalena in 1776.

PINART, ALPHONSE LOUIS, 1852-1911, *comp.*
Santa María Soamca Mission. 1732-1768.
3 folders in portfolio. 139 p. D.S. 30 cm. HHB [M-M 410]
Records compiled by various Jesuits, with some 1768 entries written by the Franciscan, Francisco Roche, of 1) baptisms, 1732-1768, with a record of mission inspection on December 19, 1737, by Martín de Elizacochea, Bishop of Durango; 2) marriages and burials, 1736-1768; and 3) baptisms and marriages, 1743-1755.

PINART, ALPHONSE LOUIS, 1852-1911, *comp.*
Santiago de Cocóspera Mission. 1822-1836.
2 folders in portfolio. 26 p. D.S. 31 cm. HHB [M-M 412]
Record of baptisms, 1822-1836, and burials, 1822-1836.

PINART, ALPHONSE LOUIS, 1852-1911, *comp.*
The *Visita* of Nuestra Señora del Pópulo del Bisanig. 1762-1803.
2 folders in portfolio. D.S. 29 cm. HHB [M-M 422]
Contains a record of marriages, 1762-1778, 20 p., and baptisms, 1780-1803, 65 p.

PINART, ALPHONSE LOUIS, 1852-1911, *comp.*
The *Visita* of San Diego del Pitaqui. 1768-1826.
4 folders in portfolio. 86 p. D.S. 29 cm.   HHB [M-M 420]
Contains: 1) burials, 1768-1797, 10 p.; 2) marriages, 1772-1778, 8 p.; 3) baptismal register, 1772-1801, 64 p.; 4) baptism, 1826, with notation of measles epidemic in that year, 4 p.

PINCHOT, AMOS RICHARDS ENO, 1873-1944
Correspondence and Papers. 1914-1941.
549 p. 19-36 cm.   [Z-Z 161]
Correspondence, press releases, and pamphlets relating to Pinchot's political interests, including activities of the America First Committee. Duplicates from the Pinchot Collection in the Library of Congress.

PINILLA Y PÉREZ, ÁNGEL
Documents and Correspondence relating to his Administration as Governor-Intendant *ad interim* of Nueva Vizcaya. 1813.
3 folders. 12 p. 21-31 cm.   [M-M 1794]
Letter concerning local administration, documents relating to the minting of *tlacos* (small copper coins) to remedy a shortage of small change, and a request that Alejo García Conde, newly appointed Governor Intendant, immediately assume his duties in Durango.

PIOUS FUND OF THE CALIFORNIAS. 1700-1857
5 items (936 p.) D.S. 22-33 cm.   [M-M 1859]
Papers, originals and copies, concerning the Pious Fund and the California missions, especially bequests and subsequent litigation. Chief centers of controversy were the estate of Francisco Lorenz de Rada, 1749-1754, with data extending from 1700 to 1805; the will of José de la Puente y Peña, Marqués de Villapuente, and the distribution of his assets among the Jesuits in the Californias and elsewhere; and miscellaneous documents on financial affairs of the Pious Fund, chiefly 1788-1789.

PIPIOLTEPEC Y ACATITLAN. EXPEDIENTE SOBRE FORMAR UN PUEBLO CON LAS RANCHERIAS DE . . . , EN LA DOCTRINA DE TEMAZCALTEPEC. MEXICO. 1709-1710
120 p. 21-31 cm.   HHB [M-M 251]
File on a proposal to form a single town from the two Indian settlements of Pipioltepec and Acatitlán, a project recommended by the parish priest, José Antonio Zúñiga, and sponsored by Lorenzo Angulo Guardamino, owner of the lands involved. Includes correspondence, orders, reports, testimony, a protest on behalf of Indian residents, certifications, and related documents.

PISCATAQUIS ASSOCIATION OF CONGREGATIONAL MINISTERS
License Issued to James Cameron to Preach the Gospel. Foxcroft, [Maine]. February 15, 1870.
1 p. D.S. 20 cm.   [Z-Z 100:50]
Written and signed by John H. Gurney, scribe. With envelope.

PLASAGARRE, M
Notes on Mexican Finance, 1851-1854. [N.p., n.d.]
2 p. 40 cm. HHB [M-M 1700:19]
Fragment from a letter-press copybook, in English. Comments on financial reform, and the payment of interest to British bondholders by M. Plasagarre, Minister of Finance.

PLYMOUTH, ENGLAND. TOWN CLERK'S OFFICE
Excerpts from Town Records of the City of Plymouth relating to Sir Francis Drake. 1580-1653.
8 p. (Photocopies and transcripts) 41 cm. [Z-G 20]
Accompanied by extract from R. N. Worth's *Calendar of Municipal Records*, explaining the significance of the so-called Black Book and White Book of Plymouth town records.

POLK, JAMES KNOX, 1795-1849
Letters to Samuel H. Laughlin and William L. Marcy. 1835-1849.
21 p. (Photocopy) 25 cm. [Z-Z 123]
Concerning his presidential career, political events in New York State, and offer of the position of Secretary of War to Marcy.

POOLE, RICHARD STAFFORD
Documents of the Third Mexican Council. . . . A Survey of Mexican Manuscripts 266, 267, 268 and 269 . . . . 1961.
32 p. (Typescript) 27 cm. [M-M 1756]
Analytical calendar of materials in the Bancroft Library relating to the Third Mexican Provincial Council, 1585. The list is arranged by manuscript and folio numbers, with a brief explanatory foreword.

PORRAS, BELISARIO, PRESIDENT OF PANAMA, 1856-1942
Invitation to William P. Vetter, Lieutenant, U.S.N. Panama, October 25, 1918.
Card and envelope. 12 cm. [Z-C 203]
Invitation to a reception celebrating the fiftieth anniversary of the Republic on November 3, 1918.

PORTER, SIR ROBERT KER, 1777-1842
Correspondence and Papers.
5 reels (On film) [Z-D 120]
Political correspondence and documents, journals, account books, and family letters, especially for the period 1825-1841 when Porter served as British consul in Caracas. Reel 5 contains an index and "key" to the collection. Original manuscripts in the Fundación John Boulton, Caracas, Venezuela.

PORTO ALEGRE, BRAZIL. PREFECTURA MUNICIPAL
Reports on Foreign Residents Wishing to Retain their Nationality. 1890-1891.
7 p. D.S. (Photocopy) 33 cm. [Z-D 134]
Reports submitted to the Junta Municipal on German and Swiss nationals resident in the state of Rio Grande do Sul.

PORTOLÁ, GASPAR DE, 1718-1786
　　Documents concerning. 1703-1785.
　　20 folders. 16-33 cm. [M-M 1811]
　　Originals and copies of documents by or about Gaspar de Portolá, relating primarily to his career as soldier, explorer, and administrator in Upper and Lower California, with some material on his career in Puebla, Mexico, and on his family and contemporaries.

PORTUGAL. ARQUIVO HISTÓRICO ULTRAMARINO, LISBON
　　Angola. Papeis avulsos. 1610-1635.
　　486 exp. (On film) [Z-A 201]
　　Documents selected for microfilming by Engel Sluiter.

PORTUGAL, JUAN CAYETANO, bp., 1783-1850
　　Pastoral Letter. Morelia. February 22, 1850.
　　131 p. A.L.S. 33 cm. HHB [M-M 200]
　　Pastoral letter, in 22 sections, regarding special services in honor of the Virgin Mary, and the desirability of a papal proclamation on the doctrine of her freedom from original sin. Prepared in response to a papal encyclical of Pius IX, Gaeta, February 2, 1849.

POTOSÍ, BOLIVIA
　　Documents for the History of. 1551-1928.
　　7 reels (On film) [Z-D 119]
　　Material relating mainly to mines and mining in Potosí, Indian labor in the mines, banking and minting of coins. Filmed by C. Gregory Crampton in Lima, Peru, and Sucre and Potosí, Bolivia.

POZO Y CALDERÓN, MARÍA CASILDA DEL, b. 1682
　　Autobiography and Other Papers relating to the Venerable María Casilda del Pozo. Mexico. 1682-1730.
　　586 p. 23 cm. HHB [M-M 202]
　　A collection of Mss. relating to the life of the Venerable Virgin, María Casilda del Pozo, consisting principally of her autobiography, written at the direction of her father confessor. It is preceded by several drafts of a life of María Casilda begun by the Jesuit, Domingo Quiroga. On p. 541 is a copy of her baptismal certificate. The remainder consists of correspondence, 1722-1727, exchanged by María Casilda, Father Quiroga, and Father Andrés de Pazos, from various points in Mexico; and a letter of 1730 addressed by Father Manuel Vicente Asencio to the nun, María Josefa de San Miguel.
　　Entered by Bancroft under "Quiroga (Domingo), Compendio breve . . . 1729;" and in the Ramírez catalogue under "Quiroga, Vida prodigiosa. . . ."

PRADILLO, AGUSTÍN, ca. 1839-
　　Hoja de Servicios. June 30, 1886.
　　8 p. 34 cm. HHB [M-M 365]
　　Service record of Brigadier General Pradillo of the Mexican Army.

PRADO Y ARZE, FRANCISCO DEL
Land Title. Valle de Santa Rosa, Coahuila, Mexico. November 16, 1809.
3 p. A.D.S. 31 cm. HHB [M-M 1700:26]
Document confirming the title of Melchor Velarde to lands purchased at auction from the estate of José Miguel Molano, deceased. Signed by Prado as Justicia Mayor.

PRATT, ALEXANDER
Letters and Papers. 1911-1938.
60 items. 28-33 cm. [Z-D 100]
Correspondence (mainly copies), reports, legal papers, maps, etc., concerning agriculture, mining, and oil interests in Colombia, Ecuador, and Panama.

[PRAYER BOOK]. DEL USO DE SOR INÉS DE LOS CINCO SEÑORES GARCIA RELIGIOSA. . . . [1835?]
61 p. 15 cm. HHB [M-M 499]
Prayer book, in Latin and Spanish, used by Sister Inés of the Convento de Santa Clara, in Mexico City; the date of use (1835) may not be that of compilation.

PRENSA ASOCIADA DE MÉXICO
Testimonial Autograph Album dedicated to Porfirio Díaz by government employees. Mexico. April 1, 1888–February 5, 1889.
65 p. 27 cm. HHB [M-M 391]
Autograph album circulated by N. Lugo Viña as an official of the Prensa Asociada, containing tributes to Díaz from prominent leaders throughout Mexico.

PRESTON, WILLIAM BALLARD, 1805-1862
Letter to Walter Booth. Navy Department. December 28, 1849.
1 p. L.S. 25 cm. [Z-Z 100:62]
Regretting that he cannot appoint Joseph Wheeler as midshipman. With newspaper clippings about Preston.

PUBLIC EDUCATION IN MEXICO. 1936
18 p. (Typescript) 28 cm. [M-M 1810]
Anonymous treatise in English on public education in Mexico during the period 1935-1936. Deals principally with the National Polytechnic Institute and vocational training, but touches also upon general primary and secondary instruction, rural education, textbooks, cultural propaganda, and other special aspects of education.

PUEBLA DE LOS ÁNGELES, MEXICO
Selected Documents from the Secretaría Municipal de. 1536-1807.
2 cartons and 1 box. (Photocopies) [M-A 12]
These documents relate primarily to the culture or manufacture of silk, wool,

and cochineal; cedulas for wool mills; ordinances for and inspection of wool mills; silk guilds; a tariff schedule for Tepeaca, 1539; references to Negroes, 1536. Collected by Woodrow W. Borah.

PUEBLA DE LOS ÁNGELES, MEXICO
Silk Culture, Wool Mills and Work Shops, and Related Materials. Puebla, ca. 1537-1807.
200 folders. (Photocopies) [M-A 12]
Selections from the Actas de Cabildo, Visitas de Obrajes, Cartas de Examen, Reales Cédulas, all related to the silk or wool industries, problems of the wool or silk factories or workshops, guilds, working conditions, treatment of Indians and Negroes, and highway thefts. One folder on Licencias de Impresores. From the Archivo del Ayuntamiento. There is a "key" to the collection.

PUERTO RICO
Letters and Documents relating to the history of Puerto Rico. 1660-1881.
2 boxes (88 folders). D., D.S. and printed. 11-54 cm. HHB [M-M 513]
1. Account book of the Real Compañía de Asiento, detailing the sale of slaves in Puerto Rico from 1768 to 1779.

2-11. Correspondence and papers of Ramón de Castro y Gutiérrez, governor from 1795-1804. The papers cover the period 1797 to 1804. They relate mainly to defense of the island (British harassment, coastal security, creation of a volunteer militia, exclusion of foreigners, etc.) and to routine local business. Mostly originals.

12-14. Papers of Toribio de Montes, governor from 1804 to 1809. The papers are for 1805-1808 and, in addition to items relating to local business, include two documents concerning the admission of French corsairs to island ports. Originals and copies.

15-16. Copies of papers of Antonio Ignacio de Cortabarría, royal commissioner sent to conduct peace negotiations with the Venezuelan revolutionaries. Concerning Venezuelan affairs, 1812.

17-36. Correspondence and papers, 1810-1818, of Salvador Meléndez Bruna, governor from 1809 to 1820. Originals and copies. Mostly concerning the Venezuelan revolt, describing defeats of the Spanish forces, requests for military and financial aid. Folder 32 contains a copy of 1810 instructions of "José Napoleon" to his agents sent to Spanish America to incite rebellion. Folder 35 contains a request for aid in holding the Spanish portion of Santo Domingo, December 25, 1816.

37-38. Papers of Gonzalo de Aróstegui y Herrera, governor from 1820-1822. Item 37 is a list of the municipalities of the island, with the number of inhabitants and officials in each, dated November 8, 1820. Item 38 is a signed letter, February 9, 1821, to the Ayuntamiento of Aguadilla, discussing plans for improving the island and for promoting an increase in its agricultural and commercial output.

39. Pinart transcripts of letters, proclamations, etc., in French and Spanish, relating to the unsuccessful attempt of H. Lafayette Villaume Ducoudray-

Holstein to free Puerto Rico from Spanish rule. 1822.

40-48. Copies of letters, and one document, all dated 1822, primarily concerning the uprising on Santo Domingo, cooperation with the French forces to restore order, and appointment of a royal representative to deal with the situation. Four items (Nos. 43-46) are communications from José de Navarro, interim governor from February to May, 1822.

49-50. Routine correspondence of Santiago Méndez de Vigo, governor from 1841 to 1844, and Rafael de Arístegui y Vélez, governor from 1844 to 1847. Two signed letters, dated February 3, 1843, and June 9, 1845, dealing with local affairs.

51-56. Papers relating to the neighboring island of Vieques, 1718-1847, and to Spanish, English, and Danish claims of sovereignty over it. Folders 52-56 contain materials descriptive of the island, including a census for 1844, maps, historical and statistical description, etc. Mostly Pinart transcripts.

57-62. Documents, some of them copies and transcripts, describing various towns of Puerto Rico and adjacent small islands, 1836-1881. Included are descriptions and charts, some topographical and some with historical notes, of San Juan, Arecibo, Utuado, Manatí, and Aguada; and descriptions and maps of the islands of Mona, Monito, and Culebra. Three items are Pinart transcripts.

63-64. Two censuses, one of the island of Puerto Rico for 1815, and one of the town of Naguabo for 1845.

65-68. Orders, proclamations, and some royal decrees, for the years 1789 to 1812. Folder 65 is a book of circulars, dated 1789, of governors Francisco Torralbo (interim governor March–July, 1789, and 1792 to 1794) and Miguel Antonio de Ustariz (governor 1789-1792). Item 66 is a book of copies of orders and decrees sent to the Teniente a Guerra in Aguada, 1691-1798, and includes orders from Miguel Antonio de Ustariz, Francisco Torralbo, and Ramón de Castro y Gutiérrez. Number 67 consists of twelve documents, sewed together, which are copies of proclamations of governors Ramón de Castro y Gutiérrez and Toribio de Montes, and copies of royal decrees, 1803-1806. Number 68 is a book of royal decrees and manifestos, concerning the Napoleonic occupation in Spain and sent to the Ayuntamiento of Aguada, 1803-1812. They are both manuscript and printed.

69-86. Transcripts of royal orders and decrees, 1717-1816, from the Archives of Puerto Rico. Folder 69 contains Pinart transcripts of royal decrees from the Archives of the Bishopric of Puerto Rico, 1717-1753, relating mainly to Capuchin missionary activities in Venezuela, especially in the province of Cumaná. Folders 70-85 contain royal decrees, 1738-1816, concerning church affairs, depredations on Cumaná by the British, and various matters of local government. Folder 86 contains two unidentified manuscript fragments, one of them dated 1813, relating to local affairs.

87-88. Fragments and excerpts from baptismal books. Item 87 is a part of the book of baptisms of the church at Coamo, 1660-1775. Item 88 is a manuscript copy, made in 1881, of an act of the Bishop of Puerto Rico, creating a parish church in Humacao, July 4, 1793.

There is a "key" to the collection.

QUERÉTARO (CITY), MEXICO
Documents concerning Elections. 1665-1668.
11 p. D.S. 31 cm. [70/81M]
Copies of royal orders, an ordinance of the Conde de Salvatierra, and petitions of members of the city government. They relate to dates of holding elections and eligibility of candidates and voters. With signatures of scribes and various officials.

QUICHÉ AND CAKCHIKEL INDIANS. GUATEMALA. 16th cent.
244 p. 19 cm. HHB [M-M 446]
Transcripts in the handwriting of A. L. Pinart of two Mss. from the collection of the Abbé Brasseur de Bourbourg, as follows:

1. Títulos de la Casa Ixcuin-Nihaib, señora del Territorio de Otzoya [1524], 30 p. An early Spanish version of a history of the Quiché Indians up to and including the time of Pedro de Alvarado. This Spanish text, for which there is no known Quiché version, is printed in Adrián Recinos, *Crónicas Indígenas de Guatemala* (Editorial Universitaria, Guatemala City, 1957).

2. Memorial escrito en lengua Cacchiquel por Dn Francisco Hernandez Arana Xahilá, cacique de Tecpanatitlan, completado y continuado por Dn Francisco Dias Xcbuta Queh . . . [16th cent.], 207 p. A legendary history of the Cakchiquel Indians, written in Cakchíquel by Indian nobles, with the portion up to 1562 by Arana and the closing portion by "Xebuta Queh" (Francisco Días Gebuta Quej).

At the beginning of the volume, Pinart has included notes on Juan de Medina, titles of works on Central American explorations, and a list of Bishops of Guatemala.

QUINTERA MINING COMPANY, LTD.
Records. 1880-1909.
16 vols. 12-45 cm. [69/19M]
Cashbook, ledgers, journals, accounts for general store, assays, record of stampmill operations, and letterpress copy books of mining operations in Aduana, Sonora, Mexico. Some letters were written by the manager of the nearby Rosario mines. List of contents available.

RADCLIFFE, MARY (VAN WAGENER)
Journal. 1860-1902.
358 p. A.D. 17 cm. [z-z 160]
Kept in a former diary of her husband, Lewis Radcliffe, with some entries, 1860-1895, copied from his diary. Describes the life of a clergyman and his family, mainly in the Middle West.

RAILWAYS. MEXICO
Tariff Schedules. Mexico City and Guadalajara. 1903-1956.
310 p. (Mimeographed and printed) 28 cm. [M-M 1876]
Freight, storage, and handling tariffs of various Mexican railway and transportation agencies, principally the administrative offices of the Mexican Na-

tional Railways, specifying rates for different types of freight. With related documents.

RAMEZAY, JEAN BAPTISTE NICHOLAS ROCHE DE, 1680-
Articles of Capitulation of Quebec. September 18, 1759.
3 p. D.S. (Photocopy) 25 cm. [z-z 100:104]
   Conditions of surrender, signed also by the British Vice-Admiral, Charles Saunders, and Brigadier General George Townshend.

RAMÍREZ, JOSÉ FERNANDO, 1804-1871, *comp.*
Documentos Historicos sobre Durango. Mexico. 1560-1847.
626 p. Ms. and printed. 32 cm. HHB [M-M 93]
   A collection of 31 items (originals, copies, summaries, and translations) relating chiefly to the religious and civil history of Durango and other portions of the Provincias Internas, from 1553 to the early nineteenth century; compiled under the personal supervision of Ramírez, a native of Durango.
   Noteworthy topics concern the military and colonizing activities of Francisco de Ibarra, governor of New Galicia, including two Mss. by Faustino Chimalpopocatl Galicia on Aztec participation in the 1563 expedition into New Vizcaya and distribution of duties among the Indians of Nombre de Dios; missionary work of the 16th and 17th centuries, with special attention to the Jesuits, Gonzalo de Tapia and Martín Pérez, and excerpts from the reports of Fathers Martín Pérez and Luis Velarde and from the history of Andrés Pérez de Rivas; establishment of Nombre de Dios; the Ávila-Santarén colonizing and missionary expedition; extracts from Juan Agustín Morfi's *Viage de Indios* relating to Teodoro de Croix; data on mining; powers of the Commandant General of the Provincias Internas; Antonio Cordero's report on the Apaches; and an expediente on the powers of Jacobo de Ugarte as commandant general.

RAMÍREZ, JOSÉ FERNANDO, 1804-1871, *comp.*
Documentos relativos á la fundacion del Hospital del Amor de Dios, ereccion de la Catedral de Mexico y promocion de su primer Obispo, D. Fr. Juan de Zumarraga, con noticias de su persona y varias piezas de su correspondencia epistolar. 1529-1658.
428 p. 23 cm. HHB [M-M 203]
   Collection of 18th-century copies relating to the activities of Juan de Zumárraga. Includes documents on the establishment of the Hospital del Amor de Dios; testamentary dispositions of Zumárraga; site of the apparition of the Virgin of Guadalupe before him; erection of the Cathedral, and installation of Zumárraga in office; and eight letters written by him to Charles V and others, 1529-1548.

RAMÍREZ, JOSÉ FERNANDO, 1804-1871, *comp.*
México y sus disturbios. Tumultos. 1621-1692.
2 vols. 24 cm. HHB [M-M 149-150]
   Collection of transcriptions in various hands, from Spanish and Mexican

sources, relating to disturbances in Mexico and dealing primarily with the outbreak of January, 1624, the related disputes of the Marqués de Gelves with the Audiencia and Archbishop Juan Pérez de la Serna, and those of the Archbishop with the religious orders; including also a letter from the royal cosmographer, Sigüenza y Góngora, to Admiral Andrés de Pez, Mexico City, August 30, 1692, concerning an Indian rebellion (cf. Sigüenza . . . Alboroto . . . , M-M 226). Intended originally by Ramírez as a supplement to *Documentos para la Historia de Méjico,* Second Series, Vols. 2-3, Mexico City, 1854-1855.

RAMÍREZ, JOSÉ FERNANDO, 1804-1871, *comp.*
Monumentos Historicos correspondientes al periodo de la dominacion Española en Mexico. Mexico. 1520-1847(?)
744 p. Ms. and printed. 32 cm.   HHB [M-M 159]

Collection of transcripts and notes relating to the history of Mexico during Spanish rule, under the following topics: chronological list of rulers of New Spain between 1521 and 1789, and summaries of events during the same period, compiled by Diego García Panes y Avellán, ca. 1791; reports on 16th and 17th century expeditions for the conquest, colonization, and conversion of Sinaloa, Sonora, and California, transcribed from the Mexican archives, 1847; the eight closing chapters from Motolinía's account of the martyrdom of three Tlaxcalan child converts, apparently a translation into Spanish of the 1601 Náhuatl translation made by the Franciscan, Juan Bautista; notes by Ramírez on various aspects of Mexico City and its environs from the 16th to the 18th centuries, with particular attention to the Huehuetoca Canal and to certain religious orders; clause from the will of Vasco de Quiroga, January 24, 1565, and news concerning his defense and acquittal on charges connected with the construction of a hospital; account compiled by José Díaz de la Vega, a Franciscan, concerning bestowal of the title of "captain general" and other honors on the 16th century Chichimeca chieftain, Juan Bautista Valerio de la Cruz; miscellaneous notes, 16th to 18th centuries, compiled by Ramírez, including such sources as Juan Mateo Mange and the Jesuit, Luis Velarde.

Entered by Bancroft under "Monumentos Históricos de la dominación Española en México."

RAMÍREZ, JOSÉ FERNANDO, 1804-1871, *comp.*
Monumentos Historicos y Politicos de la Administracion Colonial. 1480-ca. 1847.
586 p. 32 cm.   HHB [M-M 158]

A collection of documents (copies) relating principally to historical and political events in New Spain during the colonial period. Contains a list of descendants of conquistadores and their wives resident in New Spain in 1590, compiled by Andrés de Obilla from "Fragmentos de Memorias Mexicanas" in the library of the Oratory of Saint Philip Neri in Mexico City; partial record of meetings of the municipal administrative bodies of Mexico City, March, 1524, to June, 1529, also made from records in the Oratory of Saint Philip

Neri; opinion of the father provincial and other Franciscans to defend the Indians and regulate the labor exacted from them under the repartimiento system, March 5, 1594; description of the ceremonial display of the royal standard on August 12 of each year (post 1745); notes for a history of the origin and value of coinage used in Mexico during the 16th century, collected by Ramírez; and a report by Diego Clemencín (1765-1834) on the value of currency used in Castile during the time of Isabel I.

Entered by Bancroft under "Monumentos Históricos y Políticos . . . ."

RANCHO SAN RAFAEL, SONORA, MEXICO
Diseño and Other Papers.
4 items. Ms. and Photocopies.   HHB [M-M 1700:25]
1. Sketch map of Rancho San Rafael in the Altar Valley of Sonora. N.d. Two photocopies. 34x46 cm.
2. Bowman, Jacob Neibert,1875-1968. Letter of explanation of above item. Berkeley, California. March 31, 1958. 1 p. L.S. 28 cm.
3. Becker, Robert Hewitt, 1915-   . Tracing to show the location of the ranch. Berkeley. April 8, 1958. 1 p. 28 cm.
4. Waud, H. B. Letter describing the Murrietta ranch and pueblo, now known as the Rancho de San Rafael and the town of Trincheras. National City, California. February 7, 1957. 1 p. 28 cm.

RAZON . . . PARA CELEBRAR HONRAS AL . . . S.r D.n JOSEPH DE TORRES Y VERGARA ARCEDIANO . . . DE ESTA S.ta YGLESIA DE MEXICO . . . . [MEXICO CITY. 1727]
7 p. 31 cm.   [M-M 1799]
Account of the career, virtues, and benefactions of Dr. José de Torres y Vergara, Archdean of the Mexico City Cathedral, founder of the Capuchin Convent of San José de Gracia in Querétaro, et cetera.

REA, DAVID B
Human Sacrifice. Santa Cruz de Mushtli, Guatemala. December, 1889.
25 p. D.S. 28 cm.   [Z C 0]
Copy of an article, published in Charlotte, N.C., *Chronicle*, April 6, 1890, by Rea, a lawyer and miner who later taught in the "government university" of Guatemala. Describes a visit to some old sacrificial temples of the Mames and Lacandón Indians.

REAL ADUANA Y RECEPTORÍA DE ALCABALAS DE AGUASCALIENTES
Financial statement. Aguascalientes District, Mexico. January 2, 1794-January 24, 1795.
120 p. D.S. 30 cm.   [M-M 1823]
Records of receipts in 1794 from the alcabalas, as well as other receipts and expenditures, notably those for military and civil pensions.

REAL AUDIENCIA DE MÉXICO
Order. Mexico. November 14, 1586.
2 p. D.S. 43 cm. [M-M 1762]
Order issued by the Real Audiencia in the name of the king and addressed to the alcalde-in-chief of Temascal (Veracruz), Tepeque, and vicinity. Reaffirming, at the request of the Tascaltitlán Indians, the viceregal order of Martín Enríquez, August 27, 1580, on restraint of a public nuisance.

REAL CONVENTO DE JESÚS MARÍA, ORDER OF THE IMMACULATE CONCEPTION
Documents relating to. Mexico City. 1794-1811.
14 p. D.S. 21-31 cm. [M-M 1866]
Letters and circulars addressed by Viceroys Revilla Gigedo the Second, Azanza, Garibay, and Venegas to the Abbess of the Convent, dealing principally with contributions solicited from the Convent.

REDONDO, JOSÉ MARÍA
Proposal of. Sonora. 1845.
5 p. A.D.S. 33 cm. HHB [M-M 1700:10]
Requests support of the Central Government for military action by Governor José María Gaxiola of Sonora, to bring Alta California under the jurisdiction of the Department of Sonora, with a view to protecting Alta California and neighboring areas from internal disorders and foreign encroachment.

RELACION DE LA JORNADA QUE HIZO, A DESCUBRIR EN EL MAR DEL SUR EL CAPITAN HERNANDO DE GRIJALVA CON DOS NAVIOS DEL MARQUES DEL VALLE . . . 1533-1534.
11 p. 33 cm. HHB [M-M 301]
Anonymous record of the exploratory voyage in the Pacific made by the *San Lázaro* under the command of Grijalva, October 30, 1533-February, 1534, in compliance with orders from Cortés.

REMINGTON, FREDERIC, 1861-1909
Postcard Addressed to the Player's Club. New Rochelle, New York. Postmarked December 25, 1905.
1 piece. A.L.S. 8x14 cm. [Z-Z 100:74]
Concerning the Club's Christmas list.

REMÓN, MIGUEL
Descripcion, y derrotero de la Provincia de S.to Domingo de èl Darien, con noticia de los principales rios, y quebradas, pueblos de Españoles de todo color, abitaciones de los Yndios, y Franceses. . . . Real de Santa María [Panama]. April 10-June 6, 1754.
179 p. D.S. 30 cm. HHB [M-M 207]
Contemporary copy of a report prepared for the King of Spain by Governor Remón of Santo Domingo, a province in Darién, to which the author appended a record of Captain Simanca's oral report on French activities in that region. Includes two statements signed by George Butler Griffin, describing

his discovery of the document and offering it, first, to the United States Government, and subsequently, to H. H. Bancroft; an English translation by Griffin; and the translator's notes.

RESPUESTA Â LAS PREGUNTAS HECHAS [SOBRE LOS INDIOS]. N.p., n.d.
20 p. 31 cm. HHB [M-M 316]

A series of 32 questions and answers, relating chiefly to the Indians of the New World under Spanish domination, their living conditions, numbers, taxes, release from *encomiendas* and *repartimientos,* social customs, physical and moral attributes, and religious concepts, stressing the Viceroyalties of New Spain and Peru. They deal also with other aspects of the Spanish colonies, particularly the missions and monastic orders, the regular clergy, and the political status of Creoles.

REVILLA GIGEDO, JUAN VICENTE GÜÉMEZ PACHECO DE PADILLA HORCASITAS Y AGUAYO, 2ND CONDE DE, 1740-1799
2 items (28 p.) D.S., L.S. 31 cm. [70/58M]

Incomplete file relating to evaluation of the estate of the Marqués de Ayza, Mexico and Bolaños, 1792; and a letter to the magistrate of Mexico City regarding abuses in the taverns (pulquerías), Mexico, January 18, 1793, both signed by the Count of Revilla Gigedo.

REVILLA GIGEDO, JUAN VICENTE GÜÉMEZ PACHECO DE PADILLA HORCASITAS Y AGUAYO, 2ND CONDE DE, 1740-1799
Defense of Revilla Gigedo in his *Residencia,* and Other Documents. 1795-1802.
266 p. 32 cm. HHB [M-M 209]

Collection of four documents relating to the residencia of Revilla Gigedo the Younger as viceroy of New Spain. Consists of: 1) the defense of Revilla Gigedo, Mexico City, 1795, presented by his attorney, Pedro de Basave, and by Bernal y Malo, refuting point by point the accusations formulated by certain officials of the Municipal Council. Corresponds substantially to the printed "Testimonio del Escrito Presentado por el Defensor . . . de Revilla Gigedo," reproduced in Estados Unidos Mexicanos, *Publicaciones del Archivo General de la Nación,* Vol. XXII (Mexico City, 1933), pp. 98-209; 2) the judgment passed by the Council of the Indies, which posthumously vindicated Revilla Gigedo; 3) accusations against Revilla Gigedo, Mexico City, February 12, 1795, dealing primarily with alleged disrespect to a statue of Fernando VI; 4) a statement of Miguel Costansó and Ignacio Iglesias Pablo, explaining and justifying Revilla Gigedo's conduct in regard to the said statue.

REVILLA GIGEDO, JUAN VICENTE GÜÉMEZ PACHECO DE PADILLA HORCASITAS Y AGUAYO, 2ND CONDE DE, 1740-1799
Reglamento . . . para . . . el Alumbrado de las Calles de Mexico. Mexico. April 6, 1790.
12 p. 27 cm. [M-M 1892]

Contemporary copy of a decree concerning the lighting of streets in Mexico City. With a copy of a subsequent decree, November 26, 1790, on the same subject.

REVILLA GIGEDO, JUAN VICENTE GÜÉMEZ PACHECO DE PADILLA HORCASITAS Y AGUAYO, 2ND CONDE DE, 1740-1799
Ynstruccion que el Exmo Sr Conde de Revilla Gigedo, Virrey . . . de esta Nueva España dejo escrita para que . . . sus succesores tuviesen un particular modelo. . . . ca. 1794.
2 vols. 20 cm.   HHB [M-M 210-211]
  The principal item of the two volumes is a copy of the detailed instructions for the government of New Spain drawn up by Revilla Gigedo during his viceregal term, 1789-1794, for the benefit of his successors, containing pertinent financial and census tables. The instructions are preceded by copies of an anonymous prologue (n.p., n.d.) eulogizing Revilla Gigedo; a letter, Mexico City, June, 1794, from Revilla Gigedo to his successor, Branciforte; and the judgment of the Council of the Indies, Madrid, March 20, 1800(?), posthumously vindicating Revilla Gigedo, with a note on subsequent royal action, and an anonymous sonnet.

REZETAS PARA LAS NUBES DE LOS OJOS. [N.p., n.d.]
4 p. 31 cm.   HHB [M-M 1700:11]
  List of remedies prescribed for eye troubles and other ailments.

RIBADENEYRA Y BARRIENTOS, ANTONIO JOAQUÍN DE, b. 1710
Escudo Real en defensa de los Ministros de su Magestad. Ynforme Canonico Juridico Legal . . . . ca. 1763.
93 p. 30 cm.   HHB [M-M 212]
  Protest presented orally to the royal audiencia of Mexico on behalf of Domingo Valcárcel and Antonio Joaquín de Ribadeneyra, judges of the said audiencia, who had been publicly excommunicated by Archbishop Manuel Joseph Rubio y Salinas for alleged disrespect of ecclesiastical authority in connection with their examination of the Venetian, Giambattista Anovasio, a member of the Servite Order.

RICHARDS, BESSIE (LAUNDER), 1885-1969
Mining Town Memories—Colorado and Mexico. Berkeley, California. 1967.
126 p. (Photocopy) 28 cm.   [69/3PM]
  Interview conducted in 1967 for the Bancroft Library's Oral History Project. Describes childhood in Colorado mining towns of St. Elmo and Buena Vista; marriage to Edwin R. Richards, mining engineer; life at the Pinguico and La Luz silver mines near Guanajuato, 1908-1911; at Monterrey, 1923-1928; and at La Noria near Sombrerete, 1929; contacts with Mexican guerrillas and other experiences during the revolution. Illustrated with photographs.

RIDEING, WILLIAM HENRY, 1853-1918
Fragment of a Letter. December 26, 1882.
2 p. A.L.S. 20 cm.   [Z-Z 100:99]

RITOS Y CEREMONIAS JUDAICAS. [N.p., n.d.]
53 p. (Photocopy) 21 cm.   [71/21M]
  Description of Jewish rites and ceremonies, evidently prepared for the instruction of Inquisitors. Original in the Royal Danish Library.

[RIVERA Y VILLALÓN, PEDRO DE], fl. 1740
[Diario y Derrotero de lo caminado, visto, y obcervado en el Discurso de la visita general de Precidios, situados en las Provincias Ynternas de Nueva España. Mexico. 1724-1728]
29 p. 17 cm.   HHB [M-M 383]
Excerpts from Rivera's diary on his 1724-1728 tour for inspection of the northern frontier presidios. Includes only the preliminary paragraphs and the entries for the period November 22, 1724-November 3, 1725, relating to Nayarit and Nueva Vizcaya. In the handwriting of A. L. Pinart.

[RIVERA Y VILLALÓN, PEDRO DE], fl. 1740
Report, with Supplementary Documents, on the Presidios of the Provincias Internas. Mexico. 1722-1729.
228 p. 30 cm.   [M-M 1777]
Incomplete transcript of 1728 report prepared by Rivera, Governor of Tlaxcala and subsequently Governor of Guatemala, on the basis of his 1724-1728 inspection of the northern frontier presidios. It is divided into three main parts, in compliance with Viceroy Casafuerte's request for an account of presidio conditions as Rivera found them, conditions upon his departure, and measures advisable for their improvement. Stresses salaries and prices, foreshadows the noted 1729 "Reglamento para todos los Presidios de las Provincias Internas. . . ." Followed by copies of related documents (1722-1729), including a royal decree, viceregal statements, a letter from Juan de Oliván Rebolledo, Military Auditor General, and approval of the report by Palacios, the Fiscal.
For complete printed text, see Secretaría de la Defensa Nacional, Archivo Histórico Militar Mexicano, Núm. 2, *Diario y Derrotero. . .* , Mexico, 1946, p. 97 *et seq.*

ROBINSON, JUAN A
Statement. . . . [San Francisco. n.d.]
25 p. 32 cm.   HHB [M-M 375]
Statement made by Robinson, businessman and former United States Consul at Guaymas, regarding conditions and events in Mexico during his residence there from 1821 to 1864(?). Stresses silver mining and agriculture in Sonora, the activities of Raousset-Boulbon in Sonora, and Crabb's filibustering expedition of 1857.

ROBLEDO, JORGE, d. 1546
136 p. 32 cm.   HHB [M-M 449]
Copies of three reports, requested by Robledo, on early Spanish exploration and colonization in Colombia.
1. A report on Robledo's 1539-1540 expedition into Ancerma, Quinbaya, and neighboring provinces by Pedro Sarmiento, notary of the expedition. Includes an account of the founding of San Juan and Cartago. Dated at Cali, Colombia, October 12, 1540. 28 p.
2. Account of the 1540-1541 Robledo expedition into the province of Antio-

quia, including the founding of the city of Antioquia. Written by Juan Bautista Sardella, notary of the expedition. [N.p., 1541?] 78 p.

3. A description of Ancerma and nearby provinces, with comments on the towns and Indian customs. Written by a former comrade-in-arms of Sebastián de Belalcázar. [N.p., 1541?] 30 p.

RODRÍGUEZ, JOSÉ MARÍA
Appointment. Mexico City. May 18, 1859.
3 p. D.S. 42 cm.   HHB [M-M 1700:43]
Lieutenant Colonel Rodríguez's appointment as Jefe del Detall (chief of internal accounting) of the Mexico City municipal guard. Signed by Miguel Miramón, Acting President, and others.

RODRÍGUEZ, JOSÉ MARÍA
Citation. Mexico City. April 14, 1856.
2 p. D.S. 33 cm.   HHB [M-M 1700:45]
Honorary citation conferred on Captain José María Rodríguez for his services in the pacification of the country. Signed by Acting President Ignacio Comonfort and José María Yáñez.

RODRÍGUEZ CORDERO, JUAN
Power of Attorney. [Puebla] de los Angeles. September 5, 1587.
2 p. D.S. 32 cm.   [M-M 1863:1]

RODRÍGUEZ DE VILLANUEVA, GASPAR
Power of Attorney. [Puebla] de los Angeles. January 28, 1589.
2 p. D. S. 32 cm.   [M-M 1863:2]

RODRÍGUEZ GALLARDO, JOSEPH RAPHAEL
Report on the Province of Sonora. Mátape. March 15, 1750.
5 p. (Photocopy) 28 cm.   [M-A 19:2]
Report by Rodríguez to Diego Ortiz y Parrilla on conditions in the provinces under his jurisdiction.

ROJO, MANUEL CLEMENTE
Apuntes Históricos de la Baja California con algunos relativos a la Alta California. 1879.
6 items. A.D.S. 32 cm.   HHB [M-M 295]
A collection of data on the history of Lower California, with emphasis upon missions, Indian disturbances, and the biographies of political administrators, covering in a few instances events in northern California.

Contains notes supplied to the Bancroft Library by Rojo at various dates in 1879, as well as some of his correspondence on the subject with Thomas Savage, Henry L. Oak, and others.

ROMAN CATHOLIC CHURCH. GUATEMALA
Catechism. [Zacapulas (?), Guatemala. 18th cent.]
154 p. 21 cm. [M-M 1851]
A Quiché-Spanish catechism prepared for the instruction of the Guatemalan Indians in the curacy of Zacapulas and its vicinity.

A signed letter from M. J. Andrade, University of Chicago, May 25, 1939, is tipped in, and the flyleaf contains a signed note, 1939, of Alfred C. Kroeber, both dealing with the language of the Ms.

ROMAN CATHOLIC CHURCH. GUATEMALA
Doctrina y Confesionario en lengua Ixil. Precedidos de un corto modo para aprender la lengua y Ritual de Matrimonio. . . . Nebah, Guatemala. 1824.
46 p. (Photocopy) 16 cm. [M-M 1852]
A brief grammar-and-vocabulary guide to the Ixil language prepared by the parish priest of Nebaj for his successors. Contains parish accounts, text of the marriage service in Spanish and Ixil, a short catechism (with portions in Spanish or Ixil only), and appended Ixil translations of material relating to marriage preliminaries.

ROMAN CATHOLIC CHURCH. MEXICO
Collection of Documents and Letters concerning Ecclesiastical Disputes, Church Property, Inquisition Proceedings, et cetera. 1599-1815.
8 folders in box. HHB [M-M 144:1-8]
The chief documents relate to a dispute over tithes between the Mexico City Cathedral Chapter and the Society of Jesus, 1736; church repairs in old Veracruz, caused by earthquake damage, and other needs of that community, 1777-1783; controversy between the military and clergy at Our Lady of Guadalupe, 1800-1815; the will of Ramírez Ponce de León, leaving his estate to the College of San Pedro y San Pablo, 1713-1714; description of the four paintings or images of Our Lady at the four corners of Mexico City, 1754; a jurisdictional dispute in regard to the estates of three bishops of Guadalajara, deceased, 1755-1759; a vacant prebend in the collegiate church of Our Lady of Guadalupe, near Mexico City, 1779; and the Inquisition's trial and punishment of Juan Peraza, 1599-1601, on a morals charge.

ROMAN CATHOLIC CHURCH. MEXICO
[Concilios Provinciales Mexicanos Primero, Segundo y Tercero. Documentos y Actas] 1555-1773.
4 vols. Ms. and printed. 33-34 cm. HHB [M-M 266-269]
A collection of documents, in Spanish and Latin, from Mexico, Spain, the Philippines, and Peru, relating to the first three ecclesiastical provincial councils of New Spain and the Philippines, convoked respectively in 1555 and 1565 by Archbishop Alonso de Montúfar, and in 1585 by Archbishop Pedro Moya de Contreras, centering about the Third Council; bearing upon various questions—religious, social, or political—of concern to both colonists and Indians.

Volume I, 1555-1622, contains the corrected catechism of the First Council, original acts of the Second, contemporary copies of decrees of the Third, and various documents concerning the latter.

Volume II has the corrected Spanish version of the decrees and edicts issued by the Third Council, and related material.

Volume III, approximately 1555-1585, includes work papers for the Third Council—convocations, attendance, instructions, reports, relevant papal bulls, and copies or summaries of papers prepared by earlier synods in Mexico, Lima, and Spain.

Volume IV, 1581-1773, has work papers of the Third Council, but consists primarily of eight questions proposed for its consideration, together with documents of the Councils held in Lima, 1582, and Toledo, 1582-1583, and some miscellaneous matter.

For "key" to the Third Council documents in this collection, see Stafford Poole, "Documents of the Third Mexican Council in the Bancroft Library," 1961, item M-M 1756 of this Guide.

ROMAN CATHOLIC CHURCH. MEXICO
Convents. 1663-1778.
4 folders. D. and D.S. 22-31 cm.　　　　　　　　　　　　　　　HHB [M-M 521]

1. Petition (n.p., n.d.) from Francisco Núñez, minister of Molinero, requesting a loan from the Convento de la Limpia Concepción in Mexico City; followed by a report of the Abbess of the Convent and her definitors to the Archbishop-elect, explaining that they prefer a different type of investment; two annotations, one dated in Mexico City on January 12, 1664. Mexico, [1663]-1664. 3 p. 22 cm.

2. Undated petition of Alonso Rodríguez y Belasco to Rodrigo de Vivero y Peredo, requesting a loan from any Mexico City convent. Document also bears three annotations: a refusal of loan, a certification, and a receipt. [Mexico City?, 1674] 2 p. 31 cm.

3. Statement recording a ceremony in memory of Mother Ana María de Jesús, formerly a member of the Convento de Nuestra Señora de la Encarnación, marking the first anniversary of her death. Mexico, February 28, 1741. 2 p. 31 cm.

4. Documents relating to the admission of Doña María Francisco González as a member of the Convento de Santa Brígida in Mexico City. Mexico City, November, 1778. 12 p. 31 cm.

ROMAN CATHOLIC CHURCH. MEXICO
La Mitra de Sonora. March 1, 1862–October 4, 1866.
2 folders. 11 p. 32 cm.　　　　　　　　　　　　　　　　　　　HHB [M-M 362]

Material relating to the illicit exercise of spiritual functions by Juan Francisco Llevaria, who had been appointed parish priest of Mazatlán by the civil authorities during the exile of Pedro Losa, Bishop of Sonora and subsequently Archbishop of Guadalajara. Includes correspondence between the priest, Juan de Dios Zasueta, and Bishop José María Uriarte in regard to the above case.

ROMAN CATHOLIC CHURCH. MEXICO
Providencias diocesanas de Mexico, y otras superiores. [Mexico. 1648-1831]
564 p. 23 cm.   HHB [M-M 153]
Copies of decrees, orders, pastoral letters, circulars, official correspondence, and other documents relating to parochial responsibilities in Mexico with respect to various matters, such as religious ceremonies, treatment of Indians, taxation, morals, marriage, public hygiene, royal and ecclesiastical jurisdiction, the Inquisition, disposition of Jesuit property and privileges, the beatification of Juan de Palafox y Mendoza, et cetera. From the archives of Singuilucan for the period 1752-1799; Real del Doctor for the period 1778-1799; and Tezicapán for the period 1648-1831.
Entered by Bancroft under "Mexico, Providencias Diocesanas de Mexico."

ROMAN CATHOLIC CHURCH. MEXICO
Subsidio Eclesiastico en las Indias p.ª la guerra contra los Moros y otros fines .... 1721-1797; *and* Diligencias practicadas ... en orden á la Fabrica material de la Parroquial Yglecia de Tanquayalab. Mexico. 1767-1790.
2 folders. 278 p. 31 cm.; 101 p. 30-31 cm.   HHB [M-M 146:1-2]
Question of Church subsidies in the Indies for wars against the Moors, and of the removal of the town of Tancuayalab to a new site.

ROMAN CATHOLIC CHURCH. MEXICO. 1579-1822
7 folders.   HHB [M-M 147:1-7]
Documents and correspondence (originals and copies) relating to the activities of the Church or the Inquisition in Hispanic America. Comprises documents relating to the defense of Juan Nepomuceno Vasconcelos, ecclesiastical steward of the Archdiocese of Mexico, against charges of maladministration, 1821-1822; bequest of Juan Gómez Márquez for reconstruction of the Antequera cathedral, 1723-1725; royal decrees, letters, licenses, and other documents relating primarily to the promotion of Jesuit establishments and the protection of Indian converts in South America, but including one decree on the dispute between the Mexican Church and certain religious orders regarding tithes, 1579-1688; genealogy of Francisco Salbago, petitioner for a post as Familiar of the Inquisition in New Spain, 1635-1639; trial before the Inquisition of Francisco Torres del Palacio, public notary of Carrión, on charges of blasphemy, 1595-1597; dispute between Ángel Maldonado, Bishop of Antequera, and his Cathedral chapter over the use of funds for reconstruction of the cathedral, 1720-1721; Guatemalan-Mexican jurisdictional problems connected with the settlement of Mezcalapán, 1747-1802.

ROMAN CATHOLIC CHURCH. MEXICO. 1595-1831
6 folders. 448 p. 21-31 cm.   HHB [M-M 148:1-6]
Collection of documents (originals and copies), primarily of a juridical-ecclesiastical nature and relating to the Church, the monastic orders, or the Inquisition in Mexico. Topics treated comprise preservation of Church buildings, particularly at Calimaya (Tenango del Valle), 1748-1796; proposed trans-

fer to the Crown, and subsequently to the Mexican Republic, of an entailed estate bequeathed by Juan Félix Ramírez Ponce de León to the Jesuit college of San Pedro y San Pablo, 1831; trial of Santiago Hernández by the Inquisition on charges of bigamy and concubinage, 1769-1785; trial before an ecclesiastical tribunal of Canon Antonio Jiménez, vicar general of the Valladolid Cathedral Chapter, charged with maladministration by Francisco Pacheco, fiscal of the See of Michoacán, 1595; suit of Juan de Ayala, corregidor of Zumpango, against Alonso del Guijo (alias "de Arguijo," "de Alguijo"), a cleric of Jaltocán, charged with disturbing the peace and impeding administration, 1652; and two letters from Francisco Antonio de Aldama, petitioning for a canonry in the church of Nuestra Señora de Guadalupe, near Mexico City, and for other ecclesiastical favors, 1785-1788.

ROMAN CATHOLIC CHURCH. MEXICO. 1726-1811
6 folders in box. HHB [M-M 145:1-6]
Documents and correspondence relating to ecclesiastical interests in Mexico, as follows: the royal power of patronage by government officials, particularly in the Diocese of Michoacán and the University of Mexico, 1726-1742; letters and financial statements relating to reconstruction of the Chilpancingo church, 1761-1770; various documents, 1754-1769, compiled in the Diocese of Durango concerning the opposition of Vicar General Francisco Gabriel de Olivares to papal and royal orders authorizing parish priests to solemnize marriages without a license from their superiors; petition of the Cathedral Chapter of Mexico City, September 26, 1811, requesting that Father Juan Nepomuceno Castro, a rebel, be spared the death penalty; jurisdictional problems involved in the collection of ecclesiastical tithes, 1805-1811; and divorce suit of Captain José Villamil y Primo, 1802.

ROMAN CATHOLIC CHURCH. MEXICO (ARCHDIOCESE)
Ynforme general de la vicita Diosesana practicada en las Vicarias foraneas de Zacualtipan, Huejutla y Pánuco, de orden y por comicion del Ylustrisimo Señor Arzobispo de México, Dr. D. Lázaro de la Garza y Ballesteros. Años de 1855 y 1856. Curato de Santa Cruz y Soledad. Mexico. June 14, 1857.
92 p. 22 cm. HHB [M-M 104]
Report on the visits of inspection made in 1856-1857, by order of Archbishop Garza, to the parishes of Zacualtipán, Huejutla, and Pánuco. Contains an account of the condition of the churches, work of the priests, and customs of the residents in the parishes, recommendations for the establishment of missions, notes on changes effected since the inspection; and personal experiences of the inspectors, including a list of loans made and dues collected for expenses.

ROMERO, JOAQUIN
Escuadron Activo de Atlisco. Atlixco, Mexico. 1843.
3 p. 16 cm. HHB [M-M 1700:2]
Financial statement for the Second Company of the Atlixco Squadron, covering the period September 1, 1842 to February 24, 1843.

ROMERO, MATÍAS, 1837-1898
  Archivo Particular de. 1850-1899.
  72 reels. (On film) [M-A 15]
  Positive microfilm of original manuscripts in the possession of the Banco de México. Consists of letters addressed to Romero, diplomat, politician, and secretary of finance in the administrations of Presidents Benito Juárez and Porfirio Díaz.

ROSA FIGUEROA, FRANCISCO ANTONIO DE LA
  Tesoro catequistico Yndiano. Espejo de Doctrina cristiana y politica para la instruccion de los Yndios, en el idioma castellano y mexicano. . . . [Mexico. 1744-1770]
  602 p. 23 cm. HHB [M-M 100]
  Spanish text and Indian translation of a catechism and manual of religious instruction for Indians, prepared by the Franciscan friar and Inquisition familiar, Rosa Figueroa, and based in part upon the short catechism of the Jesuit, Bartolomé Castaño; with introductory material in Spanish for both language versions.
  Begun in December, 1744, in the settlement of Ixpetlaltzinco of the Federal District; corrected and expanded in 1770.

ROSA FIGUEROA, FRANCISCO ANTONIO DE LA
  Vindicias de la Verdad. Convento de Nuestro Padre San Francisco. Mexico City. January 8, 1774.
  152 p. A.M.S. 30 cm. HHB [M-M 101]
  A protest by the Franciscan friar, Rosa Figueroa, against efforts to extinguish the Indian languages, which had culminated in a report of Archbishop Lorenzana to Charles III and the resultant royal decree of April 16, 1770. Incidentally includes a defense of the work of the Franciscans in America and of the cultural claims of Indians and Creoles, with lists of American-born archbishops, bishops, and other outstanding figures.

ROUTE DU PORT DE PANAMA À CELUI D'ACAPULCO and ROUTE D'ACAPULCO À L'ISLE DE CALIFORNIA. N.p., n.d.
  20 p. 35 cm. HHB [M-M 213]
  Description of the routes leading from the port of Panama to that of Acapulco and from Acapulco to Lower California, with an account of the islands, settlements, and other features of neighboring regions; and instructions for the navigation of these routes.

ROVIROSA, JOSÉ NARCISO, 1849-1901
  El Partido de Macuspana. 1875.
  192 p. A.D. 26 cm. [71/36M]
  Geographical description of the area of Macuspana in the state of Tabasco, Mexico, with comments on the flora, agriculture, and population.
  With note by Francisco Javier Santamaría, supplying author and title. The manuscript has been published in Volume I of Santamaría's *Bibliografía general de Tabasco* (Mexico, 1930).

ROYUELA, MATÍAS
>Appointment of. Mexico City. November 16, 1843.
>3 p. D.S. 44 cm. HHB [M-M 1700:40]
>Appointment of Matías Royuela as chief accounting clerk of the Departmental Treasury of Mexico to replace Juan María Durán. Signed by Valentín Canalizo, Interim President.

RUBÍ, CAYETANO MARÍA PIGNATELLY Y DE RUBÍ, MARQUÉS DE
>Inspection of the Presidios of Nueva Vizcaya. 1765-1766.
>76 p. D.S. 30 cm. [M-M 1787]
>Documents and letters, mostly originals, relating to Field Marshal Rubí's 1766-1768 military inspection of the presidios on the northern frontier, with recommendations for redistribution of the presidios.

RUBIO, JUSTINO
>Documentos Relativos al Archivo General de Méjico. Mexico City. 1883.
>72 p. D.S. 33 cm. HHB [M-M 360]
>Data relating to the Mexican National Archives supplied by Justino Rubio, its director. Covers the establishment, development, current status, and future needs of the archives. Appended is a statement giving the number of bound volumes, papers, and maps contained therein, and an explanation of the different *ramos* into which this material is distributed. Notes the principal items of the California section and the Northwest Coast of America.

RUHEN, HEINRICH, 1718-1751
>Profession of Faith in the Society of Jesus. Tubutama, Sonora. August 15, 1751.
>4 p. (Typescript) 28 cm. HHB [M-M 1700:7]
>Text in Spanish and English of Ruhen's profession on entering the Society of Jesus, made to Jacob Sedelmeyer.

RUIZ DE APODACA Y ELIZA LÓPEZ DE LETONA Y LASQUETI, JUAN, CONDE DEL VENADITO, 1754-1835
>Letters. Mexico City. 1818-1820.
>21 p. L.S. 20-21 cm. [69/137M]
>Official communications as viceroy of Mexico. Included are a letter to the bishop of Guadalajara concerning pensions for librarians, 1818; a letter concerning funds allotted to deputies for a voyage to Spain, 1820; a printed circular communicating a royal decree on the establishment of tariffs, 1820; and letters to Mexico City customs officials relating to accounts and confiscated goods, 1820.

RUSH, RICHARD, 1780-1859
>Letter to Benjamin Austin, Commissioner of Loans of Boston, Massachusetts. U.S. Treasury Department. June 23, 1812.
>2 p. L.S. 26 cm. [Z-Z 100:22]
>Written as Comptroller, U.S. Treasury, concerning stock dividends.

RYERSON, JORGE, 1830-
Dictation of Governor Jorge Ryerson for the Historical Works of Hubert Howe Bancroft. [N.p., n.d.]
12 f. (Typescript) 34 cm.   HHB [M-M 402]
Statement of the Texas-born Mexican citizen Ryerson, who was governor of the Northern District of Lower California, giving an account of his military and political career, with some discussion of land titles in Lower California.

SÁENZ DE ESCOBAR, JOSE, fl. 1700
Breve Tratado de las mas principales Ordenanzas de Minas.... [Mexico City? ca. 1706-1740]
112 p. 22 cm.   HHB [M-M 95]
A treatise by an attorney of the Mexico City and Guadalajara royal audiencias on mining laws and measurements in the Indies; compares the old and new ordinances on the subject, contrasts them with ordinances on land measurement and ownership, specifies the advantages of expert knowledge for mine measurement, and concludes with a glossary of mining terms.
This is an extensively revised version, 1740 or later, of Sáenz's mining treatise; it is based upon a 1719 copy which gives the date of the original as "approximately 1706."
Entered by Bancroft under "Escobar, Joseph Saenz de."

SÁENZ DE ESCOBAR, JOSE, fl. 1700
Geometria practica, y mecanica dividida en tres tratados.... [Mexico City. 1706-1727?]
3 vols. (Photocopy) 26 cm.   [M-M 1747]
Also known under the title *Plática geométrica y mecánica en tres tratados....*
A group of three treatises prepared for the instruction of officials and surveyors in New Spain; with diagrams and charts. Sáenz is described on the title pages and in his own statement as merely the compiler of the work, but is generally regarded as its author in view of the preponderance of original writing. Preceded by a statement of approval from Cristóbal Guadalajara (Puebla, September 30, 1706), stating that the Ms. had been sent from Mexico City; a dedication to Captain Francisco Pérez Navas; and a note to the reader.
Vol. I. [Tratado Primero—De Medidas de Tierras], 139 p. Treatise on land legislation and measurements, with table of contents at end. For the relevant ordinances, *see* comment on Vol. III, *infra*.
Vol. II. Tratado Segundo—De las Minas . . . , 117 p. Treatise on mining legislation and measurements, with table of contents at end.
Vol. III. Tratado Terzero—De Medidas de Aguas para conducirlas y pesarlas . . . , 116 p. Treatise on measurement and distribution of water; including an "Addition" of July 14, 1727, composed of Mexico City municipal documents on irrigation requirements. With table of contents on p. 106, followed by material properly relating to Vol. I: a table of linear measurements, with an explanatory note, and texts of 1536-1580 ordinances on land measurement and distribution.
Photographed from a Ms. in the Biblioteca Nacional de México.

SÁENZ DE ESCOBAR, JOSÉ, fl. 1700
   Libro de las Ordenanzas y Medidas de Tierras, y Aguas . . . . [Mexico City. 1706?]
   305 p. 30 cm. [M-M 1746]
   Compilation containing texts of royal ordinances promulgated in 1536 and 1567 (?) by Viceroys Mendoza and Peralta on distribution and measurement of lands; Sáenz's *Geometría Práctica, y mecánica* . . . , a group of three treatises dealing respectively with interpretation and application of the ordinances on lands, measurement and distribution of water, and mining legislation and measurements; a separate treatise on legal procedure and accounting in regard to property; an appended guide for judicial commissioners; and related material. A statement approving the *Geometría* issued by Cristóbal Guadalajara in Puebla on September 30, 1706, indicates the date of these three treatises and specifies that they were sent from Mexico City. Includes diagrams, charts, documentary models, colored decorations, and a table of contents.
   A typed transcript of the above material is also available. 155 p.

SÁENZ DE ESCOBAR, JOSÉ, fl. 1700
   Ordenanzas vigentes para las medidas de Tierras y Aguas de esta America Septentrional . . . . [Mexico City(?). 18th cent.]
   10 p. (Photocopy) 24 cm. [M-M 1748]
   Data compiled by Sáenz on the basis of ordinances existing from the 16th century and relating to measurement and distribution of land or waters in North America; with interpretative comments and diagrams.
   Photographed from a Ms. in the García Collection of the University of Texas.

SAGRADAS ESCRITURAS EN LATINO-MEXICANO. [Mexico. 17th century?]
   78 p. 21 cm. HHB [M-M 463]
   Selected passages from the Old and New Testaments. Latin texts followed by translations into Náhuatl, with marginal citations.

ST. BARTHOLOMEW
   Documents relating to. 1784-1869.
   1 box (46 folders). HHB [Z-A 4]
   Transcripts, contemporary copies, and originals, relating to government under the Swedish rule. Included are passports, and proclamations mainly concerning trade and Negroes.
   Chronologically arranged. A partial "key" to the collection is available in the Library.

ST. JOHN, BELA TAYLOR, 1843-1930
   Diary. 1861-1866.
   3 vols. A.D.S. 30-32 cm. [Z-Z 146]
   Revision by St. John of his Civil War diary kept while a sergeant in the 46th Illinois Volunteer Infantry. Rewritten, 1896-1898, with annotations and supplementary material such as extracts from his letters and clippings. The original version is in the Library of Congress.

ST. JOHN, SIR SPENCER [BUCKINGHAM], 1825-1910
Remarks of Sir Spencer on the Relations between Great Britain and Mexico. [N.p., n.d.]
4 f. 32 cm.　　　　　　　　　　　　　　　　　　　　　　　HHB [M-M 343]
Record of remarks made by Sir Spencer regarding the rupture of relations between Mexico and Great Britain that had resulted from the latter's limited participation in the foreign invasion of 1861-1867.

SAINT-JURE, J　　B
El hombre espiritual ó la vida espiritual . . . . [N.p., n.d.]
212 p. 27 cm.　　　　　　　　　　　　　　　　　　　　　HHB [M-M 214]
Treatise composed by the Jesuit, Saint-Jure, and revised by the abbot and former professor of rhetoric, "J. C. de———." Part I deals with the essential traits of the spiritual or Christian man, and Part II with the basic principles of the spiritual or Christian life.

SAINT-PIERRE, CHARLES IRÉNÉE CASTEL, ABBEÉ DE (?) 1658-1743
Vida, y muerte de el Principe de Asturias D.ⁿ Carlos. Hijo Primogenito del Rey D.ⁿ Phelipe segundo. Su autor el Abad de S.ⁿ Pedro. [N.p., n.d.]
218 p. 21 cm.　　　　　　　　　　　　　　　　　　　　　HHB [M-M 397]
A biography of Don Carlos, Prince of Asturias, the son of Philip II of Spain; probably a copy of a translation from the French of the Abbé de Saint-Pierre. Another copy of what is apparently this same work is listed in the Puttick & Simpson catalogue, London, 1869, as "Hystoria de la Vida, y Muerte del Principe D. Carlos de España. . . ."

SALCEDO Y SALCEDO, NEMESIO
Proclamation. Chihuahua. August 24, 1812.
Broadside. D.S. (Photocopy) 59 cm.　　　　　　　　　HHB [M-M 1700:69]
Declaring as rebels those in opposition to the royal cause, and subject to punishment as such. General Salcedo was Commandant General of the Interior Provinces of the North.

SALVADOR
Biographies. 1886.
3 folders. (Copies) 22 cm.　　　　　　　　　　　　　　　HHB [M-M 518]
1. Manuel Delgado, b. 1853 in Cojutepeque, El Salvador. Studied law and became a lawyer of the Supreme Court. Held various offices, visited California and returned to become vice president of Salvador's Assembly. In 1886 he became Minister of Foreign Relations and later Minister from Salvador to the United States. 6 p.
2. Baltazar Estupinian, b. in Chinameca, El Salvador. He finished college in 1871 and studied law. Started several periodicals of a political nature and opposed President Raphael Zaldívar, for which he was forced to leave the country. Estupinian went to Quezaltenango, Guatemala, founded a liberal newspaper, and obtained the degree of Doctor of Jurisprudence in 1878. At the close of the Guatemalan revolution, he returned to Salvador where he supported General Francisco Menéndez and became "Ministro del Interior,

Gobernación, Fomento, Beneficencia y Instrucción Pública" in 1886. 5 p.

3. Francisco Menéndez, b. 1830 in Ahuachapán, El Salvador. Distinguished himself in military service and became general of the revolutionist army, served as president from 1885 until his death in 1890. 13 p.

SAN AGUSTÍN DE LOS AMOLES, HACIENDA DE, MEXICO
Libro donde constan por menor todos los cargos y datas de esta Haz.ª y sus anexas.... S.ⁿ Agust.ⁿ [de los Amoles]. December 31, 1803.
139 p. D.S. 30 cm. [M-M 1872]

Accounts of the San Agustín estate and dependent estates belonging to the California Missions Pious Fund, showing income, expenditures, and details regarding livestock, agriculture, and laborers. Principally for the calendar year 1803, with some data on earlier periods.

SAN FELIPE EL REAL, CHIHUAHUA
Documents relating to. 1728-1773.
3 folders. 31 cm. [M-M 1779]

Files, both copies and originals, on events in or near San Felipe el Real, Chihuahua, coming directly or indirectly under the jurisdiction of the Guadalajara Real Audiencia. Includes royal decrees, orders issued by the Audiencia or by San Felipe officials, and related documents, quoting as background material other documents dating from as early as the 17th century.

Folder 1 contains documents, 1728-1729, concerning Diego González de la Herrán, Assemblyman and Chief Constable of San Felipe. Folder 2 contains a file, 1743-1747, on the concession of land titles to residents of the district of Santa Isabel, including reports of Juan Francisco Tarín, commissioner in charge of the surveying, and decrees of Manuel de Güemes, Judge Subdelegate of land cases in much of Nueva Vizcaya. Folder 3 contains materials, 1772-1773, relating to property of the exiled Jesuits, to authorizations for its disposal, and particularly to revenue from San Felipe.

SAN FERNANDO DE VELICATÁ, BAJA CALIFORNIA
Registers of the Velicatá Dominican Mission. 1769-1821.
4 volumes. (Film and photocopies) [M-M 1766]

Registers of baptisms, 1769-1818, marriages, 1769-1817, and burials, 1773-1802, and 1803-1821, with signatures of the mission friars and of the provincial examiners.

SAN FRANCISCO DE BORJA MISSION
Libro de difuntos de la misión de San Francisco de Borja, Baja California. February, 1768–January, 1822.
143 exp. (On film) [M-M 1824]

SAN HIPÓLITO MÁRTIR, ORDER OF
Documents relating to. 1585-1771.
23 folders in box. HHB [M-M 400]

A collection of papal bulls and briefs, petitions, grants, licenses, passes, certifications, etc., originating in Italy, Mexico, or Spain and relating to the religious brotherhood of St. Hippolytus and its hospitals, particularly the hospital founded by Bernardino Álvarez in the environs of Mexico City. Includes provisions issued by Popes Sixtus V, Clement VIII, Paul V, Innocent XII, Innocent XIII, Clement XI, Clement XII, Benedict XIV, and Clement XIV, and by Cardinal-Vicar Gaspare Carpegna. The file deals with the growth of the brotherhood into an established order under the rule of St. Augustine, acceptance and reform of its constitution, recognition and installation of its officers and agents, appointment of Thomas Maria Ferrarius as its Cardinal-Protector, granting of indulgences and licenses, installation of holy relics in its buildings by Father Pedro Chirinos, procedure in regard to persons dying in its hospitals, and other matters.

Originals and certified copies, including Latin and Spanish texts and Spanish translations, many items with signatures and paper seals; some with passes of the Council of the Indies, the Real Acuerdo in Mexico City, or the Council and Commission of the Holy Crusade.

SAN HIPÓLITO MÁRTIR, ORDER OF
Documents relating to. 1742-1816.
7 items (47 p.). Ms. and printed. 20-43 cm. [M-M 1864]

Miscellaneous items relating to the Order of St. Hippolytus in Mexico. They deal with monastic abuses, property and other rights of members, and reform of the Order; notices on births in the royal family; and viceregal activities.

SAN HOMO-BONO GUILD, ECCE-HOMO GUILD, AND OTHER GUILDS. MEXICO. 1698-1814
3 folders in portfolio. 25 p. Ms. and printed. 16-31 cm. HHB [M-M 498]

Documents relating to Mexican guilds and archguilds, as follows:

1. Documents and forms of the San Homo-Bono Guild and its affiliate, the Ecce-Homo Guild. 22 p. January 24, 1698–July 5, 1807. Both of the above guilds were dependent upon the Santísima Trinidad Archguild and Church in Mexico City and were connected with the tailor's craft. Consists of five reprints, Mexico City, 1775-1806, with Ms. insertions dated as late as 1807. Includes the texts of papal briefs issued by Innocent XII (1698) and Clement XIV (18th cent.), which granted indulgences and privileges to the said guilds.

2. Receipt signed by Francisco Antonio de Horcasitas, Treasurer-Steward of the Nuestra Señora del Rosario Archguild. 1 p. Mexico City, April 30, 1796. Acknowledgment of delivery of revenue from estates formerly owned by the late Pedro Alcántara del Valle, an official of the mint.

3. Certificate of the Santísimo Sacramento Archguild. 2 p. Pachuca (Hidalgo, Mexico), January 20, 1806–January 1, 1814. Record of the entry of María Marta Sotuyo into the said guild, specifying her privileges and obligations as a member. Bears signature of José Antonio Ramírez, Steward, January 20, 1806, and notation of Miguel Eduardo Garnica, Archguild representative, January 1, 1814.

SAN MATEO IXTLAHUACA, MEXICO
   Petition. Mexico City. October 28, 1865.
   6 p. D.S. 32 cm. [M-M 1700:87]
   Concerning title to land near the town of San Mateo Ixtlahuaca, signed by six residents.

SAN MIGUEL, MARÍA DE, fl. 1682-1690
   La Dignidad de Una Espossa de Christo, mediante la profession solemne. Mexico City. 1682-[1690?]
   478 p. 25 cm. HHB [M-M 296]
   The confessions and meditations of Mother María de San Miguel, a native of Puebla attached to the Convento de la Encarnación, Congregation of the Immaculate Conception in Mexico City. It was written at the command of her confessor, who was probably Father Marcos Romero.

SAN ROMÁN Y ZEPEDA, FRAY JOSÉ DE
   Libro Beserro, o protocolo, donde se halla rason de las Escrituras . . . assi mismo noticia de los principales ympuestos, y Réditos . . . . 1787-1816.
   22 p. 30 cm. [M-M 1890]
   Record of litigation kept by the prior of the Convent of San Juan de Dios, San Juan del Río, Mexico. Concerns funds and revenue left to the convent by Nicolás José Picazo and by Luis de Silva.

SAN VICENTE FERRER, BAJA CALIFORNIA
   Registers of the San Vicente Ferrer Dominican Mission. 1780-1828.
   2 vols. (Film and photocopies) [M-M 1767]
   Registers of marriages, 1781-1800, and burials, 1780-1828, with signatures of the mission friars and of the provincial examiners.

SÁNCHEZ, D
   Half-Hour's Chat about Mexico. [N.p., n.d.]
   6 p. 33 cm. HHB [M-M 356]
   Notes on a conversation with D. Sánchez, President of the Acapulco & Vera Cruz Railroad and builder of several Mexican railways, summarizing past accomplishments of the Mexican Government and U.S. investors in regard to Mexican railway communications.

SÁNCHEZ, JOSÉ
   Derrotero y descripción de las costas del Mar del Sur. 1712.
   185 p. (Photocopy) 26 cm. [M-A 4:2]
   Description of the Pacific Coast from Cape San Jorge to the Straits of Magellan. From the Biblioteca Nacional, Mexico. There is a "key" to the collection.

SÁNCHEZ DE LA BAQUERA, JUAN
   Luz y guya para leer, escrebyr, pronunciar, y saber la lengua Othomy. . . . [Mexico. 1751]
   336 p. D.S. 23 cm. HHB [M-M 471]
   A manual for students of Otomí, compiled by a Spanish resident of San José

de Tula and comprising three books, as follows:

Orthographic guide, elementary grammatical rules, a Spanish-Otomí vocabulary, and several Otomí texts of a religious nature, including a catechism; with explanations, headings, and partial translation of the texts in Spanish. 117 p.

Spanish grammatical treatises on Otomí active verbs, 136 p., and passive verbs, 81 p., each containing eight chapters. These two sections are written in a more modern hand on newer paper than the first portion and may have been taken from another work.

SANDOVAL CERDA SILVA Y MENDOZA, GASPAR DE, CONDE DE GALVE
Legal document. Mexico City. January 30, 1696.
4 p. D.S. 31 cm. [M-M 1700:75]

Presumably a portion of a file in legal proceedings, containing copy of the deposition of Manuel de Vetetta concerning a loan of 2,000 pesos to Sebastián Díez de Posadas.

SANFORD, JAMES T
Letter book. 1863-1868.
48 p. 35 cm. [Z-Z 137]

Copies of correspondence with the Office of the Quartermaster, U.S. Army, regarding use by the government of Sanford's steamers, *Boston, Cosmopolitan, Delaware,* and *Kennebec,* during the Civil War.

SANGER CAMP & CO.
Account with Land Association. St. Louis, Missouri. May 19, 1853.
2 p. D.S. 42 cm. [Z-Z 100:81]

SANTA ANNA, ANTONIO LÓPEZ DE, PRESIDENT OF MEXICO, 1795-1876
Documents and Letters. 1822-1866.
2 vols. (15 p.) D.S. 27-35x47 cm. [M-M 1808]

Papers signed by or relating to Santa Anna, including a letter from Santa Anna to Agustín de Iturbide, 1822; military commissions conferred upon José Francisco López and Alejo Cornejo, 1842 and 1854; a letter from Joaquín Ladrón de Guevara to Manuel Castañares concerning Santa Anna, 1846; and a mortgage bond, signed by Santa Anna, 1866.

SANTA CRUZADA
Libro de las cartas acordadas de el Yll.ᵐᵒ S.ᵒʳ Patriarcha, y de el Consejo supremo de la S.ᵗᵃ Cruzada. Recibidas en el tiempo, que es commissario Subdelegado general el S. D.ᵒʳ D. Joseph Adame y Arriaga. N.º 6.º Madrid and Mexico City. [1679]-1688.
119 p. D.S. 31 cm. [M-M 1718]

Letters, decrees, orders, petitions, reports, legal documents, and related materials, originals and certified contemporary copies, dealing primarily with the appointment and work of José Adame y Arriaga, the appointment of other members of the Mexico City Crusade Tribunal, and financial administration. The material concerns the New Spain and Philippine activities of the Santa

Cruzada, a Spanish institution charged with granting indulgences, alms-collecting, distribution of dispensations, and other activities stemming from the Bulls of the Crusade.

SANTA GERTRUDIS MISSION
Libro de Bautismos . . . de Sta Gertrudis de Caducaman. . . . 1751-1811.
182 exp. (On film). [M-M 1825]

SANTA MARÍA, MIGUEL, 1789-1837
Exposicion y protesta de Miguel Santa Maria, ciudadano mejicano, ante el supremo poder judicial por atentados perpetrados contra la nacion, y notoria violacion de las leyes cometidas en la persona del protestante.
79 p. 25 cm. HHB [M-M 220]
Copy of the statement addressed by Santa María to the Supreme Court of Mexico, protesting the decree of June 23, 1833, by which he and 51 other citizens had been sentenced to exile, without judicial proceedings, on grounds of public security; and stressing the national danger under the government inaugurated by the Plan of Zabaleta, with special reference to non-compliance with the principle of separation of powers.

SANTA MARÍA LA REDONDA, MEXICO
Record of land distribution. Mexico. [N.d.]
5 p. 22 cm. HHB [M-M 453]
A record in Náhuatl of lands distributed among the Indians of the *doctrina* of Santa María la Redonda, which apparently included the ward of Teocaltitlán in Mexico City. A *doctrina* was an Indian village consecrated to the Christian religion.

SANTA ROSA DE URES SILVER MINING CO.
Correspondence, Assay Reports, and Other Papers. San Francisco, Guaymas, Hermosillo, and Santa Rosa de Ures. 1863-1865.
37 folders. [M-B 6]
Letters and reports from the mine superintendent in Mexico, R. M. Deneen, to R. Wegener in San Francisco, concerning the problem of getting the mine into operation; also assay reports and other correspondence.

SANTAMARÍA, FRANCISCO JAVIER, 1889- , *comp.*
Florilegio Tabasqueño. [Tabasco, Mexico] 1925.
131 p. 23 cm. [M-M 1817]
An anthology of unpublished poems by Tabascan poets, including several items later reproduced in Santamaría's printed compilation, *La poesía tabasqueña–Antología* . . . (Ediciones Santamaría, Mexico City, 1940).

SANTIAGO, FRAY JUAN DE
Documents relating to. 1632-1636.
4 items (14 p.) 26-28 cm. [M-M 1900]
Photocopies and notes relating to career of Fray Juan de Santiago, Dominican, in the Province of Santiago de México.

SANTIAGO, SACARIAS DE, fl. 1585
  Documents relating to. 1585-1752.
  39 p. D.S. 30 and 58x32 cm. [M-M 1898]
  Copy, made in the eighteenth century, of a patent of nobility issued in 1585 to Don Sacarías de Santiago, a Tlaxcalan chief, in recognition of his services to Cortés and the Crown. With large genealogical chart, illustrated in color, and correspondence concerning the documents.

SANTÍSIMO ROSARIO, BAJA CALIFORNIA
  Registers of the Santísimo Rosario Dominican Mission. 1744-1868.
  4 vols. (Film and photocopies) [M-M 1768]
  Registers of baptisms, 1744-1868, marriages, 1744-1868, and deaths and burials, 1775-1805, and 1805-1828, with signatures of the mission friars and of the provincial examiners.

SANTO DOMINGO
  Miscellaneous papers. 1766-ca. 1847.
  16 folders in portfolio. (Mostly copies) 26-34 cm. HHB [M-M 515]
  1. Agreement between France and Spain on the treatment of runaway Negro slaves, drawn up by Manuel de Azlor y Urries. Santo Domingo, December 11, 1766. 4 p.
  2. A judicial matter between Espinosa and Raphael de Luna. Town of San Raphael in Santo Domingo, June 16, 1768. 6 p.
  3. Proclamations by Archbishop Fernando Portello y Torres concerning emigration to Havana. Santo Domingo, 1796-1798. 8 p.
  4. Proclamation concerning taxation issued by François Dominique Toussaint L'Ouverture, in French and in Spanish. Santo Domingo, May 6, 1801. 7 p.
  5. Power of attorney dated October 28, 1802, to bring from Puerto Rico and Caracas 6,000 mules and cattle to sell in Santo Domingo. In French. 4 p.
  6. Decree by L. Ferrand concerning rebellion in Hispaniola. Santo Domingo, February 5, 1805. 1 p.
  7. Military "orders of the day" of the French army in Santo Domingo, January 20, 1807–February 13, 1809. In French. 38 p.
  8. Letter from Juan Sánchez Ramírez to Juan de Pomuseno Arredondo, concerning seizure of Santo Domingo. Santo Domingo, August 4, 1809. 2 p.
  9. Proclamation of Juan Sánchez Ramírez communicating royal cedula concerning Napoleon. Santo Domingo, November 16, 1810. 12 p.
  10. Passport issued to Francisco Amell. Santo Domingo, February 13, 1812. D. S. 1 p.
  11. Passport issued to Bernardo Rodríguez. Santo Domingo, September 12, 1812. D. S. 1 p.
  12. Pinart copy of speech by Sebastián Kindelan y O'Regan on relations between Santo Domingo and Haiti; printed in *El Telégrafo Constitucional.* Santo Domingo, March 4, 1821. 7 p.
  13. Passport issued to José Colón. Santo Domingo, November 14, 1821. D.S. 1 p.
  14. Memoirs of Sir Robert Hermann Schomburgk (1804-1865) on the re-

lations of the Dominican Republic with Haiti. Copy made by Pinart. Santo Domingo, ca. 1847. 42 p.

15. Stamped official paper of Santo Domingo. Blank. 1 p.

16. Tracings of signatures of various officials of Santo Domingo. N.p., n.d.

SANTO DOMINGO, BAJA CALIFORNIA

Registers of the Santo Domingo Dominican Mission. 1775-1850.

3 vols. (Film and photocopies) [M-M 1769]

Registers of baptisms, 1775-1839, marriages, 1776-1850, and deaths and burials, 1775-1837, with signatures of the mission friars and of the provincial examiners.

SANTO DOMINGO, CONVENT OF

Rules for the Colegio Real de San Luis. 1598(?)-1666(?).

39 p. 22 cm. HHB [M-M 219]

Copy of the statutes governing the Dominican Colegio Real de San Luis, inaugurated in Puebla in 1585, with the text of oaths to be taken by the personnel; apparently adopted in 1598, corrected in a certified copy of July 16, 1629, and expanded (see Art. 17) in 1666. The present copy contains 32 articles.

SANTORAL EN MEXICANO. [Mexico. N.d.]

498 p. 16 cm. HHB [M-M 464]

A collection in Náhuatl containing biographies of saints and miscellaneous items of a religious nature. Also included are Indian proverbs and metaphors, with Spanish translations, several Aesop's fables, and other tales.

SAWKINS, JAMES G[AY], 1806-1876

Letters and Enclosure. Washington, D.C. November 18 and 22, 1854.

11 p. A.L.S. 22-28 cm. HHB [M-M 522]

Two letters addressed to Brantz Mayer in Baltimore, describing the tombs and temple at Mitla, Mexico, as seen by Sawkins in 1837. This material was utilized in Mayer's *Observations on Mexican History and Archaeology* . . . (Washington, Smithsonian Institution, 1856).

SCHULTZ, F   C

Letter to R. C. Wells. Buenos Aires. October 16, 1926.

2 p. (Notarized photocopy) L.S. 24 cm. [z-z 100:28]

Concerning Standard Oil Company pumping of oil at Bermejo, Bolivia.

SCHURZ, CARL, 1829-1906

Letter to Emerson Venable. New York, N.Y. October 17, 1902.

2 p. A.L.S. 15 cm. [z-z 100:45]

Concerning request for copies of his speeches. With fragment of draft for a speech given September 25, 1884.

SEEBER, CHESTER, 1850-

Statement. . . . Ensenada, Mexico. 1887.

4 p. 28 cm. HHB [M-M 376]

Information dictated by Seeber, ex-Commissioner of Alaska, regarding his general career and his achievements and plans as resident land agent in Ensenada for the International Company of Mexico.

SEGESSER DE BRUNEGG, FELIPE, 1689-1761
Letters and Miscellaneous Writings. 1689-1761.
377 p. (Photocopy) 28 cm. [M-M 1805]
Letters and miscellaneous material written by, addressed to, or concerning the Jesuit missionary Segesser. Includes many letters from Segesser to his mother, or his brother François Joseph, Councilor of State in Lucerne; several from the latter; correspondence of fellow Jesuits and other persons, notably, Juan Felipe de Anza, brother of the explorer Juan Bautista; Segesser's profession upon entering the Society of Jesus; the document transferring his possessions to the Jesuits; lists of supplies received or requested for missions; and addresses of correspondents.

SEGURA, FRANCISCO DE P
San Luis Potosí. 1883.
3 items. D.S. 22-34 cm. HHB [M-M 523]
1. La Instrucción Pública primaria en San Luis Potosí. September 20, 1883. D.S. 14 p. Includes a brief survey of primary education from the time of Mexican independence.
2. La Casa de Moneda de San Luis Potosí. Development of the San Luis Potosí mint since its establishment in 1827. September, 1883. D.S. 4 p.
3. Apuntes Biográficos del Sr. Juan Ramos, b. 1848. Inspector of Schools for the state of San Luis Potosí; formerly journalist and teacher in Texas. Includes a letter from an earlier employer, Max E. Schmidt. October 12, 1883. Copy. 5 p.

SEGURA, NICOLÁS DE, 1676-1743
Defensa Canonica por las Prov.ᵃˢ de la Comp.ᵃ de Jesus, de la Nueba España, y Philipinas, sobre las censuras impuestas . . . a sus Religiosos, y a todos los que le comunicaran por los Juec[e]s Haze[do]res de rentas decimales . . . . ca. 1735.
224 p. 21 cm. HHB [M-M 221]
Copy of a statement formulated by the Jesuit, Segura, protesting the excommunication of thirteen Jesuits and other individuals by the Mexico City ecclesiastical authorities in connection with a dispute on the payment of tithes. Argues that the sentences of excommunication are morally and legally invalid. Includes copies of various related documents.

SEGURA Y SEGURA, FRANCISCO, ca. 1841-
Biography. Morelos. ca. 1896.
29 p. 22 cm. HHB [M-M 369]
Biographical notes on the career of Francisco Segura, Mexican jurist and Secretary General of the State of Morelos.

SELECTED DOCUMENTS ON SPAIN'S ACTIVITIES IN THE NEW WORLD. 1594-1849
1 box. (Transcripts and copies). 23-35 cm. [z-e 11]
Subjects include explorations and settlement of New Spain and California, 1574-1775; history of the Provincias Internas, California, and the Louisiana-Florida territory, 1606-1817; religious orders in Baja California, 1702-1768; local and state government in Mexico, 1629 and 1848-1849; description of Peru and Chile, 1634-1759; historical description of parts of Guatemala, etc., 1635. From various Spanish archives, including the Academia de la Historia, Madrid, the Archivo General de Simancas, the Biblioteca Colombina in Seville, the Biblioteca Nacional, Madrid, the Biblioteca de Palacio, Madrid, and the Biblioteca Pública, Toledo. A "key" to the collection is available in the Library.

SELECTED ITEMS ON MARITIME DISCOVERY AND EXPLORATION ON THE NORTHWEST COAST OF AMERICA. 1769-1803
3 boxes. (Transcripts) [z-e 2]
These papers, originally in the Depósito Hidrográfico at Madrid, and now in the Museo Naval, were copied for Henry Morse Stephens, ca. 1909-1910. A "key" to the collection is available in the Library.

SELECTED ITEMS PERTAINING TO DIPLOMATIC RELATIONS BETWEEN SPAIN AND THE UNITED STATES. 1817-1819
1 box. (Transcripts and copies) [z-e 3]
Copies of documents in the Archivo Histórico Nacional, Madrid, relating primarily to the Florida boundary controversy carried on by John Quincy Adams, Secretary of State, and Luis de Onís, Spanish representative in the United States. A "key" to the collection is available in the Bancroft Library.

SERMONES EN MEXICANO. [MEXICO. 16TH CENTURY?]
1,224 p. 16 cm. HHB [m-m 459]
A collection of sermons designed to include one or more for each Sunday of the year, incomplete. It is written in Náhuatl, with Latin headings and citations.

SERMONES IN FESTIS SANCTORUM. [N.p., n.d.]
884 p. 19 cm. HHB [m-m 222]
A collection of Latin sermons for the feast days of the saints and other holy days, to which are appended: 1) an alphabetical index; 2) biographical and historical sketches of saints and holy days, corresponding in order to that of the sermons. Ascribed to the 14th century. Written on vellum in Gothic script, with red and blue historiated initials, headings, and section symbols.

SERMONS. [N.p., n.d.]
240 p. 20 cm. [m-m 1736]
An anonymous collection of Lenten and Easter sermons, written in Spanish, with some Latin passages. Incomplete.

SICARD, AUGUSTIN
    Letter to the Archbishop of Haiti. Moca, Haiti. August 22, 1827.
    3 p. L.S. 30 cm.   HHB [Z-A 5:1]
    From the government agent in Moca, concerning intrigues against Father Gabriel Sanches, curate.

SIERRA OSORIO, LOPE DE
    Autos f.^{hos} por el Sr Gou.^{or} y. Capp.^{n} Genl de este R.^{no} en la Visita Genl .... Parral, San Bartolomé .... 1677-1678.
    59 p. D.S. 31 cm.   [M-M 1776]
    Documents relating to a general inspection of conditions in Nueva Vizcaya conducted in compliance with a royal order by Sierra Osorio, Governor and Captain General of that region, and subsequently a member of the Council of the Indies.

SIGÜENZA Y GÓNGORA, CARLOS DE, 1645-1700
    Alboroto y motín de los Indios de Mex.^{co} August 30, 1692.
    80 p. L.S. 31 cm.   HHB [M-M 226]
    Letter from Sigüenza to Admiral Andrés de Pez. Summarizes various events, e.g., floods, a solar eclipse, crop failure and famine, which preceded the Indian uprising of June 8 against the Spaniards, describes the revolt, and extols the remedial measures taken by civil and ecclesiastical authorities.

SIGÜENZA Y GÓNGORA, CARLOS DE, 1645-1700
    Anotaciones críticas sobre el primer apóstol de Nueva España y sobre el Imagen de Guadalupe. ca. 1699.
    69 p. 32 cm.   HHB [M-M 225]
    The foregoing title was used by Bancroft. Also entitled "Anotaciones críticas a las obras de Bernal Díaz del Castillo y de Fr. Juan de Torquemada."
    Portions of two drafts based upon the writings of Díaz del Castillo and Torquemada and dealing with early Christianization of New Spain. Concerned primarily with the legend of the Virgin of Guadalupe and the evangelical work of Fray Juan de Díaz. The second draft contains a statement showing that composition was in process on June 14, 1699.

SIGÜENZA Y GÓNGORA, CARLOS DE, 1645-1700
    Documents relating to Florida and Texas. 1691-1699.
    119 p. (Photocopy) 35-37 cm.   [Z D 501]
    Reports, orders, and letters. Originals in the Bibliothèque Nationale, Paris; the Archivo General de la Nación, Mexico; and the New York Public Library.

SKILTON, JULIUS A
    Statement. 1884.
    5 p. 32 cm.   HHB [M-M 364]
    Notes from a statement made by Skilton, formerly United States Consul General in Mexico, criticizing the conduct of John W. Foster as Minister to Mexico and, particularly, his reluctance to recommend recognition of the Díaz administration in January, 1877.

SLATER, NELSON, 1805-1886
Polemic Theology. Auburn, [New York]. 1834.
147 p. A.D. 20 cm. [z-z 110]
Questions and answers concerning various religious beliefs.

SLAVES, INDIAN AND NEGRO
Selected Documents. 1633-1638.
158 exp. (On film) [m-a 22]
Cases involving Indian and Negro slaves. From Archivo Municipal de Historia de Parral, Chihuahua.

SLUITER, ENGEL, *comp.* 1906-
Selected Documents Mostly concerning Venezuela, Peru, and Adjacent Areas. Late 16th and early 17th centuries.
1 carton. (Photocopy and transcripts) [z-d 117]
These papers deal with Spanish activities in the above areas, and treat of Indian relations, pearl fishing, trade, foreign intrusions, and defense of the Pacific Coast, notably Peru. Original depositories represented are the Algemeen Rijksarchief at the Hague; Archivo Histórico Colonial, Lisbon; Archivo Nacional, Brazil; Archivo General de Simancas, Valladolid; Archivo General de Indias, Seville; and the Biblioteca Nacional, Lima.

Many of the Peruvian documents are printed in Levillier, Roberto, ed., *Governantes del Perú, cartas y papeles, siglo XVI; documentos del Archivo de Indias.* Vols. XI and XII (1921-1926).

SMITH, JOSEPH B
Dictation of. Shreveport, Louisiana. September 9, 1887.
5 p. 29 cm. HHB [z-b 5:2]
Notes on the life of Smith, a Shreveport businessman who served in the Civil War, and comments on Reconstruction in the city.

SMITH, ROBERT, 1757-1842
Letter to Jonathan Russell. U.S. Department of State. November 15, 1810.
4 p. L.S. (Duplicate). 32 cm. [z-z 100:18]
Concerning U.S. proceedings against the French vessel *La Franchise* in New Orleans.

SOCIETY OF JESUS
Cartas escritas por el Rey de España al Papa con motibo del total exterminio de los Jesuitas de sus Reynos. . . . 1764-1767.
250 p. 21 cm. HHB [m-m 120]
A collection of five items, copies or translations, relating to the suppression of the Jesuits, including letters of Charles III of March 31 and May 2, 1767, one of Pope Clement XIII, April 16, 1767, a *Consulta* of the king's council, April 30, 1767, and an address by a member of the Burgundian Parliament upholding the 1762 edict on expulsion of the Jesuits from France, July 11, 1764.

SOCIETY OF JESUS
Father Kino and the Jesuits in California
161 p. (Typescript) 26 cm. [M-M 1716a]
Dealer's list and description of documents relating to the Jesuits in Mexico (M-M 1716), 1934.

SOCIETY OF JESUS
Father Kino and the Jesuits in California.
5 folders. [M-M 1716b]
Evaluation of the above collection (M-M 1716) by various authorities, dealer's catalog, and newspaper clipping.

SOCIETY OF JESUS
Letters and reports relating to the Jesuits in Lower California, Sinaloa, Sonora, and Arizona. 1686-1783.
75 items. (Mostly originals) [M-M 1716]
Letters and reports on the activities of the Jesuit missionaries in Lower California, Sonora, Sinaloa, and Arizona, relating to the work of Fathers Eusebio Francisco Kino, Juan María Salvatierra, Francisco María Píccolo, and others in the conversion and civilizing of the Indians. The documents contain histories of the founding of missions, explorations, Indian uprisings, and information on relations between the Jesuit missionaries and the civil and political authorities. This body of material was probably used by Andrés Marcos Burriel when he rewrote Fray Miguel Venegas' *Noticia de California*, Madrid, 1757. These documents are so important that a more detailed explanation of them is presented.

1. Altamirano, Diego Francisco, 1625-1715. Letter to Miguel Ferriz, Madrid, June 2, 1686. Altamirano spent much of his life in Peru. Later, when this letter was written, he was Procurator, in Spain, for the Paraguay mission. Gives some insight into the struggle in Rome for power, and how it was an arena for disputes between Jesuits and others. 1 p. A.L.S. 30 cm.

2. Altamirano, Diego Francisco, to Miguel Ferriz in Valencia. Madrid, July 2, 1686. Concerning arrival of the flota, and Jesuits preparing to leave for the New World. 2 p. A.L.S. 30 cm.

3. Altamirano, Pedro Ignacio. Letter to Father Silvestre Andreu in Valencia. Madrid, August 10, 1748. With regard to funds for various purposes. 2 p. A.L.S. 21 cm.

4. Andonaegui, Roque de. Report on the mission of San Joseph de Temeichi and its neighboring villages. San Joseph de Temeichi. June 21, 1744. 2 p. A.L.S. 30 cm.

5. Andonaegui, Roque de, to the Visitador, Lorenzo Gera. San Joseph de Temeichi. December 5, 1744. A full report on the history and condition of Mission San Joseph de Temeichi. 15 p. A.L.S. 30 cm.

6. Argeo, Ignacio de, to the Visitador, Juan Baptista Duquesnei. Gives a report on his mission, Santa María Bazeraca. September 18, 1744. 2 p. A.L.S. 30 cm.

7. Barba, Joseph, to the King of Spain. Mexico, April 26, 1735. A report on

the revolt of the Baja California Indians in 1734, with a ms. map of the Sonora area. 12 p. D.S. 30 cm.

8. Barco, Miguel del, 1706-1790. Informe on the mission of San Francisco Xavier in Baja California since its founding. Mission San Francisco Xavier, March, 1744. 4 p. L.S. 31 cm.

9. Bravo, Jayme: Memorial on the missions of Baja California submitted to Viceroy Marqués de Valero, with suggestions for their expansion and development. [Loreto, ca. 1717] 4 p. D.S. 30 cm.

10. Bustamante, Salvador Ignacio. Letter to the Father Provincial on the state of the missions of Nayarit, with a map, 42 x 30 cm., of the mission sites. San Pedro de Thiscatlán, October 10, 1745. 6 p. L.S. 31 cm.

11. Calderón, Phelipe. Brief account of the mission of Santa María de las Cuevas from 1692. [Santa María de las Cuevas], ca. 1720. 1 p. A.D.S. 30 cm.

12. Cancio, Lorenzo, to Joseph Lorenzo García. Personal letter. San Carlos de Buenaventura, August 9, 1766. Reports on construction of two vessels in Matandiel, ordered by José de Gálvez to transport troops and munitions. Comments on the detention of the Spanish fleet at Veracruz, probably because a powerful English fleet has left for Pensacola. Refers to the tumult in Madrid resulting in the king's withdrawal of the unpopular Prince de Esquilache from the Spanish ministry. 8 p. L.S. 20 cm.

13. David, Guillermo, to Juan Baptista Du Quesney. Letter to the Visitador reporting on the state of the mission at San Luis Gonzaga de Bacadeguatzi. Bacadeguatzi, August 21, 1744. Gives statistics from 1688 at the mission which also includes Nuestra Señora de Guadalupe de Nacori and San Ignacio de Mochopa. 2 p. A. L.S. 21 cm.

14. Díaz de Valdés, Francisco. Report on the mission of Santa Cruz and its three branch-missions, San Phelipe, San Nicolás, and San Joseph. N.d. [after 1710] 2 p. A.D.S. 31 cm.

15. Domingues, Francisco. Report from the missionary at Nabohoa on the Jesuit missions of Sinaloa. Nabohoa, February 8, 1744. A general report on the towns, rancherias, and Indian tribes of the area, with particular reference to the problems of the natives at Nabohoa. 6 p. A.D.S. 31 cm.

16. Druet, Jacobo. Account of the mission of La Purísima Concepción since its founding in 1718. November, 1744. 2 p. A.D.S. 31 cm.

17. Duque, Ignacio Xavier. Brief report on the Seri mission of Nuestra Señora del Pópulo. Nacameri, July 28, 1744. 1 p. A.D.S. 31 cm.

18. Revilla-Gigedo, Juan Vicente Güemez Pacheco de Padilla, 2nd Count of, 1740-1799. Report to the king on the missions in the territory under his command. Mexico, December 27, 1793. Text, addressed to Pedro de Acuña, of a comprehensive report requested of his predecessor, Viceroy Matías de Gálvez, by the king, but compiled by Revilla-Gigedo. Gives details of the missions of Upper and Lower California, including locations, dates of founding, descriptions of the Indians, native languages, administration, condition of the churches, crops and local economies. Detailed information is also given of the work in the missions of Sonora and Sinaloa, Durango, New Mexico, Nueva Estremadura, Texas, Nuevo León, Santander, Sierra Gorda, Nayarit, and Colotlán. 106 p. 31 cm.

19. Escalona, Joseph de. Report on the Santa María mission in Taraumara Alta. Santa María de Taraumara, June 7, 1744. 3 p. A.D.S. 31 cm.

20. Escobar y Llamas, Cristóbal de. Report to the king on the establishment of missions in California. Mexico, January 5, 1747. The Jesuit provincial tells of sending an explorer, Father Fernando Consag, to determine whether the east coast of the peninsula is joined to the mainland, and encloses Father Consag's manuscript map, dated 1746, of Lower California and Sonora. 4 p. L.S. 30 cm. With map, 64 x 74 cm.

21. Fernández de Abee, Julián Isidro. Historical report on the mission of Jesús Carichic from its founding in 1675. Mission de Jesús Carichic, July 8, 1744. Account of baptisms and other statistics, neighboring missions, and daily work. Accompanied by a rough manuscript map. 18 p. A.D.S. 31 cm. With map, 31 x 23 cm.

22. Herera, Nicolás de. Report on Santos Reyes de Cucurpe and its neighboring missions. Santos Reyes de Cucurpe, March 15, 1744. 2 p. A.D.S. 31 cm.

23. Hernáez, Gregorio, to Pedro Ignacio Altamirano. Covering letter, stating that he is sending reports of the Nayar missions. Mexico, February 28, 1746. 2 p. A.L.S. 31 cm.

24. Idiaques, Antonio de. Report on the mission Nuestra Señora de Monserrate de Nonohaba and the smaller mission San Ignacio de Humarisa. N.d. [ca. 1744] 1 p. A.D.S. 30 cm.

25. Irnaz, Patricio de. Report on mission San Andrés de Conicari. February 5, 1744. Describes condition of the Indians, with notes on the neighboring villages of San Miguel de Macoiagui and Asumpción de Nuestra Señora de Tepagui. With a rough manuscript map. 12 p. A.D.S. 31 cm. With map, 31 x 21 cm.

26. Kino, Eusebio Francisco, 1644-1711. Favores Celestiales de Jesus y de Maria SS.^{ma} y del Gloriosissimo Apostol de las Indias S. Francisco Xavier, Experimentados en las Nuevas Conquistas Espirituales y temporales o Nuevas Comverciones y Nuevas Filipinas de la America Septentrional. Nuestra Señora de Dolores, May 10, 1704. Probably the original special report, addressed to the king of Spain, describing Kino's work in Pimería, Sonora, and California, and forming the basis of a chapter of his famous *Favores Celestiales*. 11 p. L.S. 31 cm.

27. Kino, Eusebio Francisco, to Alonso Quiros. Nuestra Señora de Dolores, June 30, 1704. Conveying report (not included) on the area and suggesting more missionaries for colonization. With comments signed by Rolandegui [Bernardo Rolandegui, Jesuit Procurador]. 4 p. A.L. 30 cm.

28. Lossada, Francisco de, to Diego Francisco Altamirano. Letter concerning disputes between the Jesuits and the Inquisition. Mexico, April 20, 1686. The Jesuit Procurador in Mexico writes to the Procurador General in Madrid, asking him to use his influence with the Council of the Holy Office in favor of the Jesuits who have been falsely accused of owning mines for their own profit. 4 p. L.S. 30 cm.

29. Miguel, Domingo, to Alonso de Quiros. Letter reporting rebellion of the Taraumares. Mexico, August 26, 1697. 4 p. L.S. 30 cm.

30. Miqueo, Joseph, to Lorenzo Gera. Letter to the Padre Vistador concerning the reduction of Pamachi and the work of Padre Jocome Doye. Pamachi, October 28(?), 1744. 6 p. A.L.S. 21 cm.

31. Nentvig, Juan, 1713-1768. Guasabas, July 18, 1767. Letter to the priests of his province, concerning orders from the governor to supply Indians from Sonora and Ostimuri as auxiliaries for warfare. 2 p. L. 30 cm.

32. Ortiz, Francisco Bernardino. Informes de la Mission de Bahcon [Bacum] y Cocorin. 1745. 4 p. A.D.S. 30 cm.

33. Ossorio, Francisco. Account of the mission of Papigochi and its pueblos de visita, San Ignacio de Paguirachi and San Francisco Xavier de Moguriachi. N.d. [after 1744] 2 p. A.D.S. 31 cm.

34. Palomino, Joseph. Informe de la Mission de Guasave. Guasave, November 15, 1744. Historical account of the mission and the neighboring village of Tamazula. With manuscript map of Sonora and Sinaloa. 15 p. A.D.S. 21 cm. With map, 29 x 41 cm.

35. Píccolo, Francisco María, 1654-1729, to Alonso Quiros. Letter to the Procurador General. Mexico, May 22, 1702. Commends Joseph de la Puente y Peña, a private benefactor who has contributed generously for the founding and maintenance of missions in California. 2 p. A.L.S. 30 cm.

36. Píccolo, Francisco María, to Alonso Quiros. Letter to the Procurador General. Mexico, May 22, 1702. Urges the appointment of Andrés Pardo de Lagos as governor of California. 3 p. A.L.S. 31 cm.

37. Píccolo, Francisco María [to the viceroy?] Report on the missions of California. Mexico, 1702. Recapitulates the information given to the Audiencia of Guadalajara in compliance with their request of February 7, 1702, and reports on the work done by him and Father Juan María de Salvatierra from 1697 to 1702. 11 p. D.S. 31 cm.

38. Ramos, Francisco Xavier. Account of the mission San Pablo and the villages under its administration. San Pablo, 1745. 2 p. A.D.S. 31 cm.

39. Roldán, Joseph. Account of the mission Santa Rosalía de Onapa and its villages. Onapa, February 3, 1744. 2 p. D.S. 31 cm.

40. Roldán, Joseph. Account of the mission San Francisco Xavier de Aribechi and its neighboring village of Bacanora. Bacanora, February 25, 1744. 2 p. D.S. 31 cm.

41. Roxas, Carlos de. Account of the mission Nuestra Señora de la Asumpción de Arispe. Arizpe, July 28, 1744. Gives detailed account of the natives, the geography of the mission and its villages, and the work of the Jesuits in the area. 36 p. A.D.S. 31 cm.

42. Salmubelli, Joseph Luis. Reports on the missions Espíritu Santo de Moris and San Ildefonso de Yécora. Two brief reports. Moris, July 27, 1744. 3 p. A.D.S. 21 cm.

43. Salvatierra, Juan María de, 1648-1717, to Tirso González. Copy of a letter to the general of the Society of Jesus. Loreto Conchó de California, August 29, 1701. Reports on Loreto, describes expenses of the missions, and protests the lack of financial assistance from the crown. 4 p. A.D.S. 21 cm.

44. Salvatierra, Juan María de, to Juan Martínez de Ripaton. Account of the

California missions addressed to the Procurador General. On the road to California, October 9, 1710. 4 p. A.L.S. 30 cm.

45. Sistiaga, Sebastián de, 1684-1756, to Pedro Ignacio Altamirano. Report on the California missions. San Ignacio, April 20, 1747. Reports, as visitador of the province, to the Procurador General, giving a full account of the administration of the missions, and recommending measures to prevent the missionaries from being overshadowed by the military. 15 p. A(?).L.S. 30 cm.

46. Somera, Miguel Fernández. Report on mission Santa Cruz de Mayo and the town of Espíritu Santo de Echoloa. Santa Cruz, December 14, 1744. 1 p. A.D.S. 31 cm.

47. Téllez Girón, Luis, to Antonio de Idiaquez. Brief account of the mission San Francisco de Borja. Borja, October 29, 1744. 1 p. A.L.S. 30 cm.

48. Torres Lerca, Joseph de. Brief account of the mission San Xavier del Bac. Pimería Alta, March 16, 1744. 2 p. A.D.S. 31 cm.

49. Ugarte, Juan de, to Francisco María Píccolo. Letter describing expedition near Mulegé. Santa Rosalía, November 18, 1717. 8 p. L.S. 30 cm.

50. Vejarano, Joseph to Pedro Ignacio Altamirano. Letter to the Procurador General concerning details of sending a group of missionaries to the Philippines. Mexico, February 25, 1747. With postscript dated February 28. 4 p. A.L.S. 31 cm.

51. Vivanco, Manuel. Brief report on the mission San Joseph del Tizonazo and the town of Santa Cruz del Río. Tizonazo, April 18, 1745. 3 p. A.D.S. 21 cm.

52. Relazion de las misiones nuebas y religiosos Misioneros del tpo. del govierno del Exmo Señor Conde de Galve. December 12, 1692. Brief notes, primarily concerning salaries paid to various missionaries, with a reference to Father Kino's 1692 journey. 3 p. 21 cm.

53. Píccolo, Francisco María, 1654-1729. Copia de carta del P. Fran.^{co} María Pícolo, de la Compañía de Jhs., escrita al P. Juan María de Salvatierra, Rector de la Mission de la California acerca de un nuevo descubrimiento, hecho en aquella region por el mismo P. Pícolo. Santa Rosalía Mulegé, June 24, 1709. Report on an expedition, made at Salvatierra's request, to the opposite coast on the Pacific Ocean. 7 p. Contemporary transcript. 31 cm.

54. Píccolo, Francisco María. Copia de carta de el P. Francisco Maria Píccolo Missionero en Californias en que da razon de la ultima entrada, y descubrimiento, que hizo de aquellas tierras azia el Norte por Noviembre del año 1716. San Patricio, December 18, 1716. Gives account of his expedition and of characteristics and customs of the area. Appends a list of those rancherias which have sent representatives and those which have not. 8 p. 30 cm.

55. Razon de la Entrada a el Puerto de la Paz. Conquista de la Nacion Guaicura, y fundaz.^{on} de la Mission de N. S.^a del Pilar año de 1720. No author, place, or date. Detailed account of the voyage of Fathers Juan de Ugarte and Jayme Bravo to the port of La Paz and the founding there of the mission of Nuestra Señora del Pilar de Zaragoza. 49 p. 21 cm.

56. Nuestra Señora de Guadalupe de Guasabas Mission. Brief, unsigned account of the mission and the neighboring rancherías. 1744 (1722?). 2 p. 31 cm.

57. Letter to the Padre Rector. Mexico, December 8, 1734. Unsigned copy

of a letter, acknowledging the Rector's report of the native uprising and the murders of Fathers Lorenzo Joseph de Carranco and Nicolás Tamaral, and agreeing that military protection should be increased. 3 p. 30 cm.

58. Informe de la Mission de Tomotzi [Tomochi]. Brief, unsigned account of the mission and its villages. N.d. 2 p. 30 cm.

59. Vizarrón y Eguiarreta, Juan Antonio de. Decree concerning administration of the California missions. Mexico, July 13, 1740. Certified copy of the Archbishop-Viceroy's decree placing the soldiers at Cape San Lucas under the garrison at Loreto, in order to reduce friction between the missionaries and the military governor of Sinaloa. 7 p. 31 cm.

60. Vedoya [Licenciado] and Villavicencio, Pedro Mar[ía?] de. Report concerning the civil administration of the California missions. Mexico, July 12, 1739 [date 1734 in document is in error], and July 8, 1740. Transcript of a detailed official report by the Fiscal and the Auditor General, in response to a request by the Viceroy, outlining division of administration between the missionaries and the military. 20 p. 31 cm.

61. Vizarrón y Eguiarreta, Juan Antonio de. Copy of No. 59, without additions or certification. 4 p. 30 cm.

62. Carta de un Missionero sobre el Levantamiento de los Pimas. N.d. Unsigned letter from the missionary at Santa María Suamca, addressed to "Querido Paisano," giving details of the Pima revolt in 1751, and blaming the governor for mismanagement of the affair. 4 p. L. 30 cm.

63. Informe del Partido de Batuco, dado el A.º de 1744 por Junio. Unsigned report on San Francisco Xavier de Batuco and neighboring villages. June, 1744. 4 p. 31 cm.

64. Informe ó Estado del Partido y Mission de San Arcangel Miguel de los Ures, como se halla actualm.te dia de oi, y como se hallaba hasta oi dia l. de Julio del año 1744. En que tiempo la dha. Mission administra el p.e Philipe Segesser. Brief, unsigned report on the mission and its natives. July 1, 1744. 3 p. 30 cm.

65. Informe y padron de la Mission de N.ª S.ª de Guadalupe en la California a 21 de Nov.e de 1744. Brief, unsigned account of the mission and neighboring villages. November 21, 1744. 2 p. 31 cm.

66. Kempis, Antonio. Informe de la Mission de Santiago. 1744. Brief account of the mission and its natives. 3 p. 30 cm.

67. Altamirano, Pedro Ignacio. Informe del P.e Proc.or Pedro Ignacio Altamirano, tocante á Californias, para su mayor aumento a favor de ambas Magestades. Año de 1744. Report of the Jesuit Procurador General for the Indies in Madrid, relating to conditions in California and Pimería. Makes administrative suggestions and describes work accomplished by the missionaries. 21 p. 30 cm.

68. Informe de la Mission de N.ª S.ª de Loreto en Californias, de sus progressos y estado hasta el año presente de 1744, en que la tiene á su cargo el P. Gaspar de Truxillo. 1744. A brief history of the mission from 1697. 7 p. 31 cm.

69. Estado moderno de la Mission de Tecoripa de San Fran.co de Borja el año 1744, administrandola el P.e Phelipe Segesser de la Comp.ª de Jhs. 1744. Description of the mission and its rancherias. 4 p. 31 cm.

70. Mission de N. S.ª de los Dolores en la Nacion Waicura, su P. Missionero

actual el P.ᵉ Clemente Guillen. Informe del principio, progresso, y estado presente de la Mission de N.ʳᵃ Señora de los Dolores. 1744. History and description of the mission and its villages, listing number of inhabitants of each. 10 p. 30 cm.

71. Padron, e informe de la Mission de S.ᵗᵃ Rosalía Mulexe en Californias. Año de 1744. Brief description of the mission from its founding in 1705. 1 p. 31 cm.

72. Mission Santa Gertrudis. Report on the mission, founded in 1725, and its re-establishment under the name of María Santíssima de los Dolores. 1745. 8 p. 19 cm.

73. Californias. Sobre la arrivada de un navio Olandes en el año de 747. February, 1747. Account of the arrival of a Dutch ship at Cape San Lucas and involvement of the missionaries who allowed the crew to land illegally for refreshment and provisions. 9 p. 29 cm.

74. Roxas, Carlos de, to the governor of Sonora. San Miguel de Horcasitas, March 4, 1754. Certified copy of a letter from the Visitador of the Sonora missions, protesting the misrepresentations made against the missionaries at the time of the Pima uprising in 1751. Appends copies of various documents to support his contentions: dispatch from the viceroy, Conde de Revilla Gigedo, Mexico, October 31, 1746; decree of the Conde de Gálve, Viceroy, Mexico, August 3, 1690; letter from Gaspar Estiger to the Visitador, Carlos de Roxas, San Ignacio, April 22, 1750; and a letter from Thomas Tello to the Alcalde Mayor Juan López Valdés, Caborca, July 6, 1750. 11 p. 30 cm.

75. Disposiciones dadas en Mexico en consequencia de las ordenes reales antecedentes. Tentativas para penetrar a la Provincia del Moqui y viages del P.ᵉ Sedelmayer al Rio Gila, y Colorado. Reconocimiento de la Costa de la California hasta este Rio por el P.ᵉ Consag. Expediciones contra los Apaches, y ultimas noticias de las Missiones de California, Sonora, y Pimería hasta el año de 1752. [ca. 1755] Draft of Chapter XXII, Volume Two, of Miguel Venegas' *Noticia de la California*. 33 p. 31 cm.

SOCIETY OF JESUS

Libro para memoria de los pasos dados en esta Ciudad de Mexico . . . despues del R.ˡ Decreto de 10 de Septiembre de 1815 . . . . Mexico. 1816-1867.
174 p. 15 cm. [M-M 1763]

A running account of Jesuit history in New Spain, including Guatemala, from the date of reestablishment of the Society by Ferdinand VII to 1867. Covers reorganization under Fathers José María Castañiza, Antonio Barroso, and Pedro Cantón, dissolution in 1821, restoration in 1853, and the individual careers of many noted Jesuits. Quotes background documents and letters, from 1814 onward, of Fathers Castañiza and Francisco Arrieta, Archbishop Pedro José Fonte, Juan Francisco Castañiza (Bishop-elect of Durango and brother of José María), Viceroy Calleja, Antonio López de Santa Anna, Valentín Canalizo, and others. Contains information on the development of Jesuit educational institutions, particularly the Colegio de San Ildefonso. Initiated by Father Castañiza, continued by Francisco Mendizábal, Luis Gutiérrez Corral, and other Jesuits. Separate item is a list of the Jesuits in New Spain on January 22, 1821, when the Society was suppressed.

SOCIETY OF JESUS
   Notes on Buried Treasure. [N.p., n.d.]
   6 p. 14x20 cm.   HHB   [M-M 361]
   Notes on two treasure troves said to have been buried by the Jesuits upon their expulsion from Panama and later secretly retrieved by them.

SOCIETY OF JESUS
   Selected Documents relating to the Jesuits in Brazil, Paraguay, and Uruguay. 1634-1669.
   146 exp. (On film)   [Z-D 111]
   Letters from priests, "cartas anuas," and reports. Microfilm of originals in the Biblioteca Nacional, Rio de Janeiro.

SOCIETY OF JESUS
   Transcripts of Selected Documents relating to Jesuits in America and the Philippine Islands. 1653-1752.
   28 folders (223 p.) 30 cm.   [M-M 1846]
   Typed transcripts of letters and reports addressed to colleagues or relatives by Jesuit missionaries Pyrrhus Gerardus, Maximilian von Stein, Victor Walter, Philippus Segesser, Georgius Haberl, Theophilus Aschenbrenner, Jacobus Sedelmayer, Franciscus Xaverius Wagner, Antonius Benz, [Franciscus] Hermannus Glandorff, and Benno Dumce. These papers concern voyages to the New World; the work of Jesuits in New Spain (including California), Peru, the Philippines, and elsewhere; Indian characteristics and revolts; conflict between the Jesuits and Archbishop Vizarrón; and other matters. With a list of supplies for certain missionaries and a typed list of contents. Written in Latin or German from Santa María (Spain), Rome, Munich, Mexico City, Puebla, Ures, and localities in New Spain. A few items are accompanied by English translations.
   Transcribed from *Jesuitica*, volumes 267, 283, and 284, of the Haupstaatsarchiv, Munich.

SOCIETY OF JESUS
   Various Letters, Verses, and Documents of Protest, Criticism, and Concern for the Jesuit Order. 1605(?)-1753.
   475 p. 31 cm.   [M-M 1744]
   Collection of copies of eleven items relating to the Jesuits in the Indies and elsewhere, as follows:
   1. Mariana, Juan de, 1536-1623. Discurso sobre el regimen de la Compañía [de Jesús] . . . [n.p., 1605?], 121 p. Also known as "Discurso de las Enfermedades de la Compañía" and "Discurso de las Cosas de la Compañía." Treatise by the Jesuit historian Mariana, dealing with defects and problems of the Society and proposing remedies. Prefatory note states that this was the version found in Mariana's papers. Published posthumously in a different version.
   2. Carta de un Cavallero Romano Catholico a otro Cavallero Catholico Romano. Rome, December 28, 1728. 120 p. Treatise in epistolary form concerning a dispute between the ecclesiastical dignitaries of Spain and those of Rome on circulation of a work criticizing the Jesuits. Addressed by "An Unknown

Sage" to "A Known Idiot." With explanatory notes at beginning and end.

3. González, Tirso. Oposicion hecha al Progreso en . . . la Veatificacion . . . de . . . Juan de Palafox y Mendoza . . . . Rome, July 26, 1698. 23 p. Petition addressed to the King by the Jesuit General, González, on behalf of the Society, requesting withdrawal of royal orders on the beatification of Bishop Palafox, in view of his conflicts with the Jesuits and other groups. Appended is a circular letter on the same subject from González to the prelates of Spain.

4. Questiones Theologico-Morales sobre el Estruendoso Casso succedido en Salamanca en el Colegio de la Compañia de Jesus. . . . [N.p.] 1727. 19 p. Incomplete transcript of a refutation of criticisms concerning the celebration held in the Salamancan Jesuit College to mark the canonization in 1726 of two Jesuits, Saint Aloysius (Luis Gonzaga) and Saint Stanislas Kostka. With introductory statement.

5. Llave Maestra de los Entresijos de la Sotana, [n.p., 1720?] 21 p. Anonymous verses satirizing the Society of Jesus.

6. Robles, Antonio de. Carta escrita al Reverendísimo Padre General de la Merzed . . . . Seville, Spain, July 23, 1720. 32 p. Letter to the General of the Mercedarian Order, protesting the rumor that the author of the "Llave Maestra" (items 5, *supra*) was a Mercedarian.

7. Gaita en lugar de Lira, que con Aguardiente sè hecha á un Quartago por los Entresijos de la Sotana [n.p., 1720?] 20 p. Anonymous verse parody of the "Llave Maestra" (item 5, *supra*).

8. Procesion de Carnestolendas . . . [n.p., n.d.] 6 p. Fictitious list of persons condemned by the Inquisition, many or all of whom have been in conflict with the Society.

9. [Morán de?] Butrón, [Jacinto], 1688?-1749. Folias que ahogan á un Theatino [n.p., 1720?] 38 p. Verses ascribed to "Padre Butrón," apparently criticizing the "Llave Maestra" (item 5, *supra*), and referring to various religious orders.

10. Barreda, José de. Memorial que . . . presentó al señor Comisario Marques de Valde-Lirios . . . . Córdoba, Argentina, July 19, 1753. 35 p. Plea addressed by the Jesuit Provincial of the Province of Paraguay to Commissioner Valdelirios, requesting indulgence for the Indians in the Jesuit missions who have failed to comply with the royal order for migration, based on a 1750 treaty that ceded their territory to the Portuguese.

11. Motibos, que alegan los Yndios del Paraguay para no hacèr la trasmigracion á otras Tierras . . . . [Provincia del Paraguay, 1753?] 38 p. Summary of the explanations addressed by the Indians of the Jesuit missions in the Province of Paraguay to the Governor of Buenos Aires, concerning their failure to obey the migration order; and petition asking that their case be laid before the King so that the Indians should not be treated as rebels.

SOCIETY OF JESUS. PROVINCE OF MEXICO
Papeles de Jesuitas. 1649-1769.
528 p. Ms. and printed. 22-32 cm. HHB [M-M 193]

A collection of Spanish, Italian, and Latin letters and documents from New Spain, Italy, and Spain, relating to Jesuit affairs in the New World. Comprises the celebrated dispute between Palafox and the Jesuits; defense and exposition of Jesuit doctrines, e.g., the *Monita Secreta,* or "Secret Instructions," ascribed to the Society of Jesus; eulogies of deceased missionaries; expulsion of the Jesuits; California missions; and administration of the Colegio Máximo de San Pedro y San Pablo in Mexico City.

Bound volume containing 43 numbered items, chiefly signed originals or contemporary copies.

SOCIETY OF JESUS. PROVINCE OF SINALOA
Documentos para la Historia de Sinaloa. [Mexico. 1594-1657]
2 vols. 32 cm. HHB [M-M 298-299]

Foreword of the compiler, a priest (n.d.); anonymous introduction (n.d.), summarizing the history of the Jesuits and other Spaniards in Sinaloa, with a description of the province and its indigenous tribes. The annual reports on the province prepared by the Jesuit fathers for transmittal to Rome during the period 1594-1657; and related letters and reports of Juan Bautista de Velasco, Martín Pérez, Juan Varela, and others. Extracts copied from Vol. XV of "Historia," Archivo General de la Nación, Mexico City.

SOLÓRZANO FAMILY GENEALOGY. 1393-1604
154 p. 31 cm. HHB [M-M 424]

A file establishing the legitimacy and the Christian and noble lineage of Captain Melchior de Solórzano and Fray Luis de Solórzano, brothers residing in Mexico and descended from the Solórzano and Torres Medinilla families. Includes copies of Melchior's petition for the genealogical investigation, depositions of witnesses, royal patents, and other records, both civil and ecclesiastical, from Spain and Mexico.

SONORA, MEXICO
Planos Municipales, con Datos del Censo de 1930.
74 p. 28 cm. [69/17M]

Maps of the municipalities of the state of Sonora, containing information on size, transportation facilities, population, location of cities and villages; statistical data on births, marriages, deaths, industries, income. Based on records for 1930-1932.

SONORA, MEXICO
Selected Letters. Mexico. 1852-1853.
13 p. (Typescript) 28 cm. [M-A 23]

From the French minister in Mexico, André Levasseur, and the French consul in San Francisco, Guillaume Patrice Dillon, in regard to French filibustering activities in Sonora.

SONORA, PROVINCE OF
Libros que manifiestan el estado exacto de los diferentes ramos relativos á la Real Hacienda y Caja de la Provincia de Sonora en los años de 1770 y 1776. Real de los Alamos, Mexico. 1770-1776.
202 p. 32 cm. HHB [M-M 228]

Financial statements (copies) of the royal subtreasury in Real de los Alamos for the years 1770 and 1776, recording official income and expenditure in Sonora and neighboring provinces; with prefatory note and table of contents for each of the two sections, and explanatory note of the copyist at end of the 1770 section.

SONORA, PROVINCE OF

Materiales para la Historia de Sonora. 1658-1778.

964 p. 32 cm. HHB [M-M 229]

Collection of transcripts dealing with the history, natural features, and inhabitants of the Sonora area from 1529 to 1778. Contains letters of Father Kino and other Jesuits, official and missionary reports, official instructions, and journals such as Mange's 1694 diary. Based on originals dating from 1658 to 1778 in the Mexican National Archives. Mostly reprinted in *Documentos para la Historia de México*, 3rd and 4th series.

SONORA AND JALISCO

Newspaper Articles concerning Political Disturbances. August 11–October 20, 1935.

3 folders. (Typed transcripts and translation) 27 cm. [M-M 1720]

1. *Arizona Republic*, [Phoenix?, Arizona]. August 11–October 16, 1935. An article on the discovery of a plot to assassinate President Lázaro Cárdenas, and several reports on an uprising in Sonora against Governor Ramón Ramos and the religious and agrarian policies of the Mexican government 20 p. Typescript.

2. *Phoenix Gazette* [Phoenix, Arizona]. October 15-17, 1935. Reports on the insurrection in Sonora. 5 p. Typescript.

3. *La Opinión*, Los Angeles, California. October 29, 1935. English translation of an editorial, in Spanish, criticizing the arrest in Guadalajara of 31 Catholic priests charged with rebellion. 4 p. Typescript.

SONORAN INDIAN DOCUMENTS. MEXICO. FEBRUARY 9, 1825–MAY 11, 1827

20 folders in portfolio (84 p.) L.S. and D. 21-32 cm. HHB [M-M 495]

Collection relating principally to Yaqui and Opata disturbances in Sonora, and to Christianization of the Indians in the Gila River area; written primarily in Sonora. Contains 20 items which may be grouped as follows:

1. Urrea, Mariano de, 1765-1852. Item nos. 1, 4. Letters. Arispe (Sonora, Mexico). February 9–March 21, 1825. Two letters to Vice Governor Iriarte of Occidente, concerning the desire of the Gila River Indians for missionary instruction; one accompanied by a letter to Urrea from Pedro Ríos on the same subject, and the other with three enclosures (list of Pima settlements showing population, copy of letter to Urrea from Fray Francisco González, and list of Indian officials recognized by the Comandancia General).

2. Iriarte, Francisco, d. 1832. Item nos. 2, 3, 5, 6. Correspondence. Sonora, Mexico. February 21–April 24, 1825. Two letters, possibly drafts, from Iriarte, addressed respectively to the Congress and to Urrea, concerning transmittal to the Congress of Urrea's letter on the need for missionaries; and two letters

addressed to Iriarte, one from Tomás de Escalante and Luis Martínez de Vea on the same subject, the other from Ignacio Samaniego on Opata disturbances.

3. Elías González, Simón, 1772-1841. Item nos. 7, 9-16. Correspondence. Mexico. April 27–August 5, 1825. Includes four letters evidently from Governor Elías González regarding the threats of Opata Indian uprisings at Sahuaripa, Arivechi, San Antonio de la Huerta, and the mining camp of Jesús María; measures for protection of these places; cessation of the threat; and information of the Gila River Indians. There are also five communications to Elías González regarding the Sonoran Indians: a request on behalf of the President for information on the Indians; a letter on the Opata threat; a letter transmitting Presidential messages on navigation and colonization along the Colorado, pacification of the Sonoran Indians and the Indian practice of selling children into slavery; a letter dealing with measures to control the Opatas; and a confidential letter from Pedro de Aguayo, Mayor of Sahuaripa, concerning abandonment of plans for an Opata uprising and the disappearance of the Indian leader Solano.

4. Lumbier, Rafael. Item no. 8. Correspondence. Sonora, Mexico. June 1-4, 1825. Four letters (copies) written by or to Lumbier, concerning movements of hostile Opatas. First letter erroneously dated "1823" in copy.

5. Figueroa, José, 1792-1835. Item nos. 17, 18. Letter and order. Sonora, Mexico. August 23, 1825, and undated. A letter from General Figueroa to Governor Elías González, containing a transcript of the report sent to the Mexican Ministry of Foreign Affairs on plans for missions, friendly Indian tribes, military protection, establishment of communications with Alta California, a proposed reconnoitering expedition along the Colorado River, etc.; and a fragment of official document on security measures against the rebellious Yaquis (n.p., n.d.).

6. Occidente, State of. Item no. 19. March 25–May 31, 1827. Three copies of documents relating to finances: a receipt for taxes collected by Dionisio de Aguilar; a statement on application of taxes; and a statement on salaries paid.

7. Map of the Yaqui Valley. Item no. 20. Mexico, n.d. A map of the Yaqui Valley and neighboring territory.

SORIA, FRANCISCO DE

Ystoria y Fundacion de la Ciudad de Tlaxcala y sus quatro caveseras sacada por Francisco de Soria de lengua castellana á esta Mexicana. . . . [N.p., n.d.] *96 p. 22 cm.*   HHB [M-M 231]

A Náhuatl translation, Mexico, 1718, of a treatise in Spanish on the founding and history of the city of Tlaxcala. Authorship of the original variously ascribed to an early Christian cacique, to Juan de Torquemada, and to Diego Muñoz Camargo. This translation was copied by José Magdaleno Rosales from a 12-folio Ms. in the Archivo General del Imperio. Beristáin, *Bibliotheca Hispano Americana Septentrional*, Vol. III, p. 134, refers to a very similar work written originally in Náhuatl and translated into Spanish by Francisco de Loaysa. For a more detailed bibliographical discussion, see Charles Gibson, *Tlaxcala in the Sixteenth Century*, p. 257-258.

SOTO, MARCO AURELIO, 1846-1908
 Colección de maderas y minerales de la República de Honduras. . . . Tegucigalpa [Honduras]. May 5, 1883.
 48 p. 34 cm. HHB [M-M 357]
 Description of President Soto's collection of woods, minerals, and fibrous plants from Honduras and, in a few instances, from Nicaragua. Fifty-seven cases are described individually.

SOTO, MARCO AURELIO, 1846-1908
 Copias del editorial de "La Paz" de Tegucigalpa. . . . 1883.
 16 f. 27 cm. HHB [M-M 358]
 Copies of editorial comment in the Tegucigalpa newspaper, *La Paz*, inspired by correspondence between President Marco Aurelio Soto of Honduras and José Milla, in which the former questioned the theory that Columbus landed in Honduras or any other part of the American mainland, followed by three letters of J. Carrera, Honduran consul in Madrid, on the same subject.

SOUTH CAROLINA
 Documents for the history of. 1724-1838.
 14 folders. D.S. [z-z 122]
 Miscellaneous papers, including abstract of title for property in South Carolina; jail accounts for Orangeburg, 1775-1776; ferry charges; incomplete draft of the constitution of South Carolina, 1778; accounts for the stamping of money; military accounts; a resolution concerning pensions; contemporary copy of the ratification of the U.S. Constitution by South Carolina, 1788; wolf scalp bounty certificates; miscellaneous tax records; and legal papers in two cases relating to the non-payment of debts.

SPAIN
 Four Legal Claims. 17th century.
 130 p. D. and D.S. 29-31 cm. [z-z 19]
 Briefs and statements, three of them relating to chaplaincies and clerical duties and one concerning jurisdiction over La Torre de Juan Abad (Spain).

SPAIN. CONTADURÍA GENERAL DE DISTRIBUCIÓN
 Circular. Madrid. December 12, 1840.
 4 p. 11 cm. [z-z 100:41]
 Concerning expenditures of the Ministries of Hacienda and Gracia y Justicia.

SPAIN. LAWS, STATUTES, ET CETERA
 Cedulas relating to New Mexico and other provinces, 1609-1765.
 716 p. 31 cm. HHB [M-M 167]
 Copies of royal decrees and a few related petitions (Spain and Mexico, 1631-1765) concerning the administration of New Mexico, Lower California, New Galicia, New León, New Santander, the Provincias Internas as a whole,

and Hispaniola, with special reference to missions, treatment of Indians, and maintenance of garrisons. Arranged primarily according to geographical divisions, and chronologically within each division. Appended is an excerpt from the "Nueva Recopilación de Leyes de Indias" (Book 3, Title 2, Law 66), relating to the missions of New Mexico in 1609.

SPAIN. LAWS, STATUTES, ET CETERA
Codigo de Leyes de Indias. [ca. 1808]
788 p. 30 cm.   HHB [M-M 265]

A collection of laws on ecclesiastical and kindred affairs in the Spanish Indies, apparently corresponding to Book I of a 19th-century version of the *Recopilación de leyes de los reinos de las Indias*; marginal citations written in the same hand as the text and referring to laws dated as late as 1808.

SPAIN. LAWS, STATUTES, ET CETERA
Colección de Cédulas Reales . . . concernientes al Gobierno de las Religiones en las Americas, y especialmente en el Reyno de Guatemala, . . . November 12, 1555–May 22, 1769.
160 p. Ms. and printed. 33 cm.   HHB [M-M 437]

Primarily originals and authenticated copies of Spanish and Portuguese royal decrees, orders of the Guatemalan Audiencia issued in the name of the king, correspondence transmitting decrees, and related documents, concerning the ecclesiastical and civil government of the Indies, particularly in Guatemala, with special reference to treatment of Indians, conduct of religious orders, and expulsion of the Jesuits. The title page, in the handwriting of Brasseur de Bourbourg, erroneously limits the period covered to 1632-1769.

SPAIN. LAWS, STATUTES, ET CETERA
Extractos de cédulas en los archivos de la ciudad de México . . . . 1523-1799.
80 p. 31 cm.   HHB [M-M 151]

Summaries and extracts of cedulas in the Mexico City archives relating to the administration of New Spain, particularly Mexico City, 1523-1799. Entered by Bancroft under "Mexico, Ordenanzas de esta nobilíssima ciudad. Mexico, 1775."

SPAIN. LAWS, STATUTES, ET CETERA
Ordenanzas de esta N[obilísima] C[iudad] de Mexico aprobadas por el Rey D.ⁿ Phelipe V. . . . 1596-1797.
724 p. 32 cm.   HHB [M-M 152]

Provisions for administration of colonies in the New World: certified copy of decree issued by Philip V of Spain, Madrid, November 4, 1728, approving with some exceptions the Ordinances of Mexico City as revised June 3, 1720; copies of decrees, orders, and official correspondence, Spain and Mexico, relating to political, socio-economic, and ecclesiastical affairs in the New World, particularly New Spain, with frequent reference to the treatment of Indians and to trade with the Philippines.

Entered by Bancroft under "Mexico, Ordenanzas de esta nobilíssima ciudad. Mexico, 1775."

SPAIN. LAWS, STATUTES, ET CETERA
Reales Cédulas. . . . 1529-1812.
7 vols. Ms. and printed. 32 cm.   HHB   [M-M 170-176]
Vol. I, 1529-1812, deals with administration of the Indies; vol. II, 1529-1745, with treatment of the Indians in Tlaxcala and with the administration of religious orders, particularly the Franciscans; vol. III, 1682-1807, with stress on legal and judicial questions in the administration of the Indies; vol. IV, 1660-1751, principally with the Franciscan Order; vol. V, 1776-1803, with questions of ecclesiastical or civil jurisdiction in regard to wills, and with reform of the calendar of feast days and days honoring the Spanish royal family; vol. VI, 1707-1810, chiefly with financial, commercial, or property questions in New Spain and the Philippines, and with rulings of the Inquisition; vol. VII, 1633-1751, with a miscellany of subjects, such as the Franciscans, sale of alcoholic beverages, treatment of Indians, the royal family, and beatification of various persons.

SPAIN. LAWS, STATUTES, ET CETERA
Reales Cédulas [y documentos análogos]. July 27, 1529–June 27, 1834.
2 vols. 32 cm.   HHB   [M-M 205-206]
Collection of royal decrees, viceregal orders, and similar documents (copies or summaries), from Spain or Mexico, relating primarily to the government of New Spain. Arranged in roughly alphabetical order according to the specific topics treated, which include taxation, property questions, appointments to office, regulation of commerce, marriage, and administration of the Church and of certain religious orders, *e.g.*, the Congregation of Saint Hippolytus.

SPAIN. LAWS, STATUTES, ET CETERA
Reales órdenes que acreditan que el puerto de San Juan del Norte pertenece a Nicaragua . . . . Madrid. March 31, 1808.
4 p. (Transcript) 32 cm.   HHB   [Z-C 4:2]
Issued to promote the colonization and commercial development of the Island of Carmen and other areas. Copy of an imprint.

SPAIN. TREATIES
Convenio celebrado entre S.S. M.M los Reyes de España e Inglaterra . . . .
London. July 14, 1786.
10 p. (Typescript) 34 cm.   IIID   [Z-C 4.1]
Agreement regarding the exploitation and control of the Mosquito Coast. Transcript of an imprint.

SPICER FAMILY PAPERS. 1809-1913
1 carton.   [Z-Z 135]
Miscellaneous business and personal papers, correspondence, letter books, and clippings, mostly relating to Brigadier General Peter W. Spicer (?-1834) and his son, John W. Spicer. An important part of the collection consists of correspondence and letters of recommendation assembled by General Spicer in his efforts to secure a federal appointment from President Andrew Jackson. A

number of items, including warrants, commissions, and gold epaulets, relate to John W. Spicer's connection with the 7th Regiment of the New York National Guard.

SQUIER, EPHRAIM GEORGE, 1821-1888
Documents relating to Central America. [1519-ca. 1776]
24 items. 31-34 cm.   HHB   [M-M 300-321]

Transcripts, translations, and summaries of documents and letters relating primarily to civil and ecclesiastical administration of the Central American provinces during the sixteenth century, to the development of navigation routes and the exploration of the Pacific in that vicinity, and to the character and treatment of the Indians.

Most of these volumes bear annotations signed by Buckingham Smith, 1856-1857, and sometimes also by Martín Fernández de Navarrete or his assistant, certifying the location of the original.

STEPHENS, JOHN LLOYD, 1805-1852
Correspondence and Papers. 1795-1882.
4 boxes, 1 portfolio, and 1 reel (on film).   [z-z 116]

Concerning Stephens' travels in Mexico and Central America, his publications, and his association with the Panama Railroad Company. Included are papers concerning the settlement of his estate and family land holdings in New York state, and some correspondence of his father, Benjamin Stephens. A "key" to the collection is available.

STILES, EZRA, 1727-1795
California. December 26, 1759-1760.
7 p. A.D.S. (Photocopy) 39 cm.   [M-M 1706]

Notes on the history of the Californias in the 17th and early 18th centuries, dealing principally with Jesuit missionary work, early explorers, and the natives of the region; with an annotated map of Baja California and adjacent portion of Mexico. Said to be based on the English translation of Miguel de Venegas' history in its published and expanded Spanish version, *A Natural and Civil History of California* (London, 1759). Original in the Yale University Library.

STOCKTON, FRANCIS RICHARD, 1834-1902
Letter to Mr. Carey. Convent Station, New Jersey. February 25, 1893.
1 p. L.S. 27 cm.   [z-z 100:98]

Concerning a speech he has been asked to give.

STOUGHTON, THOMAS
Certificate. New York, N.Y. May 30, 1799.
3 p. A.D.S. 32 cm.   HHB   [M-M 1700:22]

Certificate issued by Stoughton as Consul for Spain in New York, stating that Prudencio Gutiérrez's mission of transporting armament to Veracruz aboard the American frigate *Hazard* is in accord with Spanish royal decrees.

STRINGER. WILLIAM JAMES, 1831(?)-
Indenture of Apprenticeship to Alexander Roux, Upholsterer. New York, N.Y. August 8, 1848.
2 p. D.S. 33 cm. [z-z 100:7]

STUART, HENRY C
Ferrocarril del Salvador. April, 1899–October, 1900.
1 vol. (Typescript) 28 cm. [z-c 222]
Copies of letters written by Stuart as general manager of the railroad to the board of directors in London concerning management of the company's properties.

STUART, HENRY C
Trip to Central America, 1891-1892.
344 p. A.D. 15-31 cm. [69/140m]
Journal of a trip from Denver, via New York, to Panama, Guatemala, and Salvador, and return to Denver. Describes travel, the social scene, and the mines of Guatemala. Includes programs, clippings, invitations, calling cards, autographs, letters, and many photographs.

SUÁREZ, BERNARDA MARÍA DE LOS DOLORES, 1875-
Birth Certificate. La Coruña, Spain. February 3 and 21, 1875.
6 p. D.S. 32 cm. [z-z 100:40]
Two copies of birth certificate, accompanied by copy of birth certificate of her mother, Adelaida Blasco, dated November 14, 1823.

SUASO Y COSCOJALES, DIEGO DE
Oracion Evangelica, y Panegyrica de la Purificacion de Maria SS.^{ma} . . . . Mexico City. 1703. And other items.
338 p. Ms. and printed. 21 cm. HHB [m-m 255]
The volume contains nine pieces, the first of which is the sermons of Suaso, Archdean of the Mexico City Cathedral, February 2, 1763, intended as a model for preaching in America. Then follows a "Respuesta," or detailed attack upon Suaso's model sermon, ascribed to Santiago de Henares, a pseudonym for Avendaño and his Jesuit collaborators. Other items comprise an anonymous satire dealing with the Dominican chapter meeting held in Puebla on May 5, 1714, at which Fray Antonio de la Vera was elected Provincial Vicar; verses by Father Juan Carnero; an anonymous satire, in prose and verse, relating to seating privileges in the Puebla cathedral; and other verses and satires.
Entered by Bancroft under "Zuazo, Diego de."

SUCCECION CHRONOLOGICA DE LOS PRESIDENTES . . . [Y] OBISPOS DE GOATHEMALA Y NOTICIAS CURIOSAS CHRONOLOGICAS DESTAS INDIAS. . . . GUATEMALA. 1777-[1779?]
78 p. 30 cm. HHB [m-m 442]
Anonymous Ms. relating primarily to the history of Guatemala and divided into three main sections:
1. Numbered list of the presidents and captains general of Guatemala from

1538 to 1777, with biographical comments; based upon records of the Cathedral Chapter. [Santiago de Guatemala], 1777. 8 p.

2. Numbered list of the Bishops of Guatemala from 1534 to 1745, when the diocese became an archdiocese, with some biographical data. [Guatemala, 1777?]. 2 p.

3. Roughly chronological account of important events in the Indies during the period 1492-1779. Relates chiefly to Guatemala and includes detailed accounts of the destruction of the first capital, establishment of a new capital, and the disputes on the appointment of Archbishop Francos y Monroy and the distribution of tithes. [Guatemala, ca. 1779]. 68 p.

SUGAR INDUSTRY IN MEXICO. 1910-1948
583 exp. (On film) [M-M 1841]
Typescripts of selections from various sources.

SUGAR PLANTATION AT ATLIXCO, MEXICO
Account Book. 1693-1698.
11 boxes. (Photocopy) [M-A 2]
From the Archivo General de la Nación, Mexico.

[SUN, CHING-LING (SUNG)], 1890-
Letter from Madame Sun Yat-sen to [Reo Franklin] Fortune. Hong Kong. September 2, 1938.
1 p. L., initialed. 28 cm. [Z-Z 100:70]
Concerning the China Defence League.

SUNGA Y MENDOSA, ELÍAS
Expediente posesorio promovido por. . . . San Miguel de Mayumo, Philippine Islands. 1896.
22 p. D.S. 31 cm. [70/34z]
Documents relating to Mendosa's claim for a lot in the barrio of San Vicente.

SURINAM
Notes on Dutch Colonists. 1921.
2 p. (Typescript) 28 cm. [Z-D 113:1]

SUTHERLAND, ROBERT
Letters. January–June, 1828.
38 exp. (On film) [Z-G 7]
Letters from Sutherland, British consul in Colombia. From the Foreign Office files of the Public Record Office, London.

TACUBA, MEXICO. REAL JUSTICIA
Court Records. 1680-1682.
62 p. D.S. 31 cm. [M-M 1883:1]
Records of criminal cases, mainly theft, heard before the Justice Court of Tacuba.

TAKICHI, HYOZEN TOGEN
    Mekishiko shinwa. ca. 1845.
    130 p. Ms., with colored illustrations. 26 cm. [M-M 1902]
    Account, in Japanese, of the abandoning of the wrecked ship *Eidu Maru*, in Lower California, and the experiences and observations of the survivors in Mexico, 1842-1844. The men were taken to Cape San Lucas and later to San José del Cabo, Baja California.
    Illustrated with watercolors of the rescue, landscapes, scenes of Mexican life, and local flora and fauna.

TAMARÓN Y ROMERAL, PEDRO, bp., 1695-1768
    Visita del Obispado de Durango por el Il.^{mo} Señor Don Pedro Tamaron, Obispo de su Diòcesis. Durango. 1759-1765.
    377 p. 31 cm. HHB [M-M 232]
    Copy of reports rendered by Bishop Tamarón of Durango in compliance with royal decrees regarding his inspection of his see, which comprised the present territory of Durango, Chihuahua, parts of other Mexican states, and New Mexico. Consists of an introduction and three parts. Printed as *Demostración del vastísimo obispado de la Nueva Vizcaya—1765* (ed. by Vito Alessio Robles, Mexico, 1937).

TAMARÓN Y ROMERAL, PEDRO, bp., 1695-1768
    [Visita del Obispado de Durango por el Ilustrísimo Señor Don Pedro Tamarón Obispo de Su Diócesis. Durango. 1759-1765]
    223 p. 32 cm. HHB [M-M 232A]
    A portion of the three reports regarding Tamarón's inspection of his diocese. Includes nearly all of Part I and the itineraries of Part II, but lacks the dedication and the whole of Part III; substantially identical with Tamarón y Romeral, "Visita del Obispado de Durango . . ." (M-M 232), q.v. In the handwriting of Alphonse Pinart.

TARAHUMARA. MEXICO. 1785-1791.
    3 folders. D. and D.S. 15-30 cm. HHB [M-M 520]
    Statistical and descriptive data relating to the Tarahumara region, which includes parts of Chihuahua, Durango, Sinaloa, and Sonora.
    1. Copy of a report prepared by Friar Francisco Rauzet de Jesús on the Indian population and the administration, products, climate and socio-economic conditions of 16 missions with their subsidiary communities, situated in Upper and Lower Tarahumara, principally in Chihuahua. [Chihuahua], 1785, and an annotation of 1791. 32 p. 30 cm.
    2. A census table, signed by Lasso, for a list of 46 towns in or near Chihuahua. [Chihuahua?], April 9, 1791. 1 p. 30x43 cm.
    3. A memorandum on the number of Spaniards and Indians to be sent from specific towns on forays; apparently relating primarily to towns situated in the Culiacán area. N.p., n.d. 1 p. 15 cm.

TARAHUMARA MISSIONS
Patentes y comunicaciones que se refieren a la Tarahumara (segunda parte). Mexico and Spain. 1780-1878.
113 p. (Typescript) 28 cm. [M-M 1893]
Transcript of patents, official correspondence, orders, instructions, and royal decrees concerning missions to the Tarahumara Indians.

TARAVAL, SIGISMUNDO, 1700-1763
Elogios de Misioneros de Baja California. Baja California. 1737.
2 folders in portfolio. A.D.S.? 22 cm. HHB [M-M 233A & 233B]
Eulogies of Lorenzo José Carranco and Nicolás Tamaral, Jesuit missionaries slain in Baja California in 1734 by the Pericú Indians, with two related commemorative items in Spanish prose and Latin verse; eulogy of Julián de Mayorga, also a Jesuit missionary to Baja California; letter from Taraval, July 14, 1737, transmitting this material to Father Francisco Cutillas; and certification signed by Taraval, August 12, 1737, attesting the martyrdom of Carranco and Tamaral.

TAYLOR, PAUL SHUSTER, 1895-
Notes and Papers concerning Mexican Labor in the United States. ca. 1927-1932.
2 cartons and 1 box. [Z-R 4]
Notes, pamphlets, newspaper clippings, etc., used in preparation of a series of monographs on the migration of Mexican laborers to the United States.

TAYS, EUGENE AUGUSTUS HOFFMAN, 1861-1928
Statement . . . concerning revolutionary conditions [in Mexico] prior to 1916. . . . Berkeley, California. September 1, 1916.
34 p. (Typescript) 29 cm. [M-M 1752]
Statement made by a U.S. resident of Nogales (Arizona?) and San Blas, Mexico, containing summary information on Mexico, i.e., location, area, inhabitants, history, transportation, education, and other features, but concerned principally with the property problems of foreign residents caused by the existing economic chaos, and the obligation of the U.S. Government to intervene on behalf of such residents.

TEATRO: EL ALFÉREZ . . . 1820-1838
634 p. 23 cm. HHB [M-M 88]
A collection of five plays, dealing chiefly with contemporary Mexican life, as follows: 1) El Alférez. Mexico City, 1838. 125 p. A three-act verse play by an anonymous author; 2) El Marido Joven. [Mexico, n.d.] 68 p. An anonymous three-act play; 3) Tres a un Tiempo. Mexico City. July 20, 1838. 263 p. A five-act play by an anonymous Mexican author; 4) Delavigne, Jean François Casimir, 1793-1843. Les Comédiens. Paris, 1820. 140 p. A Spanish prose translation, under the title "Los Cómicos," from the five-act French play in verse; 5) Sin-Tierra, Juan. A rio revuelto ganancia de pescadores. Sainete republicano (*pseud.*) [Mexico City, n.d.] 35 p. A one-act political farce; incomplete.

TEGGART, FREDERICK JOHN, 1870-1946
   Notes on Cartography and Early Exploration of the Pacific Coast.
   146 p. 28-33 cm. [z-r 10]

TERRALLA Y LANDA, F
   Consejos economicos, saludables, politicos, y morales, que da un amigo a otro, que intenta pasar de Mexico á Lima. ca. 1799.
   227 p. 22 cm. hhb [m-m 234]
   A long didactic poem, comprising 18 *romances*, or ballads, and containing advice for a friend who plans to move from Mexico City to Lima.

TERRAZAS, MARIANO
   Testamentaría de. Mexico. 1835-1849.
   77 p. (On film) D.S. [67/178m]
   Microfilm of papers pertaining to the settlement of the estate of Don Mariano Terrazas in Mexico City, including copy of will, documents relating to property, inventory of estate, and accounts of administrators of the estate. Originals in private possession.

TERRAZAS, SILVESTRE, 1873-1944
   Correspondence and Papers. ca. 1883-1944.
   129 boxes [m-b 18]
   Born in Chihuahua and educated there and in Mexico City, Terrazas early in life dedicated himself to a journalistic career. He founded and edited, for the Bishop of Chihuahua, Dr. Jesús J. Ortiz, the *Revista Católica*, a weekly, 1896-1901. He also founded a monthly literary review, *La Lira Chihuahuense*, in 1896 which continued until 1901. Meantime, he started his lifework with the newspaper *El Correo de Chihuahua*, 1899, issued in Chihuahua City (occasionally), but which assumed new stature with the publication of Volume I, Number 1, on January 1, 1902, and continued until the government permanently forced its discontinuance in 1935.
   In this first decade of the century, Terrazas opposed the policies of Enrique C. Creel, governor of the state of Chihuahua, and the regime of President Porfirio Díaz, and used the columns of his newspaper to this end. This led him into a long and stormy political career. In 1910, he supported Francisco I. Madero against Díaz, was sent to prison, November 22, 1910–February 10, 1911, for plotting against the government. In 1913, he opposed Victoriano Huerta, who had had Abraham González, governor of Chihuahua, murdered. Terrazas then fled to El Paso for safety, but continued publication of his paper. He supported Francisco "Pancho" Villa and was appointed his Secretario de Gobierno, or vice governor, of Chihuahua. On Villa's defeat by Carranza in 1915, Terrazas again went into exile, this time to Las Cruces, New Mexico. In the following year, he moved to El Paso, where he began publication of *La Patria*, January 1, 1919, and where he maintained a home, as well as another in Chihuahua City.
   Terrazas carried on a large correspondence with Mexican journalists, most of whom were members of the Prensa Asociada de los Estados, of which

Terrazas was one of the founders and often an officer. With them he discussed the political situation of the country, and his correspondence reflects his involvement in local and national politics. Frequently imprisoned for opposition to the party in power, and his newspaper plant locked up, he nevertheless continued the struggle in behalf of liberal causes.

The Terrazas Collection contains not only excellent files of his own newspapers, but a mass of letters and documents concerning his most active years, especially beginning with the 1910 election. Among his correspondents were such men as Miguel and Vito Alessio Robles, Venustiano Carranza, Felipe Angeles, Governor Fidel Avila of Chihuahua, the Banco Nacional de México, Plutarco Elías Calles, Enrique C. Creel, Ignacio C. Enríquez, Adolfo de la Huerta, Ricardo Flores Magón, and literally hundreds of others, many of national stature.

There is a detailed "key" to the collection.

TESTIMONIO DE LA R.¹ CEDULA, Y DILIGENZ.ᵃˢ EN SU VIRTUD EXECUTADAS EN QUE SU MAG.ᵈ MANDA . . . DAR QUENTTA DE LOS RELIGIOSOS QUE AY Y DE LOS QUE SE NESECITTAN PARA LA REDUCCION Y COMVERCION DE LOS INDIOS GENTTILES . . . . MAY 21, 1747–JANUARY 19, 1751

160 p. D. and D.S. 31 cm. [M-M 1861]

File relating to the royal decree of May 21, 1747, requesting annual reports to the Council of the Indies from civil and religious officials of New Spain, the Philippines, Peru, and New Granada, on the status and needs of missions or other religious institutions engaged in pacification and conversion of the indigenous peoples.

TEXAS

Documents relating to. 1797-1810.

195 p. D.S. 22-32 cm. [M-M 1856]

Correspondence to and from the viceroys of Mexico, mainly concerning troubles with the Apache, Comanche, and Lipan Indians in Texas, and to procuring military aid for the province. A few letters pertain to the boundary of Louisiana and to the United States' intervention in Spanish territories.

An explanatory "key" to the collection is available in the Bancroft Library.

TEXAS. COLONIZATION

Documents relating to. 1729-1730.

4 folders (210 p.) D., D.S., and typescript. [M-M 1857]

Two files of documents, copies and originals, relating to a royal decree of February 14, 1729, which provided for settlement of certain localities in the province of Texas by 400 families from the Canary Islands. This was in accordance with the recommendations of the Marqués de San Miguel de Aguayo, former governor of Coahuila and Texas, who advocated mixed colonization by Canary Islanders and Tlaxcalan natives, in view of threatened French encroachment and the potential value of the territory.

TEXAS AND CALIFORNIA
  Documents relating to. 1821-1871.
  2 vols. and 4 boxes (Typescripts) [M-A 6]
  These papers relate primarily to plans for colonization of Texas, beginning with Stephen F. Austin, and California, with some account of events in northern Mexico, the filibustering expeditions of Gaston de Raousset-Boulbon, William Walker, and Jean Napoleon Zerman to Lower California; commerce, missions, trade, and defense against frontier Indians in Sonora. From Mexico: Secretaría de Fomento, Colonización, e Industria, or Secretaría de Relaciones Exteriores.

TEXAS AND COAHUILA
  Documents relating to. Saltillo. 1688-1876.
  69 vols. (Photocopies) 29 cm. [M-A 10]
  The colonization of Texas; grants of lands to settlers; illegal trade; relations with neighboring areas; and decrees of the state of Coahuila y Texas (1824-1834, 1848-1876). From the Archivo de la Secretaría de Gobierno.
  Included are Legajos 1-54, except for Nos. 15, 18, 31, 35, 39, 46, and 47. A calendar of the documents accompanies the set.

THEVET, ANDRÉ, 1502-1590
  Le grand insulaire et pilotage d'André Thevet, angoumoisin, cosmographe du Roi. Dans lequel sont contenus plusiers plants d'isles habitées, et deshabitées, et description d'icelles. 1586.
  2 vols. (On film). [Z-F 2]
  Volume I contains descriptions of the West Indies and other islands of the New World. Volume II relates to the islands of the Mediterranean. Microfilm of original manuscript in the Bibliothèque Nationale, Paris.

TIA JUANA (TIJUANA), RANCHO DEL
  Documents concerning. Mexico. 1846-1890.
  43 p. D. and D.S. 32-46 cm. [M-M 1874]
  Legal papers, copies and originals, relating to the above rancho, owned by members of the Argüello family. Includes title to the rancho, presidential confirmation of title to the heirs, and subsequent litigation. Dated at Los Angeles, Mexico, and Ensenada.

TITULO DE MERCED Y CONFIRMACION EN FORMA DE TRES SITIOS DE TIERRA PARA GANADO MAYOR QUE COMPREHENDE EL PUESTO NOMBRADO EL TECOMATE . . . EN LA JURISDICCION DE COSALÀ, EXPEDIDO . . . À FAVOR DE D.ⁿ EUSEBIO CARDENAS, VECINO DEL PARTIDO DE CULIACÁN. ARISPE. NOVEMBER 15, 1797
  81 p. (Photocopy) 25 cm. [M-M 1844]
  File of the Land Tribunal for the Provinces of Sonora and Sinaloa confirming, with a reservation to protect Indian fishing rights, the title claimed by Eusebio Cárdenas, Culiacán tax collector, to ranch lands in the jurisdiction of

Cosalá, Sinaloa, known collectively as "El Tecomate," and purchased by him from the heirs of José Ramón Quevedo.

TLALTIZAPÁN, MORELIA, MEXICO
Libro de casamientos y entierros .... 1660-1672.
66 p. D.S. 30 cm. [71/20M]
　　Register of marriages and deaths for the town of Tlaltizapán, signed by various parish priests.

TLAXCALA
Legal Documents. 1568-1770.
126 folders in 9 boxes. 31-32 cm. [M-M 1722]
　　Miscellaneous legal papers, mostly signed originals, dealing with both civil and criminal cases, arranged in chronological order. The collection consists mainly of records from Tlaxcalan administrative tribunals, with some documents from the Real Audiencia de México and its criminal court, from the Santa Hermandad, and from the tribunal of the Santa Cruzada. Includes records of criminal, land, and inheritance cases in Tlaxcala and its environs; enlistment provisions; and one genealogical record. Many cases involve treatment of the Indians.

TLAXCALA (PROVINCE). MEXICO
El Llanto de la Puebla en la traslacion de su amabilisimo prelado el Ilustrisimo señor doctor D. Victoriano Lopez Gonzalo a la Silla de Tortosa. . . . [Puebla, Mexico. 1786]
34 p. 21 cm. HHB [M-M 129]
　　Collection of verses lamenting, on behalf of ecclesiastical and lay bodies of the province, the transfer of Bishop López Gonzalo from Tlaxcala, i. e., Puebla, to Tortosa, Spain.
　　Entered by Bancroft under "Llanto de la puebla en la traslacion de su amabilisimo prelado. Puebla [1800]." The date "1786" is suggested above as the year in which López Gonzalo was transferred.

TORO, FRANCISCO DEL
Letters Written by, or relating to. Mexico. 1912-1913.
3 folders, 3 p. 27-28 cm. [M-M 1813]
　　Letters from President Francisco Madero to José López Portillo y Rojas, 1912, offering amnesty to Toro and his men in exchange for surrender; and two letters from Toro to Carlos Cortés Ortigosa, 1912 and 1913, acknowledging safe conduct documents and requesting release of certain men from prison.

TORQUEMADA, JUAN DE, 1557(?)-1615
Primera Parte de los Veinte i Un Libros Rituales i Monarchia Indiana . . . . Madrid. 1723.
133 p. 31 cm. HHB [M-M 282]
　　English summaries and translations of selected passages from the *Monarquía Indiana*, Part I, Bks. 1-4, dealing with the origin and history of various tribes

indigenous to Mexico, the discovery of Mexico by Grijalva, and its conquest under Cortés.

Two folders, in portfolio. Written in the hand of Carlos F. Galán, one-time Governor of Lower California, and probably prepared by him in 1872 for the use of H. H. Bancroft. Entered by Bancroft under "Mexico, Aboriginal History."

TORRES, HILARIO
Letter to José Francisco Valverde. Huajuapan de León, Mexico. April 19, 1862.
1 p. A.L.S. 26 cm. [M-M 1700:86]
Thanking his friend for news of General Díaz and requesting further news.

TORRES Y RUEDA, MARCOS DE, bp., d. 1649
Disposición testamentaria. Mexico City. April 8, 1649.
4 p. 31 cm. HHB [M-M 322]
Text of the testamentary provision made on his deathbed by Bishop Torres, interim viceroy of New Spain.

Another copy of this provision is contained in "Vireyes de México. Instrucciones...." (M-M 249, item 23).

TORRES Y VERGARA, JOSÉ DE, 1661-1727
Comprobantes de la Cuenta que presentan el Bachiller Don José Sánchez y Espinosa.... [Mexico] 1802-1816.
153 p. D.S. 11-31 cm. [M-M 1704]
File of documents presented by José Sánchez y Espinosa, nephew of the deceased Dr. José de Torres y Vergara, Archdean of Mexico City Cathedral, and his son, the Count of Santa María de Guadalupe del Peñasco, as administrators of the Puerto de Nieto and neighboring estates under the will of Torres y Vergara. Apparently submitted in connection with lawsuits brought against the administrators by José Fernández Mora and others, the material deals principally with execution of Torres' provisions for religious and charitable benefactions, but refers also to funds established for similar purposes by Juan Caballero y Ocío and Juan Gerardo de Acosta. Contains accounts, reports, receipts, certifications, petition for approval of the material presented, review thereof by Juan Francisco de Farras, the accountant general for the Archdiocese of Mexico, and statements of approval from Dr. Cabeza de Vaca, Fiscal Defender, and Dr. Félix Flores Alatorre, Judge-Inspector of Wills, Chaplaincies, and Pious Works for the Archdiocese, releasing the administrators from litigation and further responsibility. Written principally in Mexico City.

TRACY, CYRUS
Family Papers. ca. 1800-1850.
2 vols. 39-44 cm. [Z-Z 107]
Notebook, mainly concerning mathematics, navigation, and philosophy, and a family genealogy probably compiled around 1848. Note on front cover of P. Tracy."
notebook: "... written by Cyrus Tracy of Windham, the father of Frederick

TRAYLOR, SAMUEL W[HITE], 1869-
Letter to R. G. Hall. Palm Beach, Florida. December 15, 1936.
1 p. L.S. (by secretary). 28 cm. [z-z 100:90]
Concerning book he has written.

TROTTER, ADA M
Earthquake Record. Summerville, South Carolina. 1887-1888.
15 p. A.D. 17 cm. [z-z 124]
Diary entries describing a series of earthquakes.

TUCKER, JOSEPH CLARENCE, 1828-1891
Papers. 1856.
84 p. A.D. and A.L.S. 28-41 cm. [69/6M]
A letter to his brother, written from Tegucigalpa, Honduras, describing traveling in Nicaragua in the wake of Walker's expedition, and Tucker's interest in silver mines in Honduras. Together with portions of manuscript for Tucker's book *To the Golden Goal* (San Francisco, 1895), relating to Nicaragua and experiences in California.

TULANCINGO, DIOCESE
Reports on the Various Parishes of the Diocese of Tulancingo. Mexico. 1865-1880.
17 folders in portfolio. 34 cm. HHB [M-M 387]
Copies of reports on the parishes and other subdivisions of the diocese which includes the present states of Hidalgo, Puebla and Veracruz. The documents were prepared primarily in reply to episcopal circular questionnaires issued on December 19, 1864, and August 27, 1870, presumably by Juan Bautista Ormaechea y Ernaiz, but also include one 1880 item made in response to a later circular from the secretariat of the diocese. These reports contain information on locations, climate, population, languages, agricultural and other products, industries and roads; some include Ms. maps.

TUMULTOS DE MÉXICO. [1624-1635]
180 p. Ms. and printed. 31 cm. HHB [M-M 236]
Documents, letters, and reports relating chiefly to the conflict between Viceroy Gelves and Archbishop Serna and the resulting disturbances of January, 1624.

Main topics include the accusation of October 20, 1635, against Viceroy Cerralvo by the Franciscan Order in New Spain; a portion of Gelves' reply to the charges against him in the conflict with Archbishop Serna; papers on the causes and origin of the Gelves-Serna dispute; a memorial of Bartolomé de Burguillos to Inquisitor Carrillo; a statement of Pedro Garcés de Portillo, vicar general of the archdiocese, regarding ecclesiastical sanctuary; report by Cristóbal Ruiz de Cabrera on the Gelves-Serna conflict; the viceroy's proclamation of December 25, 1625, on amnesty for the insurgents of the January 15, 1624, uprising; and two letters from Pope Urban VIII on the Gelves-Serna controversy.

TURPIN, PHILIP
   Genealogy and Commonplace Book. ca. 1770-1806.
   2 items. Chart, 123x23 cm., and notebook, 17 cm.   [z-z 136]
   Pocket notebook, and genealogical chart, concerning the Turpin and allied families, Henrico County, Virginia. Originally this was the account book, 1721-1759, of John Cocke. With notes in other handwritings.

TURPIN, PHILIP
   Petition to the House of Delegates concerning Property in Richmond [Virginia?]. November 17, 1795.
   4 p. 32 cm.   [z-z 100:101]

UGALDE, JUAN DE, 1727-1816
   Documentos que acompañados de vn Estado g.^{ral} pone el Coronèl D. Juan de Vgalde en las manos . . . del . . . Virrey Conde de Galvez, que todo trata sobre las quatro Provincias que se digna determinar S.E. ponèr debajo de su mando. . . . 1777-[ca. 1788]
   2 vols. 30 cm. and 46x66 cm.   HHB [M-M 404]
   Copies of documents submitted by Ugalde, ex-Governor of Coahuila, to Viceroy Bernardo de Gálvez, relating generally to needed reforms in the administration and military defense of the Provincias Internas, and particularly to a defense of Ugalde's policy in the gubernatorial post from which he was removed by Teodoro de Croix. Accompanied by a chart of troops and defenses for the northern Provincias Internas signed by Ugalde in Mexico City, May 5, 1786.

UNIÓN GENERAL DE RECLUSOS DEL PAÍS
   Estatutos Generales . . . . Zaragoza, state of Puebla. 1933.
   29 p. D.S. 17x23 cm.   HHB [M-M 1700:53]
   Constitution or rules of the "Unión General de Reclusos del País," Miguel Mondragón, Jr., president. Organized for the improvement of the lot of illiterate prisoners. With signatures of members.

UNIVERSITY OF MEXICO. 1560-1816
   660 p. 31 cm.   [M-M 1815]
   Collection of royal decrees, viceregal orders, and related documents, mainly copies, originating in Spain and Mexico and concerned principally with the University of Mexico or its relations with other educational institutions. Corresponds substantially in content with the main portion of the printed *Reales Cédulas de la Real y Pontificia Universidad de México* . . . (Mexico City, 1946) edited by John Tate Lanning, but contains several documents not in the Lanning collection.

UPSHUR, ABEL PARKER, 1790-1844
   Letter to Robert H. Nichols. U.S. Navy Department. May 20, 1842.
   1 p. L.S. 25 cm.   [z-z 100:25]
   Written as Secretary of the Navy, ordering Nichols to duty aboard a ship at Buffalo, New York.

URUEÑA, JOSÉ ANTONIO DE
Defensa de las secularizaciones autorizadas por los Sumos Pontifices. Mexico City. 1816.
52 p. 21 cm. HHB [M-M 238]
A defense of papal bulls of secularization, composed by Urueña, a secularized priest and former Mercedarian, in reply to a manuscript dissertation of José de San Bartolomé, prior of a Mexico City monastery, which impugned the validity of such bulls. Appended comments include biographical data on Urueña.

URUEÑA, JOSÉ ANTONIO DE
Defensa de las secularizaciones autorizadas por los Sumos Pontifices. Mexico City. 1816.
106 p. 21 cm. HHB [M-M 239]
A defense of papal bulls of secularization, composed in reply to the manuscript of José de San Bartolomé impugning the validity of such bulls. Substantially identical with item M-M 238.

U.S. ADJUTANT GENERAL'S OFFICE
Letter to William Henry, member of Congress from Vermont. Washington, D.C. August 4, 1848.
2 p. L.S. 27 cm. [z-z 100:6]
Reporting death in Mexico of Robert P. Raymond, Private, Company A, 6th Infantry.

U. S. ARMY
Campaign maps of military operations in northern Mexico, 1846.
Map. 63x45 cm. Copy. HHB [M-M 505]
1. Map showing the movements of the U.S. Army ... from Camargo to Monterey, Saltillo, ... an exact copy of the chart of General Arista taken at the battle of Resaca de la Palma, May 9, 1846. By Charles R. Glynn. New Orleans, September, 1846.
2. Matamoras. Sketch of Matamoras, the Rio Grande, and the area around Fort Brown. 29x22 cm. (N.d.) Copy by Geo. Fr. de la Roche.
3. Chart with the position of the French ships during the attack on the Castle of San Juan de Ulloa, November 27, 1839. 22x29 cm. Copy by Geo. Fr. de la Roche.
4. Sketch of the Battleground at Resaca de la Palma, Texas, May 9, 1846. By J. H. Eaton, 3rd. Infantry. 22x29 cm. Copy by Geo. Fr. de la Roche.
5. Sketch of Monterrey, Mexico, and vicinity. 22x29 cm. (N. d.) Copy by Geo. Fr. de la Roche.
6. Sketch map of the area immediately north of the Rio Grande at Matamoras. 29x35 cm. (N.d.) Copy by Geo. Fr. de la Roche.
7. Sketch of the Main Road from Fort Brown to Point Isabel, showing the battle grounds, May 8-9, 1846. 22x29 cm. Copy by Geo. Fr. de la Roche.
8. Sketch of the Battleground at Palo Alto, Texas, May 8, 1846. 22x29 cm. J. H. Eaton, 3rd. Infantry. Copy by Geo. Fr. de la Roche.

U.S. ARMY. 1ST ARTILLERY. COMPANY A
    Pages from an Orderly Book. Headquarters. Army of Occupation, Texas and Mexico. May 2–December 20, 1848.
    14 p. D.S. 40 cm. [M-M 1712]
    Copies of orders and court martial records, written at various headquarters points, principally Mexico and the mouth of the Rio Grande in Texas. Signed by 2nd Lieut. Daniel M. Beltzhoover.

U.S. COMMISSIONERS ON CLAIMS AGAINST MEXICO
    Note to the President of the United States. Washington, D.C. April 20, 1849.
    3 p. L.S. 21 cm.   HHB [M-M 1700:33]
    Request that certain books and documents brought from Mexico and currently on deposit in the War Department be made available to the Commissioners. Signed by George Evans, Caleb B. Smith, and Robert T. Paine. Envelope bears an annotation in the hand of President Zachary Taylor.

U.S. DEPARTMENT OF STATE
    Diplomatic Dispatches from Bolivia. 1864-1870.
    50 items (Photocopy) 35 cm. [Z-D 102]
    Include letters of Allen A. Hall, John W. Caldwell, and Leopold Markbreit, U.S. Ministers to Bolivia, with typed transcripts. Photocopies from the U.S. National Archives collected by Charles Edward Chapman.

U.S. DEPARTMENT OF STATE
    1251 exp. (On film) [M-M 1814]
    Selected documents pertaining to U.S.-Mexican affairs, 1913-1920. Originals in the National Archives.

U.S. GENERAL LAND OFFICE
    Land Grant to William Howsell. Washington, D.C. July 16, 1860.
    2 p. D.S. 25x42 cm. [Z-Z 100:52]
    Grant of bounty land in Wisconsin, in recognition of Howsell's services in the War of 1812.

U. S. INTERNAL REVENUE SERVICE
    Tax Form for 1868.
    4 p. D.S. and printed. 29 cm. [Z-Z 100:103]
    Copy of tax return of Jonathan Harshman, Dayton, Ohio.

U.S. ISTHMIAN CANAL COMMISSION, 1906-1910
    15 folders. 28 cm. [Z-C 220]
    Papers and correspondence relating mainly to the discharge of boilermaker foreman, Harry F. Cody. Contains letters by John F. Stevens, George W. Goethals, Harry F. Hodges, and others. Originals and copies.

U.S. PATENT OFFICE
  Letters Patent granted to Clark D. Page. Copy made September 23, 1879.
  9 p. and diagram. D.S. 32-71 cm. [z-z 129]
  Includes description of invention for improvement in lime kilns and drawings explaining it.

VALLEJO, MARIANO GUADALUPE, 1807-1890, *comp.*
  Colección de Documentos para la Historia de México. . . . 1821-1865.
  2 vols. Ms. and printed. 34 cm. HHB [M-M 323-324]
  Collection of 743 items, originals and copies, relating to Mexican history during the period between proclamation of the Plan de Iguala and the adoption of the 1843 Bases Orgánicas, with an additional item, no. 743, dated 1865. Covers recognition of Mexican independence by Viceroy Juan O'Donojú, the empire of Agustín de Iturbide, secession of Texas, "Pastry War" with France, and other events of the early Republic, but relating primarily to military administration, chiefly decrees and instructions transmitted through the pertinent ministries to Vallejo, Commander-in-Chief of Alta California, with some addresses, treaty texts, and miscellaneous material.

VALVERDE, GARCÍA DE, d. 1589
  Información . . . . Santiago, Guatemala. 1582.
  45 p. (Typescript) 28 cm. [z-c 209]
  A report to the king by the Governor of Guatemala concerning the excessive tribute paid by the Indians and telling of their ill treatment.

VAN LOON, HENDRICK WILLEM, 1882-1944
  Christmas Card. New York, N.Y. [December, 1920].
  1 p. A.D.S. 25 cm. [z-z 100:56]

VAN SEVERAN, ANDRÉS
  Family Papers. 1858-1893.
  7 p. (Photocopy) 28 cm. [z-c 218]
  Papers relating to affairs in El Salvador.

VARIAS ANOTACIONES A MUCHAS LEYES DE YNDIAS . . . . [MEXICO? 18TH CENT.?]
  698 p. 30 cm. HHB [M-M 126]
  The volume comprises five major items, namely, annotations to Books I-VIII of the collected Laws of the Indies; an unfinished alphabetical list of rhetorical terms and their definitions; notes on legal interpretation of various terms; treatise on the use of copper currency by José Lebrón y Cuervo, dated about 1769; a Latin treatise on legal procedure; and an 18th century subject index of terms not included in the index to the Laws of the Indies. See also "Yndice General de algunas palabras . . ." (M-M 1708) for items that correspond substantially to the above.

VÁZQUEZ, FRANCISCO, 1647-ca. 1714
  Relacion de la vida y virtudes del Venerable Hermano Pedro de S. Joseph

Betancur. . . . Por el P. Manuel Lobo, de la Compañia de Jesus. . . . Nuevamente añadida con selectas annotaciones, y constantes noticias, y ampliada, con notables corollarios. . . . Por el P. Fr. Francisco Vasquez . . . Guatemala City. 1724.

448 p. D.S. 30 cm.   HHB [M-M 280]

A biography of Pedro de San José Bethencourt, a Franciscan of the Third Order and founder of the Belemite Hospitallers' Order of Guatemala; based on the account published by the Jesuit, Manuel Lobo, Guatemala, 1667, and Seville, 1673, under a similar title, but re-written, annotated, and greatly amplified by Vázquez, Franciscan chronicler of Guatemala. There are prefaces by Vázquez and Lobo, a signed and sealed statement on behalf of the Franciscan Order, approving publication of the Vázquez version, Guatemala City, April 5, 1724, and material added by Vázquez regarding pertinent events after the death of Bethencourt.

Entered by Bancroft and in the Ramírez catalogue under the name of Lobo.

VEGA, PLÁCIDO, 1830-1878
Documentos de la Comisión Confidencial. 1858-1869.
8 boxes and 2 vols.   HHB [M-M 325-339]

These papers, originals and copies, consist of correspondence, documents, accounts, and vouchers relating mainly to General Plácido Vega's secret mission to obtain articles of war and funds in San Francisco, California, for the republican government of Benito Juárez in Mexico against the French invaders of Napoleon III. There is also material on Vega's activities in connection with volunteers from the United States in forming an expedition to invade Mexico, the Mexican "Juntas Patrióticas" in the United States, and military operations in Mexico.

An analytical "Report and Key to Arrangement" of these papers is available in the Bancroft Library. See also the published articles of Robert Ryal Miller on General Vega.

VELASCO, JOSÉ NICOLÁS(?) DE, d. ca. 1796, *comp.*
Rescriptos Reales sobre asuntos eclesiásticos. 1619-1807.
374 p. 30 cm.   HHB [M-M 208]

Collection of copies and summaries based upon royal rescripts or decrees and related material, such as viceregal orders, statements of the fiscal, a papal brief, etc., originating in Spain, the Indies, Italy, and Algeria; dealing with abuse of religious sanctuary, jurisdictional problems, Church property, taxation, treatment of Indians, and other subjects connected with the Church. The royal decree on the murder of Gregorio Corte relates to a criminal case against Father Fray Jacinto Miranda.

VELASCO, LUIS DE, d. 1564
Capitulos de Carta escrita al Rey, por D.ⁿ Luis de Velasco . . . dandole cuenta del robo que hicieron 4 navios franceses en Puerto de Cavallos, y de las prevenciones que hizo. . . . September 30, 1558.
5 p. 33 cm.   HHB [M-M 308]

Excerpts from a letter addressed by Viceroy Velasco to the King of Spain, reporting an attack by four French vessels upon the port of Caballos, Honduras, describing the measures taken and contemplated for the defense of New Spain against further attacks, summarizing the preparations for the settlement of Santa Elena (Port Royal, South Carolina?) and other points in sixteenth-century Florida, and referring briefly to plans for Zacatecas and Copala.

Bound with the above is an anonymous report, (2 pp.), "Avisos de la poderosa armada . . ." 1575, regarding French preparations for an attack on Spanish possessions in the Indies.

VELASCO, LUIS DE, MARQUÉS DE SALINAS, VICEROY OF MEXICO, 1534-1617
Land Grant Documents. 1608-1610.
23 p. D.S. 31 cm. [69/165M]
Document concerning the request of Domingo de Irita for land in Santa Cruz Tepetispam; and grant of the Hacienda de Tamariz, Chalco, with related documents.

VELASCO Y TEJADA, ANTONIO JOSÉ
Defensa Juridica por el Venerable Dean, y Cabildo de la Santa Yglesia Metropolitana de Mexico, sobre el debido assiento . . . . Mexico City. December 1, 1741.
60 p. D.S. 30 cm. HHB [M-M 143]
Document addressed by the Dean and Chapter of the Mexico City Cathedral to the Council of the Indies, complaining of the seats provided for Chapter members during the celebration of the birthday of the Prince of Asturias. Cites written and traditional sources of ecclesiastical prerogatives; and asks for recognition in seating the members, whether as a whole, as delegations, or as individuals.

VELASCO Y TEJADA, ANTONIO JOSÉ DE
Vozes juridicas, que en el Tribunal de la razon de la Justicia sentida de quatro Prebendados de la Santa Iglesia Metropolitana de Mexico. . . . [Mexico City. 1741].
120 p. 30 cm. HHB [M-M 242]
A protest composed by a canon of the Mexico City Cathedral against the action of the Cathedral Chapter which had deprived him and three other prebendaries of the right to vote on questions involving archiepiscopal jurisdiction, an action based upon their close official relationship with the Archbishop.

VELÁZQUEZ, DIEGO, 1460(?)-1523(?)
Documents relating to. 1513.
66 exp. (On film) [M-M 1843]
From transcripts in the Chacón Collection, Academia de la Historia, Havana, Cuba.

VELÁSQUEZ, DIEGO DE
    Proceso de . . . , boticario, contra Don Hernando Cortés, Marqués del Valle, sobre las medicinas. [1534]
    61 p. (Photocopy) [M-A 21]
    From the Archivo General de la Nación, Mexico, Criminal, tomo 30.

VELÁSQUEZ, PABLO
    Letters. Mexico. 1941-1942.
    4 items in folder. L.S. 28 cm.   HHB [M-M 1700:20]
    Letters, in Tarascan, written to Velásquez by Jacobo García Luis (Federal Preparatory School, Coyoacán, November 12, 1941) and Máximo Lathrop (Paracho, Michoacán, February 6, 1942); one dealing principally with politico-educational matters, the other transmitting religious works. With translations into Spanish provided by Velásquez.

VENEGAS, MIGUEL, 1680-1764(?)
    Appendice VII of his *Noticia de la California, y de su Conquista Temporal, y Espiritual, hasta el Tiempo Presente* . . . . Madrid. 1757.
    20 p. 2 maps. (Photocopy) 22x28 cm. [M-M 1733]
    Evidently a preliminary draft of Appendix VII of the above work, much abbreviated, entitled, "Razon de la construccion del Mapa particular de la California y del general de la America Septentrional, Asia Oriental, y del Mar del Sur intermedio. Traduccion de una Memoria de M.^{r} de l'Isle, leida en la Academia R.^{l} de las Ciencias de Paris en 8 de Abril de 1750, sobre los nuevos descubrimientos al Norte del Mar del Sur. . . ."

VENEGAS, MIGUEL, 1680-1764(?)
    Empressas apostolicas de los PP. Missioneros de la Compañia de Jesus, de la Provincia de Nueva-España obradas en la conquista de California. . . . [Mexico] 1739.
    713 p. 31 cm.   HHB [M-M 1701]
    A history of the Spanish exploration and conquest of the Californias, with special attention to the work of Jesuit missionaries; concerned almost exclusively with Lower California, although reference is made to voyages farther north.
    An amplified and considerably altered version, prepared by Fray Andrés Burriel, was published in Madrid, in 1757, under the title *Noticia de la California, y de su conquista temporal, y espiritual . . . sacada de la historia manuscrita, formada . . . por el Padre Miguel Venegas, de la Compañia de Jesus; y de otras Noticias y Relaciones.* . . . English and German translations of the printed version have also been published.

VENEZUELA
    Documents relating to. 187-?-1888.
    6 items (37 p.) 21-66 cm. [Z-D 129]
    Miscellaneous papers and clippings relating to pearl fisheries of Margarita, to the sinking of the *San Pedro Alcántara* in 1815 and subsequent efforts to salvage treasure aboard, to President Antonio Guzmán Blanco of Venezuela, and to the treasure hunting voyage of the steam yacht *María*.

VENEZUELA
Letters and Papers relating to Alcabalas. Caracas and La Guayra. 1816-1821.
40 items. A.L.S., L.S. and D.S. 21-30 cm. HHB [Z-D 1]
Official correspondence and papers relating to the collection of excise taxes.

VENEZUELA
Papers relating to. 1743-1826.
10 folders. 21-32 cm. D., D.S. and printed. HHB [M-M 514]
1. Royal cedula, March 19, 1743, maintaining that all curacies in the Indies are under the patronage of the crown. 12 p.

2. Depositions about the loss of the Spanish revenue cutter, *San Francisco Javier*, to three Dutch schooners off the coast of Venezuela, and the apparent desertion of its sister-ship, *San Ignacio de Loyola*. Witnesses were examined by Máximo Esteban du Bouchet and Magistrate Francisco González de Estrada. The file includes correspondence of Du Bouchet's superiors, Francisco de Garganta, commander of the squadron, González de Estrada, and Governor Felipe Ricardos. January–February, 1755. Certified copies. Received in Caracas, March 18, 1755. 130 p.

3. Report of Joseph de Abalos to Minister Joseph de Gálvez, May 14, 1778, on the island of Aruba, called Orua, Urua, or Uruba, and Spain's claim to it, though then held by the Dutch. Discusses the nature of the island and its inhabitants, and states that documents relating to Spain's claim to it had been lost in the fighting with the French. 14 p.

4. Lists of various convents and of the friars assigned to them. Caracas, July 19, 1783. In Latin. 5 p.

5. Roll of members of the Immaculate Conception convent of Caracas, and their duties. July 15, 1786. In Latin. 8 p.

6. Account of navigation between the various towns on Lake Maracaibo, i.e., Gibraltar, Mérida, and others. N.p., n.d. 3 p.

7. Report of meeting of provincials. Caracas, March 20, 1813. In Latin. 9 p.

8. Statement and sentence of Lucas Venecian, captain of the Swedish schooner, *La María*, which had been seized. Puerto Cabello, June 30, 1814. 3 p.

9. Extracts concerning the Venezuelan revolution made by Pinart. 1816-1817. 2 p.

10. Collection of 19 passports issued in various cities of Venezuela. 1810-1826.

VENEZUELA
Papers relating to. 1796-1893.
34 folders. A.L.S., D.S., and printed. 20-32 cm. [Z-D 128]
Commercial, legal, military, religious, and personal letters or documents, including one specimen of Venezuelan paper money. Noteworthy items are a file, 1796, on settlement of the estate of Juan Álvarez de Ávila and his wife, Juana Francisco de León; a dozen items relating to the sale of real estate owned by Asunción Almira Ascanio, inherited from her mother, Petronila Torres; a commission as lieutenant general to Pablo Ávila signed by President Joaquín Crespo; and a personal letter from Miguel Miranda, possibly a de-

scendant of Francisco Miranda, to his sister Estefanía. Many references to the Ávila, Blanco, and Ascanio families. Gift of Theo Crook.

VERA, PEDRO JAVIER DE
Correspondence. Spain. July 9–September 25, 1810.
5 p. L.S. 21 cm.   HHB [M-M 1700:23]
Three letters, copy and signed duplicates, of Vera and Matías Bazo, dealing principally with a remittance payable to Vera's attorney, Miguel de Nájera.

VERA DE LA VENTOSA, JUSTO
El Siglo Ylustrado. Vida de D.ⁿ Guindo Zerezo. . . . 1777.
430 p. 21 cm.   HHB [M-M 359]
Novel depicting the career of Don Guindo Zerezo, satirizing Spanish social life in the eighteenth century under French influence.
Entered by Bancroft under "Vexa. . . ."

VERAPAZ Y TIERRA DE LACANDONES
Informe de los servicios hechos por la religion de Santo-Domingo en la provincia de Verapaz y tierras de Lacandones; relacion y memoria relativa á los asuntos de la provincia de Santo-Domingo de Guatemala . . . . [Guatemala] 1724.
74 p. 30-31 cm.   HHB [M-M 440]
A report presented on behalf of the above-named Province to Antonio Pedro de Echevers y Suvisa, Captain General of Guatemala, describing the services rendered by the Dominicans in Guatemala both to the Crown and to the Indians. It stresses the poverty of the various monasteries, and protests, in the name of the Dominicans and the Mercedarians, against the threatened discontinuance of royal contributions.

VERONA, PACIENTE DE [*pseud.?*]
Paromologia de el Diphthongo de Queretaro en la procession de el Corpus desde el año de 1709. [Mexico. ca. 1712?]
290 p. 20 cm.   HHB [M-M 244]
Two dissertations by a Franciscan friar relating to the jurisdictional struggle between monastic orders and the regular clergy, upholding in particular the right of the Franciscans to precedence in the Querétaro Corpus Christi procession. Includes notes and preliminary material, largely in Latin, a dedication to the Holy Trinity, and quotations from various saints or doctors of the Church in place of the usual license and expressions of approbation.

VERTIZ, JUAN DE
Official papers. San Felipe el Real, Chihuahua. January 27–February 25, 1738.
14 p. D. S. 31 cm.   [M-M 1781]
File concerning the right of chief constables and other authorities to appoint subordinates; and petitions on conflicting claims, gubernatorial orders, official opinions, notifications, and related documents.

VICTORIA, GUADALUPE, 1789-1843
   Letter of President Victoria to Carlos María Bustamante. Mexico City. October 3, 1824.
   2 p. L.S. 21 cm.　　　　　　　　　　　　　　　　　　　　HHB [M-M 1700:41]
   Too busy to write, but has provided for Almazán's retirement.

VIDA DE LA V[ENERABL]E M[ADR]E BEATRIZ DE SILVA . . . Y LOS BREVES DE . . . INOCENCIO VIII, LEON X, SIXTO V, Y PIO V, CON LA NOTICIA DE VARIAS INDULG.ᵃˢ . . . . [MEXICO CITY]. 1830
   172 p. 20 cm.　　　　　　　　　　　　　　　　　　　　　　HHB [M-M 57]
   An account of the life of Beatriz de Silva and the development of the Congregation of the Immaculate Conception founded by her in Toledo in 1484. Includes Spanish texts of the pertinent papal bulls and briefs relating to the establishment and privileges of the Congregation (now an Order). Bound with a printed copy of *Espejo de Exemplares Obispos* . . . , Mexico, 1698, by Miguel de Castilla.

VILDOSOLA, AGUSTÍN DE
   Official Papers relating to the Administration of Sinaloa and Sonora. Mexico. 1740-1752.
   4 folders. D.S. 31 cm.　　　　　　　　　　　　　　　　　　　　　　[M-M 1782]
   Folder 1 contains documents, 1740-1752, concerning expenditures of Vildosola, Acting Governor and Captain General of Sinaloa, in connection with the conquest and pacification of the Yaquis, Mayos, and Baja Pimería Indians. They include official correspondence of Vildosola, of his predecessor, Manuel Bernal de Huidobro, and of the viceroy, Duque de la Conquista. Folder 2 relates to the accounts submitted on behalf of Vildosola by Francisco de Ortúzar for Indian campaign expenditures from January, 1742, to March, 1743. Folder 3 contains documents, 1742-1744, on the trial of Captain Gaspar Felmel, commandant of the garrison of Sinaloa (subsequently Buenavista), for various abuses of his command. Folder 4 has additional papers in the Felmel case, 1743-1752.

VILLARROEL, HIPÓLITO
   Enfermedades Politicas que padece la Capital de esta Nueva Esp.ᵃ . . . y remedios, que se la deben aplicar . . . . Mexico City. 1785-1787.
   4 vols. D.S. 21 cm.　　　　　　　　　　　　　　　　　　　HHB [M-M 245-248]
   Parts I and II of this work (1785), which consists of six parts, treat of religious affairs, among both the secular clergy and the monastic orders, and of the administration of justice. Part III (1785) concerns police problems and public morals. Parts IV and V (1787) deal with domestic and foreign commerce, agriculture, industry, and related matters. Part VI (1787) criticizes the Regulations for Intendancies proclaimed on December 4, 1786, with suggestions for their reform.
   Printed in part by Carlos María de Bustamante in 1831, and in full in 1937 by Sociedad de Bibliófolos Mexicanos.

[VINING, EDWARD PAYSON], 1847-1920
  An Inglorious Columbus, Chapter XXXVII. Recapitulation. [ca. 1885]
  69 p. (Typescript) 35 cm.　　　　　　　　　　　　　　HHB [M-M 408]
  A summary of arguments presented in preceding chapters to support the theory that Hwui Shân and other Buddhist monks visited parts of America, including Mexico, in the 5th century. This work was published in 1885.

VIÑOLAS, PEDRO
  Ya Pasó el Cólera, ó sea La vuelta de Pachuca—Comedia . . . arreglada al Teatro Mexicano por don Vidal Proseño. [N.p.] 1851.
  72 p. 25 cm.　　　　　　　　　　　　　　　　　　　　[M-M 1710]
  Romantic one-act play in various verse forms. Prefaced by dedicatory sonnet, in homage to the Conde de la Cortina y de Castro, by Viñolas, who is presumably the author of the play. Adapted for the Mexican stage by Vidal Proseño, with scene laid in Mexico City.

VIREYES DE MÉXICO. INSTRUCCIONES, RESIDENCIAS, ET CETERA. [1529-1804].
  2 vols. Ms. and printed. 31-32 cm.　　　　　　　　HHB [M-M 249-250]
  Collected documents, largely copies, relating to the viceroys and other officials of New Spain, and originating in Mexico or Spain.
  There are twenty-four numbered items in the first volume, which are: memorial in defense of the Duke of Escalona, ca. 1642; instructions of the Duke of Linares for his successor, the Marquis of Valero, 1716; documents relating to the entry of the Marquis of las Amarillas into Mexico City and of his journey from Veracruz, 1755; Viceroy Cajigal's journey from Mexico City to Veracruz, 1760, and some letters written by him; a description of the domestic quarters in the viceregal palace in Mexico City; Viceroy Bucareli's route from Veracruz to Mexico City, 1771; documents exonerating Colonel Domingo Elizondo from a charge of disobedience, 1765-1766; activities and illness of Bucareli, 1771-1779; political verses; letters of Viceroy Vizarrón y Eguiarreta to the King, 1740, regarding the arrival of a new viceroy; documents relating to proceedings of the Council of the Indies concerning the charges of Francisco de la Torre against former Viceroy Cerralvo; the "Respuesta" of Viceroy Vizarrón, 1742, in the residencia proceedings against him; decision taken in the residencia of the Duque de la Conquista, 1743; a fragment relating to the defense of Alonso de Estrada, treasurer of Hernán Cortés, 1529; funeral oration in tribute to Cardinal-Archbishop Lorenzana, 1804; Torres y Rueda's transmittal to the Audiencia of his ad interim powers, 1649; and letter of Viceroy Alburquerque, 1660, in regard to an attempt to assassinate him.
  Volume two, M-M 250, contains documents relating to the residencia of Cortés and his officials, 1528-1529; papers concerning trade with the Philippines, and for facilities at Acapulco, 1766-1768; instructions of the Duque de Linares for his successor, 1716; the Marquis de las Amarillas' journey to Mexico City; a report to the King on New Spain, ca. 1767; and duplicate of Viceroy Vizarrón's "Respuesta" to his residencia, 1742.

VIRGINIA, COMMONWEALTH OF
Legal Documents. 1788-1789.
8 p. Printed and D.S. 12-23 cm. [z-z 166]
  Miscellaneous legal papers relating to payment of debts.

VIRGINIA. LAND OFFICE
Treasury Warrant for 250 acres, Issued to John Bancker. February 22, 1847.
2 p. D.S. 26 cm. [z-z 100:12]
  On the reverse: Assignment by Bancker to Huldah Millard, Rochester, New York, April, 1869.

VIVERO, RODRIGO DE, CONDE DE ORIZABA
Documents relating to. 1576-1665.
2 reels (1,376 exp. On film). [M-M 1835]
  Microfilm of photocopies, transcripts, and original manuscripts from the private collection of George Robert Graham Conway (1873-1951).

VIZCAÍNO, SEBASTIÁN, 1550(?)-1615
Letter. Port of Monterey. December 28, 1602.
8 p. (Translation and photocopy) 20-21 cm. HHB [M-M 1700:36]
  English translation of letter, with photocopy of original, reporting the writer's discovery of Monterey, his difficulties, and the characteristics of the port and its indigenous inhabitants.

VOCABULARIOS VARIOS DE LA AMÉRICA
105 p. 35 cm. HHB [M-M 525]
  Copy of a manuscript (Add. 17631) in the British Museum. The vocabulary includes sections with Castilian, Nutkeño, and Mexican equivalents; with Castilian, Hawaiian, and Mexican; a list of Patagonian words; and others.

VOCABULARY OF LANGUAGES OF DIFFERENT PROVINCES IN SOUTH AMERICA. 1757
273 p. 25 cm. HHB [z-d 5]
  Vocabularies, theological dialogues, and catechisms in Portuguese and native Brazilian languages, especially the Manao language. Copy of Ms. 223, King George IV Library, British Museum, made in 1874 by Charles Clarke. With transcriber's note.

VON HAGEN, VICTOR WOLFGANG, 1908-
Manuscripts.
1 box. 28-75 cm. [z-z 163]
  Typewritten draft of *Quetzal Quest* (New York, Harcourt, Brace, ca. 1939) and corrected galley proofs of *Ecuador the Unknown* (ca. 1940) from printers William Brendon & Son, Ltd., Plymouth, England.

WADSWORTH, ALFRED C
Deed to Edward W. Peet for Land in Winnebago County, Wisconsin. Neenah, Wisconsin. June 10, 1859.
1 p. D.S. 41 cm. [z-z 100:93]

WAGENET, PORTIA FAYE
　Ecclesiastical Organization in New Spain. [1919?]
　Chart. 61x47 cm. [M-R 2]
　Lists of secular and regular offices and duties; bishoprics in both hemispheres; notes on church revenues and the Inquisition. With transcript.

WALKER, WILLIAM M
　Civil War Letters. 1864-1868.
　55 p. A.L.S. 7-25 cm. [z-z 139]
　Letters from Walker to his sister, Hannah, concerning his military duties and news of family and friends. With several miscellaneous items relating to other members of the family.

THE WAR OF INDEPENDENCE. MEXICO, 1811-
　10 folders (136 p.) 8-32 cm. [M-M 1830]
　Letters and documents, both originals and copies, concerning the rebellion in Zacatecas, San Luis Potosí, Cuautla, and Oaxaca. Includes reports on the army of Morelos and progress of the insurgents, a description of the geographical and economic features of Morelia, proceedings of military tribunals against Fray José Verardo Villaseñor and Manuel Sabino Crespo, and facsimiles of documents signed by Miguel Hidalgo y Costilla and by José María Morelos.

WARNER, CHARLES DUDLEY, 1829-1900
　Letter to Gideon Welles. Hartford, Connecticut. November 1, 1861.
　2 p. A.L.S. 20 cm. [z-z 100:36]
　Concerning the attitude of the government toward John C. Frémont. With typed transcript.

WATMOUGH, JAMES HORATIO, 1822-
　Letterbook and Papers. 1844-1855.
　172 p. A.D. 25-29 cm. [z-z 125]
　Contains copies of letters and accounts written as purser on U.S. naval vessels *Portsmouth*, *Perry*, and *Constitution*. Letters from the *Portsmouth* reflect service on the Pacific Coast, 1845-1847.

WEBSTER, DANIEL, 1782-1852
　Letter to Unidentified Friend. Boston. September 27, 1828.
　1 p. A.L.S. 24 cm. [z-z 100:89]
　Concerning communication from a Mr. Frost.

WESSELS, HENRY WALTON, 1809-1889
　Letters. February 24–May 2, 1847.
　14 p. (Typescript) 28 cm. [M-M 1728]
　Three letters to his brother, written by an American soldier during the Mexican War. They concern the attacks on Veracruz and Cerro Gordo, the arrival of United States forces at Jalapa, and other aspects of the war, as well as describing the countryside and referring to family matters.

WESTERGAARD, WALDEMAR CHRISTIAN, 1882-1963
Correspondence and Notes. Chico, California, and Ithaca, New York. 1907-1912.
84 p. A.L.S. and D. 15-28 cm. [z-a 205]
Letters to Henry Morse Stephens and Frederick John Teggart, and research notes, mainly on Bancroft Library materials, relating to the Danish West Indies.

WHEAT TAX
[N.p.] August, 1645.
2 p. 32 cm. hhb [m-m 1700:64]
List of persons, with wheat tax for 1645.

WHEELER, JOSEPH, 1836-1906
Letter to Porfirio Díaz. Lenox, Massachusetts. September 27, 1905.
3 p. A.L.S. 15 cm. hhb [m-m 1700:65]
Letter of introduction of "Miss String," with a recommendation of her as an English teacher.

WHEELWRIGHT, WILLIAM, 1798-1873
Diary. August, 1872–April, 1873.
107 exp. (On film) A. D. [z-d 104]
Diary kept while supervising completion of the Ensenada Port Railway in Argentina. Original manuscript in the Essex Institute, Salem, Massachusetts.

WHINERY, CHARLES CRAWFORD, 1878-
Letters to Francis Samuel Philbrick. New York City. December 21, 1907–May 13, 1908.
11 p. L.S. 28 cm. [z-a 202]
Five letters concerning preparation of articles on Cuba and other subjects for the London *Times*.

WHITTEMORE, CHARLES W
Letter. Mexico City. March 9, 1913.
8 p. D.S. (Typescript) 30 cm. [m-m 1753]
Copy of a letter to the writer's mother, dealing principally with the "Decena Trágica," or ten days of conflict in Mexico City that resulted in the overthrow of Madero's regime and his assassination. The writer mentions many prominent Mexican figures and praises the conduct of U.S. officials on the scene, particularly Ambassador Henry Lane Wilson.

[WILCOX], ELLA (WHEELER), 1855-1919
Letter to Lydia E. Houghton. Milwaukee. May 20, 18(80?).
2 p., with envelope. A.L.S. 21 cm. [z-z 100:87]
Concerning purchase of a book of her poems.

WILCOX, ELLA (WHEELER), 1855-1919
　　Letter to Messrs. Robert Clark Co. New York, N.Y. June, 1891.
　　1 p. A.L.S. 20 cm. [z-z 100:26]
　　Concerning circulars about two of her books.

WILKIE, JAMES WALLACE, 1936-
　　Oral History Interviews. Mexico. 1964-1965.
　　2 cartons. [M-M 1905]
　　Tapes and transcripts of interviews with the following Mexican leaders, conducted by Mr. Wilkie and Edna Monzón de Wilkie:
　　Salvador Abascal, Aurelio R. Acevedo, Juan Andreu Almazán, Silvano Barba González, Clementina Batalla de Bassols, Ramón Beteta, Juan de Dios Bojórquez, Alfonso Caso, Luis Chávez Orozco, Daniel Cosío Villegas, Carlos Fuentes, Francisco Javier Gaxiola, Jr., Marte R. Gómez, Manuel Gómez Morín, Martín Luis Guzmán, Luis L. León, Germán List Arzubide, Vicente Lombardo Toledano, Aurelio Manrique, José Muñoz Cota, Melchor Ortega, Ezequiel Padilla, Miguel Palomar y Vizcarra, Emilio Portes Gil, Manuel J. Sierra, Jesús Silva Herzog, David Alfaro Siqueiros, and Jacinto B. Treviño.
　　Restricted.

WILLIAMS, HERBERT O　　　　, comp.
　　Miscellaneous French Documents. 1460-1877.
　　22 p. D.S. 6-51 cm. [z-z 128]
　　Mainly documents, including passports, emanating from or pertaining to the town of Molsheim, 1460-1877; paper money and a bond from the period of the French Revolution; an official telegram, 1870, regarding the whereabouts of the Prussian troops; and a letter, 1853, describing a tri-color flag of Napoleon III.

WILLIAMS, ISAAC, 1737-1820
　　Letter to William Haymond enclosing petition to Harrison County Court, and related papers. Fort Liberty, Clarksburg, and Williamstown, West Virginia. 1792-1912.
　　9 p. A.L.S. 28-33 cm., and clipping. [z-z 105]
　　Concerning testimony to be presented in lieu of court appearance, and relating to the early history of Williamstown, West Virginia.

WILLS, INHERITANCES AND MISCELLANEOUS PAPERS. ca. 1615-1802
　　18 folders. 16-31 cm. HHB [M-M 405]
　　A collection of originals and copies pertaining to wills, inheritances, and similar matters, relating for the most part to ecclesiastical or monastic claims. Written primarily in Mexico with one item each from Peru and Spain. Contains the following:
　　1. A brief prepared by Mateo de Sande, ca. 1615, setting forth the claims of the Convento de Santa Clara, in its suit against the secular heirs of Martín Hernández for enforcement of earlier agreements and Audiencia decisions on the sum to be received by the convent.

2. Four legal briefs, ca. 1623 (Huánuco, Peru), presenting claims for ad interim appointment to a chaplaincy established by the will of Pedro de Saavedra Aguilera.

3. A brief, ca. 1626, dealing with a dispute over the chaplaincy of the Hacienda de Chilcuacán, founded in 1616 by María Galarza, and also with later claims upon her estate.

4. Documents relating to an ecclesiastical suit against Tomás Fernández Salvador, one of the executors of the will of Isabel Álvarez, with a copy of the will and a statement of costs, 1629-1651.

5a. Brief drawn up by Cristóbal Grimaldo, March 6, 1661, supporting the claims of Anna de Torres, widow of Francisco de Arellano Sotomayor, in the suit brought against her by the Mercedarian monastery named as heir in the will of her son, Alonso de Sotomayor.

5b. Statement by Felipe de Guevara (n.p., n.d.) in defense of Juan de Rosales, ousted chaplain of a charitable hospital established under the will of Hernán Cortés and dealing with jurisdictional questions which affect the hospital.

6. Documents relating to the will of Antonio de Zamudio Gastañaga, former resident of Tezcuco, who bequeathed his estate for religious purposes, 1662-1685.

7. A request addressed to Antonio Meleñdez Bazán, May 1, 1713, for an opinion on distribution of the estate of Antonio Tomás y Torty among heirs and creditors, with undated reply.

8. Documents, 1686-1714, concerning settlement of the estate of Ana Gómez, former resident of Guachinango, including a certified copy of her will and its codicil and an inventory of her possessions.

9. A file, 1715-1719, relating to a loan of 9,000 pesos from the estate of Luis Miguel Luyando y Vermeo to the Jesuit Colegio de San Gregorio.

10a. Brief filed by Salvador de Zúñiga y Barrios on January 10, 1731, on behalf of the Dominican Convent of Santa María de Gracia, seeking confirmation by the Audiencia of Guadalajara of its earlier decision regarding claims of creditors against the estate of Mimbela, deceased Bishop of Guadalajara.

10b. Statement presented in 1731 by the Durango Dean and Cathedral Chapter to the Audiencia of Guadalajara, opposing a proposal for two additional Cathedral canonries.

11. Supplementary document, ca. 1737, submitted to the Audiencia of Mexico on behalf of Alonso Prieto de Bonilla in his suit against Andrés Álvarez for possession of an entailed estate.

12. A brief, ca. 1737, presented on behalf of Antonio de Echeandía, widower of Bernarda Gertrudis Negrete, defending his claims as her executor and heir against those of Antonio de Otero Bermúdez.

13. Variant copies of a supplementary memorandum on the will of Ignacio Rodríguez y Varacijo, drafted on April 27, 1754.

14. Copy of an order of the Audiencia of .Mexico, issued in the name of Carlos III and addressed to the officials of Tulancingo District, February 29, 1771, authorizing Juan de Dios Moreno, Marquis of Valle Ameno, to take possession of the inheritance bequeathed him by his uncle, Dr. Ildefonso Francisco Moreno y Castro, formerly Dean of the Mexico City Cathedral.

15. A petition (Madrid, October 29, 1802) by Cristóbal Gómez y Güemes to the king of Spain on behalf of Matías Gutiérrez de Lanzas of Mexico City, requesting delay in the execution of a decision under review by the Audiencia of Mexico which would invalidate the will of Antonio Campa.

16. Supplementary plea by José Hurtado de Castilla (n.p., n.d.) presented on behalf of Andrés de Liceaga in a lawsuit apparently involving a conflict of claims upon the estate of Ana Sarmiento.

17. Brief presented by Miguel Zapetillo (?) on behalf of the "Santos Lugares de Jerusalén y Tierra Santa," upholding the claim of the latter to the estate of Antonio López de León and his wife, Leonor Varón de Lara, against the claims of their relatives (n.p., n.d.).

18. An undated brief presented on behalf of Juan Díaz, in his dispute with Melchor de Ribera y Vargas, regarding the conditions for a chaplaincy claimed by Díaz.

WILLSON, JAMES
Letter to John Todd. Cambridge, Ohio. March 10, 1813.
4 p. A.L.S. 19 cm. [z-z 100:21]
Concerning his own political aspirations and those of Todd in Pennsylvania.

WINN, WILLIAM WATKIN, 1874-1959
Papers relating to Ancient Battle Axe. 1909-1951.
23 items. L.S. 17-28 cm. [M-R 3]
Correspondence and papers concerning discovery of the axe, near the old presidio at Santa Cruz in Sonora, Mexico, and its authentication.

WINSLOW, ROLLIN R   , comp.
Family Papers. 1729-1848.
35 exp. (On film) [z-z 112]
Mainly deeds and other legal papers pertaining to land and property of the Doane, Hall, and Winslow families in Massachusetts and New York. With these: South Carolina paper money, 1777; two deeds to John W. Park, 1846-1850, for land in Michigan; Michigan campaign poster, 1864. There is a list of contents available.

WINTHROP, JOHN, 1588-1649
Excerpt from Journal. 1637-1639.
58 p. (Typescript) 28 cm. [z-z 142]
Transcript of portions of Winthrop's journal, *History of New England, 1630-1649.*

WORKMAN, B   F
Letter to his Sister. Camp Buena Vista, Mexico. January 16, 1847.
3 p. A.L.S. 28 cm. HHB [M-M 1700:66]
News of the Army's advance toward Buena Vista, and of possible reinforcements under General William O. Butler. Stories of outrages along the border.

XIMÉNEZ, FRANCISCO, 1666-1722(?)
Manuscrito antiguo Kiché encontrado á principios del siglo xviii° entre los indios del Pueblo de Chichicastenango. . . . [Guatemala, ca. 1721?]
106 p. 32 cm.   HHB [M-M 439]

Copy of various chapters from the history of the Provincia de San Vicente de Chiapa y de Guatemala compiled by the Dominican philologist, Ximénez. The material was subsequently published in slightly varying editions under the titles of *Las Historias del Origen de los Indios de esta Provincia de Guatemala* . . . , edited by Karl Scherzer, Vienna, 1857, and *Historia de la Provincia de San Vicente* . . . , Sociedad de Geografía e Historia, Guatemala City, 1929, Vol. I. There are two main portions:

1. Livro Sagrado del Quiché. Material translated by Ximénez from a Quiché manuscript discovered early in the eighteenth century among the Indians of Chichicastenango, containing an account of the creation of the world, the origins of Guatemala, and various aspects of Guatemalan religion and history. Corresponds to Chapters III-XXI of the 1929 printed edition. 71 p.

2. Historia del antiguo Reino del Quiché. Chapters XXVII-XXXV and part of Chapter XXXVI of Ximénez's treatise, dealing with the early history of the Province and with the religion, marriage and burial customs, and calendar of the natives. Consists largely of translations from the above-mentioned Quiché manuscript and quotations from Jerónimo Román's *República de los Indios Occidentales*. 35 p.

XIMÉNEZ, FRANCISCO, 1666-1722(?)
Primera parte de el tesoro de las lenguas Hahchiquel, Quiche y Tzutuhil en que las dichas lenguas se traducen en la nuestra española . . . . [Chichicastenango, Guatemala?, n.d.]
421 p. D.S. 31 cm.   HHB [M-M 445]

A vocabulary of the languages of the Quiché, Tzutuhil and Cakchiquel Indians of Guatemala, with a dedication written and signed by Father Ximénez.

"YANKEE DOODLE"
Words and Explanation of the Song.
3 p. (in pieces). 32 cm.   [z-z 100:10]

YAQUI AND MAYO INDIANS
Documents relating to. 1735-1745.
2 vols. (1145 p.) D. and D.S. 33 cm.   [M-M 1875]

Documents and letters, both originals and copies, concerned with the 1740 uprising of the Yaquis and Mayos and their allies, its causes, and its political or religious consequences. Written in various localities of Sonora, Sinaloa, and in Mexico City.

Included are instructions to the Indians, correspondence and reports of the Jesuit missionaries, appeals from the Indians, legal pleas and testimony, and materials relating to the trial and removal from office of Governor Manuel Bernal de Huidobro.

YNDICE GENERAL DE ALGUNAS PALABRAS QUE NO SE CONTIENEN EN EL DE LA RECOPILACION DE YNDIAS. . . . [MEXICO? 18TH CENT.?]
259 p. 31 cm. [M-M 1708]
Alphabetical subject index to the Laws of the Indies, containing words omitted from the index of the Recopilación de Indias, p. 1-93, with a supplement, p. 93-113. Contains annotations to various laws of the Indies, p. 115-254, also a treatise on copper currency by José Lebrón y Cuervo, Mexico City Honorary Assemblyman and Assessor of the Mexico City Royal Mint, p. 254-259. Internal evidence (p. 77, 101) indicates that the indexes were written after October 21, 1787, and before May 22, 1789; Lebrón's treatise was probably written about 1769.

YNDICES [DE HISTORIAS DE AMÉRICA. N. p., n. d.]
272 p. 34 cm. HHB [M-M 118]
A collection of outlines summarizing the contents of chronicles and correspondence relating to the history of America. Writers of the letters and works include Hernán Cortés, Pedro de Alvarado, Antonio Ardoino, Antonio and Francisco López de Gómara, Andrés González de Barcia, Ulrich Schmidel, Martín del Barco Centenera, Manuel de Grova, Fray Bernardino de Sahagún, and Antonio de Herrera.

YNSTRUCCIÓN SOBRE EL MODO DE MEDIR TIERRAS, . . . Y UN RÉGIMEN DE PESAR AGUAS; Y UNA TABLA PERPETUA P.ª SABER LAS HORAS . . . . [MEXICO CITY?] 1818
24 p. (Photocopy) 33 cm. [M-M 1749]
Anonymous compilation dealing principally with rules for the measurement and valuation of lands and the weighing of water. Contains early viceregal ordinances allegedly dating from 1607, but ascribed to Gastón de Peralta, Viceroy of New Spain from 1566 to 1567. Appended diagrams include a special mariners' compass to be used for estimating the time of day in different parts of the world.
Photocopy from the García Collection, University of Texas.

YORK, M L
Montezuma, a Play in Five Acts. [N.p.] 1890.
108 p. (Typescript) 27 cm. [M-M 1741]
A drama in English, dealing with the Aztec ruler Montezuma and the Spanish conquistadors, with a synopsis, and a description of characters and costumes. There are four pen-and-ink sketches, and numerous pencilled corrections and additions.

YUCATAN, MEXICO
Documents relating to. 1828-1845.
1 box. L.S., D.S., and printed. [M-A 27]
These papers relate chiefly to the early national period, including circulars

and letters from government officials to the governor of Yucatan; acts of the Yucatan assembly, 1840; official reports concerning the troops, 1834-1845; and synopsis of official correspondence, 1841-1843. There are numerous printed items.

ZACATECAS, MEXICO. APOSTÓLICO COLEGIO DE NUESTRA SEÑORA DE GUADALUPE
Escriptura de Protestacion Publica, Peticion y Concordia de este Colegio . . . de Zacatecas. [1780]
106 p. 21 cm.   HHB [M-M 66]
Copy of document protesting devotion to the Virgin of Guadalupe and Saints Michael, Joseph, and Francis of Assisi, and petitioning for their patronage; presented for signature by the members of the Zacatecas Colegio on December 11, 1780. Apparently based on a petition signed on December 11, 1728. Colored title page, two colored drawings, and illuminated lettering.

ZAMBRANA, ANTONIO, 1846-1922(?)
Education in Nicaragua. San Francisco. 1883.
12 p. 31 cm.   HHB [M-M 354]
Interview between Doctor Antonio Sambrano [Zambrana], Commissioner from Nicaragua, and John Donovan, Collector of Statistics, made for Bancroft's Histories of the Pacific States. Deals chiefly with the former's earlier career in Cuba, Costa Rica, Nicaragua, New York City, and Europe as soldier, statesman, diplomat, lawyer, author, and journalist, but touching also upon his current mission of procuring teachers in the United States for Nicaragua.

ZÁRATE SALMERÓN, GERÓNIMO DE, fl. 1626
Relaciones de todas las cossas q.ᵉ en el nuebo Mex.ᶜᵒ se han visto y se vian, assi por mar como por tierra desde el año de 1538 hasta el de 1626. [1626-1631]
136 p. 21 cm.   [M-M 1719]
Copy of a compilation prepared by the Franciscan Zárate, one-time missionary to New Mexico, which includes his personal account of Franciscan activities in the Californias, New Mexico, and elsewhere, interspersed with quoted or paraphrased reports on other land or maritime expeditions in the same area.

ZELAA E HIDALGO, JOSÉ MARIA, d. 1813
Discursos Panegiricos, ô Sermones Varios de diversos Santos, y Festividades de Jesu-Christo, y de Maria Santissima. . . . Tomo II. [Mexico. 1797-1798]
476 p. 21 cm.   HHB [M-M 253]
Collection of 26 sermons relating chiefly to events in the lives of Jesus, the Virgin Mary, and various saints; delivered by Zelaa, a secular priest of the Archdiocese of Mexico and native of Querétaro, during the period from April 13, 1797, to December 24, 1798, in the city of Querétaro and one in Salvatierra (Guanajuato).

ZEREZO Y NIEVA, ANDRÉS DE
  Document concerning Indulgences. Madrid. June 17, 1760.
  3 p. D.S. 30 cm. [M-M 1700:80]
  Printed form, filled in. Appended is note by Luis Fernando de Hoyos Mier, dean of the cathedral of Mexico City, regarding indulgence granted to Father Diego Marín de Moya.

ZUMÁRRAGA, JUAN DE, abp., 1468-1548
  Erection [*sic*] . . . Cath[edralis Mexiconensis]. Toledo. 1534.
  26 p. D.S. 30 cm. HHB [M-M 256]
  Contemporary revised copy of Zumárraga's Latin proclamation on establishment of the Mexico City Cathedral and diocese, later archdiocese. Quotes the relevant bull of Clement VII, Rome, September 2, 1530, naming Zumárraga as first bishop of the diocese, and setting forth statutes for its administration.
  Appended in Spanish are 1) a signed certification, Mexico City, June 2?, 1548, attesting Zumárraga's acceptance and signing of the revised instrument; and 2) a statement, Valladolid, November 6, 1536, signed by Queen Isabel of Portugal and Juan de Samano, transmitting this revised text to Zumárraga and requesting that it be implemented and the Council duly notified.
  Entered by Bancroft under "Pastoral sobre fundación de la Catedral de México."

ZURITA, ALONSO DE, b. 1511 or 1512
  Brebe, y sumaria Relazion, de los Señores, y diferiencias que abia de ellos, en la Nueba españa, y en otras Provinzias, sus comarcanas, y de sus leyes, usos, y customb[re]s, y de la forma que tenian en les tributar sus vasallos, en tiempo de su gentilidad, y la que despues de conquistados se ha tenido, y tiene, en los tributos que pagan á S. M. . . . [1554-ca. 1565]
  192 p. 30 cm. HHB [M-M 254]
  Copy of report to the King of Spain and his councillors on current taxation and government of Indians as compared with earlier native procedures, and on the desirability of moderating taxation. Probably begun in Mexico in 1554 and revised in Spain about 1565.
  Substantially identical with item 4 of "Morfi, Juan Agustín . . . Colección de Documentos" (M-M 162).
  Vellum-bound volume bearing the stamp of Antonio de la Rosa. Decorative t.p., and marginal annotations. A portrait of [Francisco?] Martínez de la Rosa, with the printed legend "Ancien Président du Conseil en Espagne," is pasted on the reverse of the flyleaf.

Index

Abad, Diego José, 3
Abalos, Joseph de, 250
Abarca, Felipe Antonio, 165-166
Abarca de Bolea. *See* Aranda, Conde de
Abascal, Salvador, 257
Abbott, Emma, 3
Aberdeen, George Hamilton Gordon, 4th Earl of, 3
Acapulco, 129, 253; description, 201; trade with Philippines, 122
Acatitlán, 182
Acatlán (Hidalgo), parish records, 3
Acevedo, Aurelio R., 257
Aciopari, José Querién, 3-4
Aconchi, mission, 178, 179
Acosta, Juan Gerardo de, 241
Acuña y Bejarano, Juan de. *See* Casa Fuerte
Adalid, Ignacio, 135
Adamdicosio y Cauto. *See* Pérez Adamdicosio
Adame y Arriaga, José, 209
Adames, Luciano and Pedro, 160
Adams, Charles Francis, 4
Adams, Henry Carter, 4
Adams, William, 4
Aftosa, La fiebre, 44
Agreda, Diego de, 4
Agreda, María de, 10
Agriculture
—Brazil, 52, 53
—Chile, 100
—Colombia, 185
—Cuba, 51, 66
—Ecuador, 185
—Guatemala, 54
—Mexico, 29, 57, 109, 131-132, 206, 215, 252; Californias, 218; Chiapas, 75, 82; Chihuahua, 123; government policies, 227; Provincias Internas, 50; Sonora, 44, 195; Tabasco, 201; Veracruz, 57; Zacatecas, 57
—Panama, 185
—Puerto Rico, 186
—United States, 105
Aguado, Pedro de, 4-5
Aguascalientes, 108, 191
Aguayo, Pedro de, 228
Aguiar, Francisco de, abp., 124
Aguileta Ladrón de Guevara, Juan de, 5
Aguirre, Antonio, 92
Aguirre, Francisco Xavier, 58
Aguirre y Gomiendo, Francisco, 109
Agustín Robelo, Cecilio, 131
Ahumada, Juan Antonio de, 5
Ahumada y Villalón, Agustín de, Marqués de las Amarillas, viceroy, 1755-1758, 44, 64, 135, 136, 252
Alaska Highway. *See* Inter-American Highway
Alatorre, Francisco, 5
Albiçuri (Albieuri), Juan de, 5
Albiz, Juan Manuel Comyn, Conde de, 6
Albu(r)querque, Duque de. *See* Fernández de la Cueva Enríquez
Alcabala, Mexico, 9, 191; Venezuela, 250
Alcalá, Francisco Xavier de, 6
Alcántara Pérez, Pedro, 6
Alcedo y Bexarano, Antonio de, 6
Alcoholic beverages, 36, 88, 102, 231
Aldama, Francisco Antonio de, 200
Aldrich, Thomas Bailey, 6
Alencastre Noroña y Silva, Fernando de, Duque de Linares, viceroy, 1711-1716, 135, 253
Alessandri Rodríquez, Arturo, 6
Alfieri, Vittorio, 153
Alhóndiga de Granaditas, 91
Allande, Pedro María de, 43, 174
Allen, William H., 87-88
Almazán, Juan Andreu, 257
Almira Ascanio, Asunción, 250
Altamira, Marqués de. *See* Rodríquez de Albuerne
Altamirano, Diego Francisco, 217, 219
Altamirano, Pedro Ignacio, 217, 219, 221, 222
Alvarado, Francisco de, 179
Alvarado, Pedro de, 6-7, 84-85, 151, 188, 261
Alvarado y Salcedo, Antonio de, 5
Alvarado family, genealogy, 151
Alvarez, Andrés, 258
Alvarez, Isabel, 258
Alvarez de Avila, Juan, 250
Alvítez (Albítez), Diego, 37

Alzate y Ramírez, José Antonio, 7
Amadeus, Beatus, 7
Amarillas, Marqués de las. *See* Ahumada y Villalón
Amarillas, Presidio, 141
America: bibliography, 6; description, 32; discovery and exploration, 23, 34, 42, 106, 107, 120, 229, 253; Franciscans, 92-93; geography, 32, 85; history, 32, 41, 74, 261; Indians, 32, 34, 35, 60, 73, 97, 177, 193, 197-198, 224, 230; manufactures, 79; ports, 54; Roman Catholic Church, 88, 92-93; territorial disputes, 126; trade with Great Britain, 89; water distribution, 204
Ana María de Jesús, Mother, 198
Anacreon, 163
Andagoya, Pascual de, 7
Anderson, Albin I., 7
Anderson, Robert Marshall, 7
Anderson, Thomas McArthur, 8
Andonaegui, Frank, 8
Andonaegui, Roque de, 217
Andrade, M. J., 197
Andrade, Rafael, 176
Angell, Arnold, 51
Angola, papers, 184
Angulo family, genealogy, 151
Aniñon, Felipe de, 8
Antequera (Oaxaca), 18; Cathedral, 199
Antigua Maderería del Caballito, S. A., 8
Antioquia, Colombia, 195-196
Antiquities:
—Central America, 20
—Guatemala, 42, 62, 188, 260
—Mexico, 18, 27, 29, 39, 40-41, 42, 62, 63, 67, 71, 73, 103-104, 121, 144, 150, 155-156, 212, 240-241; Chiapas, 62, 155; Maya, 63; Mitla, 212; Narnajal, Veracruz, 18; Oaxaca, 27; Yucatan, 62
—Nicaragua, 108
—Peru, 142
Antonio, Santiago, 110
Antonio de la Ascensión, Fray, 8
Anza, Juan Bautista de, 31, 72, 76, 83, 213; second expedition, 75; burial site, 95
Anza, Juan Felipe de, 213
Apache Indians, 19, 50, 63, 107, 175, 176, 189, 223, 238

Apam (Hidalgo), 171
Aparicio, José Enrique, 4
Apressa y Gandra, Domingo de, 8
Ara, Domingo de, 178
Arana, Anastasia de Vergara, 8-9
Arana Xahila, Francisco Hernández, 188
Aranda, Juan de, 130
Aranda, Marqués de, 63
Aranda, Pedro Pablo Abarca de Bolea, Conde de, 29, 170
Arauz, Clemente de, 9
Arce y Echeagaray, José Mariano de, 9
Archaeology. *See* Antiquities
Archbishops: Mexico, 24, 76; New Granada, 35
Archguilds. *See* Guilds
Architects, Mexico, 137
Arcos y Mendiola, Antonio, 128
Ardoino, Antonio, 261
Areche, José Antonio de, 170
Arén, Francisco, 115
Arévalo, Antonio de, 9
Argentina: description and travel, 4; ports, 26; railroads, 256
Argeo, Ignacio de, 217
Argüello, Manuel de, 78
Argüello family, 239
Arias, Conde de, 9
Aribechi (Arivechi), 228; mission, 220
Arista, Mariano, 30, 244
Arístegui y Vélez, Rafael de, 187
Ariza, Andrés de, 9
Arizona: history, 93; missions, 93, 217-223
Arizona Republic, 227
Arizpe (Sonora), 50, 72, 95, 175; Indians, 220; missions, 220
Arnaya, Nicolás de, 127
Arnold, Benedict, 10
Aróstegui, Nicanor, 10
Aróstegui y Herrera, Gonzalo, 186
Arpide, Antonio de, 38
Arriaga, Julián de, 10, 72
Arrieta, Antonio de, 81
Arrieta, Francisco, 223
Arrillaga, José Joaquín de, 10, 63
Arrillaga y Barcárcel, Basilio Manuel, 10
Arriola, Juan José de, 11, 140
Arteaga, Ignacio, 72, 113, 126
Artesanos, Junta de Fomento de, 57

Aruba (island), 250
Arzate, José Antonio, 11
Aschenbrenner, Theophilus, 224
Asencio, Manuel Vicente, 184
Associated Press of Mexico, 168, 185, 237-238
Astrology, 1750, Mexico, 99
Astronomy, 120; Mexico, 104-105, 144; expedition of 1769, 37; solar eclipse, 215
Asunción, Pachuca (Hidalgo), census records, 158
Ati, mission, baptismal records, 180
Atkinson, Ida I., 11
Atlases, 54, 94
Atlixco: sugar plantations, 234; squadron, 200
Atzcapotzalco monastery, 47
Audiencia de los Confines, 147
Audiencia of Guadalajara, 31, 36, 151, 206, 220, 258
Audiencia of Guatemala, 39, 66, 70, 85, 114, 142, 230
Audiencia of Mexico, 5, 23, 53, 103, 109, 134, 135, 137, 158, 168, 192, 194, 240, 257, 258, 259
Augustinians, in Mexico, 3, 78; in the Philippines, 16
Austin, Stephen F., 239
Autographs: Americans, 11-12; Mexican leaders, 185
Auza, Miguel, 5
Avaricio, Pascual de, 93
Avendaño, Suárez de Sousa, Pedro de, 12, 233
Avila, José Miguel de, 12
Avila-Santarén expedition, 60, 127, 189
Avila y Uribe, Mariano González de, 12
Avity, Pierre d', 54
Ayala, Juan de, explorer, 125-126
Ayala, Juan de, corregidor of Zumpango, 200
Ayza, Marqués de, estate of, 193
Azanza, Miguel José de, viceroy, 1798-1800, 4, 135, 152, 192; instructions to successor, 13
Aztec Indians, 189, 212; genealogy, 40-41; linguistics, 3, 16-17, 19, 30-31, 40-41, 43, 121, 123, 128, 140, 142, 146, 147-148, 154-155, 178, 201, 204, 210, 212, 214, 228; pictographs, 180; social life

INDEX

and customs, 16-17
B. G. A., 13
Bac, mission, 177, 221
Bacadeguatzi, mission, 218
Bacum (Bahcon) y Cócorin (Cócorit), mission, 220
Baja California. *See* California, Lower
Balbastro, Pablo, 179
Balboa, Vasco Núñez de. *See* Núñez de Balboa
Baldonado, Luis, 76
Balli, Nicolás, 165
Balthrope, James M., 14
Bancker, John, 254
Bancroft, George, 14
Bancroft, Hubert Howe, v, vi, vii, 15, 19, 23, 34, 42, 45, 47, 53, 56, 60, 66, 67, 69, 104, 106, 108, 121, 132, 145, 162, 164, 167, 184, 190, 193, 199, 203, 240, 241, 262, 263; conversations with Porfirio Díaz, 55; correspondence, 14; Mexican visit, 14
Bancroft, Minnie L. (Smith), 15
Banes, Isaac, 58
Bangs, Samuel, 15
Bankhead, Charles, 3
Banking: Bolivia, 184; Mexico, 109
Bankruptcy laws, 29
Bannard, William, 15
Bañuelos family, genealogy, 151
Baptismal records
—Mexico, Acatlán, 3; Ati, 180; Bisanig, 181; Caborca, 177; Caburica, 180; Caducaman, 210; Carichic, 219; Chiapas, 39, 75; Cocóspera, 181; Magdalena, 181; Nuestra Señora del Refugio, 140; Oquitoa, 180; Pitaqui, 182; San Joaquín, 165; Santa Ana Pueblo, 181; Santa Cruz, 181; Santísimo Rosario, 211; Santo Domingo, 212; Sonora, 53; Tubutama, 180, 181; Velicatá, 206
—Panama, Nata, 160; San Buenaventura de las Palmas, 160; San Juan de Penonomé, 160
—Puerto Rico, Coamo, 187
Baptista, Hierónimo (Jerónimo), 15
Barba, Joseph, 217-218
Barba González, Silvano, 257
Barbastro, Francisco Antonio, 178

Bárcena Jáuregui, Pedro de, family records, 15-16
Barco, Miguel del, 218
Barco Centenera, Martín del, 261
Bard, W. E., 66
Barillas, Manuel Lisandro, 91
Baring Brothers & Co., 16
Barlow, Samuel Latham Mitchill, 16, 84
Barreda, José de, 163, 225
Barrera y Andonaegui, Ignacio de la, genealogy, 130
Barrionuevo, Francisco, 6
Barrios, Justo Rufino, 92
Barroso, Antonio, 223
Barrutia, Ignacio Francisco, 16
Bartolache, José Ignacio, 45
Basave, Pedro de, 193
Bases Orgánicas, 28, 246
Bastida, Pedro de la, 137
Batalla de Bassols, Clementina, 257
Batangas, Philippine Islands, marriage records, 16
Battlefields, maps, Mexican War, 121
Battles, 29, 47, 115, 121, 163, 244
Batuco, mission, 222
Baudin, Charles, 74
Bautista, Juan, 16-17, 146, 190
Bavispe, 176
Bayard, Thomas Francis, 17
Bazeraca, mission, 217
Bazo, Matías, 251
Bealer, Lewis Winkler, 17
Beard, Samuel Porter, 17
Beaumarchais, Pierre-Augustin Caron de, 153
Beaumont, Pablo de la Purísima Concepción, 17
Becker, Robert H., 191
Bedford, Ed, 17
Behaim, Martin, 122
Bejarano, Félix Francisco, 17-18
Bejarano, Manuel G., 18
Béliardi, Augustin, 18
Belluga y Moncada, Luis Antonio de, cardinal, 18
Beltrán de Guzmán, Nuño, 103, 151
Benecke, Etienne, 133
Benedict XIV, Pope, 207
Benítez, Nicolás, 168
Benz, Antonio María, 18, 224
Berenguer de Marquina, Félix, viceroy, 1800-1803, 4, 13, 122, 152
Bergosa y Jordán, Antonio, bp., 18, 124

Beristáin de Souza, José Mariano, 12, 66, 69, 102, 103, 165, 228
Bernstein, Max, 18-19
Berriozábal, Felipe B., 19
Berrotarán, Joseph de, 19
Bertin, L., 19
Beteta, Ramón, 257
Bethencourt, Pedro de San José, 246-247
Bethlehemites, 19, 87; in Guatemala, 247; in Mexico, 100
Bible, 40, 90, 204; Mexican, 76; Náhuatl, 19
Biblioteca Hispano Americana Septentrional (Beristáin), 66, 102, 103, 165, 228
Bierstadt, Albert, 20
Bisanig, mission, baptismal records, 181
Bishops: Guatemala, 188; Mexico, 24, 39; Panama, 96
Black, Jeremiah Sullivan, 20
Black, John, 20, 26
Blanco Jons, Jacinto, 20
Blasco y García, Vicente, 20
Bleuler, Oton, 92
Blom, Frans Ferdinand, 20
Bloodgood, John, 20
Bluefields, Nicaragua, 150
Boban, Eugène, 61
Bocas, hacienda, 12
Bodega y Quadra, Juan Francisco de la: 1775 voyage, 125-126; 1779 voyage, 72, 126
Bojórquez, Juan de Dios, 257
Bolaños, 159-160; mining, 21
Bolaños Mining Company, 21
Bolívar, Simón, 21
Bolivia: diplomatic dispatches, 245; economic conditions, 17; Indians, 11, 184; mining, 184; petroleum, 212
Bolton, James R., 167
Bolton, Juan, 21
Bonavia y Zapata, Bernardo, 21
Bonilla, Antonio, 21, 60
Bonnin, René, 126
Borah, Woodrow W., 21, 186
Borica, Diego de, 14
Böse, Emil, 22
Bossuet, Jacobo Benigno, bp., 10
Bours & Co., Tomás Robinson, 22
Bowman, Jacob Neibert, 95, 191
Boyd, Henry, 22
Boyd, Samuel S., and William A., 22

Brackett, James L., 22
Bradford, 22
Bradley, Abraham, family papers, 23
Brambila y Arriaga, Antonio, 23
Bramer, Electa (Snow), 23
Branciforte, Marqués de. *See* Grúa Talamanca y Branciforte
Brasseur de Bourbourg, Charles Etienne, Abbé, 62, 178, 188, 230
Bravo, Jayme, 218, 221
Bravo, Nicolás, 115
Brazil, 55; agriculture, 52, 53; economics, 52; history, 52; linguistics, 52, 254; Roman Catholic Church, 52; Society of Jesus, 52, 224; treaty of limits (1757), 52
"Bread Riot," Madrid, 145
Breshwood, Captain, 57
Briggs, Lawrence Palmer, 24, 80
Bringas de Manzaneda y Encinas, Diego Miguel, 24
Brión, Luis, 24
British: in the Danish West Indies, 52-53; in the Dutch West Indies, 68; in Guatemala, 59; in Honduras, 158; in Mexico, 129, 133, 183; in the Pacific, 89; in the Philippines, 172-173; in Puerto Rico, 186; in Venezuela, 183, 187; in the West Indies, 186-187; in Yucatan, 104
British Guiana, land grants, 24
British Honduras: history, 42, 89; Indians, 42; Mosquito Coast, 89; railroads, 42; roads, 42
British West Indies: government and administration, 24; slavery and free Negroes, 24. *See also* West Indies
Brodie, John Pringle, 25
Bronimann, Emil, 25
Brotherhoods. *See* Guilds
Brown, David, 25
Brown, James, 26
Bruno, Alejandro, 60
Bucareli y Ursúa, Antonio María, viceroy, 1771-1779, 7, 26, 38, 72, 75, 102, 154, 253
Buena Vista, Battlefield of, 121
Buenos Aires, Argentina, 26
Buildings, Mexico City, 137
Bull, Frances H., 27

Bull, James Hunter, 26-27
Bulls, papal, 24, 71, 76, 136, 198, 206-207, 244, 252, 263
Burgaleta, José, 72
Burgoa, Francisco de, 27
Burguillos, Bartolomé de, 242
Burial records:
—Mexico, Acatlán, 3; Borja, 206; Caborca, 177; Caburica, 180; Chiapas, 39, 75; Cocóspera, 181; Magdalena, 181; Nuestra Señora Refugio, 140; Pitaqui, 182; San Vicente Ferrer, 208; Santa Cruz (Santa María Soamca), 181; Santísimo Rosario, 211; Santo Domingo, 212; Sonora, 53; Tlaltizapán, 240; Tubac, 181; Velicatá, 206
—Philippine Islands, Luzon, 172
Burke, Edward Austin, 27
Burt, Thomas, 27
Bustamante, Anastasio, 29, 71
Bustamante, Carlos María de, 27, 28, 29, 30, 85-86, 252
Bustamante, Ignacio de, 43, 174
Bustamante, José Alejandro de, 73
Bustamante, Salvador Ignacio, 218
Bustamante y Tagle, Bernardo Antonio de, 63-64
Butrón, Jacinto. *See* Morán de Butrón

C., M. A. d. l., 30
Caballero, José Antonio de, 18
Caballero y Ocío, Juan, 241
Caballos, Honduras, 8, 49, 66, 83, 104; attacked by French, 247-248
Cabañas, Trinidad, 150
Caborca, 80, 175; mission records, 177
Cabredo, Rodrigo de, 30
Caburica, mission, parish records, 180-181
Cacao industry, 54
Ca(c)kchiquel Indians, 85, 188, 260
Cadena, Elías, 131
Cadena, Guillén, 78
Caducaman, mission, baptismal records, 210
Caesar (vessel), 27
Cajigal de la Vega, Francisco Antonio, viceroy, 1758-1760, 253
Calderón, Martín, 38

Calderón, Miguel Joseph, 38
Calderón, Phelipe, 218
Calderón, Rodrigo de, 163
Calderón de la Barca, Pedro, 30-31
Calendar: of feast days, 231; Mayan, 62; Mexican, 67, 73, 121, 147; Quiché, 260
California, 22; colonization, 190, 239; defense 72; description, 242; discovery and exploration, 112, 113, 114, 249; economics, 79-80; Franciscans, 46, 125, 262; gold rush, 79-80, 119; history, 89, 125; Indians (linguistics), 218; settlement, 149, 214
California, Gulf of, description and travel, 159
California, Lower: administration, 58, 184; astronomical expedition, 37; census of 1851, 58; colonization, 32, 35, 86, 138; commerce, 8, 146; customs office, 51; description, 10, 27, 39, 69, 86, 201, 221, 235; discovery and exploration, 31, 61, 219, 221, 223, 249; economics, 13, 32, 40, 59; elections, 13; filibustering activities, 32, 63, 239; flora and fauna, 39; geography, 13; history, 13, 63, 86, 144, 196, 223; Indians, 14, 196, 218; Japanese shipwreck (1842), 235; lands, 35, 58, 105, 138, 203; maps, 219, 232; martyrs, 236; military affairs, 13, 14, 32, 58, 59; mining, 18-19, 59; missions, 27, 59, 65, 112, 140, 141, 196, 206, 208, 211, 217-223, 224, 226, 236, 249; piracy, 14; politics and government, 13, 58, 59, 196, 203, 229-230; war with U. S., 13
California, Upper: administration, 133, 184, 192, 246; aid to, 73; capital of, 115; communications with, 228; defense, 72, 192; discovery and exploration, 48, 72, 75, 76, 141; foreign affairs, 133; history, 48, 196; Indians, 254; missions, 72, 93, 107, 141, 218
California First Squadron, 31
Californias, 61; colonization, 31; description, 31, 218; diaries, 48; discovery and ex-

ploration, 8, 61, 156, 232; foreign intrusions, 61; Franciscans, 46, 125, 162; geography, 75; history, 61, 232, 262; Indians, 10, 46, 218, 232; military affairs, 31; missions, 10, 46, 72, 112, 125, 182, 217, 218, 219, 220, 221, 222, 232; Pious Fund, 68; Roman Catholic Church, 127-128; statistics, 98
Calleja del Rey, Félix María, viceroy, 1813-1816, 223
Calles, Plutarco Elías, 238
Caltzontzín, Francisco, 103
Calvo de la Puerta y O'Farrill, Sebastián, 117
Camacho Villavisencio, Miguel, 38
Cameron, James, 182
Campbell, W. M., 31
Campillo, José del, 163
Campos, Juan, 32
Campuzano, Antonio, 13, 43, 176
Canalizo, Valentín, 28, 202, 223
Canals, Mexico (Huehuetoca), 72, 190; Panama, 7, 22, 47, 107, 245
Cananea, disorders, 90
Canary Islands: description, 54; emigration to Cuba, 32; emigration to Texas, 238
Cancio Bonadares, Lorenzo, 83, 218
Cano Moctezuma, María de, 103
Cantón, Pedro, 223
Capuchins: in Mexico, 191; in Venezuela, 187
Carbone, João Baptista, 105
Cárdenas, Eusebio, 239-240
Cárdenas, Lázaro, 227
Cárdenas, Manuel, 92
Caribbean: description, 111; history, 44; royal expenditures in, 144
Carichic, mission, baptismal records, 219; map, 219
Carleton, James Henry, 87
Carli, Giovanni Rinaldo, Conte, 32, 74
Carlos, Prince of Asturias, 205
Carlos María Isidro, Infante, 19
Carlota, Empress of Mexico, 73-74, 115, 125
Carlson, Ruth Elizabeth (Kearney), 32
Carmelites, in Mexico, 111, 121
Carmen, Island of, 231
Carnero, Juan, 233
Carondelet, François Hector, 117
Carothers, A. G., 32
Carpegna, Gaspare, cardinal, 207
Carranco, Lorenzo José, 222, 236
Carranza, Venustiano, 32, 237-238
Carrera, Fernando de la, 33
Carrera, J., 229
Carrera, Rafael, 33, 143
Carrillo de Mendoza y Pimentel, Diego, Marqués de Gelves, viceroy, 1621-1624, 23, 70, 103, 190, 242
Carrington, J. W., 33
Carrizal, hacienda (Nuevo Léon), 93
Carvajal, Raphael, 33
Casa de Contratación de Indias, 33
Casa Fuerte, Juan de Acuña y Bejarano, Marqués de, 33, 195
Casa Grande, Gila River, ground plan, 76
Casa Mata, Plan de, 43, 174
Casa-Tilly, Marqués de, 153
Casanova y Estrada, Ricardo, abp., 91
Casas, Bartolomé de las: documents concerning, 33; works of, 34
Caso, Alfonso, 257
Casquero, Alejandro, 56
Cass, Lewis, 34
Castañeda, Gabriel de, 103, 146
Castañiza, José María, 223
Castañiza, Juan Francisco, bp., 223
Castaño, Arturo, 26
Castaño, Bartolomé, 201
Castellón, Francisco de, 150
Castera, Ignacio, 34
Castile, Royal and Supreme Council of, 163, 170
Castilla, Alonso Criado de. See Criado de Castilla
Castillo, Antonio del, 34-35
Castillo, Martín del, 78
Castillo Gadea, Juan de, genealogical documents, 35
Castillo Negrete, Francisco del, 58
Castillo y Lanzas, Joaquín María de, 131
Castro, Francisco Xavier, 141
Castro, Juan (Ivan) de, abp., 110; biography and epitaph, 34-35
Castro, Juan Nepomuceno, 200
Castro, Manuel de Jesús, 35, 58
Castro, Mauricio, 13
Castro Figueroa y Salazar, Pedro de, Duque de la Conquista, viceroy, 1740-1741, 252, 253
Castro y Gutiérrez, Ramón de, 186, 187
Catechisms, 23, 40-41; Aztec, 180; Brazil, 254; Guatemala, 197; Mexico, 123, 125, 132, 198, 201; Otomi Indian, 209; Timucuan Indian, 165; Zoque Indian, 178
Cathedrals, 12, 24, 37, 151, 164, 189, 191, 197, 200, 233, 241, 248, 258, 263
Catherine Howard (Dumas), 67
Catholic Church. *See* Roman Catholic Church
Catlin, George, papers, 35
Cattle, Santo Domingo, 211
Cavaillon, Adolfo Emilio, 45
Cavallón, Juan de, 71
Cavite (Luzon), Philippine Islands, 172; arsenal, 35-36; military affairs, 35-36
Ceballos, Pedro, 153
Cebrián y Agustín, Pedro, Conde de Fuenclara, viceroy, 1742-1746, 38
Celis, Rubín de, 64
Censuses
—Colombia, 44
—Mexico, 194; Caburica, 181; Chalcatongo livestock, 44; Chihuahua, 235; Corps of Dragoons, 36; Lower California, 58; New Mexico missions, 21; Nueva Vizcaya, 36; Pachuca, 158-159; Sonora and Sinaloa, 30
—Puerto Rico, 187
Centeno, Andrés B., 176
Central America: administration, 147, 232; antiquities, 20; botany, 129; commerce, 106; description, 17-18, 232; discovery and exploration, 188; economics, 68; history, 28, 36, 89, 106, 143, 144, 146; Indians, 9, 17-18, 63, 65, 104, 147, 155, 177, 192, 232; missions, 58-59; politics and government, 106; Ro-

man Catholic Church, 144, 147, 232; statistics, 144. *See also* Guatemala, Nicaragua, etc.
Central American Federation, 106
Cereceda (Cerezeda), Andrés de, 36, 37
Ceremonies: Cuba, 94; Mexico, 134, 191, 194 (Jewish rites)
Cermeño, Pedro Martín, 153
Cerralvo, Marqués de. *See* Pacheco Osorio
Cervantes, Ignacio Guadalupe, 167
"Cesares," city of the, 64
Chacón, José María, 92
Chacón de la Mota, Teresa, 37
Chagres River, Panama, 7
Chalcatongo (Oaxaca), 44
Chapala, Compañía Anónima de Navegación del Lago de, 45
Chappe d'Auteroche, Jean, 37
Chapultepec, Battle of, 115
Charles I of Spain, 6, 7, 24, 36, 37, 147
Charles II of Spain, 24, 38, 59, 62, 86, 163, 225
Charles III of Spain, 42, 81, 87, 114-115, 132, 137, 140, 169, 201, 216, 218, 235, 258
Charles IV of Spain, 4, 87, 218, 259
Charles V of Spain, 46, 190
Chase, E. B., 37
Chatfield, Frederick, 89
Chavero, Alfredo, 37-39
Chaves, Gabriel de, 39
Chaves, José Antonio, 35, 58
Chávez, Pedro de, 121
Chávez Orozco, Luis, 257
Cheape, George C., 101
Chiapas, Guatemala, municipal government, 128
Chiapas (city), Mexico, 62; municipal government, 39, 128; parish records, 39, 75
Chiapas (province), Mexico, 20, 75, 81-82; agriculture, 75; antiquities, 62, 155; description, 62; geography, 75; history, 58-59, 62, 260; Indians, 58-59, 62, 81-82; industry, 75; military affairs, 39; missions, 58-59, 62; politics and government, 82; Roman Catholic Church, 39, 127-128; social life and customs, 75; taxes, 39

Chicalco Indians, 46
Chichén Itzá, 58-59
Chichimeca Indians, 103, 144, 146, 148, 155-156, 190
Chickering, Allen Lawrence, 39
Chihuahua, 72; economics, 50, 123; history, 43, 173; Indians, 38, 40, 148, 176; maps and plans, 25; military affairs, 36, 40, 50, 63; mining, 21, 25; missions, 50, 235; politics and government, 39-40, 237, 251; presidios, 50; railroads, 25; roads, 25; statistical description, 235; taken by French, 126; taxes, 40; Town Council, 174
Chilcuacán, hacienda, 258
Chile, 6; agriculture, 100; description, 214; history, 40; Indians, 40; international trade, 40; politics and government, 136; relations with U.S., 40; social problems, 100
Chilpancingo, church, 200
Chimalpopocatl Galicia, Faustino, 40, 123, 146, 147, 189
China, 78, 117; Defence League, 234; foreign trade, 104
Chinese, in Mexico, 110
Chipman Stone & Co., 41
Chiquita Indians, 184; linguistics, 11
Chirinos, Pedro, 207
Chiripas, mission, 77
Chiriquí, Panama, 161-162
Chitalpopoca, Salvador Cortés Alvarado Mascarón, 46
Choco Indians, linguistics, 179
Chocolate, 41
Chole-Lacandón Indians, 59
Cholera, 28, 52, 84
Chontalcuatlán Indians, 109
Churubusco, Battle of, 115
Cicero, Marcus Tullius, 41
Cieneguilla, 174, 175; mining, 174; mission, 180
Cienfuegos, Alvaro, cardinal, 163
Cilly, John S., 41
Civil War, U.S., 116, 204, 209, 216; accounts, 99, 106; diaries and letters, 17, 22, 31, 41, 95, 106, 112, 116, 124, 255; service records, 8
Clark, Charles Upson, 41
Clark, William, 169
Clarke, 41

Clarke, George W., 41
Clavel, Salvador, 110
Clavijero, Francisco Javier, 95, 164
Clayton, John Middleton, 42
Clayton, Lloydine Della (Martin), 42
Clegern, Wayne McLauchlin, 42
Cleland, Robert Glass, 91
Clemencín, Diego, 191
Clemens, Eliza, 16
Clement VII, Pope, 263
Clement VIII, Pope, 207
Clement XI, Pope, 207
Clement XII, Pope, 207
Clement XIII, Pope, 140, 169, 216
Clement XIV, Pope, 207, 247
Clergy, 18, 87; in Hispanic America, 250; in Mexico, 13, 28, 37-39; 244, 252. *See also* Roman Catholic Church
Cleveland, Daniel, 42
Cloche, Antonino, 82
Coahuila: administration, 49-50; Indians, 50; lands, 185, 239; missions, 141, 218
Coahuila y Texas, colonization, 239
Coamo, Puerto Rico, baptismal records, 187
Coapilla (Chiapas), 75
Cobán, Guatemala, 58, 62, 78
Cochineal, 7
Cochrane Johnstone, Andrés, 113
Cocóspera, mission, baptismal and burial records, 181
Códices, Fernández Leal, 42; Mayan, 63; Mexicanus Borgianus, 73; Mexico, 147-148
Cody, Harry F., 245
Cofradía: de Nuestra Señora de la Limpia Concepción (Cuernavaca), 43; de Santa María de la Soledad (Oaxaca), 43; del Santísimo Sacramento (Cuernavaca), 43. *See also* Guilds
Coinage: Bolivia, 184; Mexico, 50, 111, 170, 182, 191, 213; Peru, 170. *See also* Mints
Coit, Daniel Wadsworth, 43
Colegio Apostólico de Nuestro Padre San Francisco, Pachuca, 159
Colegio de San Gregorio, 258
Colegio de San Ildefonso, 223
Colegio Real de San Luis, Puebla, 212

INDEX 271

Colima, description, 25; sugar mill, 143
Colina y Rubio, Carlos María, bp., *visita,* 39
Colindrés, Nicolás de, 82
College: Mexico, 41, 53, 93, 95-96, 102, 126, 133; Dominican, 212; Franciscan, 15, 68, 92-93, 141, 159, 262; Jesuit, 3, 128, 197, 200, 223, 258; Spain, Jesuit, 225
Collot, George Victor, 42
Colombia: administration, 44; agriculture, 185; censuses, 44; colonization, 4-5, 195-196; description and travel, 4-5, 69; discovery and exploration, 4-5, 195-196; history, 4-5, 44, 47, 83, 161-162, 195-196; Indians, 4-5, 195-196; laws, 44; mining, 185; petroleum, 185; politics and government, 47; relations with Great Britain, 234; residencia records, 44; slavery, 149
Colón (vessel), logbook, 159
Colonia Militar de la Frontera (Lower California), 58
Colorado River, 10, 96, 138, 223, 228
Colotlán, missions, 218
Columbus, Christopher, 34, 101, 122, 229
Columpio Silver Mining Company, 44
Comanche Indians, 238
Comisión Mexicana—Americana para la Erradicación de la Fiebre Aftosa, 44
Compagnie de Sonore, 44
Compagnie des Filles de Notre-Dame, 45
Compagnie d'Occident, 126
Compañía Restauradora, 44
Comyn, Juan Manuel, Conde de Albiz, 6
Conceptionists, 121, 192, 252
Conde y Oquendo, Francisco Javier, 45
Confederate States of America: alliance with Lower California, 58; currency, 45; prison, 99
Confraternities. *See* Guilds
Congregación de la Purísima Concepción, Mexico City, 144, 208, 252
Congresses, constituent, 28 (1842), 174
Conicari: mission, 219; Indians, 219
Conquista, Duque de la. *See* Castro Figueroa y Salazar
Consag, Fernando, 31, 223; map, 219
Constitutions
—Colombia, 161
—Mexico, of 1824, 170; of 1843, 28, 246; for the empire, 125; of 1917, 160
Contaduría General de Distribución, Spain, 229
Contreras family, genealogy, 151
Convento de la Ciudad de San Salvador, Guatemala, 65
Convento de San Agustín, Guadalajara, 46
Convento de San Francisco, Mexico City, 37-38, 80, 81; records of, 137-138
Convento de Santa Clara, Mexico City, 185, 257
Convento de Santa María de Gracia, 258
Convento Hospital de Nuestro Padre San Juan de Dios, Pachuca, 159
Convents: El Salvador, 65; Guatemala, 58-59, 62, 65, 78; Mexico, 37-38, 46, 79, 80, 81, 82, 101, 111, 121, 137-138, 152, 159, 185, 191, 192, 198, 208, 212, 257-258; Venezuela, 250
Conway, George Robert Graham, 254
Cook, Sherburne F., 83
Cooke, Rose (Terry), 46
Cooley, Tom M., 46
Copper mining, 18-19, 90, 107
Cordero, Antonio, 43, 47, 174, 189
Córdoba, Alberto de, 72
Córdoba, Antonio de, 109
Cordova, Juan de, 47
Corona, Ramón, 14, 47
Coronado. *See* Vázquez de Coronado
Corral, Ponciano, 150
Correo de Chihuahua, 237
Correoso, Buenaventura, 47
Cortabarría, Antonio Ignacio de, 186
Cortazar, Manuel, 135
Corte, Gregorio, 53, 85, 247
Corte-Miranda murder case, 85
Cortecero, Hernando, 79
Cortés, Hernando, 45, 47, 61, 67, 103, 122, 125, 130, 192, 211, 241, 249, 253, 258, 261
Cosío Villegas, Daniel, 257
Costa Rica, 262; colonization, 71; commerce, 94-95, 148; description and travel, 71, 94-95; discovery and exploration, 47, 71, 94-95; history, 47, 71, 94-95; Indians, 18, 94-95; military affairs, 94-95; mines and mineral resources, 71; municipal government, 47; railroad, 148; Roman Catholic Church, 144
Costansó, Miguel, 48, 72-73, 193
Council of Religious Orders, Spain, 163
Council of the Indies, 3-4, 6, 31, 45, 103, 147, 193, 194, 207, 215, 238, 248, 253
Courts, 14, 114, 157
Covarrubias, José María, 164
Cowley-Brown, J. S., 48
Coyotzin, Negual, 103
Coz, Bartolomé, 59
Cozzens, John B., 48
Crabb, Henry Alexander, 80, 133, 195
Crandall, Daniel M., 48
Creel, Enrique C., 237-238
Creighton, Frank Whittington, bp., 48
Creoles, 201; political appointments of, 5, 137, 162, 193; religious appointments, 56, 87, 139-140
Crescent City Bank, New Orleans, 48
Crespí, Juan, 46, 48, 141
Crespo, Antonio, 49
Crespo, Benito, 180
Crespo, Manuel Sabino, 255
Criado de Castilla, Alonso, 49, 66
Crime, 56, 109-110, 114, 157, 186, 234, 240, 247
Cristero Rebellion, 160
Croix, Carlos Francisco de, Marqués de Croix, viceroy, 1766-1771, 37, 49, 80, 81, 149
Croix, Teodoro de, Caballero de Croix, 49-50, 117, 126, 189, 243
Crook, Theo, 251
Crosman, George Hampton, 50-51
Crossman, A. W., 51
Crozat, Antoine, 126
Cruelle, Daniel de, 152
Cruillas, Marqués de. *See*

Montserrat, Joaquín
Cruz, Fernando, 91
Cruz, Sebastián de la, 151
Cruz de la Bandera, Juan Ignacio, 51
Cuautla, 255
Cuba, 171, 256; agriculture, 51, 66; history, 51, 262; immigration, 32, 211; physical and economic description, 17, 51; politics and government, 3-4; racial problems, 4; relations with U. S., 61-62; tobacco industry, 66
Cucurpe, mission, 219
Cuenca, Diego de, 82
Cuenca, Tiburcio, 164
Cuernavaca, 75; Indians, 38
Cuevas, Luis de, 51
Cuevas, mission, 218
Culiacán, 71, 72; Indians, 235
Culo Azul, Antonio, 176
Cuna Indians, linguistics, 97
Currency, 246; confederacy, 45; Mexico, 111, 261; South Carolina, 259; Spain, 191
Curtis, Samuel Ryan, diaries and papers, 51-52
Cushman, Charlotte Saunders, 52
Custer, Ferdinand V., 52
Cuyutlán Gold Mines Company, 52

Dakin, Fred H., 52
Dall & Drége Company, 52
Danish: in Vieques, 187; West Indies, 52-53. *See also* West Indies
Dardón, Manuel Joaquín, 92
Darien, 9, 192-193
Daughters of the Virgin Mary, 45
Dávalos y Braçamonte, Pedro Alonso, 156
David, Guillermo, 218
Davidson, Nathaniel, 53
Dávila, Francisco, 135
Dávila y Lugo, Francisco de, 53
"Decena Trágica," 256
DeGaland, Casimir, 105
Degollado, Santos, 5
De la Torre family, genealogy, 151
Delavigne, Jean François Casimir, 236
Delgado, José, 59
Delgado, Manuel, 205
Deneen, R. M., 210
Denhardt, Robert Moorman, 53

"Derecho de las Yglesias . . . ," 139-140
DeShields, Alf, 54
Destrada, Juan, 54
Diaries: Argentina, 256; Californias, 48, 72; Central America, 158; Far East, 77; Great Britain, 55; Mexico, 28, 30, 50, 51-52, 72, 74, 75, 76, 80, 85-86, 112, 120, 122, 126, 154, 166, 195; U. S., 17, 22, 41, 54, 55, 115-116, 170, 188, 204; West Indies, 158
Dias Ferreira, Gaspar, 55
Díaz, Domingo, 50
Díaz, Joseph Tirso, 55
Díaz, Juan, 259
Díaz, Juan de, 215
Díaz, Porfirio, 27, 41, 55, 56, 74, 115, 119, 140, 166, 185, 201, 215, 237, 241
Díaz de Armendariz, Lope, Marqués de Cadereita, viceroy, 1635-1640, 31
Díaz de la Vega, José, 127, 190
Díaz de Valdés, Francisco, 218
Díaz del Castillo, Bernal, 215
Diego, Juan, 12
Dillon, Guillaume Patrice, 226
Discovery (sloop), logbooks, 89
Dix, John Adams, 57
Doane family, 259
Doblado, Manuel, 5
Dobyns, Henry F., 57, 76
Dolores, hacienda (Nueva Vizcaya), census, 36
Dolores mission, 107 (Pimería); 222-223 (Guaicuru)
Domingues, Francisco, 218
Domínguez, Cristóbal, 37-38
Domínguez, Juan, 64
Domínguez, Juan Francisco, 102
Domínguez de Zamora y Acevedo family, genealogy, 64
Dominicans: history, 65, 82, 210; in Central America, 147; in El Salvador, 65; in Guatemala, 58-59, 62, 65, 78, 81-82, 251, 260; in Mexico, 47, 58-59, 65, 78, 79, 114, 141, 179, 206, 210, 258, 260; in California, 125; in Chiapas, 58-59, 62, 81-82; in Guadalajara, 166-167; in Lower California, 65, 208, 211, 212; in Oaxaca, 27; in Puebla, 79, 233; in Tabasco, 127-128; in Yucatan, 58-59
Dongo, Joaquín Antonio, 85

Dorve, H., 65
Dovalle, Gonzalo, 7
Doye, Jocome, 220
Doyle, John T., 118, 150
Drainage, Mexico, 72, 119, 127, 157
Drake, Francis, 145, 152, 183
Drama, 261; France, 67; Mexico, 12, 30-31, 40, 67, 115, 139-140, 153, 164, 236, 253; Spain, 30-31, 108, 145, 163-164
Druet, Jacobo, 218
Dryden, William G., 66
Duarte, Alonso, 66
Duarte, Manuel, 66
Duarte, Martín, 60, 127
Dublán y Fernández Varela, Manuel, 66
Du Bouchet, Máximo Esteban, 250
Ducatel, Professor, 67
Ducoudray-Holstein, H. Lafayette Villaume, 186
Dufau Maldonado, Pedro de, 26
Du Frechon, 67
Dumas, Alexandre, 67
Dumce, Benno, 224
Duncan family, 67
Duque, Ignacio Xavier, 218
Durán, Diego, 67
Durango, 89-90, 132; agriculture, 67; cathedral, 57, 258; coat of arms, 146; diocese, 71, 131, 200, 235; history, 43, 64, 189; Indians, 21, 89, 110; industry, 57; mining, 189; missions, 88, 218; politics and government, 21; Roman Catholic Church, 174, 189; statistical description, 235
Durasque Indians, linguistics, 78-79
Dutch: in Hispanic America, 250; in Lower California, 223; in Surinam, 234; West Indies, 67-68. *See also* West Indies

Earthquakes: Guatemala, 234; Mexico (Veracruz), 197; South Carolina, 242
East India Company, 172
Eberlein, Louis A., 68
Eberstadt, Edward Emory, 68
Ecce-Homo Guild, 207
Echávarri, Francisco Antonio de, 110
Echávarri, José Antonio, 43, 174

INDEX 273

Echavarría, Luis de, 66
Echave, José María de, 68
Echeandía, Antonio de, 258
Echevelar, Joaquín de, 68
Echeverría, Ignacio de, 110
Echeverría, Manuel, 92
Eckhardt, H. von, 133
Ecuador: agriculture, 185; description and travel, 69; mining, 185; petroleum, 185
Education, Mexico, 131-132, 138, 185, 249; of Indians, 29, 38; Jesuit institutions, 128, 223; Lancastrian schools, 25; primary, in Jalisco, 105; primary, in San Luis Potosí, 213
Edward, 69
Eidu Maru (vessel), 235
Eitel, Frederick, 69
Elections: Chiapas, 39, 82; Lower California, 13; Nueva Vizcaya, 156; Querétaro, 188
Elías González, José María, 176
Elías González, Simón, 174, 175, 228
Elías Pro, Manuel E., 176
Elizabeth I of England, 69
Elizacochea, Martín de, bp., 180, 181
Elizondo, Domingo, 72, 253
Elizondo, Ignacio, 93
El Salvador, 91, 96, 246; description, 233; Indians, 65; missions, 65; politics and government, 205-206; railroads, 233
Encomiendas, 147, 193
Enríquez, Juan Alfonso, 163
Enríquez de Almansa, Martín, viceroy, 1568-1580, 168, 192
Enríquez de Ribera, Payo, abp., 38
Ensenada, Mexico, 8, 212-213; filibustering, 32
Ensenada Port Railway, Argentina, 256
Epidemics: cholera, 28, 52, 84, measles, 182; smallpox, 21
Erb, Gabriel S., 69
Escalante, José María Vélez, 176
Escalante, Silvestre Vélez de, 127
Escalante, Tomás de, 228
Escalante y Arvizu, Manuel, 51
Escalona, Diego López Pacheco, Duque de, viceroy, 1640-1642, 253

Escalona, Joseph de, 219
Escobar y Llamas, Cristóbal de, 219
Escobedo, Mariano, 5
Escorza, Manuel Antonio de, 50
Escoto, Bartolomé de, 100; family papers, 69-70
Escoto, Juan Bautista Mendoza, 70
Espejo, Antonio de, 153
Espejo, Pedro, family papers, 70-71
Espinosa, Joachín de, 64
Espinosa, José, 164
Espinosa, Rafael, 58
Espinosa de los Monteros, Manuel, 71
Espinosa Vidaurre, José Ignacio de, 71
Espíritu Santo, Bernardo del, bp., 71, 180
Espíritu Santo de Echoloa, 221
Espíritu Santo de Moris, mission, 220
Estates: Mexico, 12, 74, 193, 197, 200, 206, 207, 237, 241, 257-259; U. S., 232; Venezuela, 250
Esteva, José Ignacio, 130-131
Estigarribia, José Félix, 17
Estiger, Gaspar, 223
Estrada, Alonso de, 253
Estrada Rávago, Juan de, 71
Estupinian, Baltazar, 205-206
Everett, Edward, 71, 97

Fabregat (Fábrega), Lino José, 73
Fabry, José Antonio, 73
Facio, José Antonio, 131
Falkland Islands, 24
Falla, Salvador, 92
Far East, 77, 78, 104, 117, 150
Farabee, Ethel, 73
Farón, Miguel, 94
Favorita (frigate), 72, 113
Felmel, Gaspar, 252
Ferdinand the Catholic of Spain, 122, 163
Ferdinand VI of Spain, 144, 193, 238
Ferdinand VII of Spain, 19, 223
Ferè, María de la, 73
Fernández de Abee, Julián Isidro, 219
Fernández de Herrera y Gómez, José María, 32, 74
Fernández de la Cueva Enríquez, Francisco, Duque de Albu(r)querque, viceroy, 1702-1711, 113, 253
Fernández del Castillo family, 74
Fernández del Castillo y de Mier, Manuel, 8, 74
Fernández Leal, Manuel, 74
Fernández Lizardi, José Joaquín, 111
Fernández Mora, José, 241
Ferrand, L., 211
Ferrarius, Thomas Maria, 207
Ferré, journal and letters, 74-75
Figueroa, José, 228
Figueroa family, genealogy, 151
Filibustering activities, 176; in Mexico, 11, 32, 63, 80, 96, 133, 195, 226, 239; in Nicaragua, 54, 106, 118, 150, 242
Filisola, Vicente, 75
First Ecclesiastical Provincial Council, 1555, 197-198
Fischer, Agustín, 141
Fleury, Claudio, 40
Floods, 26, 72, 215
Florencia, Josefa de, 110
Flores, Manuel Antonio, viceroy, 1787-1789, 135
Flores, Victor María, 75
Flores de la Torre y González, Vicente, genealogical records, 151
Flores de Rivera, José Antonio, 168
Flores family, genealogy, 151
Flores Magón, Ricardo, 238
Florida: administration, 4; boundaries, 214; history, 60, 214, 215; Indians, 165; missions, 118; racial problems, 4; settlement, 248; West Florida, 116-117
Fonseca, Magdalena de, 109
Font, Pedro, diary, 75, 76
Fontana, Bernard Lee, 76
Fonte y Hernández de Miravete, Pedro José, abp., 76, 223
Foot and mouth disease, 44
Forrest, Edwin, 76
Forsyth, John, 76, 77
Fort Calhoun [Fort Wool] (Virginia), 77
Foster, John Watson, 215
Foulke, George Clayton, 77
Fourth Mexican Provincial Council, 1771, 77, 132, 140
France, 75; description and travel, 4; miscellaneous doc-

274   INDEX

uments concerning, 257; relations with China, 78; relations with Japan, 78; relations with Korea, 78; relations with Mexico, 5, 28, 74-75, 113, 246, 247, 248; relations with Spain, 54, 211, 238, 247-248; relations with Spanish colonies, 54; relations with the U.S., 216; Society of Jesus, 216
Franciscans
—in America, 92-93, 231
—Central America, 17-18, 147
—Colombia, 4-5
—Florida, 118
—Guatemala, 54, 59, 62, 85, 128, 247
—Mexico, 15, 37-39, 48, 49, 56, 68, 77, 78, 80, 81, 95-96, 127, 128, 137-138, 140, 141, 142, 146, 147, 155-156, 162, 165, 181, 191, 201, 242, 251; in the Californias, 46, 125, 262; Chiapas, 128; Michoacán, 17; New Mexico, 262; Nueva Galicia, 46; Nueva Vizcaya, 60; Sonora, 53; Tabasco, 128; Texas, 60; Toluca, 110; Yucatan, 56, 128; Zacatecas, 262
—Nicaragua, 38
—Philippines, 162
—Spain, 92
Francisco, Prior of Viana, 78
Franco, Juan, 78-79
Franco y Ortega, Alonso, 79
Francos y Monroy, Cayetano, abp., 234
Franklin, Benjamin, 79
Freemasons, in Ireland, 79; in Mexico, 65, 79
Frelinghuysen, Frederick Theodore, 79
Frémont, John Charles, 87-88, 148, 255
French: exploration in North America, 42; in the Dutch West Indies, 68; in Hispanic America, 61; in Honduras, 248; in Mexico, 5, 74-75, 113, 126, 226, 247-248; in Panama, 192-193; in Puerto Rico, 186-187; in Santo Domingo, 211; in the West Indies, 250; filibustering activities in Sonora, 226; Revolution, 257
French Canal Company, 107
Frères, Vega, 105
Fresnillo, 159-160
Fresno, Conde del, 110

Freyre de Andrade, Gómez, 169
Frisbie, John B., 79-80
Friz, Andrés, 153
Fronteras, 176
Fuentes, Carlos, 257
Fuentes y Guzmán, Francisco Antonio de, 84
Fur trade, 96

Gabilondo, Hilario Santiago, 80
Gadsden Purchase, 61
Gaillardet, Frédéric, 67
Galán, Carlos F., 241
Galarza, María, 258
Galazo de Bárcena, Agustina, genealogical documents, 15-16
Gallardo, Luciano J., diary, 80
Gallego, Lucas, 78
Gallegos, Marán, 121
Galván family, 128
Galve, Conde de. See Sandoval Cerda Silva y Mendoza
Gálvez, Bernardo de, viceroy, 1785-1786, 116, 243
Gálvez, José de, visitor general of New Spain, Marqués de Sonora, 24, 33, 46, 81, 83, 125, 141, 218, 250; biographical materials, 80; birthplace of, 6
Gálvez, Matías de, viceroy, 1783-1784, 81, 218
Gambling, 87
Gamboa, Francisco Javier, 81
Gamio, Manuel, 81
Gándara, Manuel de la, 164
Gandullo, Luis, 79
Gante, Pedro de, 147
Garcés de Portillo, Pedro, 242
García, Gabriel, 5
García, Luis, 5
García, Nicolás Antonio, 81
García, Pedro Marcelino, 81-82, 128
García Cantarines, Francisco, 82
García Conde, Alejo, 83, 182
García de Bustamante, Doroteo, 148
García de Hermosilla, Juan, 83
García Luis, Jacobo, 249
García Panes y Avellán, Diego, 190
García Pumarino, Toribio, 158
García Torres, Vicente, 28
García Vallecillos y Ruiz, Gabriel Antonio, 83
Gardelin, Philip, 53

Garganta, Francisco de, 250
Garibay, Pedro de, viceroy, 1808-1809, 68, 192
Garrison, Cornelius K., 118
Garviso, Vicente, 84
Garza y Ballesteros, Lázaro de la, abp., 200; deportation of, 13
Gasca, Pedro de la, 147
Gastañeta, José Vicente de, biography, 84
Gatschet, Albert Samuel, 177
Gaty, Samuel, 84
Gavarrete, Juan, 84-85
Gaxiola, Francisco Javier, Jr., 257
Gaxiola, José María, 175, 176, 192
Gebuta Quej, Francisco Dias, 188
Gelves, Marqués de. See Carrillo de Mendoza y Pimentel
Genealogies: Aztec Indians, 41; Honduras, 69-70; Mexico, 15-16, 64, 70, 100, 130, 151, 156, 157, 166, 190, 199, 211, 226, 240; Peru (Inca descendants), 114; Spain, 15-16, 35, 70, 126; U. S., 22, 241, 243
Geográfica Descripción (Burgoa), 27
Geology, 143
Geometría Práctica (Sáenz de Escobar), 203-204
Gerardus, Pyrrhus, 224
Geredo, José Joaquín, 69
Germans, in Rio Grande do Sul, 183
Germany: politics and government, 90; relations with Mexico, 133
Gibson, Charles, 228
Gifford, Henry F., 85
Gila River, 76; discovery and exploration, 223; fur trade, 96; Indians, 227, 228
Glandorff, [Franciscus] Hermannus, 224
Glynn, Charles R., 244
Gochicoa y Compañía, 138
Goethals, George W., 245
Gold mining: Chiapas, 39; Durango, 90; Tepic, 52. See also Mines and mineral resources
Golson, B., 85
Gómez, Ana, 258
Gómez, José, 85-86
Gómez, Juan, 82
Gómez, Justo, 86
Gómez, Marte R., 257

INDEX 275

Gómez de Alvarado, Luis, 151
Gómez de Cervantes, Joseph, 86
Gómez de Cervantes, Nicolás Carlos, bp., 86
Gómez de Moscoso, Elvira, 143
Gómez de Orozco, Federico, 147
Gómez Farías, Valentín, 28, 57
Gómez Galván, María Teresa, 97
Gómez Márquez, Juan, 199
Gómez Morín, Manuel, 257
Gómez y Güemes, Cristóbal, 259
González, Faustino, 174, 175
González, Francisco, 227
González, J. M., 86
González, Luis, 178
González, Manuel, 41, 86, 119
González, Father Manuel, 181
González, María Francisco, 198
González, Father Pedro, 71
González, Tirso, 220, 225
González Angulo, Bernardo, 57
González Dávila, Gil, 36, 86
González de Barcia, Andrés, 261
González de Candamo, Gaspar, 165
González de Dueñas, Felipe, 70
González de Estrada, Francisco, 250
González de la Herrán, Diego, 206
González del Campillo, Manuel Ignacio, bp., 86-87
González del Castillo, Juan Ignacio, 153
González family, genealogy, 151
González Lastiri, Miguel, 134
González Ortega, Jesús, 5, 87
Goodspeed, Thomas Harper, 88
Gordon, George Hamilton, 4th Earl of Aberdeen, 3
Gorman, Willis Arnold, 95
Gorospe, Manuel Ignacio de, 88
Gostorfs, Leopold R., 149
Goupil, E. -Eugène, 61
Goya, Jesús María, 88
Graham, Daniel, 138
Grant, Ulysses S., 12, 89
Gratiot, Charles, 77
Grau, Francisco, 130

Great Britain: Colonial Office, 89; diaries, 55; Foreign Office, 84, 89; Navy, 89, 218; relations with Colombia, 234; relations with Mexico, 3, 22, 33, 75, 205; relations with Nicaragua, 150; relations with Spain, 18, 24, 104, 218, 231; relations with Texas, 3; relations with the United States, 3, 42; wills, 173
Green, Duff, 87
Green, George M., 89-90
Greene, William Cornell, 90
Greene Consolidated Copper Company, 90
Gregory I, The Great, Pope, 90
Greytown, Nicaragua, 42, 150, 231
Griffis, William E., 41
Grijalva, Hernando de, 192
Grimaldi, Jerónimo, 72
Grimaldo, Cristóbal, 258
Grimarest, Enrique de, 83
Grimm, Hans, 90
Groso, Angel, 90
Grova, Manuel de, 261
Grúa Talamanca y Branciforte, Miguel de la, Marqués de Branciforte, viceroy, 1795-1798, 9, 73, 135, 153, 194
Guadalajara, Cristóbal, 203, 204
Guadalajara (city), 21, 25, 45, 102, 167; annual accounts, 90; cathedral, 151; coat of arms, 146; history, 167; mining, 73; rebellion (1935), 227
Guadalajara (province): archdiocese, 101, 167; estates, 197; military records, 171; politics and government, 93
Guadalcázar, Diego Fernández de Córdova, Marqués de, viceroy, 1612-1621, 91, 128
Guadalupe (insurgents), 135
Guadalupe, mission (Lower California), 222
Guadalupe Hidalgo, Treaty of, 91
Guadalupe Hidalgo, church, 12
Guaicuru Indians, 221, 222-223
Guanajas Islands, Honduras, 53
Guanajuato, 91, 166; description, 25; mining, 73, 166; 194
Guasabas, 149, 220; mission (Guasave), 220, 221
Guatemala, 9, 42; antiquities, 42, 62, 188, 260; agriculture, 54; archdiocese, 234; biographies, 91-92; boundaries, 89; commerce, 54; description and travel, 58-59, 62, 84-85, 142, 233; Franciscans, 54, 59, 62, 85, 128, 247; harbors, 8, 49; history, 33, 49, 54, 62, 81-82, 83, 84-85, 92, 144, 214, 233-234, 246, 260; hospitals, 247; Indians, 42, 54, 58-59, 62, 78, 81-82, 84-85, 92, 108, 112, 142, 143, 155, 188, 191, 246, 251, 260; map, 85; marriages, 197; mining, 54, 142, 233; missions, 54, 58-59, 62, 65, 84-85, 223, 247, 251; natural resources, 58, 142; politics and government, 69-70, 134-135, 136, 205, 230; ports, 8, 49, 66; presidents and captains general, 33, 143, 233-234; Real Audiencia, 39, 66, 70, 114, 230; relations with Honduras, 91; relations with Mexico, 145, 199; roads, 42, 78; Roman Catholic Church, 95, 108, 197, 230, 234 (list of bishops); social life and customs, 233; sugar industry, 82; taxation, 58-59. *See also* Central America
Guatemala (city), 17-18, 64, 66, 70; conquest, 62; history, 62; map, 85; municipal archives, 84-85; politics and government, 84-85
Guaymas (Sonora), 51, 87, 176, 195; defense, 96; description, 25; map, 30; railroad, 87
Guaymi Indians, 61; linguistics, 78-79
Güemes, Manuel de, 206
Güemes y Horcasitas, Juan Francisco de, 1st Conde de Revilla Gigedo, viceroy, 1746-1755, 61, 63, 223
Güemes Pacheco de Padilla, Juan Vicente de, 2nd Conde de Revilla Gigedo, viceroy, 1789-1794, 9, 34, 45, 72, 118, 125, 192, 193-194, 218; instructions of, 194; residencia, 193

Guerra, García, abp. and viceroy, 1611-1612, 79
Guerrero, Vicente de, 28
Guerrero (Mexico), 132
Guevara, Felipe de, 258
Guijo, Alonso del, 200
Guilds, 21, 39, 43, 138, 142, 166, 186, 207
Guillén, Clemente, 223
Guillén II, Lord of Ariza, 163
Guirior, Manuel, viceroy of New Granada, 9, 170
Guizot, 93
Gunpowder, 10, 109
Gutiérrez, Manuel, 164
Gutiérrez Dávila, Julián, 127
Gutiérrez de Lanzas, Matías, 259
Gutiérrez Huesca, Manuel, 41
Gutiérrez Montealegre, Jerónimo, 100
Gutiérrez y Ulloa, Antonio, 93
Guyama, Honduras, 53
Guzmán, José María, 93
Guzmán, Martín Luis, 257
Guzmán, Nuño Beltrán de. *See* Beltrán de Guzmán
Guzmán Blanco, Antonio, 249

Habberton, John, 93
Haberl, Georgius, 224
Habig, Marion A., 93
Haciendas
—Guatemala, Los Llanos, 58
—Mexico, 74, 93, 206; Bocas, 12; Carrizal (Nuevo León), 93; Chilcuacán, 258; Hueyapam, 113; Illescas, 12; Isclaguacán, 113; Rocaferro, 113; San Agustín de los Amoles, 206; Santa María (Sonora), 146; Tamariz (Chalco), 248; Temisco, 152
Hack, William, 94
Haiti, 67; relations with Santo Domingo, 211-212; Roman Catholic Church, 215
Hale, Edward Everett, 94
Hall, E. A., 95
Hall family, 259
Halleck, Henry Wager, 13
Hamburg, Germany, 63
Hamilton, J. B., 94
Harding, George Laban, 94
Harris, Joseph, 105
Havana, 45; history, 94
Hawaii, linguistics, 122, 254
Haya Fernández, Diego de la, 94-95
Hayes, Benjamin, 60

Heceta (Hezeta), Bruno de, 125-126
Heizer, Robert Fleming, 95
Henares, Santiago de, 12, 233
Henderson, Simeon Reddick, 95
Henríquez, Joseph Andrés, 95
Henry, William, 244
Heraldry, Guatemala, 64; Mexico, 64, 146, 151; Spain, 64, 126
Heredia y Sarmiento, José Ignacio, 95
Herera, Nicolás de, 219
Herize, Ignacio de, 95-96
Hermosillo (Sonora), 96
Hernáez, Francisco Javier, 96
Hernáez, Gregorio, 219
Hernández, Juan, 96
Hernández, Santiago, 200
Hernández Cházaro, Francisco, 18
Herrán, Jerónimo, 175
Herrera, Vasco de, 37
Herrera y Montemayor, Juan, 96
Herrera y Tordesillas, Antonio de, 261
Hervas, Santos, 96
Hidalgo: history, 158-159; Indians, 177
Hidalgo y Costillo, Miguel, 84, 255
Hieroglyphics: Mayan, 63; Mexican, 71, 73
Hierro, Simón del, 141
Hildebrand, Milton, 96
Hill, Roscoe R., 97
Hinchman, 97
Hintze, P. von, 133
Hispanic America: Franciscans, 231; French activities, 61; history, 234; laws, 88; mining, 203-204; missions, 193; Roman Catholic Church, 23-24, 56, 139-140, 193, 230, 247; slave labor, 60; wills, 231
Hispaniola (Española): Indians, 155; politics and government, 229-230; rebellion in, 211
Hodges, Harry F., 245
Holmer, Nils Magnus, 97
Honduras, 20; description, 108, 242; drawings, 108; economics, 27; genealogy, 69-70; harbors, 8, 49; history, 36, 37, 49, 69-70, 84-85, 104; Indians, 9, 37, 70, 168; land, 168; mining, 229, 242; natural resources, 229; politics and government, 69-70, 142; ports, 8, 49, 66, 85, 104; presidents, 27; relations with Guatemala, 91. *See also* Central America
Hope (sloop), log, 169
Horcasitas, Francisco Antonio de, 207
Hospital de Jesús Nazareno, Mexico City, 28
Hospital del Amor de Dios, 189
Hospitals: Guatemala, 247; Mexico, 26, 28, 43, 121, 132, 138, 142, 162, 189, 190, 207, 258
Hovey, Charles Mason, 97
Howard, Thomas, 97
Hoyos Mier, Luis Fernando de, 263
Huantajaya Mine, Tarapacá, Peru, 98
Huarochiri (province), Peru, 112
Huehuetoca Canal, 72, 190
Huejotzingo (Puebla), taxation, 63
Huejuquilla (Nueva Vizcaya), 63-64; lands, 98
Huerta, Adolfo de la, 238
Hueyapam, hacienda, 113
Hugo de Omerick, Ignacio Joseph de, 98
Huidobro, Manuel Bernal de, 252, 260
Humacao, Puerto Rico, 187
Humarisa, mission, 219
Humboldt, Alexander, Freiherr von, 98, 122
Hunter, Dard, 99
Hurtado de Castilla, José, 259
Hurtado de Mendoza, Diego, 163
Hyde, Albert A., 99

Ibáñez, José Manuel de, 99
Ibarra, Francisco de, 189
Ibarra, Roque, 175
Idiaquez, Antonio de, 219, 221
Iglesias, José María, 55, 99
Iglesias, Miguel, 119
Iglesias Pablo, Ignacio, 193
Illanes, Mario, 100
Illarregui, Miguel Francisco de, 99
Illescas, hacienda, 12
Immaculate Conception, Order of the. *See* Conceptionists
Immaculate Conception Con-

INDEX 277

vent, Caracas, Venezuela, 250
Inca Indians, 114, 142
Indians
—America, 35, 97, 193; conversion of, 34; customs, 34, 177; legends, 177; linguistics, 73; origins, 32, 73; revolts, 224; treatment of, 60, 197-198, 230
—Bolivia, 11; labor, 184
—British Honduras, 42
—Californias, 10, 46, 218, 232
—Central America, 9, 18, 104, 155, 192, 232; culture, 63; expedition against, 17-18; linguistics, 177; treatment of, 65, 147
—Chile, 40
—Colombia, 4-5, 195-196
—Costa Rica, 18, 94-95
—El Salvador, 65
—Española, 155
—Florida, 165
—Guatemala, 42, 54, 58-59, 62, 78, 84-85, 92, 108, 112, 142, 143, 155, 188, 191, 251, 260; disturbances, 62; human sacrifice, 191; religion and mythology, 84, 188, 260; social life and customs, 260; treatment of, 246; uprising in Chiapas, 81-82; — of Chiapas, 81-82; Chichicastenango, 260; Cobán, 58-59; Quiché, 260; Verapaz, 62, 78, 142
—Honduras, 9, 37, 70, 168
—Louisiana territory, 116-117
—Mexico, 3, 40-41, 43, 67, 71, 77, 88, 95, 114, 127, 174, 182, 193; antiquities, 39; biographies, 127; conscription, 220; conversion, 98, 217, 238; culture, 155-156, 201; education, 29, 38; genealogy, 156, government, 144, 263; health, 38; history, 42, 240-241; labor, 38, 57, 82, 191; marriage, 123; pacification, 19, 61, 252; religion and mythology, 62, 67, 110, 127, 155-156; rights, 83, 239; slavery, 216, 228; social life and customs, 103; taxation, 263; treatment of, 36, 37-39, 55, 57, 64, 100, 114, 134, 174, 199, 229-230, 231, 240, 247; tribute, 37-39, 100; uprisings, 49-50, 51, 81-82, 154, 181, 190,

196, 215, 217, 218, 219, 222, 227, 228, 260; —of Atempa, 122; Bacalar (Yucatan), 59; Baja Pimería, 252; Caborca, 177; Californias, 10, 46, 232; Chiapas, 58-59, 62, 81-82; Chihuahua, 38, 40, 148, 176; Chontalcuatlán, 109; Coahuila, 50; Cuernavaca, 38; Culiacán, 235; Durango, 21, 89, 110; Gila River, 227, 228; Hidalgo, 177; Huejotitán, 47; Lower California, 14, 196, 218; Mexico City, 38; Meztitlán, 39; Michoacán, 5, 100; Morelia, 100; Nativitas, 39; Nueva Galicia, 46, 93, 146; Nueva Vizcaya, 16, 19, 50, 63, 64, 154, 189; Oaxaca, 27, 42; Ostimuri, 220; Pátzcuaro, 57; Provincias Internas, 49-50, 83; Puebla, 152, 186; San Andrés de Conicari, 219; San Ignacio, 177; San Luis Potosí (state), 177; Sinaloa, 5, 61, 127, 218, 226, 239, 260; Sonora, 51, 53, 61, 174, 175, 176, 220, 227-228, 239, 260; Tabasco, 127-128; Tascaltitlán, 192; Texas, 100, 145, 238; Teziutlán, 122; Tlaxcala, 38, 127, 211, 231, 238, 240; Toluca, 38, 48; Tonalá(n), 46; Tubutama, 177; Upper California, 254; Yucatan, 58-59, 62; Zinacantepec, 38
—New Granada, 238
—Nicaragua, 9, 42
—Panama, 9, 78-79, 97, 192
—Paraguay, 225
—Peru, 33, 114, 170-171, 193; conversion, 238; forced labor, 98; religion and mythology, 112, 142; treatment of, 57; —of Huarochiri, 112
—South America, 199, 216
See also Aztec Indians, Pima Indians, etc.
Indian Linguistics. See Linguistics
Indulgences, Mexico, 55, 76, 207, 210, 263; Philippine Islands, 210
Industry, 57, 86, 100, 185-186; gunpowder, 10; sugar, 82, 143, 234
Inga (Inca), Bernardo, 114
Innocent XI, Pope, 92

Innocent XII, Pope, 207
Innocent XIII, Pope, 207
Inquisition, 194, 231, 255; Honduras, 69-70; Mexico, 68, 70, 96, 98, 100-101, 130, 151, 197, 199, 200, 201, 219; Philippine Islands, 101; Portugal, 7; Spain, 7, 163, 225
Institute of Pacific Relations, 150
Intendancies, 72, 81, 252
Inter-American Highway, 101
International Company of Mexico, 8, 18-19, 69, 86, 101, 213
Iriarte, Francisco, 43, 175, 227-228
Irnaz, Patricio de, 219
Irrigation, 72; Mexico City, 203; Querétaro, 106
Isabel I, La Católica, 101, 122, 191
Isclaguacán, hacienda, 113
Isla, José Francisco de, 140
Islas, Francisco, 43, 176
Isunza, Francisco J., 101-102
Iturbide, Agustín de, 29, 102, 174, 209, 246
Iturmendi, Ignacio, 181
Iturria, María Amo, 158
Iturrigaray y Aróstegui, José Manuel de, viceroy, 1803-1808, 36, 102, 134
Itzá Indians, 59, 62, 104
Ixil Indians, 112; linguistics, 197
Ixtlilxochitl, Fernando de Alba, 103-104
Izaguirre, Pedro de, 104

Jackson, Andrew, 104, 231
Jackson, Robert Houghwout, 104
Jackson & Company, 104
Jacobinism, in Mexico, 170
Jacobs, E., 104
Jaillandier, Père, 104-105
Jails, 57, 164, 243
Jalapa, 64, 128, 130, 255
Jalisco, 20, 105, 167; presidents of, 167
Jamapa River, 72
Jamieson, Stuart, 105
Janos presidio, 40, 43, 64, 154; Indians, 176
Janssens, Jan, 105
Japanese, in Lower California, 235
Jáuregui y Aróstegui, María Inés, 134
Javero, José María, 131

Jecker, Jean Baptiste, 119
Jerez, Máximo, 150
Jesuits. *See* Society of Jesus
Jesús Arce, José Ignacio de, 105
Jesús María, mining camp, 228
Jewitt, H. J., 105
Jicaque Indians, 70, 92, 168
Jiménez, Antonio, 200
Jiménez, Francisco. *See* Ximénez, Francisco
Jiménez Caro, Francisco, 38
Jiménez de Quesada, Gonzalo, 4-5
Jiménez Moreno, Wigberto, 157, 178
Jones, John R., 105
Jones, Moses Z., 106
José, Martín, 121
Joseph Napoleon, 186
Journalism, 29, 41, 237-238
Juana Inés de la Cruz, Sor, 121
Juárez, Benito, 5, 13, 41, 55, 66, 74, 105, 115, 126, 129, 201; action against the French, 247
Juchipila, 151
Julius III, Pope, 87
Junker von Langegg, Ferdinand Adalbert, 106
Junta de Aguas de la Zanja Madre del Río de Querétaro, 106
Junta de Fomento, 132-133
Junta de Minería, 132-133
"Juntas Patrióticas," 247
Juzgado de Indios, 106

Kautz, Albert, 106
Keith, William, 26
Kempis, Antonio, 222
Kerr, Clark, 106
Kewen, Edward John Cage, 106
Kidder, D. G., 107
Kindelan y O'Regan, Sebastián, 211
Kingsborough, Edward King, 73, 103
Kinnaird, Lawrence, 107, 116
Kino, Eusebio Francisco, 77, 107, 181, 217, 219, 221, 227
Klein, John C., 107
Kleinschmidt, Heinrich, 107
Knight, William Henry, 130
Korea, 78; relations with France, 78; relations with U. S., 77, 150
Kunstmann, Friedrich, 107
Kuykendall, Ralph Simpson, 107

Labor, 38, 82, 105, 130, 147, 191, 236
Lacandón Indians, 59, 108, 191, 251
Lacayo, Marco H., 108
Lacy (Lasci), Conde de, 72
Ladrón de Guevara, Joaquín, 209
Lafora, Nicolás de, 72
Lagos, 102
La Harpe, de, 126
Lamar, Mirabeau Buonaparte, 66
Lamburu, Marcos, 82
Lancaster, Joseph, 25
Lancaster-Jones, Alfonso, 141; Collection, 120, 141
Land
—British Guiana, 24
—Honduras, 168
—Mexico, 98, 168, 239, 240; distribution, 128, 174, 204, 210; grants, 35, 58, 128, 239, 248; laws, 36, 98, 203-204; measurement, 88, 203-204, 261; public, 137; reform, 130; titles, 128, 130, 134, 137, 146, 147-148, 156, 177, 203, 206, 208, 239-240; in Coahuila, 185, 239; Lower California, 35, 58, 105, 138, 203; Nueva Galicia, 46, 151; Nueva Vizcaya, 98, 206; San Mateo Ixtlahuaca, 208; Santa Isabel, 206; Santa María la Redonda, 210; Sonora, 146, 174, 175, 239-240; Texas, 239; Zacatecas, 119
—Philippine Islands, 234
—United States, 104, 229, 245, 254, 259
—Venezuela, 250
Land Tribunal (Sonora y Sinaloa), 239-240
Landero, José Juan, 131
Lanning, John Tate, 243
Lansing, Robert, 108
La Opinión, 227
La Patria, 237
La Paz, 229
Lapérouse, Jean François de Galaup, Comte de, 61, 108
Laredo, Domingo, 56
Larraguiti, Juan Nicolás de, 134
Larrañaga, Juan Ignacio, 110
Lasuén, Fermín Francisco de, 141
Lathrop, Máximo, 249
Latorre, Carlos, 108

Laughlin, Samuel H., 183
Laws of Burgos, 155
Laws of the Indies, 29, 230, 246; index to, 261
Lazo, J. S., 108
Lebrón y Cuervo, José, 246, 261
Lee, Robert Edward, 89
Leebrick, Karl Clayton, 173
Lefebvre, Alfred, 109
Legal cases, 53, 56, 58, 84, 109-110, 156, 157, 168, 240, 241
Legaré, Hugh Swinton, 111
Lemos, Manuel Gayoso, 117
Lench, Patricio, 111
León, Alonso de, 60, 126
León, J. J., 111
León, Luis L., 257
León y Gama, Antonio de, 111
Leonard, Henry P., 111
Lerdo de Tejada, Sebastián, 41, 115
Lerma, Duque de, 169
Letona, Lisandro, 91
Levasseur, André, 226
Liceaga, Andrés de, 259
Liga Nacional Defensora de la Libertad Religiosa, 160
Lima, Peru, 237; description and travel, 96
Linares, Duque de. *See* Alencastre Noroña y Silva
Linck, Wenceslaus, 112
Lincoln, Jackson Steward, 112
Lingayen Gulf, 7
Linguistics: American Indians, 73; Aztec, 3, 16-17, 19, 30-31, 40-41, 43, 121, 123, 128, 140, 142, 146, 147-148, 154-155, 178, 201, 204, 210, 212, 214, 228; Cackchiquel, 188, 260; Chiquita, 11; Choco, 179; Cuna, 97; Durasque, 78-79; Guaymi, 78-79; Ixil, 197; Matlatzinca, 15, 179; Mazahua, 125, 180; Mixtec, 42; Opata, 118, 178 (Hehué and Tehuima dialects), 179; Otomí, 6, 40-41, 125, 157, 179, 208-209, (Pame dialect) 180; Pápago, 179; Pima, 18, 178; Pokoman, 143; Quiché, 197, 260; Seri, 179; Tarascan, 249; Timucuan, 165; Tzental, 178; Tzotzil, 178; Tzutuhil, 260; Yaqui, 51; Yunga, 33; Zapotec, 42; Zoque, 178; of Brazil, 52, 254 (Manao); California, 218; Central America, 177;

INDEX

Hawaii, 122, 254; Mexico, 109, 121, 177-179; Nootka, 122, 254; Patagonia, 254; San Luis Potosí, 177
Lipan Indians, 50, 154, 238
Lira Chihuahuense, La, 237
List Arzubide, Germán, 257
Literature: Mexico, 10, 139-140, 205, 208, 212, 214; Spain, 163-164. *See also* Drama, Poetry, etc.
Livestock: Mexico, 44, 61, 81; Santo Domingo, 211
Livingston, Edward, 113
Lizana y Beaumont, Francisco Javier de, viceroy, 1809-1810, 113, 123-124
Llave, Pablo de la, 69
Llevaria, Juan Francisco, 198
Llisa, Pedro de, 177
Loaysa, Francisco de, 228
Lobato, José María, 43
Lobo, Manuel, 247
Logbooks, 89, 113, 159, 169
Lombardo Toledano, Vicente, 257
Lope de Vega. *See* Vega Carpio
López, Domingo Antonio, 49
López, Francisco, 113
López, Gregorio, 113-114
López, Patricio Antonio, 114
López de Gómara, Antonio and Francisco, 261
López de Haro, Gonzalo, 114
López de la Mota Padilla. *See* Mota Padilla
López de León, Antonio, 259
López de Solís, Juan Francisco, 87
López Gonzalo, Victoriano, bp., 87, 240
López Matoso, Antonio Ignacio, 114
López Pacheco, Diego. *See* Escalona
López Portillo, Antonio, 11, 114-115
López Portillo y Rojas, José, 240
López Rayón, Ignacio, 115
López Uraga, José, 115
Lorca y Villena, Melchor Vidal de, 111
Lorenz de Rada, Francisco, 182
Lorenzana y Butrón, Francisco Antonio, abp. and cardinal, 77, 98, 201, 253
Loreto, 65; mission, 222
Loreto Conchó, 220

Los Angeles (California), proclamation of capital, 115
Losa, Pedro, abp., 198
Lossada, Francisco de, 219
Loudon, De Witt Clinton, diaries, 115-116
Louisiana: administration, 116-117, 126; boundaries, 238; defense, 117; exploration, 145; history, 60, 116-117, 125, 214; Indians, 116-117, 126; trading posts, 116
Louisiana Papers, 116-117
Lovatt, William Nelson, 117
Lower California. *See* California, Lower
Lowery, Woodbury, 118
Lowfeld, Battle of, 163
Lowrie, Mrs. John R., 118
Lucio, Antonio, 109
Ludlow, Volney P., 118
Lumbier, Rafael, 228
Luna, Espinosa and Raphael de, 211
Luna, Felipe S., 118
Luyando y Guerrero, Manuel Monrroy de, 118
Luyando y Vermeo, Luis Miguel, 258
Luzon, burial records, 172

Macati, Philippine Islands, 172
Macdonald, Charles J., 118
Macdonough, Thomas, 118
Machado, Doctor, 110
MacKenzie, Robert Shelton, 119
Macuspana (Tabasco), 201
Madallán, Mother Clara de, 45
Madero, Francisco I., 237, 240, 256
Madison, James, 119, 126
Madrid, José Francisco de la, 94
Madrid, Manuel de la, 102
Madrid, Manuel J., 119
Magallanes, Francisco, Juan, and Mariano, 119
Magallanes, José Yrineo, 119
Magdalena, mission, baptismal, marriage, burial records, 181
Magnus, A. von, 133
Maguey cultivation, 23
Maguire, John, 84
Mail routes, 50, 151, 175
Maison de Mexique, 109
Maison de Paris, 109
Maldonado, Angel, bp., 199
Maldonado, Simón, 119

Mame Indians, 191
Manero, Vicente E., 119
Mange, Juan Mateo, 120, 190, 227
Mangin, Antide, 120
Mangino, Fernando José, 125, 164
Maniau y Torquemada, José Nicolás, 69, 120
Manila: archdiocese, 167; Battle of, 68; capture by British, 172-173; elections, 120; galleons, 128-129; military affairs, 75, 113; municipal administration, 120; public ceremonies, 120
Mañozca, Lucas de, 121
Manrique, Aurelio, 257
Manso y Zúñiga, Francisco, abp., 3, 121
Manuel de los Angeles, 121
Maps and charts
—America (Behaim and Humboldt), 54, 122
—Canary Islands, 54
—Colombia, 185
—Ecuador, 185
—Guatemala, 84-85
—Mexico, battles, 29, 115, 121; California, 249; Chalcatongo, 44; Chihuahua, 25; frontier presidios, 72; Gila River, 76; Guaymas, 30; Jesús Carichic mission, 219; Lower California, 219, 232; Matamoros, 29, 244; Mazatlán, 30; Mexican towns and states, 25; Mexico City, 34, 127; mining, 25, 203-204; Nayarit, 141; Nayarit missions, 218; northern Mexico, 25, 244; Provincias Internas, 24, 243; Puebla, 6, 13; San Andrés de Conicari, 219; San Feliz de Mazatlán, 30; San Francisco, 76; Sinaloa, 30, 220, 226; Sonora, 24, 30, 191, 218, 220, 226; Tlahuac, 147-148; Tulancingo, 242; U. S. army campaign maps, 244; Veracruz, 162, 168; Yaqui Valley, 228
—North Pacific Coast, 13
—Pacific Coast, 131, 237
—Panama, 185
—Portugal, 54
—Puerto Rico, 187
—Spain, 54
—Vieques, 187
—West Indies, 54
Maracaibo, Lake, 250

280 INDEX

Marcos, Diego, 43
Marcy, William L., 183
Margil de Jesús, Antonio, 60, 162
María (steam yacht), 249
María Luisa de Borbón, 163
María Magdalena, Mother, autobiography, 121-122
María Santísima de los Dolores, mission. *See* Santa Gertrudis mission
Mariana, Juan de, 224
Marín, Enrique, 56
Marín de Moya, Diego, 263
Marín de Porras, Primo Feliciano, bp., 165
Mariscal, Manuel, 82
Marriage, 15, 36; Guatemala, 197, 260; Mexico, 77, 87, 95, 96, 123-124, 154, 199, 200, 231
Marriage records
—Mexico, Acatlán, 3; Bisanig, 181; Caborca, 177; Caburica, 181; Chiapas, 39, 75; Magdalena, 181; Nuevo León, 165; Pitaqui, 182; Real de San Ildefonso de Cieneguilla, 180; San Vicente Ferrer, 208; Santa Ana Pueblo, 181; Santa Cruz (Santa María Soamca), 181; Santísimo Rosario, 211; Santo Domingo, 212; Tlaltizapán, 240; Tubac, 181; Velicatá, 206
—Panama, Panama City, 160; San Francisco Xavier de Cañazas, 160
—Philippine Islands, Batangas, 16; Pasig, 167
Martínez, Esteban José, 113, 114, 122; voyage, 72
Martínez, Francisco, 60
Martínez, Manuel, 122
Martínez de la Rosa, Francisco, 263
Martínez de Piña, Alonso, 109
Martínez de Vea, Luis, 228
Martínez Pacheco, Rafael, 50
Martínez Velasco, Antonio, 76
Martyrs, 127, 146, 190, 222, 236
Mascaró, Manuel Agustín, diary, 72
Masons. *See* Freemasons
Massanet, Damián, 60
Matamoros, 52, 88, 122-123; battle of, 29; maps, 29, 244
Mateo, Lucas, 123
Mathers, Alonzo M., 123

Matlatzinca Indians, linguistics, 15
Matthews, Robert L., family papers, 124
Matzahua. *See* Mazahua
Maurits, Johan, 55
Maximilian, Ferdinand, Emperor of Mexico, 33, 71, 73-74, 87, 115, 119, 125, 139, 157
Maya Indians, 63, 252, 260
Mayer, Brantz, 60, 125-126, 212
Máynez, Alberto, 174
Mayo, mission, 221
Mayorga, Julián de, 236
Mayorga, Martín de, viceroy, 1779-1784, 87
Mazahua Indians, linguistics, 125, 180
Mazateve Alvarado family, genealogy, 126
Mazatlán, 88, 167, 198; description, 159; map, 30
Mazurriaga, Juan de, 87
Measles, 182
Media Anata, 133
Medicine, 111, 194, 249
Medina, Baltasar de, 127
Medina, Juan de, 188
Medina, María Teresa de, 110
Mediterranean Sea: description, 27, 239; trade, 63
Medrano y Peñaloza, Manuel, 126
Mejía, Ignacio, 19, 126
Mejía, Tomás, 139
Meléndez Bazán, Antonio, 258
Meléndez Bruna, Salvador, 186
Melero y Fernández, José Honorato, 111
Mellon, W. L., 68
Mendes da Silva, João. *See* Amadeus, Beatus
Méndez, Juan N., 55
Méndez de Hinostrosa, Diego, 37
Méndez de Vigo, Santiago, 187
Mendieta Rebollo, Gabriel de, 138
Mendigure, Andrés, 112, 170
Mendoza, Antonio de, Conde de Tendilla, viceroy, 1535-1550, 7, 103, 144, 146, 148, 204
Mendoza, Baltasar de, 70
Mendoza, José María, 177
Mendoza, Mateo Antonio de, 63-64
Menéndez, Francisco, 205-206

Mercedarians: in Guatemala, 251; in Mexico, 53, 100, 135, 244, 258; in Spain, 225
Merchant's Board of Seville, 109
Mercury. *See* Quicksilver
Merelo, Angel María, 130
Mescalero Indians, 50, 154
Mexía, José Antonio, family papers, 129
Mexía, Ynés, 129
Mexican Company, The, 129
Mexican Immigration to the United States (Gamio), 81
Mexican National Railway System, 97, 188-189
Mexico: agriculture, 29, 44, 50, 57, 75, 82, 109, 123, 131-132, 195, 201, 206, 215, 218, 227, 252; antiquities, 18, 27, 29, 39, 40-41, 42, 62, 63, 67, 71, 73, 103-104, 121, 144, 150, 155-156, 212, 240-241; archdiocese, 164, 241; army, 26, 36, 113, 184, 200; banking, 109; botany, 109; boundary disputes, 42; colonization, 77; commerce, 7, 8, 18, 52, 53, 86, 98, 109, 128-129, 144, 252, 253; congress, 64; conquest, 69, 103, 240-241; courts, 14, 114, 157; description and travel, 7, 14, 22, 23, 25, 27, 31, 89-90, 102, 104-105, 195, 232, 236; diaries, 28, 30, 50, 51-52, 72, 74, 75, 76, 80, 85-86, 112, 120, 122, 126, 154, 166, 195; discovery and exploration, 149, 153, 214, 217, 241; economics, 29, 68, 80, 131-132, 236, 252; education, 25, 29, 38, 105, 128, 131-132, 138, 185, 213, 223, 249 (*see also* Education); estates, 12, 74, 193, 200, 206, 207, 237, 241, 257-259; European intervention, 33, 119, 126, 129, 133, 139, 205, 244, 247; filibustering activities, 11, 32, 63, 80, 96, 133, 195, 226, 239; finances, 68, 86, 91, 131, 134, 164, 183, 194; foreign investments, 208; foreign relations, 133, 228 (*see also* Mexico, relations with France, etc.); foreign trade, 109, 119, 130; foreigners, 91; genealogies, 15-16, 41, 64, 70, 100, 130, 151,

156, 157, 166, 190, 199, 211, 226, 240; geography, 85, 98, 103; history, 11, 17, 23-24, 28, 29, 30, 41, 43, 55, 57, 61, 67, 103-104, 104-105, 107, 112, 115, 125, 129, 130, 130-131, 133, 144, 174-177, 190-191, 236, 239, 242, 246, 253, 261; immigration, 88; independence, 43, 246; Indians, see Indians, Mexico; industry, 10, 57, 82, 86, 100, 143, 185-186, 234; jurisprudence, 14, 43, 57, 99, 114, 252; land, see Land, Mexico; legal cases, 53, 109-110, 156, 157, 168, 240, 241; linguistics, see Linguistics, Mexico; local government, 5, 130, 214; military affairs, 19, 30, 32, 43, 47, 63, 64, 80, 98, 138, 140, 174-177, 246; mining, see Mines and mineral resources, Mexico; mints and coinage, 50, 88, 111, 170, 182, 191, 213, 261; natural resources, 17; northern states, 43, 61, 63, 129, 174-177, 239; "Pastry War," 28, 74-75, 246; politics and government, 5, 27, 29, 30, 33, 39-40, 41, 43, 55, 74-75, 85-86, 99, 129, 130, 134, 140, 143, 144, 145, 157, 164, 174, 175, 210, 227, 229-230, 238, 246, 252; population, 86, 98; ports, 30, 76, 83; presidents, 33, listed, 130; public health, 38, 130; publications, 28, 29, 30; race problems, 130; railroads, 25, 41, 80, 87, 97, 145, 157, 188-189, 208; relations with France, 5, 28, 74-75, 113, 246, 247, 248; relations with Germany, 133; relations with Great Britain, 3, 22, 33, 75, 205; relations with Guatemala, 145, 199; relations with the U.S., 28, 41, 52, 58, 85, 87-88, 125-126, 129, 131, 145, 176, 215, 245, 256; revolution, 29, 43, 147, 194; rivers, 10, 45, 76, 96, 131-132, 138, 223, 227, 228, 244; roads, 13, 25, 30, 104-105, 151, 157, 162; Roman Catholic Church, see Roman Catholic Church; slavery, 100, 131, 151, 216, 228; social conditions, 14, 131-132, 157; social life and customs, 74, 85-86, 90, 115, 129, 237; social reforms, 29; statistics, 75, 86, 98, 194; street lighting, 193; Supreme Court, 57, 99, 210; tariffs, 175, 186, 188-189, 202; taxation, 9, 34, 39, 40, 60, 63, 91, 98, 109, 111, 121, 122, 130, 133, 134, 136, 144, 159, 199, 231, 263; tobacco, 29, 36, 60, 130, 164; trade with the Philippines, 230, 253; Tumult of 1624, 23, 189-190; War with the U.S., 13, 15, 16, 28, 29, 30, 48, 51-52, 59, 79-80, 118, 129, 131, 139, 143, 167, 170, 245, 255, 259, maps, 115, 244; Wars of Independence (1812-1821), 64, 112, 205, 255; water, 72, 106, 203-204, 261; wills, 156, 168, 174, 182, 190, 197, 237, 241, 257-259. See also New Spain

Mexico City, 45, 75, 190; Department of Health and Welfare (records), 138; fiscal affairs, 138; hospitals, 28, 121, 207; Indians, 38; irrigation, 203; Junta de Fomento de Artesanos, 57; laws, 230; maps and plans, 34, 127; markets, 57; municipal government, 136, 137, 138, 155, 190-191; parishes, 38; public works, 34, 138, 193; real estate records, 97; Roman Catholic Church, 37, 241; social life and customs, 14; viceregal palace, 153

Mexico City Cathedral, 12, 37, 164, 189, 191, 197, 200, 233, 241, 248, 258, 263

Mexico City Crusade Tribunal, 209

Mexico, Gulf of, 75

Mexico, Valley of, 72; drainage, 119; maps and charts, 119

Mezcalapán, 199

Mézierès, Athanase de, 60, 116, 126

Meztitlán (province), 39

Michoacán, 57, 103, 132; diocese, 5, 200; Franciscans in, 17; Indians, 5, 100; missions, 5; tribute, 100

Mier, Servando, 29

Miguel, Domingo, 219

Milatovich, Antonio, 138
Milla, Juan Esteban, 176
Milla y Vidaurre, José, 229
Miller, William, 139
Mimbela, Manuel de, bp., 258
Mines and mineral resources
—Bolivia, 184
—Colombia, 185
—Colorado, 194
—Costa Rica, 71
—Ecuador, 185
—Guatemala, 54 (Zapotitlán), 142 (Verapaz), 233
—Honduras, 229, 242
—Indies, 203-204
—Mexico, 22, 25 (maps), 36, 44, 73, 80, 89-90, 98, 107, 111, 129, 130, 132-133, 135, 139, 147, 203-204 (maps); Bolaños district, 21; Chihuahua, 21, 25; Cieneguilla, 174; companies, 21; Durango, 189; Guanajuato, 73, 166; Jesuit ownership of, 219; legislation, 110; Lower California, 18-19, 59; northern frontier, 174; Nueva Galicia, 93; Pachuca, 73, 158, 159-160; Real de Santa Eulalia, 81; Sinaloa, 44; Sonora, 22, 44, 46, 90, 107, 174, 188, 195, 210; Tepic, 52; Zacatecas, 73
—Nicaragua, 36
—Panama, 78-79, 185
—Peru, 98
—Yukon Territory, 97
See also Gold mining, Silver mining, etc.

Mints, 88, 213, 261. See also Coinage
Miqueo, Joseph, 220
Mira de Amescua, Antonio, 31
Miramón, Joaquín, family papers, 139
Miramón, Miguel, 139, 196
Miranda, Francisco Javier, 139
Miranda, Francisco Montero de. See Montero de Miranda
Miranda, Francisco Palacios, 13
Miranda, Jacinto, 53, 56, 85, 247
Miranda, Miguel, 250-251
Miró, Esteban, 116-117
Missionaries, Mexico, 24, 46, 48, 49, 50, 189, 213, 217, 218, 219, 221, 222; Venezuela, 187. See also Missions, Franciscans, Society of Jesus, etc.

Missions
—Central America, 58-59
—El Salvador, 65
—Florida, 118
—Guatemala, 54, 58-59, 62, 65, 84-85, 247, 251
—Hispanic America, 193
—Mexico, 28, 46, 71, 77, 78, 123, 125, 140, 141, 180-181, 200, 210, 213, 217, 238; Arizona, 93; Californias, 10, 46, 72, 125, 182, 219, 220, 221, 222; Chiapas, 58-59, 62; Chihuahua, 50, 235; Coahuila, 141, 218; Colotlán, 218; Durango, 88, 218; frontier, 112, 174; Lower California, 27, 59, 65, 112, 140, 141, 196, 206, 208, 211, 217-223, 224, 226, 236, 249; Michoacán, 5; Nayarit, 77, 218, 219; New Mexico, 21, 149, 218, 229-230; Nueva Galicia, 93, 141; Nueva Vizcaya, 16, 36, 60, 88, 141; Nuevo León, 141, 218; Nuevo Santander, 141; Pame Indians, 180; Pimería, 53, 57, 107, 175, 180, 222, 223; Provincias Internas, 24; Sahuaripa, 110; San Joseph de Temeichi, 217; Santander, 218; Sierra Gorda, 218; Sinaloa, 5, 77, 217-223, 226; Sonora, 24, 53, 57, 77, 93, 217-223, 227-228, 239; Tarahumara, 77, 235, 236; Texas, 60, 125, 141, 145, 218; Tumacácori, 123, 175; Upper California, 72, 93, 107, 141, 218
—New Granada, 238
—Nicaragua, 38
—Paraguay, 163, 224, 225
—Peru, 238
—Philippine Islands, 213, 221, 224, 238
—Uruguay, 224
See also individual mission names
Mississippi River: exploration, 42, 145; Valley, 116-117
Mitla, 150, 212
Mixco, Guatemala, 84
Mixtec Indians, linguistics, 42
Mixteca Alta, parish archives, 21
Möbius, Paul, 141
Moctezuma, 46, 131, 261
Moctezuma, Conde de. *See* Sarmiento Valladares

Moe, Alfred Keane, 142
Molina, Alonso de, 142
Molina, Cristóbal de, 142
Molina de Salama, Simón, abp., 58-59
Molino del Rey, Battle of, 115
Molsheim, France, 257
Monarchy, 134; in Mexico, 29
Monasteries: El Salvador, 65; Guatemala, 54, 62, 251; Mexico, 38, 39, 47, 56, 68, 128, 136, 244, 257-258; Peru, 56; Philippine Islands, 56
Moncada, Ramón de, 142
Mondragón, Miguel, Jr., 243
Monopolies: Guatemala, 134-135; Mexico, 134, 135, 136; tobacco, 164
Montaño, Dolores, 32
Montaño, Sebastián, 79
Montemar, Count of, 163
Monterey, California, 72; discovery and exploration, 46, 76, 254; port of, 46, 48, 72; settlement, 75
Montero, Nicolás, 100
Montero, Simón, 142
Montero de Miranda, Francisco, 142
Monterrey, Conde de. *See* Zúñiga y Acevedo, Gaspar de
Monterrey, 194; battlefield, 121; map, 244
Montes, Francisco, 143
Montes, Miguel, 175
Montes, Toribio de, 186, 187
Montes de Oca family, 48
Monteverde, Manuel, 143
Montgomery, Jim Lane, 14
Mon(t)serrat, Joaquín, Marqués de Cruillas, viceroy, 1760-1766, 51
Montúfar, Alonso de, abp., 197-198
Moore, Nathan, 143
Moralia, 90
Morán, Pedro, 143
Morán de Butrón, Jacinto, 225
Morán y del Villar, José, Marqués de Vivanco, 143
Morazán, Francisco, 143
Morelia, description, 255; Indians, 100; tribute, 100
Morell de Santa Cruz, Pedro Agustín, bp., 144
Morelos: conditions, 132; history, 131; politics and government, 213
Morelos y Pavón, José María Teclo, 255; death of, 29

Moreno, José Demetrio, 69
Moreno, José Matías, 13
Moreno, José R., 58
Moreno, Juan de Dios, Marqués de Valle Ameno, 258
Moreno de Ocío, Antonio, 158
Morete, José de Jesús, 144
Morfi, Juan Agustín, 60, 104, 127, 144-145, 146, 189, 263
Morga, Juan, 143
Morgan, Charles, 118
Morgan, Philip Hicky, 145
Moriana, Conde de, 145
Morris, James, 145
Morris, William Alfred, 145
Morshead, Owen F., 145
Mosquito Coast, 89, 150, 231; Territory, boundaries, 89
Mosquito Indians, 9, 18
Mota, Andrés de la, 37
Mota (López) Padilla, Matías Angel de la, 104, 146
Motolinía, Toribio, 127, 146, 156, 190
Mott, Talbott and Company, 146
Moulin, Henri, 74-75
Mourelle, Francisco Antonio, 72
Moya de Contreras, Pedro, abp. and viceroy, 1584-1585, 197-198
Moyano, Francisco, 123, 178
Mulattoes, 38
Mulegé, 221; mission, 223
Munguía, Mariana, 146
Muñoz, Juan Bautista, 146-147
Muñoz Camargo, Diego, 228
Muñoz Cota, José, 257
Munuera, Esteban, 110
Murray, John, 147
Murrietta ranch, 191
Music: Nicaragua, 150; Panama, 147

Nagualismo, 62
Náhuatl. *See* Linguistics, Aztec Indians
Nájera, Manuel de, 128, 251
Nájera Yanguas, Diego de, 180
Nanne, Henry F. W., 148
Napoleon, 211; and Spain, 187
Narbona, Francisco, 176
Nasatir, Abraham P., 40
Nata, Panama, baptismal records, 160
A Nation Without Room (Grimm), 90
National Polytechnic Institute, Mexico, 185

Native languages. *See* Linguistics
Nativitas: Indians, 39; monastery, 38
Natzmer, Bruno von, 150
Nava, Pedro de, 117, 148
Navarra, Juan, 9
Navarrete, Pedro M., 13
Navarro, Francisco, 68
Navarro, José de, 187
Navarro y Noriega, Fernando, 28
Navas Quevedo, Andrés de las, bp., 59, 62, 85
Navigation, 94; Caribbean, 111; Chagres River, 7; Pacific Coast, 114; routes, 54, 83, 232
Nayarit, 195, 218; maps and charts, 141; missions, 77, 218, 219
Negrete, Francisco de, 110
Negroes: British West Indies, 24; Danish West Indies, 52; Hispanic America, 211; Mexico, 100, 151, 186, 216; Panama, 119; St. Bartholomew, 204; Santo Domingo, 211; South America, 149. *See also* Slavery
Neira y Quiroga, José de, 148-149
Nentvig, Juan Bautista, 149, 220
New Granada, 4-5, 9, 83, 158; administration, 149; boundary questions, 89; Indians, 238; missions, 238; slavery, 149; Veraguas and Chiriquí, 161-162
New Laws of the Indies, excerpts from, 129
New Mexico: attempted annexation by Texas, 66; description, 21, 169; discovery and exploration, 72, 149, 153; Franciscans, 262; history, 21, 66, 127, 149, 262; missions, 21, 149, 218, 229-230; politics and government, 229-230; settlement, 149
New Spain: administration, 4, 5, 13, 33, 36, 39-40, 44, 47, 49, 65, 81, 88, 136, 137, 155, 190, 194, 229-230; commerce, 13, 230; fiscal affairs, 31, 136, 231; governors, 125; intendancies, 72, 98; laws, 8, 9, 13, 36, 109-110, 203-204, 231; military, 13, 72, 75, 136, 248; residencias, 171, 253; social conditions, 230; viceroys (and chiefs of state), 149, 190
New York: city jail, 145; National Guard, 232; state politics, 183
Newspapers, 29, 41; Arizona, 227; Honduras, 229; Mexico, 168, 237-238; U. S. Army, 15
Nicaragua: antiquities, 108; description and travel, 42, 86, 242; discovery and exploration, 86; education, 262; filibustering activities, 54, 106, 118, 150, 242; Franciscans, 38; history, 36, 42, 54, 86, 106, 118, 150; Indians, 9, 42; mining, 36; missions, 38; natural resources, 229; patriotic songs, 150; ports, 83; relations with Great Britain, 150; Roman Catholic Church, 144. *See also* Central America
Nicholson, Robert, family papers, 150
Nicoya (ecclesiastical province), 144
Niño, Andrés, 36, 86
Noble, Harold Joyce, 77, 150
Noble, Robert Watson, diary, 166
Nolan, Philip, 96
Nombre de Dios (Nueva Galicia), 151, 189
Nombre de Dios, Panama, 8, 66, 83
Nonohaba, mission, 219
Nootka, linguistics, 122, 254
Noriega y Vicario, Ana María, 154
Norris, James R., 20
Norton, Charles Eliot, 150
Noticia de la California (Venegas), 217, 223, 249
Nuestra Santísima Madre de la Soledad (brotherhood), 166
Nuestra Señora de Regla, map, 13
Nuestra Señora del Carmen Presidio, Tris, 26
Nueva Estremadura. *See* Coahuila
Nueva Galicia, 72; colonization, 189; description, 93; genealogy, 151; history, 46, 93, 146, 167; Indians, 46, 93, 146; land, 46, 151; mining, 93; missions, 93, 141; politics and government, 229-230
Nueva Vizcaya, 5, 72, 175, 195, 215; censuses (1786-1821), 36; dispute with Sonora, 175; history, 60, 154, 175, 189; Indians, 16, 19, 50, 63, 64, 154, 189; inspection, 215; land, 98, 206; military affairs, 16, 19, 60, 63; missions, 16, 36, 60, 88, 141; politics and government, 16, 19, 49-50, 60, 182; presidios, 50, 63-64, 154; Roman Catholic Church, 60, 235
Nuevas Filipinas. *See* Texas
Nuevo León: hospital, 132; missions, 141, 218; politics and government, 229-230
Nuevo Santander, 229-230; missions, 141
Núñez, Francisco, 198
Núñez Arica, Alonzo, genealogical documents, 15-16
Núñez de Balboa, Vasco, 86
Núñez de Haro y Peralta, Alonso, abp. and viceroy, 1787, 53, 87, 110, 152
Núñez de la Vega, Francisco, bp., 62
Nuttall, Zelia Magdalena, 94, 115, 152

Oak, Henry Lebbeus, 196
Oaxaca (state), 18, 28, 55, 131, 152; antiquities, 27; Church, 23; Indians, 27, 42; rebellion during War of Independence, 255; taken by French, 126
Oberndorfer, Leonora (Levy), 152
Obilla, Andrés de, 190
Obras Públicas, Guanajuato, 91
Obregón, Baltasar de, 153
O'Brien, Joseph J., 153
Occidente (state), 228
Ochoa, Gaspar de, 43, 174
Ochoa y Aaña, Anastasio María de, 153
O'Conor, Hugo de, 154
Ocotopec (Chiapas), 75
O'Donojú, Juan, viceroy, 1821, 246
O'Gorman, Charles Thaddeus, marriage of, 154
Old Providence Island, Company of, 89

284 INDEX

Oliván Rebolledo, Juan de, 195
Olivares, Conde-Duque de, 163
Olivares y Benito, Francisco Gabriel, bp., 56, 200
Olivera y Angulo, Sebastián de, 59, 62
Olivera y Pardo, Jacinto, bp., 82
Olives y Sintes, Sebastián, 154
Olliffe, H., 154
Olmos, Andrés de, 154
Onapa, mission, 220
Oñate family, genealogy, 151
Onís, Luis de, 214
Opata Indians, 25, 227, 228; linguistics, 118, 178, 179 (Hehué and Tehuima dialects)
Oquitoa, mission, 123; baptismal records, 180
Oratory: Mexico, 45, 56, 87, 134; Spain, 45
Order of the Immaculate Conception. See Conceptionists
Ordóñez, Juan, 158-159
Ordóñez y Aguiar, Ramón de, 62, 155
Orduña, 84
O'Reilly, Alexander, 116
Orica, Honduras, 168
Orizaba, 22; diary, 112; history, 112
Ormaechea y Ernaiz, Juan Bautista, 242
Orozco, José de, 70
Orozco Cervantes, Manuel de, family estate papers, 156
Orrantia, Juan de, 156
Ortega, Francisco de, 156
Ortega, José Francisco, 46
Ortega, Melchor, 257
Ortega Montañés, Juan de, abp. and viceroy, 1696, 158
Ortega Moro, José, 102
Ortigosa, Vicente, 156
Ortiz, Francisco Bernardino, 220
Ortiz, Jesús J., bp., 237
Ortiz Parrilla, Diego, 61, 157, 196
Ortúzar, Francisco de, 252
Osorio, Lorenzo, family estate papers, 156
Ossorio, Buenaventura Francisco de, 157
Ossorio, Francisco, 220
Ostimuri: description, 72; Indians, 220
Osuma, Conde de, 163
Otero, Mariano, 157

Otomí Indians, 157; linguistics, 6, 40-41, 125, 157, 179 (Matlatzinca branch), 180 (Pame dialect), 208-209
Our Lady of Guadalupe, church, 197
Ovando, Juan de, 60
Oyarvide y Heredia, Antonio de, 158

Pacheco, Francisco, 200
Pacheco Osorio, Rodrigo, Marqués de Cerralvo, viceroy, 1624-1635, 156, 242, 253
Pacheco, Solís, Miguel, 109
Pachuca (Hidalgo): history, 158-159; mining, 73, 158, 159-160
Pacific Coast: description and travel, 201, 208, 255; discovery and exploration, 46, 48, 61, 72, 89, 113, 114, 122, 125-126, 149, 214; foreign intrusions, 149; maps and charts, 13, 237; navigation, 201
Pacific Mail Steamship Company, 159
Pacific Ocean: canal, 7; discovery and exploration, 6-7, 86, 96, 192, 232, 249; navigation, 94
Padierna, Battle of, 115
Padilla, Ezequiel, 257
Padilla family, genealogy, 151
Páez, Federico G., 94
Páez, José Antonio, 21
Pagüichique (Chihuahua), Indians, 148
Paine, Robert T., 50-51, 245
Paintings, 148, 197; Indian, 156
Palacios, Cristóbal, 159
Palafox y Mendoza, Juan de, bp. of Puebla, viceroy, 1642, 21, 42, 102, 144, 159, 163, 164, 199; beatification of, 225; portrait, 164
Palenque, 20, 62, 108; antiquities, 155
Palermo, patron saint of, 11
Palmer, Walter William, 159-160
Palmerston, Lord John Henry Temple, 89
Palo Alto, Battle of, battleground, 244; map, 29
Palomar y Vizcarra, Miguel, 160, 257
Palomino, Joseph, 220
Palóu, Francisco, 46, 125, 141

Pamachi, 220
Pame Indians, 180
Pan American Federation of Labor, 147
Panama, 7, 67, 163; agriculture, 185; baptismal records, 160; commerce, 7; description and travel, 69, 233; flora and fauna, 78-79; French activities, 192-193; harbors, 8, 201; history, 47, 160-161 (Veraguas and Chiriquí); Indians, 9, 78-79, 97, 192; map, 185; mining, 78-79, 185; petroleum, 185; politics and government, 7, 47, 119; popular songs, 147; ports, 8, 66, 83; presidents, 47; railroads, 232; Roman Catholic Church, 96, 119, 160; social conditions, 119; Society of Jesus, 224; vital statistics, 160. See also Darien
Panama (city), 7, 8, 66, 78-79, 83, 160
Panama Canal, 22, 47, 107, 153, 245
Panama, Isthmus of, 78-79, 159
Panama-Pacific Exposition, 153
Panes y Avellán, Diego García, 162
Pantepec (Chiapas), 75
Pápago Indians, 176; linguistics, 179
Papalotla, 164
Papeles del Padre Fischer, 141
Paper-making, 99
Papigochi, 21; mission, 220
Paraguay: Indians, 225; missions, 163, 224, 225; president, 17
Pardo, Diego, 140, 165
Parián, 57
Parish records: Mexico, 36, 80; Acatlán, 3; Chiapas, 39; Nuestra Señora de Guadalupe de Reinosa, 165-166; Pachuca, 158-159; Santa María la Redonda, 38; Teposcolula, 21; Tulancingo, 242; Mixteca Alta, 21. See also Burial records, Marriage records, etc.
Park, John W., 259
Parke, John Grubb, 166
Parker, Achsa Snow, 23
Parkman, Samuel Paul, 166
Parkes, C. E., 166
Parra, Francisco, 166-167

INDEX 285

Parras, Matías, 179
Parrott, John, 167
Parrott, William Stuart, 73
Pasig, Philippine Islands, 167
Paso y Troncoso, Francisco, 88
Pastraño, Juan, 46
"Pastry War," 28, 74-75, 246
Patiño, Pedro Pablo, 167
Patiño de Avila, Alvaro, 167-168
Patterson, W. E., 51
Patton, Perry, 170
Paul III, Pope, 87
Paul V, Pope, 207
Pavy, Francis, 101
Paxson, Frederic Logan, 168
Payno y Flores, Manuel, 99
Paz, Ireneo, 168
Paz, Pedro de, 168
Paz Baraona, Miguel, 168
Paz Cortés y Monroy, María Josefa de, 168
Pazos, Andrés de, 184
Pearl fisheries: Mexico (California), 156; South America, 216; Venezuela (Margarita), 249
Pearson, Norman Holmes, 168
Pease, Isaac D., 169
Peirce, Silas, 169
Peláez, Felipe, 8
Peña, Juan Antonio de la, 60, 126
Peña, Manuel de la, 110
Penonomé, Panama. See San Juan de Penonomé
Peralta, Gastón de, viceroy, 1566, 204, 261
Peraza, Juan, 197
Perea, Estevan de, 169
Pérez, Antonio, 169
Pérez, Francisco, 170
Pérez, Juan, 72, 125
Pérez, Martín, 127, 189, 226
Pérez Adamdicosio y Cauto, José María Alejo de, 170
Pérez de la Serna, Juan, abp., 190
Pérez de la Torre, Diego, 151
Perry, Oliver Hazzard, diary and papers, 170
Peru, 257; antiquities, 142; army, 139; coinage, 170; description and travel, 69, 83, 214; economics, 17; genealogy (Incas), 114; history, 6-7, 129, 147, 170-171, 216; Indians, 33, 57, 98, 112, 114, 142, 170-171, 193, 238; mining, 98; missions, 224, 238; newspapers, 57; politics and government, 136; race relations, 57; Roman Catholic Church, 109, 197-198; social life and customs, 237
Pesa y Casas, José Mariano de la, 171
Pesquera, Felipe, 171
Petroleum, Bolivia, 212; Colombia, 185; Ecuador, 185; Panama, 185
Philbrick, Francis Samuel, 61-62, 171, 256
Philip I of Spain, 155
Philip II of Spain, 31, 47, 54, 83, 155, 163, 192, 205, 246, 247-248
Philip III of Spain, 35, 38, 49, 163
Philip IV of Spain, 156, 163, 169
Philip V of Spain, 5, 18, 38, 45, 54, 89, 171, 217, 219, 230, 238
Philippine Islands, 7; administration, 54, 134, 172, 173; Battle of Manila, 68; British expedition, 172-173; commerce, 54, 122, 128-129; description and travel, 23; economics, 134, 136, 231; Franciscans, 162; geography, 54; history, 172-173; land, 234; Manila galleons, 128-129; military and naval affairs, 10, 35-36, 75, 172-173; missions, 221, 238; natives, 238; Roman Catholic Church, 136, 197-198, 213; Society of Jesus, 213, 221, 224; Spanish American War, 8; trade with Mexico, 230, 253; trade with Spain, 18, 128-129; witchcraft, 101
Phoenix Gazette, 227
Píccolo, Francisco María, 217, 220, 221
Piernas, Pedro, 116
Pijijiapa, parish (Chiapas), 39
Pilar de Zaragoza, mission, La Paz, 140, 221
Pilcher, Thomas, will, 173
Pima Indians, 61, 77, 107, 175, 227; linguistics, 18, 178; Revolt of 1751, 222, 223
Pimentel, Manuel Francisco, 128
Pimería Alta, 219; missions, 53, 57, 107, 175, 180, 222, 223; —Baja, 252
Piña y Mazo, Pedro, 77, 132
Pinart, Alphonse Louis, 9, 11, 33, 43, 52-53, 57, 59, 62, 67, 117, 142, 150, 162, 165, 171, 173-182, 188, 195, 211-212, 235, 250; biographical, 94
Pinart, Zelia Nuttall. See Nuttall
Pinchot, Amos Richard Eno, 182
Pineda, Juan de, 83
Pineda, Manuel, 13
Pinedo y Alarcón, Martín de, 111
Pinilla y Pérez, Angel, 182
Pinolillo, El, 131
Pious Fund, 68, 182, 206
Pipioltepec, 182
Piracy, 59; in Lower California, 14
Piscataquis Association of Congregational Ministers, 182
Pitaqui, visita, 182
Pius IV, Pope, 87
Pius VII, Pope, 76
Pius IX, Pope, 184
Pizarro, Francisco, 122, 147
Plan de Ayutla, 11; de Casa Mata, 43, 174; de Cuernavaca, 170; de Iguala, 246; de Orizaba, 170; de Zabaleta, 210
Plasagarre, M., 183
Plymouth, England, town records, 183
Poetry, 4, 12, 46, 69, 224-225; America, 99; Guatemala, 85; Mexico, 11, 12, 28, 42, 56, 68, 69, 82, 88, 101-102, 111, 114, 134, 139-140, 145, 164, 165, 167, 194, 210, 233, 236, 237, 240, 253; Spain, 99, 163-164; United States, 256-257
Pokoman Indians, linguistics, 143
Polk, James Knox, 12, 52, 183
Poole, Richard Stafford, 183, 198
Popocatépetl, 67
Population figures. See Censuses
Pópulo, mission, 218
Porras, Belisario, 183
Portello y Torres, Fernando, abp., 211
Porter, Sir Robert Ker, 183
Portes Gil, Emilio, 257
Porto Alegre, Brazil, municipal government, 183
Portolá, Gaspar de, biographical material, 184; expedition, 72
Ports: America, 54; Argenti-

na, 26; Canary Islands, 54; Guatemala, 8, 49, 66; Honduras, 8, 49, 66, 83, 104; Mexico, 30, 76, 83; Nicaragua, 83; Panama, 8, 66, 83; Portugal, 54; Spain, 54; West Indies, 54
Portugal, Juan Cayetano, 184
Potosí, Bolivia, history, 184
Pozo y Calderón, María Casilda del, 184
Pradillo, Agustín, 184
Prado y Arze, Francisco del, 185
Pratt, Alexander, 185
Prayer books, 185
Presidios, 72, 195; Amarillas, 141; Chihuahua, 50; Conchos River, 64; inspection by the Marqués de Rubí, 202; inspection by Pedro de Rivera, 16; Janos, 40, 43, 64, 154; maps and plans, 72; Nuestra Señora del Carmen (Tris), 26; Nueva Vizcaya, 50, 63-64, 154; Rio Grande, 144; San Ignacio, 177; Santa Barbara (California), 102; Santa Cruz (Sonora), 259; Tubac, 176; Tubutama, 177; Tucson, 176
Preston, William Ballard, 185
Princesa (frigate), 113 (logbooks), 114, 122
Protomedicato, Tribunal del (Mexico City), 38
Provincia de San Diego, 165; de San Hipólito de Oaxaca, 27; de San José, Yucatan, 56, 128; de San Pedro y San Pablo, 17; de San Vicente de Chiapa y de Guatemala, 58-59, 82, 260; de Santiago de México, 47, 65, 210; de Santo Domingo, Guatemala, 59; del Santísimo Nombre de Jesús, Guatemala, 62, 128; del Santo Evangelio, 15, 37-39, 49, 78
Provincial Councils (Ecclesiastical): First (1555), 197-198; Second (1565), 197-198; for New Spain, Third (1585), 132, 183, 197-198; Fourth (1771), 77, 132, 140
Provincias Internas, 205; administration, 49-50, 83, 229-230, 243; agriculture, 50; Comandancia General, 148; description, 31, 195; exploration, 149; history, 125, 173, 189, 214; Indians, 49-50, 83; local affairs, 21; mail service, 50; map, 24; military affairs, 47, 243; missions, 24; settlement, 50, 149; statistics, 98
Puebla de los Angeles (city), 15-16, 102, 110, 184; description, 6; history, 6; Indians, 185-186; manufactures, 185-186; road map, 13
Puebla de los Angeles (diocese), 6, 42, 87, 139, 240; bishop of, 169; cathedral, 169, 233; history, 6
Puente y Peña, José de la, Marqués de Villapuente, 182, 220
Puerto Rico, 155; agriculture, 186; censuses, 187; commerce, 186; defense, 186-187; economics, 17, 186-187; French activities, 186-187; history, 186-187; maps, 187; municipal government, 186; Roman Catholic Church, 187; slavery, 186
Pulgar, Jerónimo, 135
Pulque, 9, 23, 193; regulations, 88
Purísima Concepción, mission, 218

Quebec, 10; capitulation of, 189
Querétaro, 113; feasts and celebrations, 251; lands, 128; municipal government, 122, 188; recruiting, 75
Quiché Indians: history, 188; linguistics, 197, 260; marriage records, 260
Quicksilver, 73, 109, 135, 136, 144, 148-149, 158
Quijar, Antonio Anselmo, 110
Quiñones Osorio, Alvaro, 70
Quintera Mining Company, Ltd., 188
Quiroga, Domingo de, 184
Quiroga, Vasco de, 11, 190

Racine, Jean Baptiste, 153
Radcliffe, Mary (Van Wagener), diary, 188
Railroads: Argentina, 256; British Honduras, 42; Costa Rica, 148; El Salvador, 233; Mexico, 25, 41, 80, 87, 97, 145, 157, 188-189, 208; Panama, 232; South America, 69
Ramezay, Jean Baptiste Nicholas Roche de, 189
Ramírez, José Fernando, 66, 137, 167, 189-191
Ramírez, Juan, bp., 79
Ramírez de Arellano, Domingo, 176
Ramírez Ponce de León, Juan Félix, 197, 200
Ramón, Domingo, 60, 125, 126
Ramos, Francisco Xavier, 220
Ramos, Juan, 213
Ramos, Ramón, 227
Rancho Bejarano, 102; de San Lucas (Chol Province, Guatemala), 59; San Rafael (Sonora), 191
Raousset Boulbon, Gaston Raoul, Comte de, 44, 195; filibustering activities, 133, 239
Rauzet de Jesús, Francisco, 235
Rea, David B., 191
Real Aduana y Receptoria de Alcabalas (Aguascalientes), 191
Real Casa de Moneda, Potosí, Peru, 170
Real Compañía de Asiento, Puerto Rico, 186
Real Convento de Jesús María, 192
Real del Monte y Pachuca, 159-160
Real Hacienda, 73, 136, 226 (Sonora)
Real Justicia, Nueva Vizcaya, 151; Tacuba, 234
Rebecca (sloop), 169
Redondo, José María, 192
Refugio, mission (Matamoros), 140
"Registro Yucateco," 62
Reglamento of 1816, 43
Reinosa: mission, 165-166; parish records, 165
Religious orders: America, 56, 193, 230, 231; France, 45; Guatemala, 247, 251; Mexico, 53, 78, 100, 110-111, 121, 127, 135, 146, 159, 187, 190, 191, 192, 194, 206, 207, 214, 231, 244, 251, 252, 258; Philippine Islands, 127; Spain, 225, 252; Venezuela, 187. *See also* Dominicans, Franciscans, Society of Jesus, etc.
Remesal, Antonio de, 59, 62
Remington, Frederic, 192
Remón, Miguel, 192-193
Repartimiento system, 55, 191, 193

INDEX 287

Resaca de la Palma, Battle of, map, 244
Residencias, Colombia, 44; Mexico (New Spain), 171, 253
Resources and Development of Mexico (Bancroft), 131-132
Revilla Gigedo, 1st Conde de. See Güemes y Horcasitas
Revilla Gigedo, 2nd Conde de. See Güemes Pacheco de Padilla
Rey y Alarcón, Bartolomé, 130
Reynosa, W. S. Gregory, 51
Ribadeneyra y Barrientos. See Rivadeneira
Ricardos, Felipe, 250
Richards, Bessie (Launder), 194
Richthofen, E. K. H., 133
Ricketson, Asa, 126
Rideing, William Henry, 194
Rieloff, F. C., 133
Rincón, Manuel, 115
Rio Grande Presidio (Coahuila), 144
Rip(p)erdá, Juan María, Barón de, 60, 117, 126
Riva, Juan Antonio de la, 114
Rivadeneira y Barrientos, Antonio Joaquín de, 77, 132, 140, 194
Rivas, Andrés de, 127
Rivas y Solar, José Francisco de, 152
Rivera, Juan Antonio, 28
Rivera, Pedro de, 16
Rivera Cambos, Manuel, 130
Rivera y Alarcón, 130
Rivera y Moncada, Fernando de, 14
Rivera y Villalón, Pedro de, 9, 195
Rivers, 10, 45, 76, 96, 131-132, 138, 223, 227, 228, 244
Roads: British Honduras, 42; Guatemala, 42, 78; Mexico, 104-105, 151, 157; Chihuahua, 25; Northwest Mexico, 25; Puebla, 13; Sonora and Sinaloa, 30; Veracruz, 162
Robinson, Juan A., 195
Robledo, Jorge, 195-196
Robles, Antonio de, 225
Rocaferro, hacienda, 113
Roche, Francisco, 181
Rochel, Francisco Antonio, 165
Rodríguez, Antonio, 152
Rodríguez, Bernardo, 211

Rodríguez, José María, 196
Rodríguez, Juan J., 91
Rodríguez, Trinidad, 47
Rodríguez Cordero, Juan, 196
Rodríguez de Albuerne, Juan, Marqués de Altamira, 61
Rodríguez de Villanueva, Gaspar, 196
Rodríguez Gallardo, Joseph Raphael, 196
Rodríguez y Belasco, Alonso, 198
Rodríguez y Varacijo, Ignacio, 258
Roehm, Mrs. H. G., 35
Rojas, Diego José de, 82
Rojo, Manuel Clemente, 196
Rolandegui, Bernardo, 219
Roldán, Bartolomé, 179
Roldán, Joseph, 220
Roman Catholic Church: catechism, 23; Congregation of Propaganda Fide (Rome), 93; ecclesiastical asylum, 242, 247; history, 23-24; organization, 215, 217; relations of church and state, 230; theology, 66, 81, 88, 90, 216. See also Tithes
—America, 88, 92-93
—Brazil, 52
—Central America, 144, 147, 232
—Costa Rica, 144
—Guatemala, 95, 108, 197, 230, 234
—Haiti, 215
—Hispanic America, 23-24, 56, 139-140, 193, 230, 247
—Mexico, 15, 17, 18, 19, 21, 28, 36, 37-39, 40-41, 42, 43, 55, 57, 68, 71, 86, 87, 88, 98, 102, 109, 121, 134, 140, 169, 189, 197-200, 212, 213, 215, 230, 244, 252, 257-259; administration, 23-24, 38, 39, 76, 132, 231, 248; appointments, 131, 169; archbishops, 24, 76; catechisms, 123, 125, 132, 180, 198, 201; cathedrals, 24, 37; celebrations, 120; ceremonies, 248; chapels, 121; chaplaincies, 86; church and state, 23, 57, 132, 160, 164, 175, 194, 200, 217, 242, 248; churches, 24; Congregation of Rites, 167; curacies, 28; ecclesiastical tribunal, 110; fiscal affairs, 136, 138; Fourth Mexican Provincial Council (1771), 77, 132, 140; government

policies, 227; institutions, 138; lands, 46; law, 77, 96; liturgy, 139, 154-155, 167, 214, 233, 251, 262; patronage, 114-115; property, 164; theology, 111, 113-114, 132, 184; Third Mexican Provincial Council (1585), 132, 183, 197-198; in the Californias, 218; Chiapa (diocese), 127-128; Chiapas, 39; Durango, 174, 189; Guadalajara (diocese), 167; Guatemala (diocese), 127-128; Mexico City, 37, 241. (See also Mexico City Cathedral); Nueva Vizcaya, 60, 235; Oaxaca, 18; Sonora, 198; Sonora y Sinaloa, 30; Tabasco, 127-128; Tlaxcala, 240; Yucatan (diocese), 127-128. See also Parish records
—New Granada, 35
—Nicaragua, 144
—Pacific Islands, 136
—Panama, 96, 119, 160
—Peru, 109, 197-198
—Philippine Islands, 136, 197-198, 213
—Puerto Rico, 187
—Spain, 87, 197-198, 224-225, 229, 230
See also Clergy; Franciscans; Dominicans; Missions; Religious Orders, etc.
Romero, Joaquín, 200
Romero, Maías, 201
Ronda, Agustín, 94
Rosa y Figueroa, Francisco de la, 38, 201
Rosales, Juan de, 258
Rovirosa, José Narciso, 201
Rowe, John H., 171
Roxo, Andrés Joseph, 120
Royuela, Matías, 202
Rozas, Luis de, 169
Ruanco, Domingo, estate of, 33
Rubí, Marqués de, 174, 202
Rubio, José F., 50
Rubio, Justino, 14, 202
Ruhen, Heinrich, 202
Ruiz, Santiago, 64
Ruiz de Apodaca, Juan, viceroy, 1816-1821, 19, 202
Ruiz de Cabrera, Cristóbal, 242
Rush, Richard, 202
Ryerson, Jorge, 203

Saavedra Aguilera, Pedro de, 258

288 INDEX

Sáenz de Escobar, José, 203-204
Sahagún, Bernardino de, 261
Sahuaripa, mission, 110
Saint Aloysius (Luis Gonzaga), 225
St. Bartholomew, island, 204
Saint Bonaventure, 68
Saint-Denis, 60, 126
St. Hippolytus, Order of. See San Hipólito Mártir
Saint Jan of Nepomuk (San Juan Nepomuceno), 120
St. John, Bela Taylor, 204
St. John, Sir Spencer [Buckingham], 205
Saint John the Divine, 113-114
Saint-Jure, J. B., 205
St. Louis (Missouri), 84, 107, 116, 209 (lands)
Saint Philip Neri, Oratory of, Mexico City, 190-191
Saint-Pierre, Charles Irénée Castel, Abbé de, 205
Saint Stanislas Kostka, 225
Salazar, Gabriel de, 58-59
Salbago, Francisco, genealogy, 199
Salcedo, Manuel Juan de, 117
Salcedo y Salcedo, Nemesio, 205
Salinas, Juan de, 109
Salmubelli, Joseph Luis, 220
Salt: regulations, 18; mines, 59
Salvatierra, Conde de. See Sarmiento de Sotomayor
Salvatierra, Juan María, 144, 217, 220, 221
Samaniego, Ignacio, 228
Samborombón Bay, Argentina, 26
Sambo-Mosquito Indians, 9
Sambrano, Antonio. See Zambrana
San Agustín de los Amoles, hacienda, 206
San Blas, 113, 122; description, 25
San Buenaventura de las Palmas, Panama, baptismal records, 160
San Diego (California), 10, 48, 72
San Felipe de Jesús, 162
San Felipe el Real (Chihuahua), 156, 206
San Francisco, 44, 51, 113; discovery and exploration, 75, 76; harbor, 76; Panama-Pacific Exposition (1915), 153
San Francisco de Borja, mission, 112, 221; burial records, 206
San Francisco Javier (revenue cutter), 250
San Francisco Xavier, mission, Baja California, 218
San Francisco Xavier de Cañazas, Panama, 160
San Hipólito, Church of, 137
San Hipólito Mártir, Order of, 206-207, 231; hospital, 207
San Homo-Bono Guild, 207
San Ignacio Caburi, 175
San Joaquín, mission, baptismal records, 165
San José Mine, Pachuca, 158
San Juan de Penonomé, Panama, baptismal records, 160
San Juan de Ulúa, 72, 74-75; chart, 244; fortifications, 144; military problems, 13; report of mutiny, 131
San Juan del Norte. See Greytown
San Juan del Río (Querétaro), flood, 26
San Juan Nepomuceno (sloop), 158
San Juan Santa Cruz, Manuel de, 81
San Lázaro (vessel), 192
San Luis Potosí, 213; description, 164; education, 213; history, 164; Indians, 177; mint, 213; population, 177; rebellion, 255; towns, 177
San Marcos, Guatemala, 58
San Mateo Ixtlahuaca, 208
San Miguel, María Josefa de, 184, 208
San Miguel (Nueva Galicia), 151
San Miguel de Aguayo, José de Azlor, Marqués de, 60, 238
San Miguel Tzinacantepec, *doctrina*, 38
San Pablo, mission, 220
San Pedro Macati, Philippine Islands, 172
San Pedro Mártir: description and travel, 39; mission, 65
San Pedro Tlahuac (Xochimilco), codices, 147-148
San Pedro y San Pablo, Colegio Máximo de, Mexico City, 3, 197, 200, 226
San Román y Zepeda, José de, 208
San Salvador, Convento de, 65
San Vicente Ferrer, mission, burial records, 208

Sánchez, D., 208
Sánchez, José, 208
Sánchez, Manuel Eliseo, 91
Sánchez Chamuscado, Francisco, 153
Sánchez de la Baquera, Juan, 208-209
Sánchez Ochoa, Gaspar, 87
Sánchez Ramírez, Juan, 211
Sande, Mateo de, 257
Sandoval Acazitli, Francisco de, 103, 144, 146
Sandoval Cerda Silva y Mendoza, Gaspar de, Conde de Galve, viceroy, 1688-1696, 209, 223
Sanford, James T., 209
Sanger Camp & Co., 209
Santa Ana Pueblo, baptismal and marriage records, 181
Santa Anna, Antonio López de, 22, 28, 29, 64, 115, 143, 209, 223
Santa Cruz, Antonio Marín de, 12
Santa Cruz, mission, 181, 218, 222
Santa Cruz Tepetispam, 248
Santa Cruzada, 207, 240; Mexico, 209-210; Philippine Islands, 209-210
Santa Gertrudis: mission, 223; Indians, 14
Santa Gertrudis Mine (Pachuca), 158
Santa Isabel, land titles, 206
Santa María, Miguel, 210
Santa María de la Soledad (cofradía), 43
Santa María la Redonda: *doctrina*, 38; land distribution, 210
Santa María Soamca (Suamca), mission. See Santa Cruz
Santa Rosa de Ures Silver Mining Company, 210
Santa Rosalia de Palermo, biography, 11
Santamaría, Francisco Javier, 201, 210
Santiago, Juan de, 109, 210
Santiago, Sacarías de, genealogy, 211
Santiago, Provincia de, 47, 65, 210
Santiago, mission, 222
Santísimo Rosario, mission, 211
Santo Colegio de Cristo . . . , Guatemala (City), 92-93
Santo Domingo, 186-187, 211-212; emigration to Cuba,

211; French activities, 211; history, 211-212; relations with Haiti, 211-212; slaves, 211; taxation, 211
Santo Domingo (province), Darien, 192-193
Santo Domingo, mission, 212
Santo Evangelio, Provincia de, 15, 37-39, 49, 78
Santo Tomás (Lower California), 32
Santo Tomás del Castillo, Honduras, 104
Santos y Salazar, Manuel de los, 40
Sariñana, Isidro, bp., 127
Sarmiento, Joseph, 141
Sarmiento de Sotomayor, García, Conde de Salvatierra, viceroy, 1642-1648, 128, 135, 144, 188
Sarmiento Valladares, José, Conde de Moctezuma, viceroy, 1696-1701, 75
Satire, 12, 101-102, 233
Savage, Thomas, 196
Sawkins, James Gay, 212
Schlözer, K. von, 133
Schmidel, Ulrich, 261
Scholes, France V., 61, 149
Schomburgk, Sir Robert Hermann, 211-212
Schools. *See* Education
Schultz, F. C., 212
Schurz, Carl, 212
Scott, William Anderson, 150
Scott, Winfield, 28, 115
Second Ecclesiastical Provincial Council (1565), 197-198
Sedelmayer, Jacobo, 202, 223, 224
Seeber, Chester, 212-213
Segesser de Brunegg, François Joseph, 213
Segesser von Brunegg, Philipp, 213, 222, 224
Segura, Francisco de P., 213
Segura, Nicolás de, 213
Segura y Segura, Francisco, 213
Seiffart, F., 133
Seri Indians, 61, 77, 176, 181, 218; linguistics, 179
Sermons: Cuba, 45; Mexico, 12, 15, 42, 45, 56, 69, 87, 95-96, 125, 178, 214, 233, 262; Spain, 45
Serna, Juan Pérez de la, abp., 23, 242
Serna, Pedro de la, 175
Serra, Junípero, 46, 72, 141
Seymour, Sir George F., 89

Sherman, William Tecumseh, 116
Ships, Boston Register of, 22
Shipwrecks, *Eidu Maru* (1842), 235; *Union* (1851), 58
Shipyards, Cavite, Philippine Islands, 36
Sicard, Agustín, 215
Sierra, Manuel J., 257
Sierra Osorio, Lope de, 59, 215
Sigüenza y Góngora, Carlos de, 66, 127, 136, 144, 190, 215
Silk: culture, 185-186; guilds, 186
Silva, Beatriz de, 252
Silva Herzog, Jesús, 257
Silver mining: Guanajuato, 194; Honduras, 242; Mexico, 111; Peru, 98; Sonora, 46, 195, 210
Simpson, Lesley B., 92, 155
Sin-Tierra, Juan, 236
Sinaloa, 51; administration, 6, 225; defense, 61, 252; description, 72, 132, 157, 227, 235; ecclesiastical province, 226; finances, 61; history, 5, 61, 127, 226, 227; Indians, 5, 61, 127, 218, 226, 239, 260; mining, 44; missions, 5, 77, 217-223, 226; settlement, 190; Society of Jesus, 30, 127, 217-223, 226, 260; statistics, 235; towns and rancherías, 218. *See also* Sonora y Sinaloa, Free State of
Siqueiros, David Alfaro, 257
Sisemble Indians, 110
Sistiaga, Sebastián de, 221
Sixtus V, Pope, 163, 207
Skilton, Julius A., 215
Slater, Nelson, 216
Slavery: British West Indies, 24; Hispanic America, 60; Mexico, 131, 151; Indian, 216, 228; Negro, 100, 216; New Granada, 149; Puerto Rico, 186; Santo Domingo, 211; South America, 149; Venezuela, 149
Sluiter, Engel, 63, 184, 216
Smith, Joseph B., 216
Smith, Robert, 216
Sociedad de Amigos de Aguas Calientes, 108
Society of Jesus, 45, 216-226; educational institutions, 223; expulsion of, 80, 230; history, 216, 223, 224, 225, 226
—America, 120, 162-164, 224, 225, 226
—Brazil, 52, 224
—Chile, 40
—France, 216
—Guatemala, 223, 247
—Mexico, 3, 5, 28-29, 30, 37-38, 77, 88, 112, 122, 144, 189, 199, 200, 202, 205, 213, 217, 218, 219, 233; annual reports, 30; assets, 49; disputes regarding tithes, 159, 197; disputes with Inquisition, 219; educational institutions, 128, 223; expulsion, 80, 140, 141, 206, 226; history, 223-224; mine ownership, 219; missions, 141; property, 49, 110, 206; reports of Father Kino, 107; in Arizona, 217-223; in the Californias, 112, 182, 217, 218, 232; Durango, 88; in Lower California, 112, 217-223, 224, 236, 249; Nayarit, 218; Nueva Vizcaya, 60, 88; Puebla, 87; Santa María Soamca, 181; Sinaloa, 30, 127, 217-223; Sonora, 53, 120, 217-223, 227; Sonora y Sinaloa, 260; Tepozotlán, 128
—Panama, 224
—Paraguay, 163, 224, 225
—Peru, 224
—Philippine Islands, 213, 221, 224
—Spain, 169-170, 216, 217, 219, 224-225
—Uruguay, 224
Soledad (brotherhood), 166
Solier, Micaela de, 100
Solís, Gaspar José de, diary, 60
Solórzano, Luis de, 100; genealogy, 226
Somera, Miguel Fernández, 221
Sonora, Marqués de. *See* Gálvez, José de
Sonora, 51; administration, 61, 176, 252; agriculture, 44; Comandancia General, 13; commerce, 239; conquest and colonization, 190; defense, 51, 61, 177, 239; defense of Upper California, 192; description, 72, 143, 157, 196, 227, 235; dispute with Nueva Vizcaya, 175; exploration, 72, 120; filibustering activities, 80, 96, 226; finances, 61, 176, 226-227;

history, 43, 44, 61, 83, 93, 96, 173-174, 227; Indian uprising (1740), 260; Indians, 51, 53, 61, 174, 175, 176, 220, 227-228, 239, 260; insurrection (1935), 227; land, 146, 174, 175, 239-240; maps and charts, 218, 226; mining, 22, 44, 46, 90, 107, 174, 188, 195, 210; missions, 24, 53, 57, 77, 93, 120, 217-223, 227-228, 239, 260; politics and government, 143; resources, 143; Roman Catholic Church, 198; statistics, 226, 235; tariffs, 175; transportation, 226
Sonora y Sinaloa, Free State of: description, 30; maps, 30, 220
Soria, Francisco de, 228
Soria, José de, 69
Soriano, Juan Guadalupe, 180
Sosa, Juan Alonso de, 129
Soto, Marco Aurelio, 229
South America: botany, 129; commerce, 43, 216; defense, 215; description, 208; economics, 17; foreign intrusions, 215; history, 21, 153; Indians, 199, 216; railroads, 69; slavery, 149. *See also* Chile, Peru, etc.
South Carolina, 229; earthquakes, 242; land, 104, 229
South Sea Waggoner (Sharpe), 94
Spain: activities in America, 214; administration of the colonies, 10, 36, 44, 54, 60, 83, 155, 193, 229-230, 231, 246, 252; commerce, 8, 18, 142; constitution, 21; finance, 18; foreign relations, 18; relations with France, 54, 211, 238, 247, 248; with Great Britain, 18, 24, 104, 218, 231; with the U.S., 214, 232; genealogy, 15-16, 35, 70, 126; history, 162-164; laws and legal affairs, 4, 7, 14, 36, 192, 231, 246, 247; military and naval affairs, 10, 163, 172, 218; Napoleonic occupation, 187; navy, 35, 36; politics and government, 44, 87, 140, 145, 162-164, 218; ports, 54; relations of Church and state, 230; Roman Catholic Church in Spain, 87, 92, 197-198, 224-225, 229; royal family, 207, 231; social life and customs, 162-164, 251; Society of Jesus, 216, 217, 219, 224-225, expulsion of, 169-170; Spanish-American War, 8, 68; trade with the colonies, 18, 54, 128-129; War of the Austrian Succession, 163
Sperry, Leavenworth (Lem) Porter, 90
Spicer, John W., family papers, 231-232
Squier, Ephraim George, 232
Standard Oil Company (Bolivia), 212
Stearns, Abel, 26
Stephens, Benjamin, 232
Stephens, Henry Morse, 54, 214, 256
Stephens, John Lloyd, 232
Stevens, John F., 245
Stiles, Ezra, 232
Stockton, Francis Richard, 232
Storrs, Augustus, 166
Stoughton, Thomas, 232
Stringer, William James, 233
Stuart, Henry C., 233
Suárez, Bernarda María de los Dolores, 233
Suaso y Coscajales, Diego de, 12, 233
Sugar industry: Guatemala, 82; Mexico, 82, 143, 234
Suma Indians, 19, 63
Sun, Ching-ling (Sung), (Madame Sun Yat-sen), 234
Sunga y Mendosa, Elías, 234
Surinam: Dutch colonists, 234; economic conditions, 17
Sutherland, Robert, 234
Swedish in St. Bartholomew, 204

Tabasco, 32, 84; exploration, 20; Indians, 127-128; Roman Catholic Church, 127-128
Tacotalpa, pueblo, 127-128
Tacuba, 234
Takichi, Hyozen Togen, 235
Talamanca, Costa Rica, 94-95; Indians, 17-18
Tamaral, Nicolás, 222, 236
Tamariz, José, 110
Tamarón y Romeral, Pedro, 235
Tamaulipas, 122-123
Tamazula, 220
Tancuayalab, 199
Tapalapa (Chiapas), 75
Tapia, Gonzalo de, 5, 189
Tarahumar Indians, 16, 77, 219, 235, 236
Tara(h)umara region, 77, 235, 236; mission, 219
Taraval, Sigismundo, 236
Tariffs, 202; railroad, 188-189; in Sonora, 175; in Tepeaca, 186
Tarín, Juan Francisco, 206
Tascaltitlán, Indians, 192
Taxation, 193, 247, 256; Guatemala, 58-59; Mexico, 63, 98, 109, 111, 121, 122, 130, 134, 136, 144, 159, 199, 231; in Chiapas, 39; in Chihuahua, 40; excise, 9; of Indians, 263; Media Anata, 133; paving assessments, 34; pulque, 9; "royal fifth," 91; tobacco, 60; Santo Domingo, 211; United States, 245; Venezuela, 250
Taylor, Paul Shuster, 236
Tays, Eugene Augustus Hoffman, 236
Techialoyan codices, 147-148
Tecomate, El, 239-240
Tecoripa, mission, 222
Tecpán, Guatemala, 84; plans, 85
Teggart, Frederick John, 237, 256
Tegucigalpa, Honduras, 9, 70, 142
Tejeda, Enrique, 175
Téllez Girón, Luis, 221
Tello, Thomas, 223
Temeichi, mission, 217
Temporal, Bartolomé, 178
Tenochtitlán, 136
Tepeaca, 186
Tepic: description, 25; mining, 52
Teposcolula (Oaxaca), municipal government, 152
Terán, Domingo, 60
Terralla y Landa, F., 237
Terrazas, Mariano, 237
Terrazas, Silvestre, 237-238
Texas, 26, 116; attempt to annex New Mexico, 66; biography, 73; colonization, 122-123, 149, 238, 239; description, 145; discovery and exploration, 60, 149; filibustering, 96; foreign relations, 3, 57; history, 28, 60, 61, 66, 122-123, 125, 144-145, 215, 238, 239, 246; Indians, 100, 145, 238; land grants, 239;

missions, 60, 125, 141, 145, 218; relations with Great Britain, 3; revolt, 28; secession, 246
Thevat, André, 239
Third Mexican Provincial Council (1585), 132, 183, 197-198
Thomas, J. L., 51
Tia Juana (Tiajuana), Rancho del, 239
Tierra Firme. *See* Panama
Timucuan Indians, linguistics, 165
Tithes: Guatemala, 234; Mexico, 109, 134, 136, 159, 197, 199, 200, 213; Philippine Islands, 213
Tizonazo, mission, 221
Tlahuac, 147
Tlaltelulco, 15, 38, 39
Tlaltizapán (Morelia), parish records, 240
Tlaxcala, 231; child martyrs, 146, 190; ecclesiastical province, 37-39; founding, 228; genealogy, 240; history, 127, 146, 228; Indians, 38, 127, 211, 231, 238, 240; legal cases, 240; Roman Catholic Church, 240
Tobacco industry, Cuba, 66; Mexico, 29, 36, 60, 130, 164
Toledo, Alvarez de, 78
Toltec Indians, 103
Toluca: description, 48; expulsion of Franciscans, 110; Indians, 38, 48; Valle de, 180
Tomochi (Tomotzi), mission, 222
Toro, Francisco del, 240
Torquemada, Juan de, 215, 228, 240-241
Torquemada, Martín de, 128
Torralbo, Francisco, 187
Torre, Francisco de la, 253
Torre, Martín de la, 144
Torre-Campo, Toribio José de Cosío y Campa, Marqués de, 82
Torres, Alonso de, 100
Torres, Anna de, 258
Torres, Hilario, 241
Torres del Palacio, Francisco, 199
Torres Lerca, Joseph de, 221
Torres Medinilla family, genealogy, 226
Torres y Rueda, Marcos de, bp. and viceroy, 1648-1650, 241, 253

Torres y Vergara, José de, 123, 191, 241
Torrubia, José, 162
Toussaint L'Ouverture, François Dominique, 211
Tracy, Cyrus, 241
Traylor, Samuel White, 242
Treaties
—Brazil, treaty of limits of 1757, 52
—Mexico, peace treaty with France, 75; Treaty of Guadalupe Hidalgo, 91; treaty texts, 246
—Spain, treaty with France, 211; treaty with Great Britain, 231
—U.S. and Great Britain, 42
Tres Palacios y Verdeja, Felipe José de, abp., 94
Treviño, Jacinto B., 257
Tribute, Guatemala, 246; Mexico, 37-38, 63, 100, 122
Trigo, José de, 49
Trincheras (Sonora), 191
Troncoso, María Francisca, genealogy, 130
Trotter, Ada M., 242
Truxillo, Gaspar de, 222
Tubac, 72; military affairs, 175; mission records, 181; population, 176; presidio, 176
Tubutama, mission records, 180, 181
Tucker, Joseph Clarence, 108, 242
Tucson, 176-177
Tulancingo, 113, 177, 258; description, 242; maps, 242; parish records and reports, 242
Tumacácori, mission, 123, 175; chapel inventory, 177
Tupac Amaru, Diego Cristóbal, 170
Tupac Amaru, José Gabriel, 170
Tupac Amaru (Amaro), Mariano, 112, 170
Turpin, Philip, 243
Tzental (Tzendal) Indians, 81-82, 155; linquistics, 178
Tzutuhil Indians, vocabulary, 260

Ugalde, Juan de, 50, 243
Ugarte, Juan de, 141, 221
Ugarte y Loyola, Jacobo de, 125, 154, 189
Ulloa, Antonio de, 116

Umerez, José de, bp., 160
Union (steamship), 58
Unión General de Reclusos del País, 243
United States: Adjutant General's Office, 244; agriculture, 105; aid to Mexico, 87-88, 247; boundary question (1855), 176; citizens in Mexico, 236; Civil War, 8, 17, 22, 31, 41, 95, 99, 106, 112, 116, 124, 204, 209, 216, 255; colonists in Tamaulipas and Texas, 122-123; Commission on Claims Against Mexico, 245; diaries, 17, 22, 41, 54, 55, 115-116, 170, 188, 204; Diplomatic Service, 8, 20, 26, 84, 215; in Bolivia, 245; in Brazil, 53; in Colombia, 44; in Honduras, 142; in Mexico, 195 (Guaymas), 167 (Mazatlán), 122-123 (Tamaulipas and Texas); elections (1860), 116; General Land Office, 245; immigration from Mexico, 81; Internal Revenue Service, 245; intervention in Spanish territories, 238; intrusions in Mexico, 176; Isthmian Canal Commission, 245; lands, 104, 229, 245, 254, 259; Navy, 77, 118, 243; Patent Office, 246; politics and government, 182, 183, 259; relations with Bolivia, 245; with Chile, 40; with European countries, 108; with France, 216; with Great Britain, 3, 42; with Mexico, 28, 41, 52, 58, 85, 87-88, 125-126, 129, 131, 145, 176, 215, 245, 256; with Spain, 214, 232; Secretary of State, 77; settlers in Louisiana territory, 116-117; Spanish-American War, 8, 68; taxes, 245; Treasury Department, 57, 202; War Department, 101; War with Mexico, 13, 15, 16, 28, 29, 30, 48, 51-52, 59, 79-80, 118, 129, 131, 139, 143, 167, 170, 245, 255, 259, maps, 115, 244
United States Army, 15, 22, 26, 48, 50-51, 95, 116, 170, 204, 245; campaign maps of northern Mexico, 244; finances, 77; newspapers, 15; occupation of Mexico, 30;

292 INDEX

Office of the Quartermaster, 209; withdrawal from Mexico, (1916), 85
University: of Guadalajara, 36; of Mexico, 87, 200, 243 (history); of Valencia, 20; reforms (Spain), 164
Unzaga y Amezaga, Luis de, 116
Upshur, Abel Parker, 243
Urban VIII, Pope, 242
Urcullu, Manuel de, 93
Ures (Sonora), 43, 75, 149, 176; mission, 222
Uriarte, José María, bp., 198
Uroza y Bárcena, José de, genealogical documents, 15-16
Urrea, Mariano de, 175, 227
Urueña, José Antonio de, 244
Uruguay, description, 4; history, 169; Society of Jesus, 224
Ustariz, Miguel Antonio de, 187

Valcárcel y Formento, Domingo, 110, 194
Valdivia, Luis de, 40
Valerio de la Cruz, Juan Bautista, 190
Valero, Marqués de. *See* Zúñiga, Baltasar de
Valle, Blas del, 62
Valle de la Poana (Nueva Galicia), 151
Valle de San Buenaventura, 63
Valle de San Juan Bautista de Pesquería, 93
Vallejo, Mariano Guadalupe, 132, 246
Vallina, Joseph de la, 38
Valverde, García de, 54, 246
Valverde y Mercado, Francisco de, 66
Van Loon, Hendrick Willem, 246
Van Severan, Andrés, 246
Vaño, Juan, 175
Vargas Machuca, Juan, 135
Vasconcelos, Juan Nepomuceno, 199
Vásquez Prieto, José, 144
Vázquez, Francisco, 62, 246-247
Vázquez, Matheo, 163
Vázquez de Coronado, Juan, 47
Vedoya [Licenciado], 222
Vega, Martínez de la, 102
Vega, Plácido, 247
Vega Carpio, Lope Félix de, 31

Vega y Salazar, Jerónimo de, residencia of, 5
Vejarano, Joseph, 221
Velarde, Luis, 120, 189, 190
Velarde, Melchor, 185
Velasco, José Nicolás, 247
Velasco, Juan Bautista, 127, 226
Velasco, Luis de, viceroy, 1550-1564, 247-248
Velasco, Luis de (II), Marqués de Salinas, viceroy, 1590-1595, 128, 248
Velasco y Tejada, Antonio José (de), 248
Velásquez, Diego de, 249
Velásquez, Joaquín, 72
Velásquez, Pablo, 249
Velázquez, Diego, 248
Velez de Escalante. *See* Escalante
Velicatá, mission, records, 206
Venecian, Lucas, 250
Venegas, Francisco Javier de, viceroy, 1810-1813, 192
Venegas, Miguel, 217, 223, 232, 249 (map)
Venezuela, 186, 249, 250-251; Capuchin missionaries, 187; history, 4-5, 186-187, 216; land, 250; laws, 88; passports, 250; revolution, 24, 186, 250; slavery, 149; taxation, 250; treasure, 249
Vera, Pedro Javier de, 251
Vera de la Ventosa, Justo, 251
Veracruz (city), 49, 74, 144, 232, 255; defense, 13, 72, 133, 158; description, 167-168; detention of Spanish fleet, 218; earthquake damage, 197; garrison, 162; history, 162; maps and plans, 162, 167-168; roads, 162; water supply, 72
Veracruz (state), 22, 132; agriculture, 57; antiquities, 18; industry, 57
Veraguas, Panama, 17-18; history, 161-162
Verapaz (province), Guatemala, 62, 251; description, 58-59, 62, 78, 142; history, 58-59; mining, 142; missions, 58-59; natural resources, 78, 142
Verona, Paciente de, 251
Vertiz, Juan Miguel de, 109, 251
Veta Grande, 159-160
Viceroys, New Spain, 24, 39, 125, 149, 192, 207, 253; Antonio de Mendoza, 1535-1550, 7, 103, 144, 146, 148, 204; Luis de Velasco, 1550-1564, 247-248; Gastón de Peralta, 1566-1568, 204, 261; Martín Enríquez de Almansa, 1568-1580, 168, 192; Pedro Moya de Contreras, 1584-1585, 197-198; Luis de Velasco (II), 1590-1595, 128, 248; Gaspar de Zúñiga y Acevedo, Conde de Monterrey, 1595-1603, 143; García Guerra, 1611-1612, 79; Diego Fernández de Córdoba, Marqués de Guadalcázar, 1612-1621, 91, 128; Diego Carrillo de Mendoza y Pimentel, Marqués de Gelves, 1621-1624, 23, 70, 103, 190, 242; Rodrigo Pacheco Osorio, Marqués de Cerralvo, 1624-1635, 156, 242, 253; Lope Díaz de Armendariz, Marqués de Cadereita, 1635-1640, 31; Diego López Pacheco Escalona, Duque de Escalona, 1640-1642, 253; Juan de Palafox y Mendoza, 1642, 21, 42, 102, 144, 159, 163, 164, 199, 225; García Sarmiento de Sotomayor, Conde de Salvatierra, 1642-1648, 128, 135, 144, 188; Marcos de Torres y Rueda, 1648-1650, 241, 253; Gaspar de Sandoval Cerda Silva y Mendoza, Conde de Galve, 1688-1696, 209, 223; Juan de Ortega Montañés, 1696, 1701-1702, 158; José Sarmiento Valladares, Conde de Moctezuma, 1696-1701, 75; Francisco Fernández de la Cueva Enríquez, Duque de Alburquerque, 1702-1711, 113, 253; Fernando de Alencastre Noroña y Silva, Duque de Linares, 1711-1716, 135, 253; Baltasar de Zúñiga, Marqués de Valero, 1716-1722, 135, 218, 253; Juan de Acuña y Bejarano, Marqués de Casa Fuerte, 1722-1734, 33, 195; Juan Antonio de Vizarrón Eguiarreta, 1734-1740, 135, 222, 224, 253; Pedro de Castro Figueroa y Salazar, Duque de la Conquista, 1740-1741, 252, 253; Pedro Cebrián y

Agustín, Conde de Fuenclara, 1741-1746, 38; Juan Francisco de Güemes y Horcasitas, Conde de Revilla Gigedo, 1746-1755, 61, 63, 223; Agustín de Ahumada y Villalón, Marqués de las Amarillas, 1755-1758, 44, 64, 135, 136, 252; Francisco Antonio Cajigal de la Vega, 1758-1760, 253; Joaquín Montserrat, Marqués de Cruillas, 1760-1766, 51; Carlos Francisco de Croix, Marqués de Croix, 1766-1771, 37, 49, 80, 81, 149; Antonio María Bucareli y Ursúa, 1771-1779, 7, 26, 38, 72, 75, 102, 154, 253; Martín de Mayorga, 1779-1783, 87; Matías de Gálvez, 1783-1784, 81, 218; Bernardo de Gálvez, 1785-1786, 116, 243; Alonso Núñez de Haro y Peralta, 1787, 53, 87, 110, 152; Manuel Antonio Flores, 1787-1789, 135; Juan Vicente Güemez Pacheco de Padilla, Conde de Revilla Gigedo, 1789-1794, 9, 34, 45, 72, 118, 125, 192, 193-194, 218; Miguel de la Grúa Talamanca y Branciforte, Marqués de Branciforte, 1794-1798, 9, 73, 135, 153, 194; Miguel José de Azanza, 1798-1800, 4, 13, 135, 152, 192; Félix Berenguer de Marquina, 1800-1803, 4, 13, 122, 152; José Manuel de Iturrigaray, 1803-1808, 36, 102, 134; Pedro de Garibay, 1808-1809, 68, 192; Francisco Javier de Lizana y Beaumont, 1809-1810, 113, 123-124; Francisco Javier de Venegas, 1810-1813, 192; Félix María Calleja del Rey, 1813-1816, 223; Juan Ruiz de Apodaca y Eliza López de Letona y Lasqueti, 1816-1821, 19, 202; Juan O'Donojú, 1821, 246

Victoria Guadalupe (Félix Fernández), 29, 252; administration of, 27
Vieques, Puerto Rico, 187
Vifquain, Victor, 107
Vildósola, Agustín de, 51, 252
Villa, Francisco ("Pancho"), 52, 237

Villalvaso y Rodríguez, Germán Ascensión, bp., 39
Villaroel, Hipólito, 252
Villaseñor, José Verardo, 255
Villavicencio, Pedro María, 222
Villiers, Baltazar de, 116
Vining, Edward Payson, 253
Viñolas, Pedro, 253
Virgin of Guadalupe, 11, 12, 40, 43, 44, 45, 95, 127, 189, 215, 262
Virginia, Commonwealth of, 254
Vivanco, Manuel, 221
Vivanco, Marqués de. See Morán y del Villar
Vivero, Rodrigo de, Conde de Orizaba, 254
Vizarrón Eguiarreta, Juan Antonio de, abp. and viceroy, 1734-1740, 135, 222, 224, 253
Vizcaíno, Sebastián, 8, 254
Von Hagen, Victor Wolfgang, 92, 99, 254
Von Stein, Maximilian, 224
Voyages, Californias, 8; Gulf of California, 159; Mediterranean, 27; Mexico, 27; Northwest Coast, 214; Pacific Coast, 113; transatlantic, 15; West Indies, 27, 158

Wadsworth, Alfred C., 254
Wagenet, Portia Faye, 255
Wagner, E., 133
Wagner, Franciscus Xavierus, 224
Waldteufel, J. A., 25
Walker, Hannah, 255
Walker, William: activities in Lower California, 63, 239; in Nicaragua, 54, 106, 118, 150, 242
Walker, William M., 255
Walter, Victor, 224
Wangenheim, H. von, 133
War of Independence, 64, 112, 255
Warner, Charles Dudley, 255
Water, Mexico: legislation, 203-204; measurement, 203-204, 261; North America, distribution, 204; supply, 72
Watmough, James Horatio, 255
Waud, H. B., 191
Webster, David, 255
Welles, Edgar Thaddeus, 101
Welles, Gideon, 255
Wessels, Henry Walton, 255

West Indies: description, 23, 25, 27, 54, 158, 239; discovery and exploration, 239; economic conditions, 17; French activities, 250; ports, 54; trade with Spain, 18; voyages to, 27, 158
Westergaard, Waldemar Christian, 256
Whaling, 85, 169
Wheat tax, 256
Wheeler, Joseph, 185, 256
Wheelwright, William, 256
Whinery, Charles Crawford, 256
Whittemore, Charles W., 256
Wilcox, Ella (Wheeler), 256-257
Wilkie, Edna Monzón de, 160, 257
Wilkie, James W., 160, 257
Williams, Herbert O., 257
Williams, Isaac, 257
Wills: Great Britain, 173; Hispanic America, 231; Mexico, 156, 168, 174, 182, 190, 197, 237, 241, 257-259
Willson, James, 259
Wilson, Henry Lane, 256
Winckler, E. von, 133
Winn, William Watkin, 259
Winslow, Rollin R., Family papers, 259
Winthrop, John, 259
Witchcraft: Mexico, 110; Philippine Islands, 101
Wool: culture and manufacture, 185-186; guilds, 186; Morelia mills, 100
Workman, B. F., 259

Ximénez, Francisco, 260

"Yankee Doodle," 260
Yaqui Indians, 25, 51, 227, 228, 252, 260; Valley (map), 228
Yécora, mission, 220
Yepes, Diogo de, bp., 92-93
York, M. L., 261
Yucatan: antiquities, 62; description, 58-59, 62, 132; disturbances, 29; Franciscans, 56, 128; history, 104, 261-262; Indians, 58-59, 62; politics and government, 261-262; Roman Catholic Church, 127-128. See also Central America
Yunga Indians, linguistics, 33

Zacatecas, 21, 73, 248; agricul-

ture, 57; Franciscan college of, 262; industry, 57; lands, 119; mining, 73; powder factory, 10; rebellion, 255
Zambrana, Antonio, 262
Zamudio Gastañaga, Antonio de, 258
Zapotec Indians, 42, 114
Zapotitlán (province), Guatemala, 54
Zaragoza, Ignacio, 5
Zárate Salmerón, Gerónimo de, 127, 262
Zasueta, Juan de Dios, 198
Zavala (Zabala), Lorenzo de, 43
Zelaa e Hidalgo, José María, 262
Zerezo, Guindo, 251
Zerezo y Nieva, Andrés de, 263
Zerman, Juan Napoleon, 11, 239
Zinacantepec, 38
Zoque Indians, linguistics, 178
Zorlado y de Haro, Francisco de, 152
Zubiría y Escalante, José Antonio, bp., 71
Zuleta, Christóbal de, 80
Zumárraga, Juan de, bp., 12, 156, 189, 263
Zúñiga, Baltasar de, Marqués de Valero, viceroy, 1716-1722, 135, 218, 253
Zúñiga, y Acevedo, Gaspar de, Conde de Monterrey, viceroy, 1595-1603, 143
Zúñiga, y Barrios, Salvador de, 109-110, 258
Zurita, Alonso de, 144, 147, 263
Zuza, José Tomás de, 174